THE ATLAS OF THE
ANCIENT
WORLD

THE ATLAS OF THE
ANCIENT
WORLD

CHARTING THE GREAT CIVILIZATIONS OF THE PAST

MARGARET OLIPHANT

SIMON & SCHUSTER
NEW YORK LONDON TORONTO SYDNEY TOKYO SINGAPORE

SIMON & SCHUSTER
Simon & Schuster Building
Rockefeller Center
1230 Avenue of the Americas
New York, NY 10020

A Marshall Edition
Conceived, edited and designed by
Marshall Editions
170 Piccadilly, London W1V 9DD

The publishers would like to thank Iris Barry for writing the section on the Americas (*pp. 178–201*).

Editor	James Harpur
Art Director	David Goodman
Picture Editor	Richard Philpott
Research	Heather Magrill
	Jazz Wilson
Editorial Director	Ruth Binney
Production	Barry Baker
	Janice Storr

Typeset by Servis Filmsetting Limited, Manchester, UK
Originated by Scantrans Pte Limited, Singapore
Printed and bound in the UK by Butler & Tanner, Frome, Somerset

10 9 8 7 6 5 4 3 2 1

Library of Congress Cataloging-in-Publication Data

Oliphant, Margaret.
    The atlas of the ancient world / Margaret Oliphant.
      p. cm.
    ISBN 0-671-75103-4
    1. Geography, Ancient–Maps. I. Title.
  G1033.05 1992 ⟨G&M⟩   91–38075   CIP
  911–dc20

ISBN: 0-671-75103-4

Contents

PREFACE

This is a book that takes the reader back over several thousand years through many lands and their very different ancient cultures. As a specialist in the civilizations of the eastern Mediterranean and the Near East, I have found it as absorbing to explore cultures from those parts of the world not in my specific field of study as those which fall within it. As such, mindful of the people I have accompanied as lecturer on tours of archaeological sites, I have seen my role as that of a guide and interpreter.

In writing about matters as varied as the influence of Hellenism on the Roman world, Shang burial customs in ancient China or the gods of Egypt, my aim has been to stir the readers' interest and imagination, with the hope that they will go on to read more specialized works, some of which have been listed in the bibliography. Illustrations and maps have been carefully chosen, and chronological tables provide a means of comparing the different civilizations. The importance of this was brought home to me on my first tours to Turkey. Here, the remains of ancient cultures span thousands of years, and visitors to sites such as Hattusas or Sardis invariably wanted to know what was happening in the world when these ruins were the living cities of the Hittites and Lydians, respectively. The past survives in archaeological sites, books and museums, but a historical imagination is required to enjoy the pursuit of antiquity to its fullest. And imagination often needs to be stimulated, something which this book will, I hope, achieve.

MARGARET OLIPHANT

This polychrome brick frieze from the palace of the Persian king Darius (522–486 B.C.) shows a line of archers, who served as the king's bodyguard. A detail from the frieze is shown opposite.

INTRODUCTION

In the political turmoil of the late 20th century, rapid changes in governments and political systems and the redrawing of national boundaries have brought a greater sense of insecurity. One result of this is a resurgence of nationalism and the accompanying need to turn to historical antecedents for the collective reassurance and sense of tribal identity they bring. In Russia, for example, in 1991, the decision of the people of Stalingrad to rename their city St. Petersburg – a name associated with the height of Russian culture before the Revolution – was symbolic of an urge to return to roots and a need for a spiritual revival.

Indeed, the establishment of a national myth of a glorious or culturally significant past has always been salutary for a country's psychic welfare: it is no accident that the flag of Mexico incorporates an ancient Aztec icon, or that the seal, flag and currency of India bear the symbol of the Buddhist wheel of *dharma*, first used as a government symbol by the great Indian emperor Ashoka more than 2,000 years ago. And monuments from the ancient world still serve as rallying points for national pride and foci of a cultural heritage. For Britons, the gaunt megaliths of Stonehenge

evoke the same ineffable emotions as the pyramids, the Parthenon or the Colosseum do for Egyptians, Greeks or Italians.

This book aims to introduce the great civilizations of the past, tracing the rise and fall of each people, and describing important aspects of their lives, deaths and dreams. The nine civilizations covered are indicated on the map (BELOW) along with some of their principal sites. Prehistoric Europe, Egypt, Mesopotamia and the Near East, Persia, India and China can be found on the main relief map, with the Americas, the Roman world, and Greece and the Aegean on the inset maps. Page numbers for each section are given after the headings.

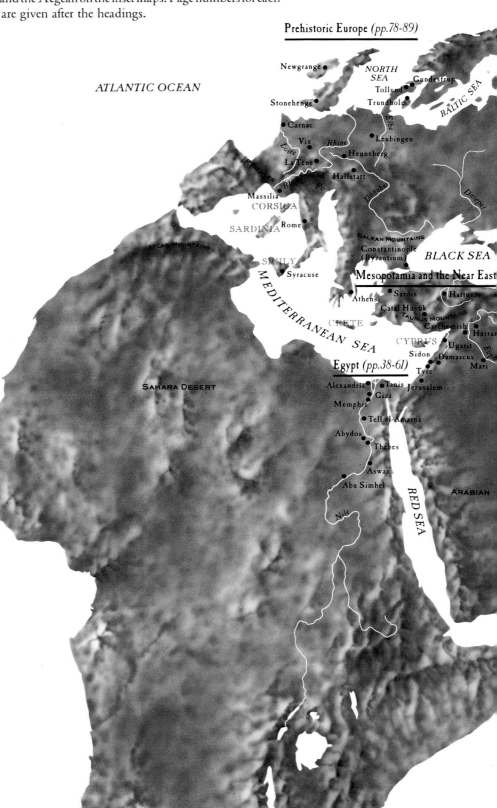

MESOPOTAMIA AND THE NEAR EAST

"So the Lord scattered them abroad from thence upon the face of all the earth: and they left off to build the city. Therefore was the name of it called Babel; because the Lord did there confound the language of all the earth . . . ." GENESIS 11:8–9

The ancient Near East, an area which stretched from the eastern Mediterranean coast to the Iranian plateau, was the home of a number of brilliant civilizations, from the Sumerians to the Neo-Babylonians, which lasted about 3,000 years to the middle of the first millennium B.C. Until archaeological discoveries in the mid-19th century and, later, the decipherment of the Babylonian script, the area and its history were known only through the inevitably biased accounts of the Bible and the inaccurate narratives of classical authors.

The fantastical painting of the Tower of Babel, for example, by the 16th-century Flemish artist Pieter Bruegel, was actually based on the Roman Colosseum and typifies the many imaginary scenes of Babylonian life depicted by later artists. In fact, German excavations at Babylon from the early years of this century have shown that the city of King Nebuchadrezzar II (604–562 B.C.) was probably more splendid than later creations of the mind.

It was in the Near East, particularly in Palestine and the Levant, that the transition from hunter-gatherer to farmer first took place, a crucial step in the history of humankind. This fundamental change in food provision created conditions suitable for a settled existence and therefore the first villages. Later, in southern Mesopotamia, the land which lay between the Tigris and Euphrates, the first cities and states developed with the hallmarks of civilized society: literacy, organized religion and monumental architecture in the form of huge pyramidlike ziggurats. In Mesopotamia, too, the first writing was invented. This was a picture script that developed into cuneiform – an abstract "wedge-shaped" script whose decipherment marks the dawn of historical records.

The Sumerians were the first people to establish cities in Mesopotamia. They were followed by Akkadians, Amorites, Hurrians and others who infiltrated or invaded the region. These peoples all adapted and contributed to a culture that survived for over 3,000 years. To the west of Mesopotamia, the Canaanites of Palestine and the Levant came into contact with Egyptian culture, and the art of the Levant reflected this. In general, however, the Canaanites retained their distinctive culture until, in the first millennium A.D., they were displaced by the Philistines, Israelites and Aramaeans, largely known from the Bible.

North of Palestine the powerful Hittites of Anatolia ruled as far as Syria over what has sometimes been called an empire. But the first real empire was that of the Assyrians, a warlike people who ruled most of the Near East for over 200 years until the beginning of the sixth century B.C. The Assyrians were succeeded by the Babylonians, who in turn fell to the Persians in 539 B.C. These last Mesopotamian empires vanished under later conquests by Greeks and Romans, their imperial histories becoming unreliable memories in the accounts of the Bible and Greek authors.

This glazed-brick bull, *representing the Near Eastern sky god Adad, was one of the reliefs decorating the Ishtar Gate at Babylon, built in the reign of Nebuchadrezzar II. Dragons, symbolizing the god Marduk, also adorned the gate.*

The ziggurat at Ur, *built by the great Sumerian king Ur-Nammu (2112–2095 B.C.) is the best preserved temple tower in Mesopotamia. Originally cased with baked brick, the ziggurat symbolized the sacred mountain of the god – in this case, Nanna, the moon god.*

This huge structure measured 190 by 130 feet at its base and, from its high terrace within the sacred precinct, dominated the city of Ur. It is thought the ziggurat had three stories, connected by external staircases, with the topmost surmounted by a shrine.

The minaret of the Great Mosque of Samarra in Iraq (RIGHT) was built by the Abbasid caliph al-Mutawakkil in A.D. 848. The baked brick minaret has an external spiral ramp and clearly shows that its Muslim builders were following the architecture of the ziggurats of ancient Mesopotamia.

A Nubian is attacked by a lioness in this gilded Phoenician ivory, which was used as an inlay in furniture. The ivory was one of a pair found in the Assyrian city of Nimrud. It dates from the eighth century B.C., when quantities of Phoenician and Syrian ivories were plundered by the Assyrians.

THE FIRST FARMERS

Between the end of the Ice Age around 10,000 B.C. and the emergence of the first civilization in the Near East, profound changes occurred in the way that people lived. At the outset, small bands of hunter-gatherers roamed in search of plants and animals for food. Yet within a few thousand years, with the introduction of farming, a very different world of villages and cities had emerged. Farming altered society radically, creating not only a settled way of life, but also the conditions in which new technologies, such as pottery and metalworking, would develop. In short, it provided the economic base for civilization.

In the uplands of the Fertile Crescent, the region extending in a broad curve from Palestine eastward to the Zagros Mountains, there grew various cereals, such as wheat and barley. Discoveries of sickle blades indicate that by 15,000 B.C. hunter-gatherers were reaping these grains. By about 10,000 B.C. this process had intensified, and in Palestine and Syria, settled communities were storing wild grain in pits and producing flour with grindstones.

About 1,000 years later, the Neolithic people of the Near East made one of the most important contributions to the evolution of society when they began to cultivate plants. Through generations of selective harvesting and sowing, wild species were domesticated. Precisely when and where planting began is uncertain. Jericho, the famous biblical city conquered by Joshua, is the earliest known agricultural community. But the first extensive evidence for cultivation is in southeast Anatolia and the Zagros Mountains, and by 7000 B.C., it was practiced in much of the Near East. Animals were also now domesticated, showing that the dog is not only man's best friend, but also his oldest.

Farming villages gradually developed, and in Palestine, where earlier communities had lived in huts, people now dwelt in houses with plastered and painted floors. They made baskets, wove textiles from flax, and carved vessels from stone. Such skills developed because the increased food supply from farming

A typical scene (BELOW LEFT) *of winnowing and threshing in present-day Iran is living proof that traditional farming methods stretching back several thousand years are still in use today.*

Ancient Mesopotamia and the Near East *from prehistory to the second half of the first millennium B.C. Mesopotamia means "[the land] between the rivers" — the Tigris and Euphrates — and it was in this region that the first cities arose.*

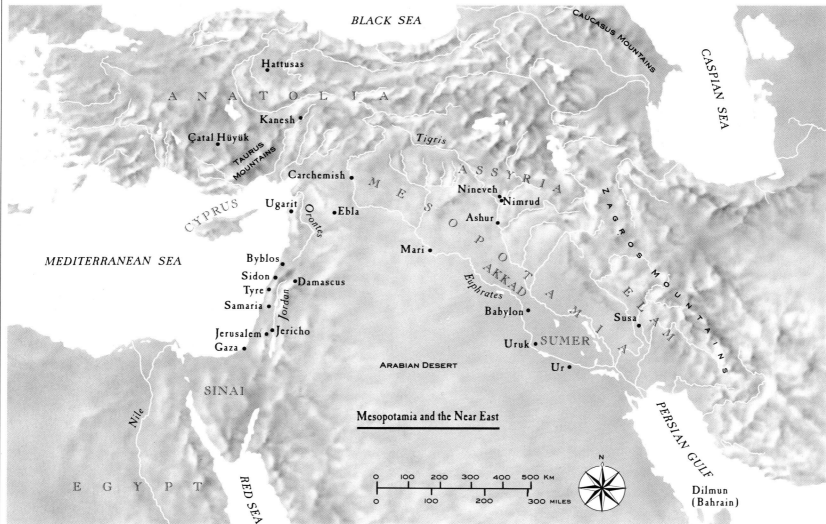

Mesopotamia and the Near East

supported more people than those working the land. In this way, craft specialization began.

Nor, it seems, did these first farming communities "live on bread alone." In 1983, a remarkable discovery was made at the site of Ain Ghazal in Jordan, of several large male and female statues modeled in lime plaster over reed frameworks; their purpose is unknown, but a ceremonial or religious usage is likely. Also, human skulls with faces shaped in plaster and shell-inlaid eyes have been found at Jericho and elsewhere, and are thought to be connected with ancestor worship. Certainly, they show the increasing importance of religion.

The impressive site of Jericho had, by 9000 B.C., grown into a settlement near a perennial spring. It then developed suddenly into a town of some ten acres in extent around 8000 B.C. At about this time, a huge stone wall and a stone tower on its interior were built, possibly for defense or as protection against flooding. This construction would have required many workers and the means to support them, and it is thought that the town population was probably about 1,500 people, although it might have been as many as 3,000. The source of Jericho's wealth is not known, but it probably came from trade in salt and bitumen, which were obtainable from the nearby Dead Sea. The importance of trade was certainly apparent at this time.

These striking statues were found in one of a number of pits excavated at Ain Ghazal, a site in the outskirts of the Jordanian capital of Amman. Similar statues have also been discovered at Jericho. Their specific function is as yet unknown, but their form suggests that they were probably used in some sort of religious cult.

DOMESTICATING ANIMALS

The domestication of animals took place shortly after the beginning of agriculture in about 9000 B.C. As animals evolved from wild to domesticated species, they gradually changed – zooarchaeologists can distinguish wild from domestic varieties from bone analysis. Bones can also show changes in the proportion of different species, another sign of domestication. The table (BELOW) shows this process at Jericho between 8000 and 6000 B.C. Not all wild species can be domesticated, but, by 7000 B.C., several Near Eastern animals had evolved from their wild ancestors, including the dog, goat, sheep, pig, cow and cat, which were descended from the wolf, Bezoar goat, Asiatic moufflon, wild boar, auroch and wild cat, respectively. The donkey and horse were domesticated by 4000 B.C.

The earliest farmers continued to hunt even after they had begun to herd and breed livestock. Because of their suitability for hunting, dogs were already domesticated by about 10,000 B.C., slightly before plant cultivation. The herding of animals such as the goat provided a further source of food from milking. Goats were popular because they grazed widely and needed little fodder. Sheep were valued for their fleeces, and cattle and donkeys proved more than their worth to their owners as draft animals.

Farming at Jericho, 8000 – 6000 B.C.

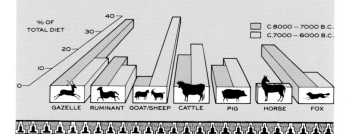

| | | C.8000 – 7000 B.C. |
| | | C.7000 – 6000 B.C. |

% OF TOTAL DIET

GAZELLE RUMINANT GOAT/SHEEP CATTLE PIG HORSE FOX

FROM VILLAGE TO CITY

A view from a mudhif, *a communal village meeting house of contemporary marsh Arabs of southern Iraq. It shows boats and buildings made of woven reeds, a material used in Mesopotamia 5,000 years ago. The boats are of identical design to models found in the Royal Tombs of the city of Ur. The* mudhif *resembles a reed hut depicted on a gypsum trough (*RIGHT*) found at Uruk and dating from about 3000 B.C. The trough was probably a temple offering to the goddess Inanna, and the hut is characterized by poles topped with loops and tassels protruding from the roof, symbolizing Inanna.*

The development of new skills and crafts in the Near East from 7000 B.C. onward stimulated both trade between communities and the exploitation of natural resources. Obsidian from Anatolia (Turkey), for instance, has been discovered at Jericho, 500 miles away. This volcanic glass was used to make cutting tools and has been found widely diffused from its source in central and eastern Anatolia. Semiprecious stones, shells and bitumen have also been found at sites far from their places of origin. Whether goods were carried by professional traders or by other means is not known, but it is clear that trade increased as time went by and as villages became more prosperous.

Once farming became widespread around 7000 B.C., so too did pottery, which is not surprising, given the many uses to which it can be put. Although clay was worked before this time, its use was limited and did not extend to fired vessels. Baked clay is virtually indestructible, and archaeologists can obtain much information from comparing different types of pottery. Metalworking was another major technological advance during this period and further increased people's control over their environment. At first, naturally occurring nuggets of copper were simply hammered and cut with stone tools. Such early pieces have been found in southeast Anatolia at Cayonu, not far from copper mines of a later period. But the revolutionary discovery, sometime after 7000 B.C., was that pure metal could be extracted by heating the ore. The earliest known object cast from copper also comes from Anatolia and was made around 5000 B.C.

ÇATAL HÜYÜK: A NEOLITHIC TOWN

Excavations at Çatal Hüyük, a seventh-millennium town in Anatolia, have revealed a picture of Neolithic life richer than that of any earlier settlement. It is the largest Neolithic site in the Near East, and the artistic achievements of its people are a testament to the skills and creativity of Neolithic man. The earliest levels have not been excavated, but the 14 that have been cover some 600 years from about 6800 B.C. The economy of this town of 5,000 people was based on farming, although specialized and luxury craftsmanship was also important. Çatal Hüyük conducted an extensive trade in obsidian, a volcanic glass, which perhaps came from the nearby volcanoes of Hasan Dağ (BELOW) and Karaca Dağ. People lived in houses made of brick and timber, built adjoining each other and entered from

above by ladders. Each consisted of a storeroom and living room with built-in furniture, usually a bench and platforms for sleeping, sitting or working, under which the dead were buried. At one end was the kitchen with an oven and hearth.

Several buildings are thought to be shrines. Although they have no altars, the presence of statuettes of deities and rich paintings and reliefs with symbolic motifs indicates a religious function. Wall paintings of bulls seem to represent ritual festivities, and bulls' heads carved from plaster are also attached to the walls of niches. Paintings of vultures picking at corpses and the finding of human skulls in a shrine whose paintings are interpreted as priests disguised as vultures suggest some sort of funerary ritual.

Hasan Dağ, an extinct volcano northeast of Çatal Hüyük, was probably the principal source, along with Karaca Dağ and Erciyes Dağ, of the town's obsidian. The latter is a volcanic glass which was made into sharp cutting tools. Excavations in the Near East have shown that most of the region's obsidian was imported from eastern and central Anatolia.

Although by 7000 B.C. there were farming communities in much of the Near East, they were usually small and, like earlier communities (with the exception of Jericho in the eighth millennium), were villages rather than towns. However, the extraordinary site of Çatal Hüyük in western Anatolia had grown to a town of over 5,000 inhabitants before 6000 B.C. Although at present this site seems to be an isolated phenomenon, this may not in fact be the case, and there may simply be gaps in knowledge concerning Anatolia during this period.

It was in Mesopotamia, however, where farming had spread by 6500 B.C., that the invention of irrigation permitted cultivation to be extended to the rain-free, but fertile, alluvial plains of the south. The increased crop yields in turn supported larger

populations and transformed the region later known as Sumer.

In historic times, Mesopotamian people believed that Eridu was the first city created. According to the Babylonian *Epic of Creation*, "A reed had not come forth,/A tree had not been created,/A house had not been made,/A city had not been made,/All the lands were sea./Then Eridu was made." Excavations have confirmed the antiquity of the site: it was settled in the fifth millennium, when a small shrine was built with features, such as an altar niche and offering table, that would later become standard in Mesopotamian temples. At Eridu and other sites, the increasingly sophisticated stoneware, ceramics and metal indicated prosperity and wide trading links. It was from these centers that the world's first cities would rise.

THE FIRST CITIES

Between 4000 and 3000 B.C., the world's first known cities developed in southern Mesopotamia, later known as Sumer. The earlier adoption of irrigation methods had substantially increased food supplies and population, which in turn gave rise to cities. This urban development was accompanied by an increase in area and population, but it was also marked by dramatic changes in social, political and economic life. Thus, while farming had provided the economic base for civilization, it did not in itself account for it.

Although the reasons for the emergence of cities are not yet fully understood, a number of factors seem to have played a part. The region's alluvial soil was deposited each spring when the Tigris and Euphrates rivers flooded their banks, so farmers had to build a complex canal system to control the annual inundation. This required a high degree of cooperation and organization. Inevitable variations in the fertility of the soil would have led to differences in individual wealth; as a result, society became stratified into different social classes.

Before this time, in village communities a sufficient food surplus had allowed some people to become craftsmen. In southern Mesopotamia, the irrigated alluvial plain yielded a considerable surplus, so even larger numbers of specialists evolved. In a community of farmers, craftsmen, laborers, merchants, and an emerging class of administrators, society became too complex to function without, for instance, laws and, in turn, some mechanism by which to impose them. In other words, all these developments created the need for centralized decision-making and a structure for implementing its resolutions.

Linked to these dynamic changes in society was the invention of writing to record business transactions — receipts, records of crop yields, quantities delivered, and the like. They are dated to about 3300 B.C. and were found at the site of the ancient city of Uruk. Writing developed (p. 18) from simple pictures of objects and numbers to a more complex abstract system, and writing skills remained in the hands of scribes, who in turn became an elite. The first texts that can be read and express a language are in Sumerian.

At much the same period (c. 3500–3000 B.C.), the buildings became progressively large and elaborate. Archaeological evidence has revealed that by the late fourth millennium, there were a number of cities in Sumer with a central temple or temple complex, each with an economic authority centered on the temple. Although more is known about Uruk than the other cities, Kish was of equal, if not greater, importance at this time.

Little is known of the early development of Nippur, but by the third millennium, it was the most important religious center. Each city was placed under the protection of a particular god, whose home was the temple. Physically and socially, the city was dominated by the temple complex, which owned much of the land and livestock. The scribal elite was trained in the temple schools and in turn became its administrators.

Uruk, the best known of these city sites, now lies some 12 miles from the Euphrates, a branch of which once ran by the city. Here, the White Temple on its raised terrace is the best example of a Sumerian high temple. Inside was a stepped altar and a central table for burnt offerings. Staircases on the side gave access to the roof, where certain prayers had to be said. A feature of this period was the colored mosaic made of clay cones. These were set into walls to form a pattern, as, for example, in the court beside the temple at Uruk. The beautiful limestone and marble carvings from late Uruk also demonstrate a great deal of sensitivity and technical skill.

This white marble mask is almost life-size and was found in the temple precinct at Uruk. It is possible that it belonged to a statue or a relief composed of several parts. The back is flat and there are drilled holes that suggest it was fastened to something. The eyes and eyebrows would have been inlaid, as well as, possibly, the hair. Uruk is the best known of the early Sumerian cities and an important religious center. It was also the city of the legendary king Gilgalmesh, whose daring exploits are told in the eponymous Epic.

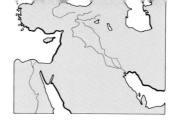

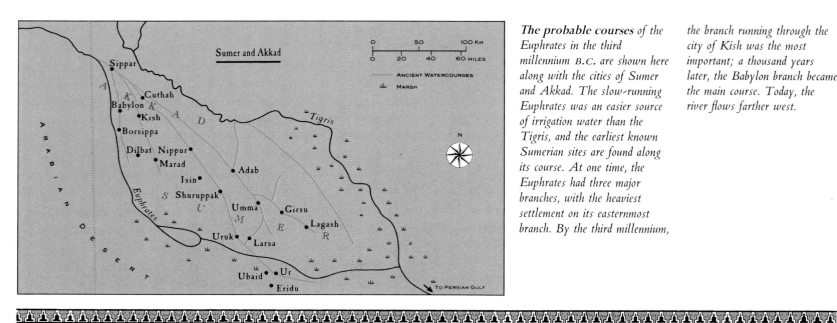

Sumer and Akkad

ANCIENT WATERCOURSES
MARSH

The probable courses of the Euphrates in the third millennium B.C. are shown here along with the cities of Sumer and Akkad. The slow-running Euphrates was an easier source of irrigation water than the Tigris, and the earliest known Sumerian sites are found along its course. At one time, the Euphrates had three major branches, with the heaviest settlement on its easternmost branch. By the third millennium, the branch running through the city of Kish was the most important; a thousand years later, the Babylon branch became the main course. Today, the river flows farther west.

INVALUABLE POTS

The earliest known pottery in the Near East was discovered in Syria and is dated to about the beginning of the eighth millennium B.C. The pots were made by hand and lightly fired. By the fifth millennium, craftsmen were using the slow, hand-turned wheel, and about a thousand years later, the fast-spinning potter's wheel had been invented. It is at about this time that mass-produced pottery makes an appearance.

Pottery was an extremely valuable craft for settled communities, providing the means for cooking, eating, drinking and storage. It is also immensely useful to archaeologists, because although pots break easily, potsherds are virtually indestructible and can provide much information. Chemical analysis can identify the source of the clay, the type of vessel, the way it was made, the decoration and level of expertise – all this reveals something of the activities and technology of the people who made it. And because ceramic styles change fairly rapidly, pottery is also useful for distinguishing one archaeological period from another.

A Bahrain potter (FAR RIGHT) *uses the time-honored fast-spinning wheel to ply his craft. The jar* (RIGHT) *dates from about 2700 B.C. and was* found at Khafajeh near the Tigris. Its naturalistic and geometric motifs were painted in red and black.

SUMER AND AKKAD

THE FIRST WRITING

The earliest known writing in the world was found on tablets at Uruk and dates from about 3300 B.C. They comprise economic records and are pictographic: an ox was drawn as an ox head and so on. A pictographic script can be seen on the 5,000-year-old tablet (BOTTOM). Such a system cannot convey complex ideas, and in time pictographic signs evolved into a system that used syllables. Pictures could express simple ideas, so "mouth" came also to mean "speak" (to avoid confusion a sign, called a determinative, was added to indicate the general class to which the word belonged). Also, signs were combined; for example, the signs for mouth and water together meant "drink."

A crucial step came when a word symbol came to express the sound, but not the meaning, of that word. These sound signs, for instance, would represent the English word "belief" with pictures of a bee and a leaf. Gradually, the picture signs became abstract symbols, as the chart (BELOW) shows. Sumerian was the first language to be expressed in syllabic writing, which was later adapted to write Eblaite and Akkadian.

sag	gin/gub	gu	anše	ud	a
HEAD	WALK/STAND	OX	DONKEY	DAY	WATER

The chart (TOP) *shows the progression from pictograms to an early cuneiform (c.2400 B.C.) and Late Assyrian cuneiform (c.650 B.C.). How the signs sounded in Sumerian is shown with what they mean in English below.*

The Sumerian city-states came to prominence during the third millennium in southern Mesopotamia. They are known primarily from excavated temples and their environs. These sacred areas were constantly rebuilt, so the resulting mounds, or *tells*, were highly visible and have attracted archaeologists since the 19th century. Little is known of the cities that once surrounded the temples; consequently, the large role the temples appear to have had may simply reflect the available evidence. Nevertheless, the temples were clearly important, possibly as self-sufficient organizations that were economically, but not politically, dominant.

Not much is known about early Sumerian kingship and political administration of the first city-states. Kingship seems to have developed from the time when war leaders were appointed as strong men to direct others in fights over boundaries and other disputes. The title designating king, *lugal*, means "great man," and perhaps goes back to this original function, which in time became permanent. Certainly the history of these Early Dynastic states is characterized by almost incessant warfare. One result of this was the construction of large city walls for protection; another was the development of military equipment.

The fortunes of these cities fluctuated as they struggled with each other, and this seems to be reflected in the Sumerian Kinglist, a later text that records the earliest Sumerian dynasties. Thus, Eridu, known to be one of the oldest cities, is where kingship was first "lowered from heaven." After a great flood, (for which, as yet, there is no evidence, although it might have been a particularly bad annual spring flood), kingship was taken to Kish, another very early site; and next was Uruk, contemporaneous with Kish. Lagash, Ur and Umma are all other cities involved in these early struggles. Then, with the conquest of Uruk by Lugalzaggesi of Umma, the latter became "king of the land of Sumer" at the head of a confederation of 50 cities.

This political unity was short-lived, for in about 2370 B.C., Sumer was conquered by Sargon of Akkad. The legend of Sargon's birth is the earliest of other similar stories about the births of heroic men, including Moses. Sargon's mother placed him in a pitch-covered basket to float down the Euphrates, from which he was rescued by a shepherd, who raised the boy as his own. As a young man, Sargon became cup-bearer to the king of Kish, whom he later overthrew. He conquered all of Mesopotamia, parts of north Syria, and Elam to the east. He founded a new city called Agade as the capital of his state, Akkad, and he and his successors spoke a Semitic language now known as Akkadian. The Sumerian cuneiform script was adapted to write Akkadian, which was used officially. It later superseded Sumerian as the dominant language of the region.

Sargon's dynasty was ephemeral, and although his grandson Naram-Sin was also a warrior and good ruler, the empire was subjected to both internal and external pressures. In about 2200 B.C., it was overrun by the Gutians, a mountain people from the east. After 100 years of anarchy, the Third Dynasty of Ur (c.2112–2006 B.C.) was founded by Ur-Nammu. He and his successors were great warriors and ushered in a century of prosperity. The kings created an efficient centralized administration, rebuilt temples and encouraged a renaissance in Sumerian art and literature. In 2006, however, Ur was sacked by the Elamites, a people living east of Sumer in present-day Iran.

Sir Leonard Woolley
(1880–1960) was one of the greatest British archaeologists of the 20th century. At the age of 27, he began digging for Egyptian antiquities in the Sudan and, five years later, worked with T.E. Lawrence ("Lawrence of Arabia") on the Hittite city of Carchemish in Syria. The high point of his career was undoubtedly the excavation of Ur, which shed enormous light on the Sumerian civilization.

THE ROYAL TOMBS OF UR

Between 1922 and 1934, the British archaeologist Leonard Woolley directed the excavations at the Sumerian site of Ur on behalf of the British Museum and the University of Pennsylvania. This work has given the most complete picture there is of a Sumerian city. Woolley discovered, in a cemetery of 1,840 graves, 17 that were of particular interest. Only two of these were unplundered, but the names of the kings Meskalamdu and Akalandu made it clear that they were royal tombs, dating from about 2500 B.C. However, even without the names, the immensely rich contents would have made their owners' royal status evident.

The tomb chambers were also much larger than those of the other burials and were made of brick or stone. Apart from the tombs' contents and size, the most interesting discovery was that these royal personages had been accompanied in death by attendants, whose numbers varied between 3 and 74. It was clear from the evidence that these attendants had taken poison after walking into the tombs and arranging themselves according to rank. In one tomb, a female attendant was found with a ribbon of her headdress in her pocket, where she had presumably placed it to put on later. As these are the only unplundered tombs found, it is not known whether

The helmet (BELOW) *belonged to King Meskalamdu of Ur and dates from the mid-second millennium B.C. On the inside were found traces of cloth padding, which was fastened through holes drilled around the edge. The hairstyle, with its neat plait held by a fillet at the back, is also found on the famous bronze Akkadian head thought to be of Sargon or his grandson Naram-Sin, and so was probably a sign of high rank.*

this burial custom was peculiar to Ur, or whether it also occurred in other Sumerian cities.

The largest of the tombs, called the Great Death Pit, contained 74 skeletons, as well as three lyres, two of silver and one of gold. One of the most interesting finds was the helmet belonging to Meskalamdu, which resembles those worn by soldiers of Eannatum I of Lagash as depicted on the Stele of the Vultures. The so-called Standard of Ur, probably the sounding box of a lyre, is decorated with shell and lapis lazuli inlaid in bitumen. On one side (BELOW LEFT) the scene is of war, with chariots and a phalanx of soldiers. In the top register, prisoners are being brought to the king, who is represented as a larger-than-life figure. The reverse side shows a celebration, perhaps after the victory. A singer, who seems to be blind, holds a lyre similar to those found in the tombs.

Also unearthed were large quantities of jewelry, necklaces, headdresses and hair rings of gold, silver, lapis lazuli, carnelian and agate. These were luxury goods that the people of Ur clearly had the wealth to import from places as distant as the Indus Valley and Afghanistan, the source of lapis lazuli. Where the gold came from is unknown, but it certainly was not Sumer, for none of these goods originated here.

The Standard of Ur was probably the sounding box of a lyre. On its "war side" (LEFT), in the bottom register, teams of onagers draw two-man chariots into battle; in the middle, helmeted soldiers drive captives before them; and at the top, the large figure of the king receives his prisoners.

Even before the sack of Ur by the Elamites in about 2000 B.C., nomads from the west had infiltrated Mesopotamia and had taken over large areas of land. These newcomers, usually identified with a people known in the Bible as the Amorites, eventually took control of several cities. These included Mari on the upper Euphrates, Ashur, farther north, and Babylon, where an Amorite dynasty ruled after 1900 B.C. At this time, Babylon (meaning the "gate of the gods") was a small provincial city until the reign of its great king Hammurabi (1792–1750 B.C.), who unified Mesopotamia for a short time, under the hegemony of Babylon.

Hammurabi's diplomatic and trading links with other cities in the region are known from a cache of letters found at the site of Mari, in modern Syria. When the city was excavated, more than 13,000 cuneiform tablets were found. These Mari letters illuminate the international situation during the first 30 years of Hammurabi's reign. They portray a picture of constantly shifting alliances as the most powerful cities tried to gain control over their rivals. But Hammurabi was more than a match for his opponents and by about 1750 B.C. Babylon had destroyed Mari.

Mari's prosperity, like that of the city of Ebla farther west, rested on trade. Founded some time in the third millennium, Mari became an important city in the Sumerian period. As the wealthy cities of the south grew and required supplies of raw materials, such as timber, stone and metals from the west, trading networks developed in Syria. Ebla, for instance, controlled the cutting and transporting of timber, while Mari grew rich from the tolls it levied on river-borne traffic.

While the letters found at Mari provide a picture of the complex politics of the various Amorite kingdoms, the remains of the palace help to shed light on the lifestyle of these wealthy rulers. The Sumerian influence on the art and sculpture of Mari can clearly be seen in the remains of the palace. Built of mud brick, this huge structure contained more than 260 ground-floor rooms, with more upstairs. The rooms were arranged around an outer public courtyard and an inner private one for the ruler and his family.

Painted plaster fragments show that many rooms were decorated with colorful scenes. One such fragment, which dates from the time of the last king, Zimri-Lim, shows bulls being led for

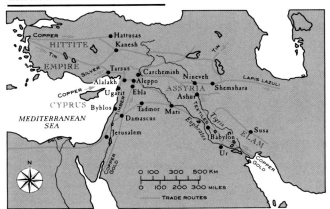

Trade routes of the second millennium B.C.

During the second millennium B.C., an extensive trade network existed throughout the Near East and Mesopotamia. Among the most important trading cities was Mari, which prospered as a result of tolls levied on vessels on the Euphrates.

GODS AND GODDESSES OF THE NEAR EAST

The religions of the ancient Near East were polytheistic. They began as nature religions, but in time, the sky, wind, water, earth and other natural elements that were worshipped became personified. Often, however, the earlier non-human elements were retained in the depiction of deities, for example rays of light piercing the sun god's shoulders, or the fork of lightning held by the sky god Ba'al. The aniconic, or anti-image, tendency in Canaanite religions, in which stones were the objects of worship, may reflect this reverence for elemental forces.

Certain deities were linked to particular cities. Some became more important as the city became powerful, as was the case with Marduk, Babylon's city god. There were specific cults and festivities for the various deities, who dwelt, it was believed, in

their temples. Here they were attended by their human servants, created specifically for this purpose. The city rulers were the agents of the gods, representing them on earth.

In Mesopotamia, the taking of omens and various forms of divination were important elements of religion. Animals were sacrificed to secure divine favor, and among the Phoenician descendants of the Canaanites, there is evidence of child sacrifice. The ancients were generally tolerant in religious matters and usually identified their city gods with those of other cities, so that the same god would appear under different names. Thus An, Anu, Adad, Ba'al, Hadad and Teshub were, respectively, the Sumerian, Akkadian, Assyrian, Canaanite, Aramaean and Hurrian forms of the sky deity.

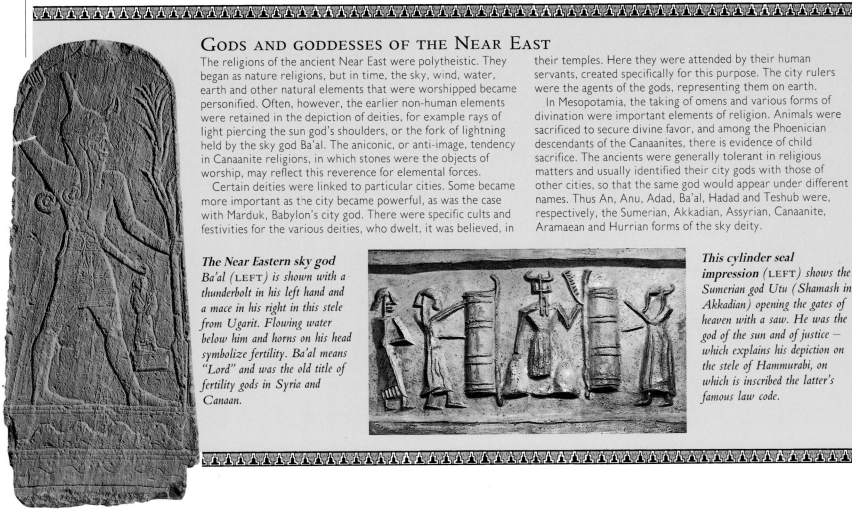

The Near Eastern sky god Ba'al (LEFT) is shown with a thunderbolt in his left hand and a mace in his right in this stele from Ugarit. Flowing water below him and horns on his head symbolize fertility. Ba'al means "Lord" and was the old title of fertility gods in Syria and Canaan.

This cylinder seal impression (LEFT) shows the Sumerian god Utu (Shamash in Akkadian) opening the gates of heaven with a saw. He was the god of the sun and of justice — which explains his depiction on the stele of Hammurabi, on which is inscribed the latter's famous law code.

sacrifice. There were also decorations of shell mosaics, which had been popular during the Sumerian period. The palace was added to over some 300 years. Near the palace was a temple and beyond it, there were the private houses. The city was surrounded by a massive brick wall and covered about 250 acres.

The Amorite ruler of Ashur, the capital of Assyria, in northern Mesopotamia, is also known from the Mari letters as an adversary of the city. And another set of documents, many of them letters, provides a fascinating insight into the lives of several generations of Assyrian merchants. These tablets were found in Anatolia at the site of an Assyrian trading colony on the edge of the town of Kanesh, ruled by a local prince. Between about 1950 and 1750 B.C., merchants from Ashur traded with several such towns. Textiles and tin were sent by caravans of black donkeys across the Taurus Mountains to Assyrian agents living in the trading colony. These goods were then sold locally, and the profits, in gold and silver, were sent back to Ashur.

The site of Mari lies on the west bank of the Euphrates in modern Syria. The city became prosperous through its trading links with other cities of the period, shown on the map (OPPOSITE PAGE), and its control of the river traffic. Timber, copper, silver and textiles from the west, and tin from the northeast, bound for the cities of Sumer and Akkad passed through Mari, as did the westward trade of lapis lazuli from Afghanistan. Agriculture was important, and irrigation cultivation was carried out on the city's river terrace.

Found at the site of Çatal Hüyük, this figurine of a woman (ABOVE) is typical of statuettes found in early agricultural communities. These images cannot be precisely interpreted, but they were often of fat or pregnant females or of women giving birth, and thus were probably linked to fertility.

The goddess Ishtar (Sumerian Inanna) combined the qualities of earlier goddesses. She is shown (BELOW) as a deity of war, standing on a crouching lion and holding a bow and arrows. The palm trees are linked to her Sumerian origin as goddess of the date storehouse.

Astarte (RIGHT) was the Canaanite form of Ishtar and, as a fertility goddess, was often depicted naked. She also had warlike qualities and in coastal cities, such as the ports of Tyre and Sidon, she was called the "Lady of the Sea."

21

ANATOLIA AND THE HITTITES

In the second millennium B.C., the Hittites of Anatolia became a great power in the Near East. At various times, they dominated the area over four centuries, successfully challenging Egyptian hegemony over Syria, until their eclipse shortly before about 1200 B.C. From their capital Hattusas (modern Boğhaz-köy), in central Anatolia, they controlled an empire whose history was marked by expansions and contractions, which at times reduced their domains to the environs of their capital.

Hattusas was originally a Hattic settlement; although little is known of these people, Hattic influence on Hittite culture is reflected in the names of their capital and country, which was called Hatti. The origins of the Hittites are uncertain and the evidence for the early period is fragmentary. However, around 1800 B.C., Hattusas was devastated by the Hittite king Anitta of Kussara, who placed it under a curse, forbidding his successors to settle there. Nevertheless, this dictate was ignored, for by the era of Hammurabi (1792–1750 B.C.), the city, situated on a high commanding promontory, had become Hittite.

The Hittite archives, which were found at Hattusas and date back to about 1650 B.C., show that the Hittites spoke an Indo-European language. Most of the texts, which concern history, politics, legal matters, literature and religion, were written in Hittite on clay tablets in cuneiform script. There were also tablets inscribed in other languages, including Akkadian, which was the language of diplomacy.

Under Hattusilis I (c.1650 B.C.), north Syria, important for its trade routes and access to the ports of Byblos and Ugarit on the Mediterranean coast, was conquered. It was later lost and then

Yazilikaya was a Hittite religious center lying just over a mile to the northeast of Hattusas. Reliefs carved on the sides of limestone outcrops show processions of deities. In the frieze (BELOW LEFT), the Hittite king Tudhaliya is embraced by the god Sharruma, who is wearing a tall crown. The Yazilikaya sanctuary was built in the 13th century B.C. under the orders of Tudhaliya's father Hattusilis III.

This procession of male deities (RIGHT), carved out of the rock in high relief, forms part of the sacred art at the Hittite shrine Yazilikaya. The gods wear pointed crowns, kilts and turned-up shoes and are holding scimitars or maces.

regained. In about 1550 B.C., Mursilis I raided and plundered Babylon, contributing to the fall of Hammurabi's dynasty. With the emergence of the Mitannian Empire, the Hittites lost territory and for nearly a century were considerably weaker. Following the accession of Suppiluliumas in 1380 B.C., Hittite power was reasserted, and the next century witnessed the golden age of their empire. Once again, they took Syria and, ruling it through vassal states, they controlled the strong cities of Carchemish and Alalakh; at the same time, they made treaties with Ugarit and Alalakh.

After the open conflict between the Hittites and Egypt at the indecisive Battle of Qadesh (pp.54–55), a peace treaty was signed some years later, in about 1269 B.C. By this Egypt confined its interests to Palestine. Incredibly, both the Hittite (written in Akkadian) and Egyptian copies of the treaty have survived. The peace lasted until the disappearance of the Hittite Empire shortly before 1200 B.C. The reasons for this sudden eclipse are not fully understood, but are probably connected with the arrival of the marauding Sea People (pp. 28–29), internal disturbances and the raiding Gaska people of the north, who are usually identified with the Phrygians of northwestern Anatolia.

There is no evidence that the Hittites were powerful because of their supposed monopoly of iron production. Much of their success in war was in fact due to the horse and chariot. The king was commander of the army and maintained large numbers of infantry and a bodyguard on a feudal basis. He was also the supreme judicial authority and chief priest, the role in which he was usually represented on monuments. Hittite queens had a strong, independent position.

In this and other ways, the Hittites differed from their Near Eastern neighbors – despite the fact that they had absorbed parts of foreign cultures. From Mesopotamia came their script and some of their literature, while their religion shows Hurrian influences. In spite of their sudden demise, certain features of the Hittite world survived for three centuries in the small Neo-Hittite kingdoms of southeastern Anatolia and northern Syria.

WINKLER AT HATTUSAS

Sculpted lions give their name to a major gate (ABOVE) at Hattusas. The city's main gates were typically flanked by watchtowers (BELOW) built on deep foundations.

In October 1905, Dr. Hugo Winkler, a German Assyriologist, began excavating the site of Boğhazköy, north of the Turkish capital of Ankara. The journey from Ankara had taken five days and vermin-infested nights, and Winkler, always a difficult personality, complained incessantly. Despite rain, which turned the site into a sea of mud in the first week, Winkler found 34 fragments of clay tablets. His initial success continued in 1906 and, in a year's time, his excavations had exceeded all expectations: more than 10,000 cuneiform tablets had been found and parts of a city uncovered. Mary tablets were in Akkadian and, reading them, Winkler realized that some were letters between Egypt and the king of the Hatti. He saw clearly that he had unearthed the Hittite royal archive and that Boğhazköy was Hattusas, the Hittite capital.

Winkler had been very ill while working on these tablets, but he persisted with his work. It was 1907 when he published his readings of the texts; and although he had translated many Akkadian tablets, there remained a large number in a language that could not be read. However, after Winkler's death in 1913, a young Czech scholar named Bedrich Hrozny deciphered this Hittite language and made the astounding discovery that it belonged to the Indo-European languages (which include most modern European languages) and was possibly the oldest.

EMPIRES AND DIPLOMACY

Between about 1600 and 1200 B.C., powerful empires in the Near East contended with each other for control of the region through military and diplomatic means. There was a balance of power between the Kassites in Babylonia, the Mitannians in eastern Syria and Palestine, the Egyptian Empire in Palestine and southern Syria, the Assyrians in northern Mesopotamia and the Hittites in Anatolia and northern Syria.

The empire of Mitanni was at its height between 1430 and 1350 B.C., at which time it stretched from the Zagros Mountains to the Mediterranean. The capital Wassugani has not been found, but it is thought to be in the region known as the Nairi lands, east of the great bend in the River Euphrates. The population of Mitanni was predominantly Hurrian, but the ruling aristocracy seems to have consisted of Indo-Aryans. One reason for Mitanni's prominent position in the Near East at this time was the effective use made of the two-wheeled, horse-drawn war chariot. However, Mitanni eventually fell to attacks by its former Assyrian vassals and the Hittites.

After the fall of Hammurabi's dynasty, following the Hittite raid on Babylon in about 1550 B.C., a people of obscure origin known as the Kassites ruled Babylonia. They first appear in historical records around 1700 B.C., usually as expert handlers of horses, which were beginning to revolutionize warfare. One of their chieftains seized the throne after the Hittites sacked Babylon. There are few documents from the Kassite period, but Babylonia seems to have been remarkably stable in the 400 years of Kassite rule. The capital was moved to the strategic site of Dur-Kurigalzu, which has only been partially excavated.

For the first thousand years of its history, Assyria was dominated by Sumer. When the Third Dynasty of Ur fell in about 2000 B.C., Assyria became independent, and its merchants traded with Anatolia. The Amorite Shamshi-Adad I became king of Assyria in 1814 B.C. and established Assyrian control over most of northern Mesopotamia, including Mari, which was later recaptured by its native prince. But with the emergence of Hammurabi, Babylon eclipsed Assyria, which gradually weakened and came under the control of the newly arrived Mitannians. This domination was, however, short-lived.

During this period, cuneiform, which had earlier spread to much of the Near East when Mesopotamia was the dominant power, became the international script. Akkadian was the language of diplomacy. A 14th-century archive of cuneiform letters found at the site of Tell el-Amarna in Egypt (pp.52–53) reveals the correspondence between the great kings of the region. They frequently sent each other letters and gifts and sometimes married each other's daughters.

The Egyptian pharaoh was for a time the most powerful ruler, but during the reign of Akhenaten (1379–1362 B.C.), Egypt lost her dominant position. The Amarna letters were found in 1887 by a peasant woman looking for old bricks, which make good fertilizer. The scholars who saw them quickly realized that this was the correspondence of the "State Department" of Akhenaten. However, there were earlier letters, too, probably brought there from Thebes when the capital was moved.

Through the tablets, it is possible to follow the international events of this time. The Hittites of Anatolia had broken the power of Mitanni and were plotting with Egypt's vassals in Syria. Loyal vassals were asking Egypt for help, but Akhenaten seems to have ignored their pleas; and by the end of his reign, the Egyptian empire in Syria had been lost, never to recover.

The ziggurat of Dur-Kurigalzu, north of Babylon, was a Kassite foundation, probably built in about the early 14th century B.C.

Most of the tablets from Tell el-Amarna, the site of the short-lived Egyptian capital Akhetaten, are letters from the archives of Akhenaten and his father, Amenophis III. Many concern affairs in Palestine, where, by the end of Akhenaten's reign (1362 B.C.), Egypt had lost her empire. The attempts of loyal vassals, such as Rib-Adda of Byblos, to get help from Egypt against cities supporting the Hittites were in vain. Another group of letters, quotes from which are keyed into the map (RIGHT), are from rulers of other regional powers. They reveal that Egypt was first among equals, linked to some states by marriages, and that, for a time, the status quo in the Near East was maintained by diplomacy and gift exchange.

MEDITERRANEAN SEA

> ❝ Rib-Adda speaks to the King of Lands, of many lands, the Great King...to the King my Lord. I bow at my Lord's feet – the Sun God – seven times... the city Byblos his handmaid faithful to the King has gathered because of the allies who are his foes. And I am ill at ease: behold the King lets slip from his hand the chief city that is faithful to him. Let the King smite the lands of those ❞ who rob him....

LETTER FROM RIB-ADDA OF BYBLOS TO AMENOPHIS IV

Nile

Tell el-Amarna •

E   G   Y

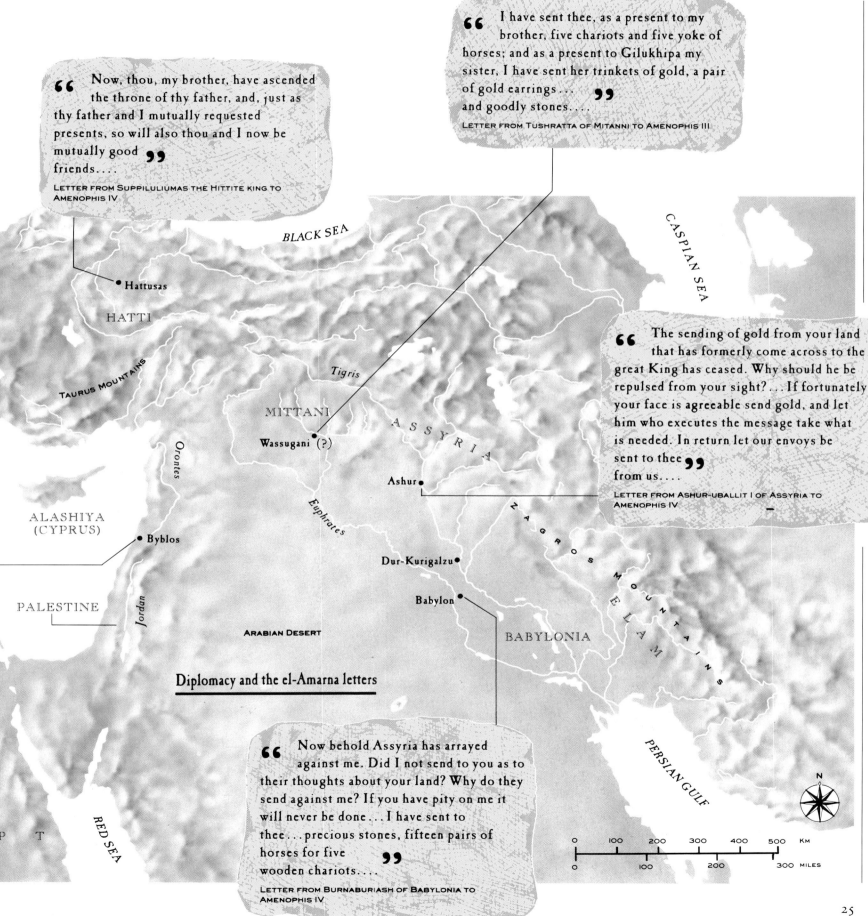

" I have sent thee, as a present to my
brother, five chariots and five yoke of
horses; and as a present to Gilukhipa my
sister, I have sent her trinkets of gold, a pair
of gold earrings . . .
and goodly stones. . . . "

LETTER FROM TUSHRATTA OF MITANNI TO AMENOPHIS III

" Now, thou, my brother, have ascended
the throne of thy father, and, just as
thy father and I mutually requested
presents, so will also thou and I now be
mutually good
friends. . . . "

**LETTER FROM SUPPILULIUMAS THE HITTITE KING TO
AMENOPHIS IV**

BLACK SEA

CASPIAN
SEA

• Hattusas

HATTI

TAURUS MOUNTAINS

Tigris

MITTANI

• Wassugani (?)

ASSYRIA

" The sending of gold from your land
that has formerly come across to the
great King has ceased. Why should he be
repulsed from your sight? . . . If fortunately
your face is agreeable send gold, and let
him who executes the message take what
is needed. In return let our envoys be
sent to thee
from us. . . . "

**LETTER FROM ASHUR-UBALLIT I OF ASSYRIA TO
AMENOPHIS IV**

Orontes

Ashur •

ALASHIYA
(CYPRUS)

• Byblos

Euphrates

ZAGROS MOUNTAINS

PALESTINE

Jordan

Dur-Kurigalzu •

Babylon •

ELAM

ARABIAN DESERT

BABYLONIA

Diplomacy and the el-Amarna letters

" Now behold Assyria has arrayed
against me. Did I not send to you as to
their thoughts about your land? Why do they
send against me? If you have pity on me it
will never be done . . . I have sent to
thee . . . precious stones, fifteen pairs of
horses for five
wooden chariots. . . . "

**LETTER FROM BURNABURIASH OF BABYLONIA TO
AMENOPHIS IV**

PERSIAN GULF

N

P   T

RED SEA

0   100   200   300   400   500 KM

0   100   200   300 MILES

SYRIA, PALESTINE AND THE LEVANT

From about 1650 B.C., the history of Syria, Palestine and the Levant (the coastal area from Egypt to Anatolia) was closely linked to their powerful neighboring empires. Egypt to the south, the Hittites to the north and Mitanni to the east were all vying for the region's prosperous city-states and the trade routes they controlled. The area was inhabited by Semitic Amorites and Canaanites, who, despite cultural differences, spoke virtually the same language. The Canaanites, who lived in the Levant and Palestine and were probably descendants of earlier Amorites, came under the influence of Egyptian culture through trade. Farther north, the Amorites were influenced by Mesopotamian and Hurrian culture through the east-west trade between the Euphrates valley and the Mediterranean.

The ancient Syrian city of Ebla, south of Aleppo, is known from Akkadian texts of the late third millennium B.C. Archive texts found at Ebla — some of which are written in cuneiform Eblaite, the earliest known form of written West Semitic — show that by about 2500 B.C., it was a prosperous trading city. Its inhabitants preceded the nomadic Amorites, once thought to have been the earliest Semitic people in Syria. In about 2000 B.C., the Amorites sacked Ebla, and by about 1800 B.C., there were several Amorite kingdoms in Syria and Palestine, including Byblos and Ugarit. The largest kingdom was Yamkhad (Aleppo), which encompassed an area from the Taurus Mountains to the Euphrates and governed with subject rulers, such as the king of Alalakh.

At the beginning of the 16th century B.C., the Hittites destroyed Aleppo, which later came under the control of Hurrian Mitanni. The Hurrians, a non-Semitic people, possibly from eastern Anatolia, settled in Syria as far south as Alalakh in the early second millennium, although it was not until the 16th century B.C. that their kingdom of Mitanni was formed. By 1480 B.C., Alalakh was vassal to Mitanni, now allied to Egypt.

The subsequent decline of Egyptian influence in Syria allowed the Hittite king Suppiluliumas (1380–1346 B.C.) to defeat Mitanni and its vassals, Aleppo and Alalakh. By the end of the century, the Hittites controlled much of the region, including Ugarit, formerly a vassal of Egypt. Egypt had long traded with the Levant, and between about 1900 and 1788 B.C., links with Byblos were close. Objects discovered in the Byblos Royal Tombs, for example, show the beginnings of Egyptian influence on Canaanite-Amorite culture (something which can also be seen in the later art of the Phoenicians, the cultural descendants of the Canaanites).

For about two centuries up until 1570 B.C., Egypt was controlled by rulers known as the Hyksos. After their defeat, however, strong Egyptian rulers established control of Palestine, the Levant and part of Syria, reaching as far as the Euphrates in about 1525 B.C. But peace was established in the region only after the campaigns of Amenophis II (1450–1425 B.C.) against Mitanni. During this period of Egyptian hegemony, trade flourished. Canaanite and Syrian products included timber, dyed cloth, wine jars, oil flasks, metalwork and cattle. The reign of Akhenaten (1379–1362), however, saw Egypt lose much of the region. It never regained its former frontiers, in spite of later efforts that culminated in the peace between Egypt and the Hittites in about 1269 B.C. Within a century, Egypt's decline was such that the Canaanite and Syrian cities were left to develop on their own.

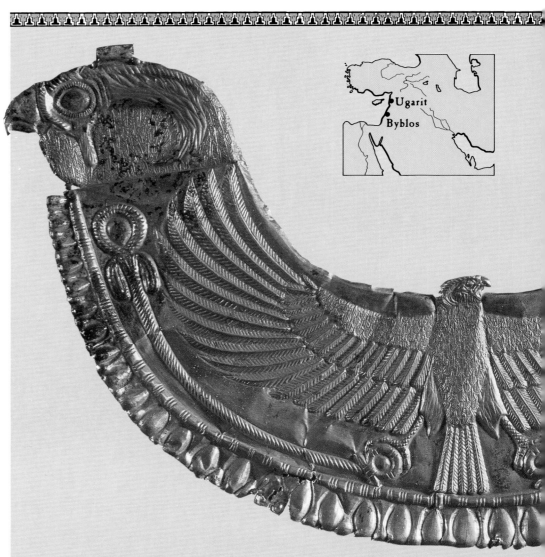

BYBLOS AND THE EGYPT CONNECTION

The ancient coastal city of Byblos grew wealthy from trade, particularly with Egypt to whom it exported timber from 2600 B.C. and perhaps earlier. Later, the relationship with Egypt was close and had a longstanding effect on the art and culture of the city. In the Royal Tombs of Byblos, the city's Amorite rulers were buried with Egyptian objects, among them an obsidian box decorated with gold and bearing the name of Pharaoh Amenemhet IV (1798–1740 B.C.) in silver hieroglyphs.

The golden Horus chest ornament (ABOVE), from another tomb, was probably made locally, for although of Egyptian design, it shows Canaanite stylistic details. At the temple, the pieces found were of Amorite style and work, including the golden scabbard sheath of an ivory-handled dagger showing three men herding a strange flock of animals, including a goat, lion, baboon, dog and fish. The city is mentioned in Mesopotamian texts of 2100 B.C., and about 400 years later, it traded textiles and garments, doubtless of the purple subsequently made famous by the Phoenicians, with the city of Mari. There was also trade with the Minoans of Crete.

The influence of Egypt on the art of Byblos is well illustrated by this magnificent gold chest ornament or pectoral (ABOVE). On it are depicted images of Horus, the Egyptian hawk-god, but stylistic details indicate that it was fashioned by local craftsmen. The pectoral was found in the Royal Tombs.

This exquisite pendant of gold inlaid with precious jewels (RIGHT), discovered in the tomb of one of the kings of Byblos, also shows Egyptian motifs, including the god Horus.

UGARIT AND TRADE

The port of Ugarit on the Syrian coast was a major trading city which, like Byblos, was under Egyptian influence in the early second millennium. Its period of greatest prosperity began during the peace between Mitanni and Egypt, to which it was nominally subject. However, it also acknowledged Hittite authority and, as with all the Levant cities, seemed able to keep trading no matter which great power was dominant. Ugarit also had links with the Aegean world of the Mycenaeans (pp.96–99). Much of its wealth came from trade in Cypriot copper and metalworking. Purple dye from the murex shell, salt and grain were other items that were exported.

The archive found at Ugarit contains texts in several languages, some written in a cuneiform alphabetic script. They include material on Ugaritic religion and myths that have cast light on Canaanite religious practices. The city was destroyed, probably by the Sea People (pp.28–29), in about 1200 B.C.

This 14th-century B.C. gold dish (ABOVE) *from Ugarit shows vigor and fluidity in its depiction of a hunting scene. The chariot is similar to those of the Egyptian New Kingdom. By the 14th century B.C., Ugarit* (RIGHT) *controlled some 30 miles of coastland, including four ports, and was well placed for sea trade. At this time, it was at its greatest extent, with a massive rampart enclosing an area of some 50 acres. The palace complex included 67 rooms and 5 courtyards on the ground floor, making it probably the largest contemporary palace in Syro-Palestine.*

The angular statuette (RIGHT) *probably depicts an Ugaritic king. He is holding what appears to be a mace, a characteristic symbol of royal power.*

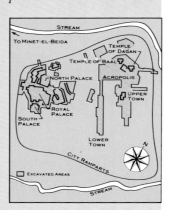

PEOPLES OF THE OLD TESTAMENT

In about 1200 B.C., the Hittite Empire disappeared suddenly, and cities of the eastern Mediterranean coast were laid waste. Some, such as the wealthy Canaanite city of Ugarit on the Syrian coast, were completely abandoned. These disturbances are thought to have been caused by roving bands of marauders known as the Sea People. Although it is not certain, it is possible that the Sea People were also linked to the destruction of Troy and cities of Mycenaean Greece. It is known from Egyptian accounts that they twice attacked Egypt and were defeated, for the second time, in about 1186 B.C.

Some of the Sea People evidently settled on Egypt's borders, later becoming mercenaries, while a group known as the Peleset settled in southern Canaan around Gaza. These people, who were subsequently known as the Philistines, gave the region its name, Palestine. The remains of their iron weapons bear out Old Testament accounts of their fighting with large spears and their reputation as fierce warriors.

Events in the Near East in the century before about 1000 B.C. are unclear, and there is a break in the archaeological record. But when records are again available, the map of the Near East has changed. The former great powers, such as Egypt, Babylonia and Assyria, have weakened, and the Hittites have vanished from the political map. Nomadic tribes have settled in Syro-Palestine and gradually formed into small states. In an area normally dominated by stronger neighbors, these states were later to be conquered by Assyria, but they nevertheless made lasting contributions to future societies.

The nomadic Aramaeans settled in Syria and along the Euphrates River. By the tenth century B.C., their kingdoms spread even into Assyrian territory. But the kingdom of Damascus, centered on its oasis, was to become the greatest and, before its defeat by Assyria in 732 B.C., was regularly in conflict with Israel. The legacy of the Aramaeans was their language, which became the common tongue of the Near East, until the introduction of Arabic after the seventh century A.D. The Aramaic script was adapted from the Phoenician alphabet (pp.30–31) and, because it was easy to write, displaced cuneiform. Aramaic was also the language spoken at the time of Jesus Christ, and parts of the Bible were originally written in it.

To the north of the Aramaean territories, partly in Syria and reaching into southeast Anatolia, were the Neo-Hittite states, so called because their world shows certain links with the earlier Hittites. These people, too, were absorbed by the Assyrian Empire in the ninth century, and it is thought that some of their architectural traditions might have been borrowed by the Assyrians. For example, it is at this time that the first carved stone relief sculptures appear in the Assyrian palaces.

The settlement of the Hebrew tribes in ancient Canaan, their conflicts with neighboring people, and the division of David and Solomon's kingdom into the separate states of Israel and Judah are known from the Bible. From the eighth century B.C., the history and laws of these people were written down and preserved, some as part of the Hebrew Bible – the Christian Old Testament. Although, politically, the Hebrews played a relatively insignificant role in the Near East, their most enduring legacy was their religion. Judaism, the world's first monotheistic religion, was the cornerstone of Christianity and Islam, and thus its influence on western history and culture was immense.

Nomadic life has always been a feature of Near Eastern society, and modern nomads, such as those (LEFT) in Iraq, still exist, albeit in decreasing numbers. The black tents of nomads referred to in the Bible can still be seen today. The Amorites, Aramaeans and other ancient peoples practiced a type of nomadism which was essentially short-range pastoral transhumance: that is, the group, usually an extended family unit, traveled according to the seasons in search of pasture, sometimes stopping to plant or reap. These nomads coexisted with settled people, who provided markets for their livestock and produce.

Although nomadic life was unsuitable for keeping historical records, it is known from the texts of urban dwellers that nomads were often very wealthy. Indeed, members of groups might actually settle in a city for a time, or even permanently.

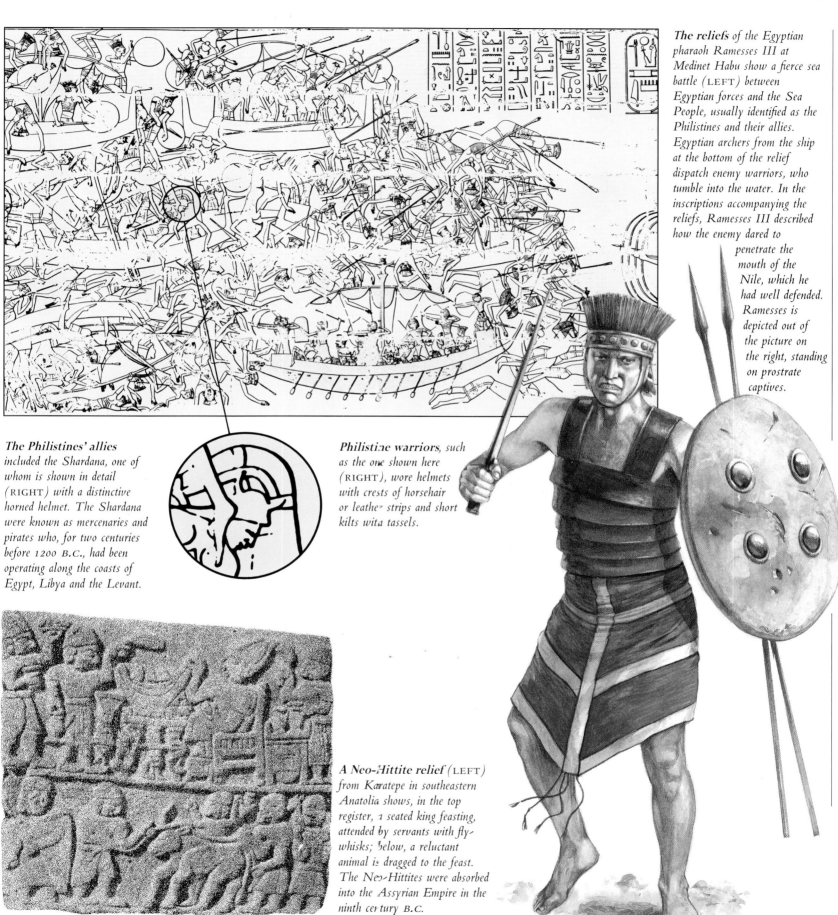

The reliefs of the Egyptian pharaoh Ramesses III at Medinet Habu show a fierce sea battle (LEFT) between Egyptian forces and the Sea People, usually identified as the Philistines and their allies. Egyptian archers from the ship at the bottom of the relief dispatch enemy warriors, who tumble into the water. In the inscriptions accompanying the reliefs, Ramesses III described how the enemy dared to penetrate the mouth of the Nile, which he had well defended. Ramesses is depicted out of the picture on the right, standing on prostrate captives.

The Philistines' allies included the Shardana, one of whom is shown in detail (RIGHT) with a distinctive horned helmet. The Shardana were known as mercenaries and pirates who, for two centuries before 1200 B.C., had been operating along the coasts of Egypt, Libya and the Levant.

Philistine warriors, such as the one shown here (RIGHT), wore helmets with crests of horsehair or leather strips and short kilts with tassels.

A Neo-Hittite relief (LEFT) from Karatepe in southeastern Anatolia shows, in the top register, a seated king feasting, attended by servants with fly-whisks; below, a reluctant animal is dragged to the feast. The Neo-Hittites were absorbed into the Assyrian Empire in the ninth century B.C.

29

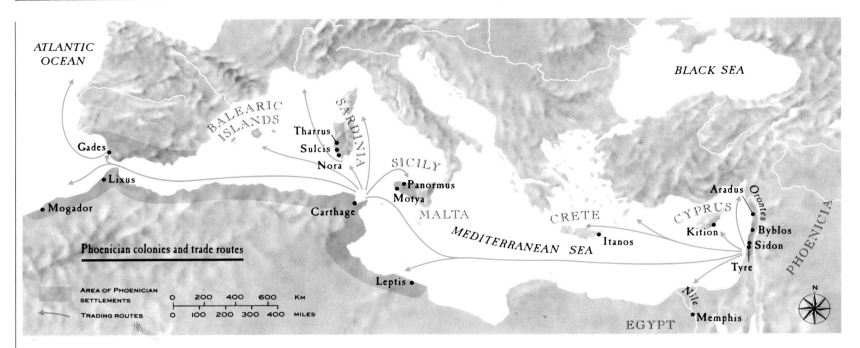

ATLANTIC
OCEAN

BLACK SEA

BALEARIC ISLANDS

SARDINIA

Tharrus
Sulcis
Nora

SICILY

Panormus
Motya

Gades

Lixus

Mogador

Carthage

MALTA

CRETE

CYPRUS

Aradus
Orontes
Kition
Byblos
Sidon

PHOENICIA

MEDITERRANEAN SEA

Itanos

Tyre

Leptis

Nile

EGYPT
Memphis

N

Phoenician colonies and trade routes

AREA OF PHOENICIAN
SETTLEMENTS

0   200   400   600   KM

TRADING ROUTES

0   100   200   300   400   MILES

The Phoenicians were highly skilled mariners and, according to the Greek historian Herodotus, they sailed around Africa. As the map (ABOVE) shows, they founded trading colonies in northern Africa, Spain, Sardinia and Sicily and, much earlier, on Cyprus, where they mined copper. Later, when the colony of Carthage was the greatest power in the western Mediterranean, gold was brought from west Africa and tin from Portugal. A somewhat less exotic, but clearly profitable, trade was in dried fish, and the distinctive long pots in which these were transported are found at many coastal sites.

The ancient people of the eastern Mediterranean coastal lands were linked to each other by the sea. The earliest Egyptian historical document records the import of "forty ships of cedar logs" in the reign of Sneferu (c.2950 B.C.). This doubtless refers to the famous cedars of Lebanon which, with their precious oils, were one of the earliest goods traded by the people of that coast. Much later, in the first millennium B.C., the Phoenicians of the coastal cities still exported cedarwood and oils, but they were also now the foremost traders, mariners and craftsmen in the region.

The Phoenicians were a Semitic people who called themselves *Kinahu*, or Canaanites, after the whole region, although their cities were only located on the narrow coastal strip of modern Lebanon. They were known to the Greeks as *Phoinikes*, the "purple men," perhaps because one of their most coveted products was the famous Tyrian purple cloth, named for the city of Tyre. The dye for this was made from the *Murex* sea snail and could range in color from the palest pink to the deepest purple, later made famous by the Roman aristocracy.

Phoenician cities were independent states, although they would sometimes form alliances with each other. Tyre was to become the greatest of these cities, although others, such as Byblos and Aradus, were also very prosperous. These cities were built, whenever possible, on land jutting out into the sea or on offshore islands. High stone walls and towers protected the inhabitants, who lived in two-story houses with balconies. The Phoenicians were in fact famous for their skills as builders and craftsmen and were, for instance, employed to build King Solomon's temple at Jerusalem in the tenth century B.C.

Phoenician ivory carvings, glassware, jewelry and metal goods have been found widely spread, from Mesopotamia to Spain. Their ivory carvings, for example, decorated the palace built by Omri, the king of Israel, at his capital Samaria, and a huge collection of ivories, many of them in the Phoenician style, were found at the Assyrian capital Nimrud, where they had been taken as plunder or booty. Carved ivory often decorated expensive furniture and was sometimes gilded – indeed, the later Greek

use of gilded ivory cult statues might be derived, in the opinion of some historians, from Phoenician practice.

Apart from producing their own exports, the Phoenicians also acted as middlemen in trade. From the tenth century B.C., Phoenician ships sailed off in search of metals. Their first mining activities – for copper – took place on Cyprus, where they founded the colony of Kition. Later, rich deposits of silver in Spain led to the foundation of Gades, modern Cadiz. But the most famous of their colonies was Carthage, founded by Tyre, according to tradition, in 814 B.C. This city of the legendary Queen Dido was originally a staging post on the long journey to Spain; but in time it grew to be a great city, eclipsing even Tyre itself, until its defeat by Rome in the Punic Wars (pp.128–29), which finally ended in 146 B.C.

For posterity, however, the greatest contribution of the Phoenicians was their alphabetic writing system. First invented by the Canaanites in the second millennium, this simple script was taken abroad by Phoenician merchants wherever they traveled. From them, it was adopted by the Greeks, who made small changes to suit to their language. Later, the Romans adapted the Greek alphabet, and it is the Roman alphabet that forms the basis of modern western scripts.

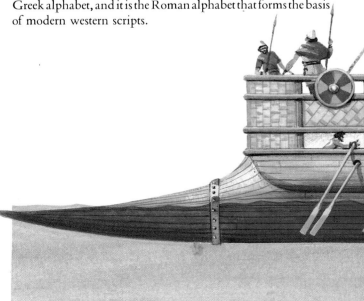

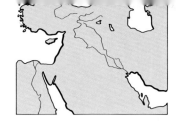

Until the end of the Bronze Age (c.1200 B.C.), the sea lanes of the Mediterranean had been dominated by the Mycenaeans of mainland Greece. However, after their demise, seaborne trade in the region came under the control of the Phoenician cities of the Levant. The hinterland that they controlled was confined to a narrow coastal strip extending inland to the mountains and generally less than 20 miles wide. With minimal land area to exploit, the Phoenicians took to the sea, trading and colonizing from the ninth century onward.

The Phoenician warship (BELOW), which would have escorted merchant ships, is based on an Assyrian relief. Its speed derived from a combination of sail and two banks of rowers, one of which could not be seen from the outside.

Natural resources formed the basis of many Phoenician industries. On nearby mountain slopes, cedars and pines grew, providing their earliest export, particularly to Egypt, where wood of sufficient length and quality was scarce. The resins also provided oils and unguents for trading. Later, other

Phoenician products circulated throughout the Mediterranean. Their famous purple dye was derived from the shellfish *Murex trunculus*, and their highly prized textiles were woven from the fleeces of their own sheep and from imported Egyptian flax.

From about 600 B.C. onward, the Phoenicians used their abundant supplies of sand to make glass that was almost colorless, as well as gaudy colored trinkets and amulets, which have been found in regions as far apart as Egypt and the Black Sea.

THE FIRST ALPHABETS

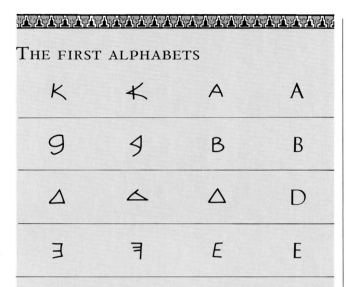

Stages in the development of the alphabet are charted here. The first column shows four letters of the Canaanite script of the late second millennium. These progressed in various stages, including Early Phoenician and Greek, shown in the second and third columns, to the Roman letters of most modern western scripts.

Alphabetic writing was invented in the Levant in about 1600 B.C. In the alphabetic system, a single sign represents a sound and so, unlike early pictograms, which were used to represent objects, the number of characters needed for written communication is considerably reduced. At the town of Ugarit, in modern Syria, a cuneiform alphabet with 32 symbols was in use by about 1400 B.C., and there were attempts at this time to simplify the Egyptian hieroglyphic system. By the early tenth century, the earliest known fully alphabetic Canaanite system had evolved, as evidenced by an inscription on the sarcophagus of Ahiram, ruler of Tyre. Phoenician and early Hebrew alphabets are related to this lesser known Canaanite system. When the Greeks adopted the alphabetic system, they introduced and adapted signs for representing vowels, since the Canaanite system used only consonants.

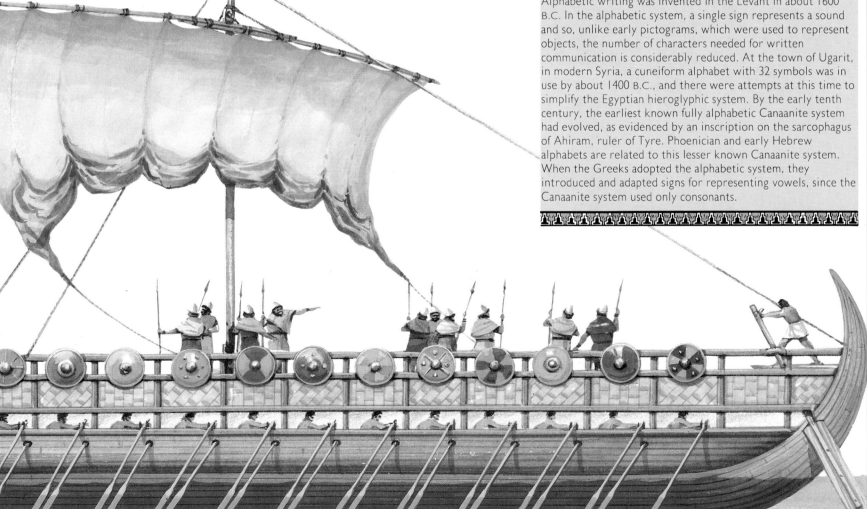

The first people to unite most of the Near East in one empire were the Assyrians. Although both the Hittites and the Egyptians had expanded their territories, they had controlled their foreign subjects through vassal rulers, whereas the Assyrians developed a system of provincial government. The Assyrian Empire also differed from these earlier expansions in the scale of its conquests and in its highly organized system of imperial administration.

The heartland of Assyria was in northern Mesopotamia, on the Tigris River. Here, there had been sanctuaries since about 3000 B.C. at Ashur, the capital, and Nineveh, the city of Ishtar. During the first thousand years of its history, Assyria, lying on important trade routes to Anatolia, was dominated by Sumer. With the accession of the Amorite king Shamshi-Adad I in about 1814, the Assyrians established control over much of northern Mesopotamia. The rise of Babylon under Hammurabi (1792–1750 B.C.) reduced Assyrian power, and later, for a short while, Assyria was dominated by the kingdom of Mitanni.

Centuries later, following the end of the Hittite Empire in about 1200 B.C. and the decline of Egypt, Assyria filled the political vacuum, emerging as a dominant power and regaining territory that had been lost to the Aramaeans. Acquisition of new lands began in the reign of Ashurnasirpal II (883–859 B.C.). Under him and his successor Shalmaneser III (858–824 B.C.), Assyria's boundaries were established at the Euphrates, and the kingdoms of north Syria were brought under control as vassals. Revolt in Assyria at the end of Shalmaneser's reign helped the kingdom of Urartu, lying to the northeast, to expand and dominate the eastern trade routes as well as the Syrian vassals on whom Assyria depended for manpower and for the supply of metals and horses from Asia Minor.

A period of weak central government marked the first half of the eighth century, when provincial governors acted as virtual independent rulers. Then, in 745 B.C., Tiglath-Pileser III came to the throne, marking the beginning of a century of Assyria's greatest expansion. To resolve long-standing border disputes

*From about 800 to 650 B.C., the domains of Assyria expanded from the upper Euphrates region to an empire embracing much of the Near East. This expansion first began in the ninth century when Ashurnasirpal II reclaimed from Aramaean tribes territory up to the Euphrates. Under Esarhaddon, the empire reached its greatest extent (*RIGHT*).*

***Ashurbanipal**, mounted on his horse, dispatches a lion single-handed in a relief (*RIGHT BELOW*) from Nineveh dating from about 650 B.C.*

LAYARD: EXCAVATING ASSYRIA

Sir Henry Austen Layard (1817–94) began excavations at the Assyrian site of Nimrud (ancient Kalhu) in November 1845. In fact, Layard had traveled widely in the Near East before starting this venture, which he had persuaded Sir Stratford Canning, the British ambassador at Istanbul, to finance. This in itself was no mean achievement for a young man of 28. Fortunately, in view of the difficulties with the local pasha and tribesmen, his previous experience and understanding of the local people were a great advantage when handling the many problems that arose.

At Nimrud, Layard uncovered the great Northwest Palace of Ashurnasirpal II (883–859 B.C.) and the later palaces of Esarhaddon (680–669 B.C.) and Tiglath-Pileser III (745–727 B.C.), as well as the remains of other buildings. He excavated briefly at Ashur and, in 1849, began to uncover Sennacherib's (704–681 B.C.) palace at Nineveh, where, he later calculated, he unearthed about a mile and a half of stone reliefs. He also organized the difficult task of transporting to Great Britain sculptures that included huge winged bulls weighing ten tons apiece. Layard left Mesopotamia for the last time in 1851. His earlier book, *Nineveh and its Remains*, was a popular success and gives a lively account of his work at Nimrud, which he at first thought to be Nineveh. On his return to Britain, Layard went into politics and eventually became British ambassador in Turkey from 1877 to 1880. He was knighted in 1878.

A party of children in the British Museum is shown some of the fruits of Layard's excavations in this Victorian illustration.

***Sir Henry Layard**, shown (*LEFT*) dressed in Persian clothes standing next to his servant Salah, began excavations at Nineveh (*RIGHT*) in 1849. Some of the human-headed winged bulls which he uncovered eventually reached the British Museum, as shown in the engraving (*ABOVE LEFT*).*

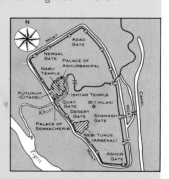

with Babylonia, Tiglath-Pileser asserted Assyria's position and moved the border farther south. Later, he captured Babylon and, in 729 B.C., became its king. He campaigned against the kingdom of Urartu, but this rival power was not neutralized until the reign of Sargon II (721–705 B.C.). In the west, Tiglath-Pileser recaptured the Syrian states and placed them under direct Assyrian rule. He later took Damascus, turning it and outlying parts of Israel into provinces. From then on, in later reigns, direct provincial rule was imposed with each military expansion.

Under Sennacherib (704–681 B.C.), the Assyrians entered Palestine, defeated the coastal cities, repelled Egypt, overran Judah and besieged Jerusalem. Although Jerusalem was not taken, its people were forced to buy off their aggressors with tribute. Once again there was trouble in Babylonia. So Sennacherib marched on Babylon and sacked it. His son Esarhaddon (680–669 B.C.), however, rebuilt Babylon and, farther east, made vassal treaties with princes of the increasingly powerful Medes, realizing that they could be potential allies against Elam, Babylon's old foe. (The Elamites were eventually eliminated by Esarhaddon's successor, Ashurbanipal, in 647.) In 675 B.C., Esarhaddon attacked Egypt under Pharaoh Taharqa, took Memphis and proclaimed himself king; but on his departure, Taharqa returned to power. Finally, the maximum extent of

(Continued p.34)

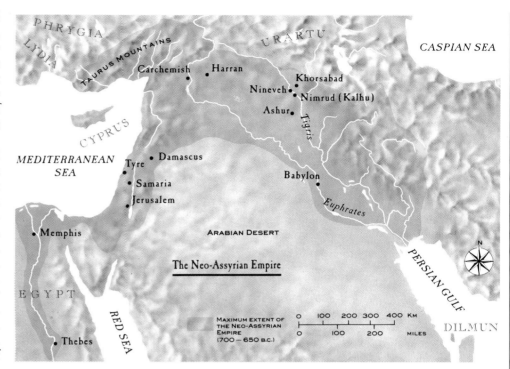

The Neo-Assyrian Empire

MAXIMUM EXTENT OF THE NEO-ASSYRIAN EMPIRE (700–650 B.C.)

33

Assyrian expansion was reached when the army of Ashurbanipal (668–627 B.C.) sacked the Egyptian city of Thebes.

Echoes of these turbulent events are heard in the Bible; and long before the excavations of Sir Henry Layard in the 19th century, which uncovered numerous Assyrian reliefs of battle scenes, the Assyrians had been branded as "warlike" by posterity. This image has been perpetuated, for example, in Lord Byron's poem "The destruction of Sennacherib," which begins:

"The Assyrian came down like the wolf on the fold
And his cohorts were gleaming in purple and gold;
And the sheen of their spears was like stars on the sea,
When the blue wave rolls nightly on deep Galilee."

Indeed, this view of the Assyrians as rapacious conquerors is partially true. Their vassals had to swear obedience and pay tribute, and the penalties for rebellion were dreadful: when cities were taken, they were looted and sometimes totally destroyed; and, even when they were not, citizens were often deported to some other part of the empire.

The Assyrians, however, despite their image, did embrace the arts of civilization. When Ashurnasirpal II moved his capital from Ashur to Nimrud, he built a great palace using workmen from conquered territories. After its completion, he celebrated by throwing a huge banquet for 69,574 guests. Nimrud remained the royal center until Sargon II built a new capital farther north, but this was only used for a short time. His son, Sennacherib, built yet another palace at Nineveh, which he called "The Palace without Rival." Booty and tribute were used to adorn the temples and palaces of Nineveh, famed for its wealth and splendor. The palace had beautiful gardens interlaced with streams, and plants were brought to it from distant lands.

The palaces were administrative centers as well as home to the king, his family and the court. There were numerous advisors, as well as diviners to read the omens before decisions were taken on matters of state. Earlier kings had led campaigns—indeed Sargon was killed on one—but later kings remained at court. Ashurbanipal, who had scholars copy and gather ancient texts for his library, was proud of his literacy and scholarship.

Originally, the Assyrian army consisted of peasants, but as the empire expanded, a standing army of conscripted soldiers was organized. Provincial governors, whose authority did not extend to the garrisons of local fortresses, were responsible for raising conscripts and supplying the army on campaign — a task that included the provision of fodder for horses. And a system of roads and grain storage depots helped the army and the king's messengers to move swiftly. The governors also had to raise the corvée (forced labor) for road building and maintenance, as well as collecting the taxes.

The constant collection of taxes from provinces or of tribute from vassals led time and again to rebellions that were harshly put down. But each subjugation further stretched Assyria's resources. Ultimately, faced with external pressure and internal civil strife, the country was too weak to withstand the alliance which had been formed between the Babylonian resistance movement under Nabopolassar and the Medes. With the fall of Nineveh in 612 B.C. to a combined force of Medes and Babylonians, the might of Assyria ended, although it was at the city of Harran west of Nineveh that Nabopolassar finally defeated the last remnants of the Assyrian army.

On the completion of his palace at Nimrud in 865 B.C., Ashurnasirpal II held a large banquet in a courtyard adjoining his throne room to celebrate the occasion. The details of this feast, reconstructed here, are known from a stele discovered at the palace during excavation, more than 2,500 years after the original event.

Ashurnasirpal (1) would have entered the courtyard, the facade of which was decorated with reliefs and large sculpted lamassu (3) — hybrid winged creatures. The king, sheltered from the sun by a parasol, would have been flanked by the crown prince and chief eunuch, immediately to his left and right, respectively. A line of Phoenician tribute bearers (2) brought the king valuable produce, such as wood, ivory and textiles.

Guests reclined on ivory and gilded couches and stools (5 and 4) and were regaled by musicians (6) playing lyres and double pipes. Much wine would have been quaffed, and the food consisted of various types of meat, such as venison, duck, lamb and goose; vegetables, such as turnips, lettuces and onions; and fruits, including quinces, plums, pears and pomegranates. The banquet took place over ten days and was attended by almost 50,000 guests.

BABYLON

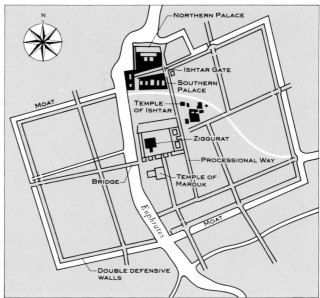

An aerial view of the site of Babylon shows the foundations of the great ziggurat, which lay in a sacred area south of the Ishtar Gate. The ziggurat was probably built in the early second millennium by Hammurabi, the king who made Babylon and its god Marduk supreme in the area.

Babylon was well planned (BELOW RIGHT). The main streets, most of them named after gods, ran parallel or at right angles to the river. The main entrance to the city was through the Ishtar Gate.

After the final defeat of Assyria in 609 B.C., the ancient city of Babylon once more became the greatest city of Mesopotamia. Under its new dynasty, whose first king, Nabopolassar (625–605 B.C.), had led the campaigns against Assyria, it also became the center of an empire that reached to the borders of Egypt. Although its empire did not last for even a century, it is this Babylon that was preserved in later literature.

Since the great days of Hammurabi (1792–1750 B.C.), Babylon had been sacked and looted several times. Indeed, a large stele on which the famous law code of Hammurabi had been inscribed was taken by the Elamites to Susa, where it was later found in the 19th century. More than a thousand years after Hammurabi, Nabopolassar, a Chaldaean sheikh who had seized the Babylonian throne, and his successor, Nebuchadrezzar II (604–562), rebuilt the city in greater splendor than before.

Babylon was surrounded by huge outer and inner walls, which the Greek historian Herodotus claimed were so wide that a chariot with four horses could be driven along it. Excavation has borne out this statement. There were several city gates, each named after one of the gods. The Euphrates River divided the city into two parts, which were connected by a bridge. In the eastern city lay the temples and palaces, which faced the river and to which the Processional Way led from the great Ishtar Gate.

Both the gate and sacred way were covered with brilliant, blue-glazed tiles on which were depicted lions, bulls and dragons in raised relief. These animals represented the gods most important to the city. Marduk, the city deity, was the dragon; Adad, the god of the sky and weather, the bull; and Ishtar, the goddess of love and war, was symbolized by the lion. Next to the great ziggurat was the temple of Marduk, and there were several other temples nearby. The palace was also decorated with glazed tiles. Nearby, on man-made terraces, were the Hanging Gardens, one of the seven wonders of the ancient world.

Within a few years of defeating Assyria, Nebuchadrezzar II had taken control of the lands from Mesopotamia to the Levant. In 597 B.C., he captured Jerusalem and forced King Jehoiachin and the greater part of the Jewish nobles into exile. He then appointed Jehoiachin's uncle Zedekiah as the city's new ruler. Shortly, however, Zedekiah was openly espousing anti-Babylonian policies, spurred on by the Egyptians, Babylon's rivals for Near Eastern hegemony. But Zedekiah's strategy badly misfired: Nebuchadrezzar attacked Jerusalem again in 587 and, after an 18-month siege, broke the resistance of its inhabitants. A second group of Judaeans was sent into exile.

This policy of deportation was in fact a common practice in the ancient Near East, since it kept the leaders of defeated people under direct control. The conquered provinces were ruled by Babylonian governors, although some were left in the care of local rulers whose loyalty to Babylon could be relied on. Local taxes covered the cost of administering the provinces, and the temples had to give one-tenth of their income (from temple lands) to the king. It is possible that the temple priests' resentment at this tax later resulted in their support of Cyrus of Persia, who, according to the Babylonian Chronicle, captured Babylon "without a battle" in 539 B.C.

BABYLONIAN IMAGES

The imaginary Babylon of western art has been largely conjured up, until the beginning of this century, from biased accounts of the Old Testament or Greek authors. It was not until the rediscovery of Mesopotamian civilization, which began in the mid-19th century, that artists, used to an accepted literary tradition, were able to utilize a nonliterary source. Until then, both painter and viewer knew the familiar stories, and, over the centuries, as art reinforced biblical and Greek literature hostile to Babylon, a stereotyped image of Babylonian

depravity developed. In fact, there is nothing in the texts or artifacts of the Babylonians that confirms this negative image, and yet it has persisted. And even when there has been knowledge of newly discovered Mesopotamian art and culture, it has often been used to give only a spurious authenticity to the subject matter depicted. The typical, but inaccurate, image of Babylon has thus been further reinforced and perpetuated.

In *The Babylonian Marriage Market* (BELOW), for example, painted by Edwin Long in the late 19th

century, the scene is based on the Greek historian Herodotus's account of the supposed Babylonian custom of selling girls to the highest bidder at the marriage market. The painter has faithfully followed the text, in which an auctioneer offers each girl individually, starting with the best-looking. Long was obviously familiar with Assyrian palace reliefs and used them as a source for the mural that decorates the room in the painting. Certainly he was unfamiliar with any Babylonian reliefs since at this time the city had not been excavated.

In this still of the Babylonian marriage market (BELOW RIGHT) *from his epic film* Intolerance, *made in 1916, D.W. Griffiths used the latest archaeological material for his portrayal of antiquity. In this scene, he has updated the painting* (RIGHT) *by Edwin Long and has incorporated decoration based on German excavations at Babylon from 1905 to 1914, including the ceramic panel* (BELOW) *from the throne room. Griffiths manages to achieve a highly ingenious misrepresentation of "Babylonian life." For although*

the Babylonian material, reconstructed in Berlin, has been used to add an aura of authenticity, this is undermined by the pharaonic fans, the Assyrian garden secene (*adapted from Long's picture*) *and an assortment of Egypto-Syrian-Mesopotamian garments.*

Edwin Long's painting (RIGHT) *of the Babylonian marriage market was based on an unreliable account by Herodotus in Book I of his* Histories. *The mural decoration is derived from Assyrian, not Babylonian, reliefs.*

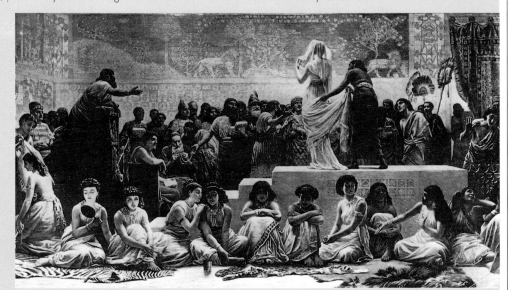

EGYPT

"Hail to you O Nile!
Sprung from earth,
Come to nourish Egypt!" ANCIENT EGYPTIAN HYMN

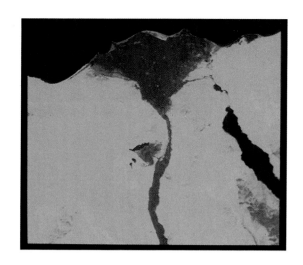

Between about 3100 and 332 B.C., one of the oldest and richest civilizations of the ancient world flourished in the Nile Valley. Here, Egyptian royal dynasties ruled from the First Cataract of the Nile to the Mediterranean Sea and at times controlled an empire, which, at its greatest, reached from Syria in the east to Nubia (Sudan) in the south. After thousands of years, the pyramids, temples and royal tombs still speak of the wealth and power of these rulers – the pharaohs who were god-kings, lords of the two lands, Upper and Lower Egypt.

The two lands, united by the shadowy first ruler, Menes, balanced each other economically and culturally, and were unified by the Nile. From the granite outcrops at Aswan – the traditional southern frontier – to the papyrus thickets and fertile fields of the delta, the Nile was Egypt's source of life. In the fifth century B.C., the Greek historian Herodotus called Egypt "the gift of the Nile," an apt description that the Egyptians themselves were well aware of. For they called their land *Kmt*, meaning "the Black Land," referring to the rich black mud deposited each year by the Nile flood.

The desert beyond the river valley they called *Dsrt*, "the Red Land," and here the dead were buried. In their tombs, the "houses of eternity," they were provided with everything needed to continue the pleasures of life in the next world. Much of what is known about ancient Egypt comes from the paintings, writings and objects found in these tombs, where they were preserved by the dry conditions of the desert. Evidence for this long-lost world also comes from the great stone-built monumental structures – the pyramids, obelisks, temples and statues.

The distinctive culture of ancient Egypt was unique in its continuity, and it retained its identity until it finally succumbed to Christianity during the third and fourth centuries A.D. But it did not completely die, for Coptic, the last form of the ancient language was used (and still is) in the services of the Christian Coptic Church. The last inscription in Egyptian hieroglyphics was made in A.D. 394, and, in the following year, when the Roman Empire was divided into two halves, Egypt became part of the eastern Roman – later, Byzantine – world.

Long before the demise of the ancient Egyptian world, classical authors visited and wrote about this fascinating land. However, for scholars, one of the most important literary works from this period was written in Greek by an Egyptian priest in the third century B.C.: Manetho's *Chronicle of Kings*, preserved by later writers, lists Egyptian rulers from the time of Menes to the conquest of Egypt by Alexander the Great in 332 B.C. Manetho estimated the length of each reign and divided the list into 31 dynasties. This system is used today as the basic framework for the history of ancient Egypt. For ease, Egypt's long history is divided into several phases, the main ones being the Old, Middle and New Kingdoms.

Until the decipherment of hieroglyphic writing in 1822, classical and biblical accounts were the main sources for knowledge of ancient Egypt. From the 15th century, European travelers visited and wrote about Egypt, but it was Napoleon Bonaparte's invasion in 1798 that marked the beginning of serious Egyptian studies. Accompanying Napoleon were 200 scholars, whose duty it was to explore and describe the country. With the publication of their works, later scholars could study copies of ancient texts. Among them was the Rosetta Stone, from which the French scholar Champollion (pp.60–61) deciphered hieroglyphs and so made it possible for Egyptian texts to be read.

A satellite photograph of the Nile and its delta vividly shows the contrast between desert and Egypt's life-giving river.

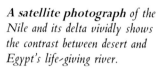

A figurine dating from about 3500 B.C., found in a grave of the predynastic Naqada culture, shows a female bird deity, or perhaps a dancer, with arms aloft in fluid expressiveness.

The temple of Isis, painted by the British artist David Roberts in 1843, was built in Ptolemaic times and was one of the most sacred places in Egypt. Since the construction of the Aswan Dam, it has been moved to a neighboring island.

A loving couple (RIGHT), possibly Meritaten, daughter of Akhenaten (1379–1362 B.C.), and her husband Smenkhkare', stroll in a garden on this limestone relief.

THE LAND OF EGYPT

The importance of the River Nile to both the people of ancient Egypt and their land cannot be underestimated. It is well expressed in an ancient Egyptian hymn, which pays homage to the life-giving river, describing it as: "Food provider, bounty maker,/Who creates all that is good." In a land where there is virtually no rainfall, except for a little near the coast, the Nile literally nourished Egypt, providing water and food as well as the chief means of transportation. Without the Nile, the region would be desert, as it is on both sides of the river oasis.

Of the world's great rivers, the Nile is one of the most predictable, since the timing and volume of its flood are, generally, reliable. Rains in the highlands of Ethiopia and central Africa feed the White and Blue Niles, causing the Nile in Egypt to rise in the summer and fall. Until the river was regulated by dams, particularly the Aswan Dam in 1970, the river rose in late July and, from mid-August to late September, flooded the valley. Salts were washed out of the soil and a layer of fertile silt was deposited.

Agriculture was the chief occupation of peasants, and the Nile flood determined the farming seasons. The year began in late summer with the "Inundation," when the land could not be worked. Then followed the season of cultivation, or "Going

Egypt has been irrigated by the waters of the Nile for thousands of years. The shaduf (BELOW) was introduced in the time of the New Kingdom (c.1567–1085 B.C.). A bucket is dipped into the water and then lifted by means of a counterweight. This primitive machine is still used, especially in Upper Egypt, although it is effective only for light irrigation.

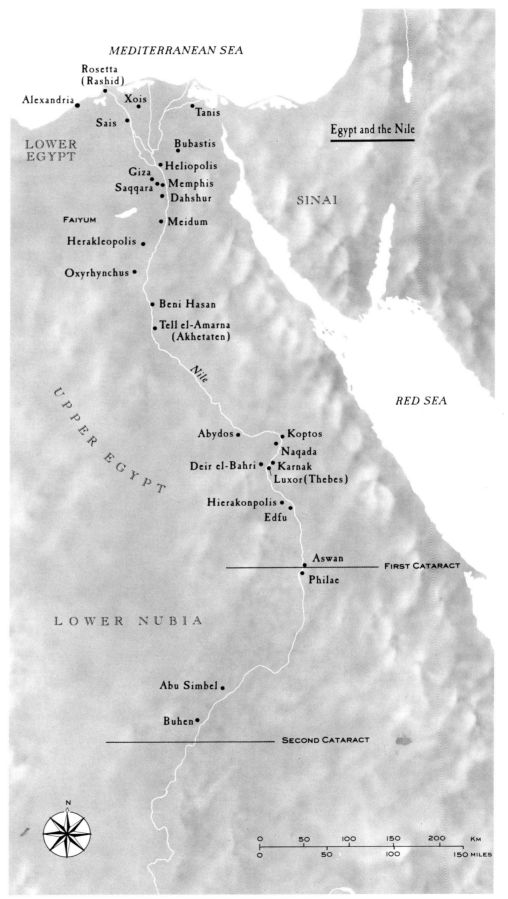

Egypt and the Nile

down of the Inundation," and finally the harvest in the "Drought" season. Although usually dependable, the Nile, if it was exceptionally low or high, could cause famine or devastate the land. Control and regulation of the river were immensely important, and irrigation was practiced from the earliest times. Banks were built to prevent the river from flooding over, and canals were cut to lead the water to otherwise unusable land. There were instruments known as Nilometers for measuring and recording the flood levels, and from them, the state's officials could calculate the likely harvest and thus the amount of tax they should impose upon the people.

The cultivated land provided rich yields and was the basis of Egypt's wealth. Several types of cereals were grown, and grain later became a major export. There were many types of vegetables, herbs and oil-producing crops for cooking and lighting. Flax for linen clothing and papyrus, which was made into paper, were also important crops.

Various water-lifting devices were invented – and can still be seen today. New Kingdom paintings show the shaduf, a bucket suspended from a pole with a counterweight. The *sakiye*, a large rotating wheel onto whose rim were attached water pots, was certainly used in Ptolemaic times and perhaps earlier. Later, the *tambour*, or Archimedes screw, was used to lift water over a short distance. The Egyptian people could feed themselves on the Nile's abundant fish, as well as on game and a variety of domesticated animals and poultry.

In the dry lands beyond the cultivated areas, there were hard and soft stones for building and for carving statues and vessels. They ranged from the hardest granites and diorite to soft and translucent alabaster. There were semiprecious jewel stones such as carnelian, agate, onyx and jasper. Turquoise came from Sinai and amethyst from Nubia. There was also copper and, above all, gold from the eastern desert and later from Nubia in the south. Natron, a sulfur used for mummification, came from the western desert, and salt pans were situated on the delta coast. The desert oases provided pasture and water for cattle-breeding nomads, although the oasis of the Faiyum, which was linked to the Nile, was extremely fertile and heavily populated.

Found in a Middle Kingdom tomb of about 2000 B.C., this ancient model (ABOVE RIGHT) shows a farmer working his field with a wooden plow and oxen. Four thousand years later, virtually the same scene (RIGHT) can be found in present-day Egypt.

The ancient civilization of Egypt was, in the words of the Greek historian Herodotus, the "gift of the Nile." This great river, with its annual inundations, provided the fertile soil needed for agriculture to flourish. The map (LEFT) shows the principal sites, from the delta to the Second Cataract, of Egypt's long history.

BEFORE THE PHARAOHS

Egyptian culture had its roots in Africa. However, the gradual formation of the land of Egypt – partly the result of climatic change – distinguished it from the cultural basis of the rest of northern Africa. In the last centuries before the dynastic period of Egyptian history that began in about 3100 B.C., there was a rapid development of civilization, including the appearance of monumental buildings and writing. Some scholars link these changes to contacts with western Asia; others see them as a natural progression of native Egyptian culture.

After the last Ice Age, in about 10,000 B.C., the grasslands of northern Africa gradually became deserts. As the plains and river courses dried up, animals and people, who were nomadic hunters, moved into the Nile Valley. Compared with the Near East, Neolithic farming developed relatively late in Egypt, but by about 5000 B.C., plants were being cultivated, animals were being bred, and people built houses and made baskets and pottery. It is clear that at this time the Egyptians already believed in life after death, for the dead were buried with food, drinking vessels, tools, beads, palettes used for grinding cosmetics, and other objects for the afterlife.

During this early period, there were a number of different groups of people. Their cultures, which are named after the sites where they were first found, are recognized by their pottery and increasingly sophisticated objects, including carved ivory and glazed stone vessels. Simple copper tools began to be used, and increasing quantities of copper and gold formed part of the jewelry buried with the dead.

Around 3500 B.C., there came a turning point which marked the end of a period of gradual change and local village culture. For the first time, there were contacts with other countries; a uniform culture spread over the entire Nile Valley and the delta, and a number of larger centers emerged, particularly Naqada, Koptos, Abydos and Hierakonpolis. There was also social change, for richer and more powerful groups of people became evident. Writing developed and large building works appeared; and some architectural elements and certain artistic motifs of this period suggest contacts with Mesopotamia, as does the introduction of writing. Maceheads, slate palettes, cylinder seals and the great recessed brick tombs of the earliest dynasties show affinities with Mesopotamian art, but the method of cultural transmission is not known. Trade, small-scale immigration and invasion have all been proposed.

Later historical sources suggest that before the First Dynasty (c.3100–2890 B.C.), kings had ruled the whole of Egypt after the two formerly separate kingdoms of Upper Egypt in the south and Lower Egypt in the north had been unified. Little is known of these kingdoms, whose capitals were reputedly Buto in the north and Nekheb, near Hierakonpolis, in the south. Knowledge of their rulers is scant; fragments of a macehead from Hierakonpolis, belonging to a king called Scorpion, depict scenes of his irrigation works and victory over his enemies.

It is possible that Scorpion preceded Na'rmer, who conquered the north and then became king of a united country. However, it is also possible that the idea of two predynastic kingdoms stems from the dualistic nature of Egyptian ideology and does not reflect historical reality. In this case, there might have been a gradual, not a sudden, unification, reflected in the spread of single culture.

One of the oldest painted scenes of ancient Egypt, this mural was discovered on an early brick-built tomb of a chief at Hierakonpolis, situated on the Nile south of Thebes. Dating from about 3400 B.C., the painting shows a variety of motifs, including different types of ships, animals such as antelope, and men with weapons. Also visible at the bottom left is a scene of a hero subduing two lions, reminiscent of Mesopotamian depictions of the legendary king Gilgamesh, Lord of the Beasts.

This richly carved ivory handle (LEFT) belongs to a ripple-flaked flint knife which was found at Gebel el-Arak and dates from about 3400 B.C. The side shown here depicts a battle on water; the boats in the bottom row are like Egyptian boats of this period, while the ones immediately above them have vertical prows and sterns rather like the boats of the Tigris.

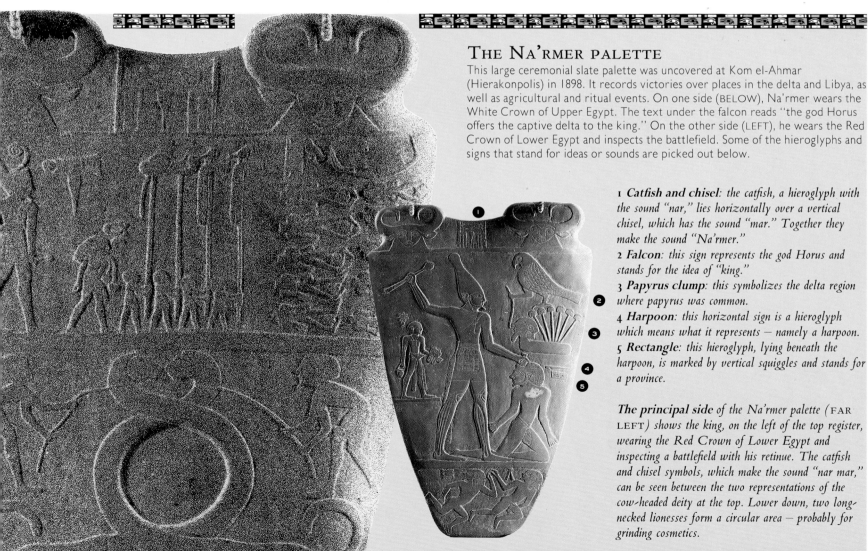

THE NA'RMER PALETTE

This large ceremonial slate palette was uncovered at Kom el-Ahmar (Hierakonpolis) in 1898. It records victories over places in the delta and Libya, as well as agricultural and ritual events. On one side (BELOW), Na'rmer wears the White Crown of Upper Egypt. The text under the falcon reads "the god Horus offers the captive delta to the king." On the other side (LEFT), he wears the Red Crown of Lower Egypt and inspects the battlefield. Some of the hieroglyphs and signs that stand for ideas or sounds are picked out below.

1 **Catfish and chisel:** *the catfish, a hieroglyph with the sound "nar," lies horizontally over a vertical chisel, which has the sound "mar." Together they make the sound "Na'rmer."*

2 **Falcon:** *this sign represents the god Horus and stands for the idea of "king."*

3 **Papyrus clump:** *this symbolizes the delta region where papyrus was common.*

4 **Harpoon:** *this horizontal sign is a hieroglyph which means what it represents — namely a harpoon.*

5 **Rectangle:** *this hieroglyph, lying beneath the harpoon, is marked by vertical squiggles and stands for a province.*

The principal side of the Na'rmer palette (FAR LEFT) *shows the king, on the left of the top register, wearing the Red Crown of Lower Egypt and inspecting a battlefield with his retinue. The catfish and chisel symbols, which make the sound "nar mar," can be seen between the two representations of the cow-headed deity at the top. Lower down, two long-necked lionesses form a circular area — probably for grinding cosmetics.*

The first king of the newly unified Egyptian state was the legendary Menes, known from later Egyptian king lists and classical sources. This first ruler of the First Dynasty, who lived around 3100 B.C., is shrouded in mystery and identified by some scholars with Na'rmer, the unifier of the two kingdoms. Little is known about the 500 years from the reign of Menes to the first great pyramid builders of the Fourth Dynasty (c.2613–2494), but this time marked the start of Egyptian civilization.

A centralized system of administration was developed, and the country was governed from Memphis, traditionally said to have been founded by Menes. During this period, the Egyptian script began to evolve into its classic form, and papyrus was used by the scribes for writing on. As irrigation works were extended, Egypt became increasingly prosperous. The classical southern frontier at the First Cataract was established. Craftsmen produced fine stonework, jewelry and furniture, as shown by finds in the tombs of the first two dynasties at Abydos and Saqqara.

This was also a period of artistic experimentation – a good example is the Step Pyramid at Saqqara, tomb of the Third Dynasty ruler Djoser. Designed by the architect and vizier Imhotep, the pyramid rose in several stepped stages and was a novel architectural form, built with new materials and techniques. It is also the oldest stone building of its size in the world.

By the Fourth Dynasty, kings were being buried in true, smooth-sided pyramids. Sneferu, the first ruler of this dynasty, built pyramids at Dahshur and Maidum. Such vast projects required great wealth and a highly efficient system of organization. During the Nile inundation, therefore, the peasants, who

This diorite statue of about 2500 B.C. depicts Khafre (Khephren), the fourth ruler of the Fourth Dynasty. The royal god Horus, in the shape of a falcon, sits on the top of the throne, giving his protective strength to the king.

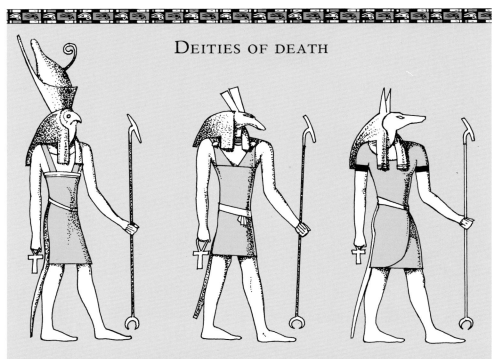

DEITIES OF DEATH

There were countless Egyptian gods, whose functions, as varied as their appearances, were often interchangeable or overlapped. For this reason, they are difficult to classify. There were both universal and local gods; some of the former are found entirely or partly linked to death and burial. Osiris, the mummiform god and ruler of the underworld, depicted wearing the white crown and carrying the crook and scepter, was also the dying god of vegetation. Killed and dismembered by his brother Seth, lord of the desert and the cruel god of battle, Osiris was resurrected by Anubis, the jackal-headed god of embalming, and by his wife-sister, Isis, whose wings wafted the breath of life into him. As the father of the living Horus, the dead king became Osiris. The complex symbolism changed over time, and later, all the transfigured dead became Osiris, symbol of resurrection.

The principal Egyptian deities of death were (CLOCKWISE, FROM TOP LEFT) the falcon-headed Horus; Seth, the brother of Osiris; the jackal-headed Anubis; Osiris, wearing the white crown and holding the crook and scepter; and Isis, who was both sister and wife of Osiris.

made up most of Egypt's population, were employed on such great building projects. They were always liable for corvée (forced labor), for the land on which they worked for most of the year belonged, in theory, to the king. In Sneferu's reign, there are records of trade with Byblos in the Levant for cedarwood, and there was a campaign into Nubia, which led to the foundation of a settlement at Buhen, probably used as a base for mining expeditions and trade.

The pyramids built at Giza for the succeeding Fourth Dynasty rulers, Khufu, Khafre and Menkaure', although stripped of their fine stone facings and gilded capstones, still dominate the skyline near Cairo. Even today, the building of Khufu's Great Pyramid would be a technological feat. It has been estimated that every year during his 23-year reign, 100,000 large stone blocks, each weighing about two and a half tons, had to be quarried, dressed, taken to the site and set in position.

The pyramids were intended to protect the bodies of the kings and their jewelry, tomb furnishings and other objects placed with them for the afterlife. Smaller separate pyramids were built for the queens. Pyramid complexes included a mortuary temple linked by a causeway to a valley temple where parts of the funerary rituals were performed. The boat found near Khufu's pyramid is thought to have been used to carry the dead king to the valley temple. There was also, perhaps, a symbolic link between this boat and the solar barque in which, according to Egyptian mythology, the sun god traveled through the sky by day. The solar religion was important in the Fourth and Fifth Dynasties, and it is likely that the pyramid was a solar symbol.

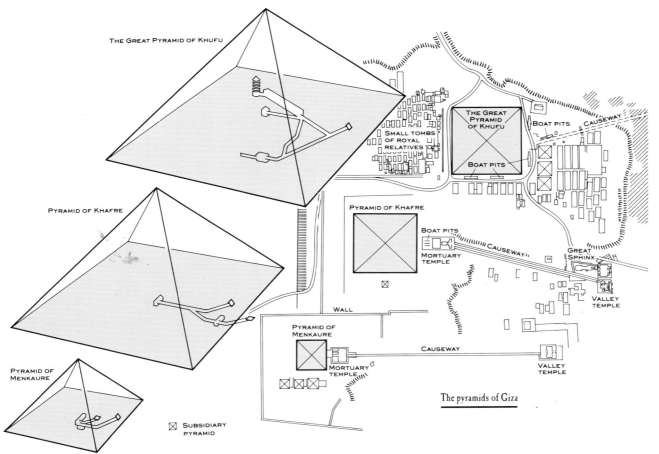

THE GREAT PYRAMID OF KHUFU

PYRAMID OF KHAFRE

PYRAMID OF MENKAURE

⊠ SUBSIDIARY PYRAMID

SMALL TOMBS OF ROYAL RELATIVES

THE GREAT PYRAMID OF KHUFU

BOAT PITS

CAUSEWAY

BOAT PITS

PYRAMID OF KHAFRE

BOAT PITS

CAUSEWAY

MORTUARY TEMPLE

GREAT SPHINX

VALLEY TEMPLE

WALL

PYRAMID OF MENKAURE

MORTUARY TEMPLE

CAUSEWAY

VALLEY TEMPLE

The pyramids of Giza

Measuring more than 138 feet long, this wooden boat (ABOVE) was found, dismantled, in a pit on the south side of Khufu's pyramid in the 1950s. It was later easily reassembled and is now housed in a museum next to the pyramid. The boat was made from more than 1,200 pieces of timber, mainly cedarwood from the Lebanon. It was probably used to take the deceased ruler to the place of purification and embalming and then to the valley temple.

The largest of the Giza pyramids (LEFT) is that of Khufu, although the pyramid of Khafre appears taller, since it was constructed on slightly higher ground. Surrounding these giant structures are smaller pyramids belonging to queens, countless mastaba ("bench-shaped") tombs of nobles, mortuary and valley temples, and causeways.

BELZONI: A STRONG MAN IN EGYPT

Giovannin Battista Belzoni was born in Padua in 1778, but was forced to leave his home town when the French invaded in 1798. In 1803, he arrived in England where his great height of six and a half feet enabled him to earn his living as a strong man on the vaudeville stage. As "Patagonian Samson," he appeared in a human pyramid act – an ironic fact in view of his subsequent connection with Egypt.

In 1815, chance took Belzoni to Egypt. Here, his prior training in hydraulics and his size and strength helped him in his new role as collector of antiquities for the British Museum, a task he performed on behalf of Henry Salt, the British consul. Belzoni's first commission was to remove the granite bust of the Younger Memnon from the Ramesseum at Thebes, in the face of considerable opposition. He then traveled up the Nile and opened the Temple of Ramesses II at Abu Simbel. Back at Thebes, he discovered several tombs in the Valley of the Kings, including that of Seti I. After finding the colossal head of an Eighteenth Dynasty pharaoh, he traveled northward; and, at Giza, he entered the pyramid of Khafre, which until

then was thought to be a solid mass.

Belzoni left Egypt in 1819 and, two years later, arranged an exhibition of his finds, drawings and casts at the Egyptian Hall, Piccadilly, in London. Later, tiring of the attentions of London society, he set off on an expedition to find the source of the Niger, but died of dysentery in 1823.

The huge scale of the Fourth Dynasty pyramids and the extensive resources that made their construction possible are a measure of the power and wealth of the pharaohs at this time. The cult of the sun god Re' had gradually increased in importance and, from the time of Khafre, the pharaoh was called "son of Re'." The temples at Heliopolis, the cult center, were among the most influential in Egypt, and by the Fifth Dynasty (c.2494–2345 B.C.), its priests had become very powerful. At the same time, the stature of the pharaoh decreased, the royal tombs became smaller and some rulers built sun temples. Although important for the ideology of kingship, the cult of the sun had a limited appeal and consequently became less prominent by the end of this dynasty.

Earlier kings had delegated some of their duties to highborn officials, usually royal relatives. After their deaths, these nobles were laid in tombs close to the royal pyramid, the most favored situated in its shadow. At Giza there are rows of flat-topped *mastaba* tombs, symbols of the nobles' closeness to their rulers in death as in life. But, gradually, as the royal strength diminished, the courtiers grew in power and independence.

The nobles became a wealthy group, receiving gifts of land from the king. As these gifts were endowments for the upkeep of family tombs and funerary rituals, they were often exempt from taxes. The lands given to them were hereditary, so crown lands were gradually owned by children of former courtiers. The latter, who were no longer dependent for their positions upon the king, made their positions hereditary. In the case of the *nomarchs*, or provincial governors, they became extremely independent – some had their own private armies – particularly in the more remote areas of the country.

The Great Pyramids of Giza (RIGHT) *are still an awesome sight, more than 4,000 years after their construction during the Fourth Dynasty. The Step Pyramid at Saqqara (ABOVE), built for the Third Dynasty king Djoser, was a precursor of the true, smooth-sided pyramid.*

The *nomarchs* increasingly chose to be buried in impressive rock-cut tombs in cliffs of the regions where they had lived and governed. For instance, a Sixth Dynasty governor of Upper Egypt, Weni, was buried at Abydos, and the inscriptions in his tomb give an account of his deeds, including his military campaign to Palestine in the reign of Pepi I. Trading expeditions were regularly sent to Nubia for exotic products such as incense, ivory and skins. Cattle and slaves were also brought back. A later governor, Harkhuf, buried at Elephantine, recorded his four expeditions to Nubia and, on one occasion, he returned with a dancing pygmy for the young pharaoh Pepi II.

The last king of the Sixth Dynasty, Pepi II, reigned for over 90 years. Following his death in about 2181 B.C., there was a period of crisis and social upheaval known as the First Intermediate Period. A series of low floods and resultant famines during the Sixth Dynasty had undermined the stability of the state and perhaps provoked rebellion. The Egyptian people always looked back on the Old Kingdom as a Golden Age and a measure for all later cultural achievements. Apart from innovations in architectural monuments, some still visible after thousands of years, there were developments in painting and sculpture, as well as in medicine, literature and theology.

The period that followed was one of rapid decline. With no central power, the provinces became independent states, often at war with each other. The situation was made worse by the penetration of nomadic foreigners into the delta region. The writings of this period reflect the insecurity and sorrow of a people for whom "Laughter has perished. Grief walks the land."

THE FATHER OF MODERN EGYPTOLOGY

Unlike the colorful Belzoni (OPPOSITE PAGE), the austere British Professor Flinders Petrie (1853–1942) rarely made the headlines. Although he began as an amateur archaeologist, Petrie ended up being called the Father of modern Egyptology. Until his pioneering work in archaeological method, most excavators were intent on the acquisition of great treasures – such as those Belzoni had removed from Egypt – to display in museums. Petrie's understanding that excavation was about retrieving information, rather than finding beautiful objects, is now taken for granted, but this was not always so.

Petrie was originally a surveyor who was interested in pyramidology and the British Israelites, a supposedly lost tribe of Israel. From this somewhat unconventional background, he became the foremost excavator in Egypt, working at numerous sites. Although he did make spectacular discoveries, his work was important in providing a framework of information about the different areas and periods of Egyptian history. He understood the value of small objects and the importance of recording everything found.

One of his major contributions to archaeology was his invention of sequence dating. On the assumption that pottery styles changed gradually, he arranged pots from 900 tombs into chronological order and then divided the sequence into equal sections, numbered to allow for future discoveries. Petrie's long life was spent digging, recording and bringing order to Egypt's past. In later life, he lived and worked in Palestine, where he died, at the age of 89, in 1942.

Sir Flinders Petrie, despite an eccentric streak, pioneered new standards in excavation and in the analysis and publication of finds. Wherever he worked, whether in Egypt or, later in life, in the Near East, he imposed the highest standards on himself and his workers.

D'ISRAEL-I IN TRIUMPH; OR, THE MODERN SPHYNX.

A cartoon from the 1867 issue of the British magazine Punch *(LEFT) uses Sir Edward Poynter's painting,* Israel in Egypt *(BELOW), to satirize the British statesman Benjamin Disraeli (1840–81). Instead of Poynter's lion, the* Punch *cartoonist has depicted Disraeli in the form of a sphinx being dragged by slaves who bear the faces of famous contemporaries.*

ISRAEL IN EGYPT

Painted in 1867, *Israel in Egypt* (LEFT BELOW) established Sir Edward Poynter's reputation as an artist when he was only 31. Although the subject matter, the Israelites working as slaves in Egypt, does not illustrate a specific Bible story, the content was well understood. Such themes were popular with the Victorians, who were familiar with the Old Testament and interested in ancient Egyptian culture. Like other painters of this genre, such as Edwin Long and Sir Lawrence Alma-Tadema, Poynter never visited Egypt, but had access to books and museum collections (he even managed to live opposite the British Museum) to assist him in this elaborate "reconstruction" of pharaonic Egypt.

Although his depiction of Egypt is imaginary, the details have been carefully researched and accurately copied; the whole, however, is a mixture of buildings and elements from widely different places and periods. The lion in the foreground is modeled on one of a pair of the Eighteenth Dynasty in the British Museum; the temple on the right is a mixture of the temples of Luxor and Edfu, and the Great Pyramid of Giza looms on the horizon of the Theban hills. The painting has been described as a "conglomeration of unassimilated facts" which, while true, is irrelevant, for the artist was not attempting to portray absolute reality, but the essence or image of a place. Complete accuracy, stripped of extravagant artistic licence, would have diminished the dramatic impact achieved by the juxtaposition of Israelite slavery amid pharaonic opulence.

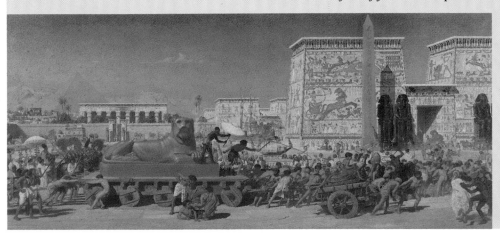

KING AND COURT

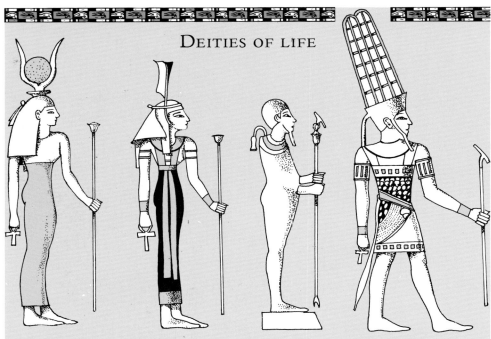

DEITIES OF LIFE

Some of the greatest and best-loved Egyptian gods were the children of deities, symbolizing the basic physical elements in the various creation stories. Although Osiris was god of the underworld (p.44), he was also the god of vegetation, believed to have introduced agriculture and wine-growing to Egypt. His brother was Seth, and his wife Isis was also his sister. Horus, the son of Isis and Osiris, was the heavenly falcon god and the living king. Another god closely associated with the king was Amun of Thebes, who ultimately became the supreme state god. He was identified with the sun god Re', as Amun-Re'.

Some gods were associated with love and prosperity; Hathor, the goddess of love, music and dancing, carried a sistrum, a musical instrument. She was usually shown in human form with a sun disk and cow horns on her head, because she had once raised the youthful sun to heaven on her horns. Hapi, god of the Nile in flood, brought fertility to the land. He was shown as a long-haired man with papyrus on his head and carried offering tables laden with produce. Ma'at personified the basic laws of existence and brought order and harmony. She was the goddess of truth and law.

There were also gods associated with the activities of ordinary people: Ptah was the local god of Memphis, inventor of the arts and patron of craftsmen. Two deities who were popular with women and associated with new life were Bes, the dwarf god of the family and the protector of pregnant women, and the hippopotamus goddess, Taweret, protectress of pregnant women.

Egyptian religious ideas were complex and developed over a long period. At different times and places, certain gods were more or less important. Some of these were (CLOCKWISE, FROM TOP LEFT) Hathor, shown with cow horns and a sun disk on her head; Ma'at, the personification of order and harmony; Ptah, patron of craftsmen; Amun-Re', chief god of the New Kingdom; Bes, the dwarf god; and Taweret, the hippopotamus goddess.

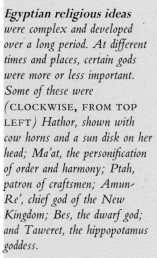

The accession in 2060 B.C. of Mentuhotep II of Thebes, the first pharaoh of the Middle Kingdom, ended 90 years of conflict with a dynasty established at Herakleopolis, south of Memphis. This strong Eleventh Dynasty ruler restored order in Egypt and consolidated the borders. He drove the Asiatics from the delta and campaigned against the Libyans and nomadic tribes in Sinai and the eastern desert. Trading expeditions were sent to Syria and Palestine; and in Nubia, where Egyptian authority had lapsed since the Sixth Dynasty, tribute was levied and the trading route made safe. Mentuhotep II reigned for 50 years and was buried at Deir el-Bahri in an unusual tomb that comprised a temple and a pyramid.

During Mentuhotep III's reign, Egyptian ships once again sailed the Red Sea to Punt – whose location is unkown, but was possibly Ethiopia – where the precious incense grew. During the brief and troubled reign of Mentuhotep IV, a quarrying expedition to the Wadi Hammamat was led by the vizier Amenemhet, who usurped the throne five years later. For two centuries from 1991 B.C., Egypt prospered under the Twelfth Dynasty of able and energetic rulers. Amenemhet I moved the court to Itjtowy, a town situated somewhere between Memphis and Maidum. He and his successors built their pyramids in the vicinity of the Faiyum, where, under Sesostris II (1897–1878 B.C.), a great land reclamation project was begun. Later, the lake was drained and thousands of acres were brought under cultivation.

At such times of powerful rulers, Egypt was governed by an efficient administration. Taxation provided much of the wealth and was carefully organized. A census of fields and of all cattle was taken every two years. From Nilometer readings, the probable height of the inundation was calculated to work out the likely harvest of each field for tax assessment. In addition to tax calculation and collection, another important official function was the building up of reserve grain stocks to avoid famine after a bad harvest. The state controlled all foreign trade and owned the mines and quarries.

The chief official was the vizier who directed the departments of agriculture, justice, labor and the treasury. Also under his control were the central government departments administering the provinces of Upper, Middle and Lower Egypt formed under Sesostris III (1878–1843 B.C.). This king had shorn the wealthy *nomarchs* of their privileges and rendered them politically impotent. At the same time, a middle class of craftsmen, traders and small farmers emerged.

Sesostris III personally led three campaigns to Nubia and consolidated Egypt's control there. To protect trade and assure access to the gold of Nubia, fortresses had been established earlier as far south as Buhen, above the Second Cataract. Several forts were built at the frontier. Expeditions were sent to Sinai to mine turquoise, and there was trade with Syria and the Levant where, at Byblos, several Twelfth Dynasty objects have been found.

Little is known of the end of the Twelfth Dynasty; but for more than a century after the queen who was last of the line, the Thirteenth Dynasty rulers resided at It-towy. For later Egyptians, the Middle Kingdom was renowned as being the Golden Age of literature, when the language attained its classical form. Indeed, it is still the case that Middle Egyptian is the form of the language that aspiring Egyptologists are first taught.

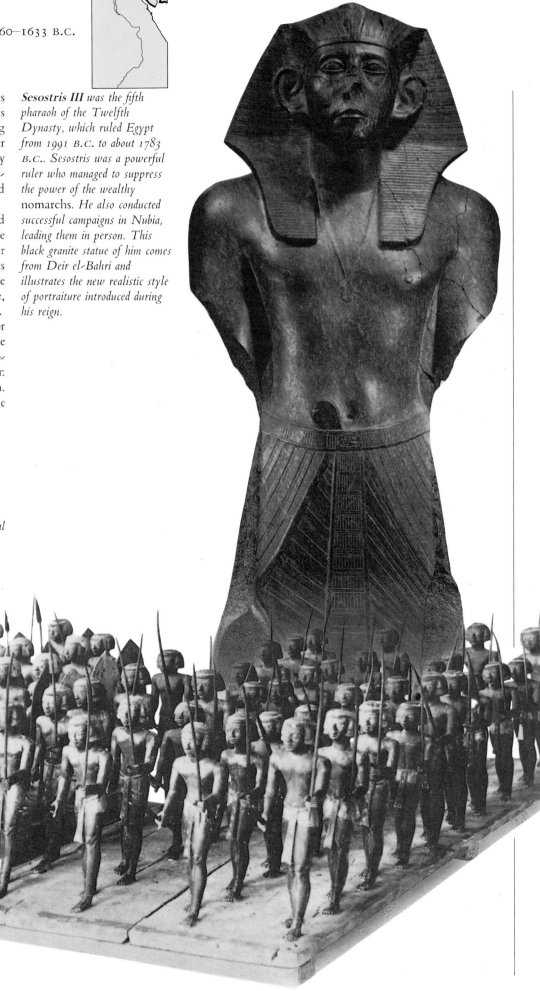

Sesostris III was the fifth pharaoh of the Twelfth Dynasty, which ruled Egypt from 1991 B.C. to about 1783 B.C.. Sesostris was a powerful ruler who managed to suppress the power of the wealthy nomarchs. He also conducted successful campaigns in Nubia, leading them in person. This black granite statue of him comes from Deir el-Bahri and illustrates the new realistic style of portraiture introduced during his reign.

Wooden models (BELOW) *from the tomb of Prince Mesekhti, probably of the Twelfth Dynasty, portray Nubian soldiers, against whom Sesostris III's army would have fought. The Nubians are dark* *skinned and are armed with shields, spears, and bows and arrows. Such models were put in tombs in the belief that they would perform services for the owner — in this case a provincial noble — in the afterlife.*

49

THE RISE AND FALL OF THE HYKSOS

Following the end of the Thirteenth Dynasty in 1633 B.C., much of Egypt came under the control of Asiatic people known as the Hyksos, from the Egyptian *heka-haswt*, meaning "rulers of the foreign lands." These people ruled from the city of Avaris, which has not yet been found, although it probably lay near Qatana in the eastern delta. The identity of the Hyksos is not known, and there is no evidence that they invaded Egypt. It is more likely that their takeover was peaceful and came as a result of an increased Asiatic population in the delta, a phenomenon which coincided wtith the decline of the Thirteenth Dynasty. During the Middle Kingdom, Asiatics were employed by the state, at first in the Sinai mines and increasingly in Egypt itself.

With the disappearance of a strong central government, Egypt, once again, was a land divided. Throughout the Thirteenth Dynasty, and for some time afterward, a line of local

kings ruled from Xois in the western delta. These Fourteenth Dynasty kings seem to have maintained their independence when much of the country had submitted to the Hyksos, who formed the Fifteenth and Sixteenth Dynasties. In the south, a new line of princes arose at Thebes, and these Seventeenth Dynasty rulers formed a semi-independent state. Although they paid tribute to the Hyksos, they retained their autonomy. And, after about a century, it was these princes who overthrew the Hyksos and drove them from Egypt.

Later tradition, probably based on the propaganda of the Theban victors, claimed that there was anarchy under the Hyksos, who were accused of burning temples and cities. In fact, there is no evidence for this and, indeed, everything points to their respect for Egyptian culture, which they clearly adopted. They used Egyptian titles, wrote their names in hieroglyphs,

The mortuary temple of Queen Hatshepsut, at Deir el-Bahri, is partly rock-cut and partly free-standing. Its colonnaded courts are on three levels and lead, by way of two ramps, to the sanctuary cut into the hillside. Hatshepsut was the third Eighteenth Dynasty ruler after Ahmosis, the pharaoh who expelled the Hyksos from Egypt.

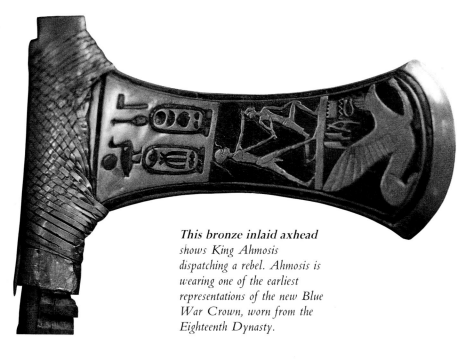

This bronze inlaid axhead shows King Ahmosis dispatching a rebel. Ahmosis is wearing one of the earliest representations of the new Blue War Crown, worn from the Eighteenth Dynasty.

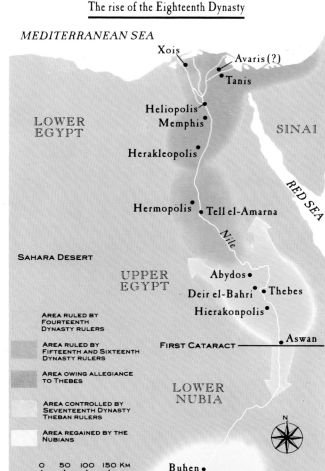

The rise of the Eighteenth Dynasty

MEDITERRANEAN SEA

Xois
Avaris (?)
Tanis
Heliopolis
Memphis
Herakleopolis
Hermopolis
Tell el-Amarna

LOWER EGYPT

SINAI

RED SEA

SAHARA DESERT

UPPER EGYPT

Nile

Abydos
Deir el-Bahri · Thebes
Hierakonpolis

FIRST CATARACT — Aswan

AREA RULED BY FOURTEENTH DYNASTY RULERS

AREA RULED BY FIFTEENTH AND SIXTEENTH DYNASTY RULERS

AREA OWING ALLEGIANCE TO THEBES

AREA CONTROLLED BY SEVENTEENTH DYNASTY THEBAN RULERS

AREA REGAINED BY THE NUBIANS

LOWER NUBIA

Buhen ·
SECOND CATARACT

0   50   100   150 KM
0   50   100 MILES

Western Asiatics (LEFT), in a wall painting from Beni Hasan, bring eye paint to trade with an Egyptian governor during the reign of Sesostris II. An increase of Asiatics in the delta occurred during the decline of the Thirteenth Dynasty.

In 1633 B.C., after the end of the Thirteenth Dynasty, the Asiatic Hyksos, who formed the Fifteenth and Sixteenth Dynasties, ruled much of Egypt from Avaris in the delta. In the same region, an independent dynasty, the Fourteenth, for a while governed from Xois until 1603 B.C.. In the south, Nubia regained its autonomy and, in Thebes, a series of princes (the Seventeenth Dynasty) maintained a semi-independent rule. The last of these princes began the struggle against the Hyksos, who were eventually expelled from Egypt by Ahmosis, first ruler of the Eighteenth Dynasty. Ahmosis then moved south to fight the Nubians.

appointed Egyptian officials and maintained the administrative system. During this time, many new developments and practical skills were introduced into Egypt. These included advanced methods of bronze making, a vertical loom for weaving, an improved potter's wheel, the lyre and lute, hump-backed cattle, new vegetables and fruits, and most important, new weapons and the horse-drawn chariot.

But whatever the reality of the nature of their rule, the Hyksos' presence was probably not popular; throughout Egypt's history, as reliefs and inscriptions make clear, foreigners were looked on unfavorably. However, one of the consequences of Hyksos rule was the dramatic change in Egypt's attitudes to warfare and foreign conquest. From now on, Egypt would pursue an aggressive military and foreign policy, backed by a full-time and extremely professional army.

The Theban prince Seqenenre' began the struggle against the Hyksos, dying in battle of fatal head wounds. His son Kamose drove them from Middle Egypt and took Avaris. In 1570 B.C., he was succeeded by his younger brother Ahmosis, who drove the Hyksos out of Egypt, pursued them into Palestine and eliminated them in a series of campaigns. He then turned south and fought the Nubians, who had supported the Hyksos.

After a decade of fighting, Ahmosis became the first Eighteenth Dynasty ruler of the New Kingdom. His first task was to restore Egypt's economy after the years of war. Raw materials from other countries appeared again, for silver, gold, lapis lazuli and turquoise have been found in burials of this time, and they were also presented to the god Amun-Re', whose cult Ahmosis fostered. The founder of this most illustrious of Egyptian dynasties died in 1546 B.C.

THE EIGHTEENTH DYNASTY

Under a series of able Eighteenth Dynasty rulers, Egypt established control over Syria and Palestine and became the leading power in the Near East. Provincial governors, often local princes, were placed in charge of the newly conquered Asian territories, and in some states Egyptian garrisons were installed. As a guarantee of loyalty, the sons of local princes were taken to Egypt, where their education meant that they would develop pro-Egyptian sympathies. A royal messenger acted as an intermediary between the pharaoh's court and the Asiatic provinces, from whom annual tribute was exacted.

Once again, Nubia was subjugated, and by the end of the reign of Amenophis II (1450–1425 B.C.), Egyptian control reached beyond the Fourth Cataract. The province was ruled by an official called the "King's son of Kush," and Egyptian domination was symbolized by the construction of walled towns, each with its own temple, which replaced the Middle Kingdom fortresses. The mines of Kush now provided the gold of Egypt, and Nubia also supplied other luxury goods, such as copper, ivory, ebony and animal skins.

The wealth from booty, tribute and trade stimulated cultural life, as did increasing contacts with other countries. There were new fashions in clothing and jewelry, and new customs and gods. Thebes was now the capital, and although little is left of the brick-built palaces, the remains of painted and gilded plaster decoration of Amenophis III's (1417–1379 B.C.) pleasure palace reveal something of the elegance of this building. From the time of Tuthmosis I (1546–1526 B.C.), the temple of the state god Amun was enlarged and enhanced, and it was here that the pharaohs dedicated booty from victorious campaigns.

The temple was also the main treasury of the state. Kings were buried in rock-cut tombs near Thebes and the only intact burial found, that of the young king Tutankhamun (1361–1352 B.C.),

gives some idea of the sumptuous treasures doubtless buried with more important rulers and of the wealth and brilliance of this period. The queens and princes were buried in neighboring valleys, as were the nobles, whose tombs were painted with charming scenes of daily life.

Egypt's power and prosperity were largely the result of the exploits of a few kings. Tuthmosis I campaigned as far as the Euphrates and first brought Syria and Palestine under Egyptian control. Following the reign of Hatshepsut (1503–1482 B.C.), the widow of Tuthmosis II, her nephew and stepson Tuthmosis III (1504–1450) reasserted Egyptian authority over kingdoms in Asia, and came into conflict with Mitanni. Under Tuthmosis IV (1425–17), a peace treaty was concluded between these powers and sealed by dynastic marriages. Toward the end of Amenophis III's reign, the Hittites sacked Mitanni's capital and began to dominate Syria, which they took control of during the reign of Amenophis IV (1379–1362). Egyptian influence in the region now lapsed.

Amenophis IV abandoned the worship of Amun, claiming divine guidance from the Aten, or sun's disk. He took the name Akhenaten, meaning "beneficial to the sun-disk," but failed to introduce the new religion at Thebes, where there was opposition from the powerful priests of Amun. He moved his capital to the newly built city of Akhetaten, "the horizon of the Aten," about 200 miles north of Thebes, and which is now known as Tell el-Amarna. Here the Aten was worshipped at an open-air altar in the Great Temple. Akhenaten, his beautiful wife Nefertiti and their children lived at the Royal Residence and at the Maru-Aten, a pleasure palace with a lake, south of the town. A new and distinctive naturalistic style was used in the decoration of the palaces and nobles' villas, as well as in the reliefs and sculptures of this period.

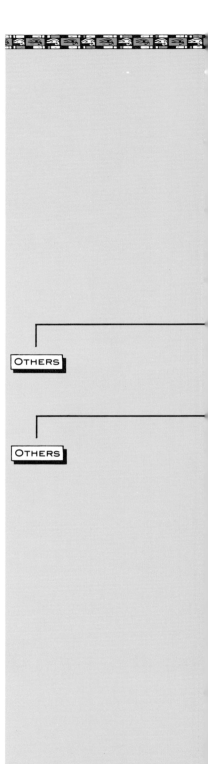

The site of Tell el-Amarna, which gives its name to the Amarna Age, was the ancient capital of Akhetaten ("the horizon of the Aten"), built by the pharaoh Akhenaten. Situated on the east bank of the Nile, it is surrounded on three sides by steep cliffs, in which have been discovered rock-cut tombs intended for the royal courtiers. The city was abandoned soon after the accession of Tutankhamun, who rejected Akhenaten's cult of the Aten and returned to the old religion of Amun.

THE FAMILY OF AKHENATEN

There are several unresolved historical problems about the Amarna Age, which partly result from attempts by later rulers to eliminate all traces of Akhenaten. The chronology is difficult to establish because some rulers elevated their heirs to the position of co-regent. The genealogy of Akhenaten, shown here, is complicated since, for example, the Eighteenth Dynasty pharaohs often married the Great Royal Daughter, who was usually their own full or half-sister. Amenophis III married a commoner, Tiy, and they had several children, including Akhenaten and their eldest daughter, Sitamun. She seems to have married her father, by whom she had several children, including Smenkhkare', who briefly succeeded Akhenaten, his uncle and half-brother.

Akhenaten married Nefertiti and they had six daughters, the eldest of whom died young. Later, Nefertiti either died or was banished and Akhenaten married his second daughter, Meritaten. As the royal heiress, Meritaten was subsequently married to Smenkhkare', and Akhenaten took his third daughter, Ankhesenpaaten, as wife. Both Akhenaten and Meritaten died, and Smenkhkare' married Ankhesenpaaten, the widowed princess. Tutankhamun, his young successor, also married Ankhesenpaaten. They were either uncle and niece or half-siblings, depending on whether Tutankhamun was the brother of Smenkhkare', as suggested by tests carried out on their mummies, or Akhenaten's son by a secondary wife, Kiya. The young king died childless, as did his much-widowed queen.

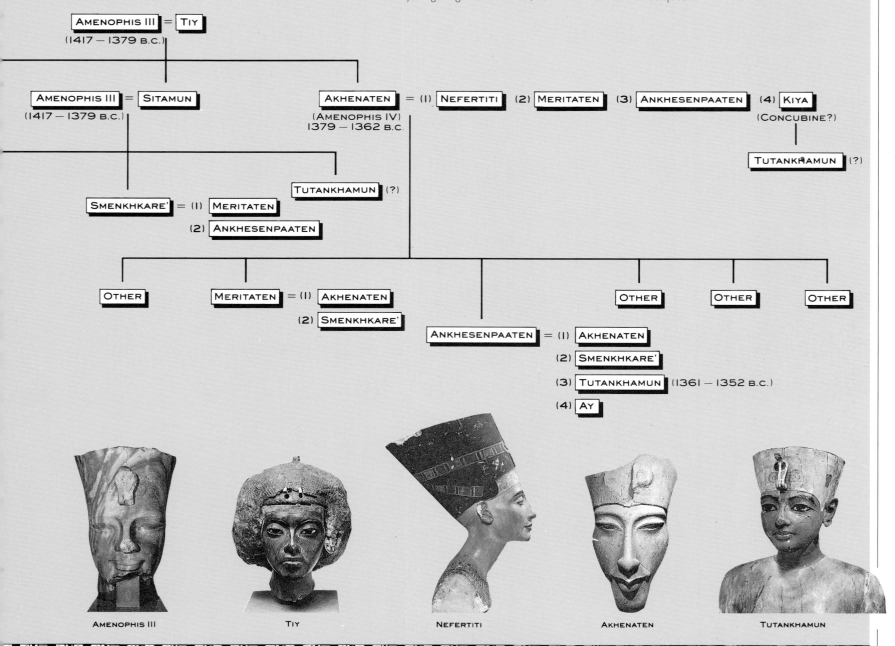

AMENOPHIS III   TIY   NEFERTITI   AKHENATEN   TUTANKHAMUN

After the death of Akhenaten, the Eighteenth Dynasty was continued by the short reign of Smenkhkare'. On the latter's death, the nine-year-old Tutankhaten (1361–1352 B.C.) became pharaoh. As custom decreed, he was married to the royal heiress, and soon afterward the court moved to Memphis. While the king was a minor, the vizier and regent was Ay, who had been Akhenaten's Master of the Horse. There was a return to traditional policies, and the worship of Amun was restored. In honor of the Theban god, the royal couple changed their names to Tutankhamun and Ankhesenamun.

On his death, the young king was buried in a small tomb. (Its discovery by the British archaeologist Howard Carter and his sponsor Lord Carnarvon in 1923 made Tutankhamun the most famous of pharaohs.) His widow wrote to the Hittite king asking that one of his sons be sent to marry her and become the new pharaoh. The suspicious king delayed, but finally sent a prince, who was killed on his way to Egypt. Instead, the elderly vizier Ay secured the throne by marrying Ankhesenamun, and nothing is heard of her after Ay's death in 1348 B.C.

Following Ay's brief reign, the former commander of the army, Horemheb (1348–1320 B.C.), came to the throne. Although he is regarded as the last ruler of the Eighteenth Dynasty, there are indications that Egyptians in later times treated him as the founder of the Nineteenth Dynasty. The details of his reign are sparse, but it seems to have been devoted to restoring the old order and destroying all traces of Akhenaten and his family.

The first ruler of the new dynasty, Ramesses I, was the son of a low-ranking military officer. He was appointed vizier by Horemheb, who named him as his successor. He reigned for two years and was succeeded by his son, Seti I (1318–1304 B.C.), who did much to restore Egypt's prestige. There was one campaign against the Libyans, and he also campaigned in the east and restored Egyptian control over Palestine. Egypt came into conflict with the Hittites in Syria, but by the end of Seti I's reign, the two powers seem to have reached an understanding.

Seti's son, Ramesses II (1304–1237 B.C.), resumed hostilities and, in the fifth year of his reign, fought the Hittites under their

In the spring of 1300 B.C., an Egyptian expeditionary force under Ramesses II, camped near the city of Qadesh, was nearly overrun by the Hittites. But according to Ramesses, the day was saved by his fierce counterattack.

Wearing his blue war helmet, Ramesses (6) and his chariots (4 and 8) scattered the three-man Hittite chariots (5 and 7), already softened up by volleys of arrows from Egyptian archers. On the other side of the Orontes (1), not far from Qadesh (3), the Hittite king Muwatallis (2) looked on with his 8,000-strong reserve.

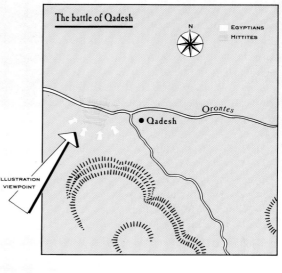

king Muwatallis at Qadesh. The details of this encounter for the control of Syria are known because Ramesses had it recorded as a great victory on several temple reliefs. In fact, the result was indecisive, and both armies suffered heavy losses. The city of Qadesh, on the Orontes River, was the Hittites' southern defense bastion. On the march north, Ramesses detached a special task force to secure one of the seaports, from where it was to join the main army at Qadesh. Misled by false information, the main army of four divisions continued northward along the Orontes, unaware that the Hittites were waiting just beyond Qadesh.

The division of Amun, led by Ramesses, was the first to reach its destination and set up camp. As the next division approached, it was charged by the Hittite chariotry, broke ranks and scattered. The third division was too far away to help, the camp was overrun and heavy losses were sustained. However, Ramesses, according to his own accounts, led a spirited counterattack. The task force which had been detached now came to the rescue, and, with another division, defeated the Hittites. Both sides withdrew, and some years later, they signed a treaty.

DECLINE AND CIVIL WAR

The remainder of Ramesses II's long reign was relatively peaceful and prosperous. Nubia was still under his control, although there seem to have been difficulties in maintaining the earlier levels of gold production. Ramesses' many new buildings included the temple at Abu Simbel, his mortuary temple at Thebes and monuments at Tanis. He also moved the capital north to Pi-Ramesse. Under his successors, Egypt entered a long period of decline. Merneptah (1236–1223 B.C.) fought and defeated invading Libyans, who were allied to the Sea People (pp.28–29). In the reign of the Twentieth Dynasty pharaoh Ramesses III (1198–1166 B.C.), Egypt was again attacked by Libyans and the Sea People. Three campaigns were fought in the delta before the invaders were beaten.

Although most of Ramesses III's reign was prosperous and the king made many gifts to the temples, toward the end there were problems. One was the first recorded strike in history, which occurred when the monthly food rations paid to the royal tomb workers were overdue and the vizier himself had to inter-vene. More serious was the discovery that several of the king's wives and officials of the harem were involved in a plot to kill him. As punishment, some of the plotters were allowed to kill themselves, while others had their nose and ears cut off.

The next eight rulers were all called Ramesses, and under them Egypt lost what was left of her empire and became increas-ingly unstable. During these years, the Theban royal tombs were plundered by robbers and the account of their trial survives. When the thefts were discovered, 36 royal mummies were removed from their tombs by officials and hidden in a remote rock shaft, where they were only discovered 3,000 years later. Such thefts were partly the result of reduced policing of the royal necropolis caused by a shortage of funds.

The last ruler of the Twentieth Dynasty was Ramesses XI (1113–1085 B.C.), and during his reign Egypt was virtually divided between the powerful High Priest of Amun at Thebes and the vizier of Lower Egypt, Smendes, who ruled from Tanis. Although he was still recognized as the pharaoh, the last Ramesses no longer had any authority and withdrew to his

The statue of Ramesses II (1304–1237 B.C.) (RIGHT), holding an offering table, shows this vigorous ruler to be serene and smiling and in the prime of life. It is in stark contrast to his mummified head (BELOW LEFT). Tests on Ramesses' mummy, which was found in Deir el-Bahri, reveal that the pharaoh, arguably Egypt's greatest, suffered from dental problems, heart disease and arthritis. His distinctive hooked nose is a characteristic feature of all the other Ramesside pharaohs of the Nineteenth Dynasty.

residence in the delta. Following his death, Egypt was once again ruled by rival kings from different cities and the country's days of greatness were over. Initially, the descendants of Smendes ruled as kings at Tanis for about 100 years, until 945 B.C., and at Thebes there was a line of rulers who were descended from the High Priest. Marriage ties strengthened the alliance between these two dynasties, and this period was relatively uneventful.

However, as always at times of weak central authority, new groups of people moved into Egypt. The Libyans, who formerly had been repulsed so frequently, settled in the western delta and the Faiyum. In time, they were Egyptianized and many of their leading families became powerful. Some Libyans were the descendants of captives settled in Egypt by Ramesses III.

One such family, a line of Libyan chiefs, became established in about 945 B.C. at Bubastis, halfway between Memphis and Tanis. Sheshonq, the head of this family, became the first ruler of the Twenty-Second Dynasty. He renewed Egyptian interest in Nubia, traded with Byblos and invaded Israel in about 925 B.C. But the authority of his successors was challenged in Thebes and elsewhere. Within a century, the various Libyan dynasties were at odds with each other and civil war broke out. As Egypt disintegrated during this confused period, in Nubia a Kushite kingdom, centered on Napata close to the Fourth Cataract, gradually moved its influence northward.

PRESERVING THE BODY

The Egyptian practice of mummification to preserve bodies after death was founded on their belief in an afterlife. They believed that the *ka*, the life force created at the same time as the body, would not survive unless the body was preserved in a recognizable form. The most elaborate and expensive form of mummification began with the purification of the body, first by washing and then by removing the vital organs. It was then covered with natron, a compound of sodium and carbon, for 40 days, to dry it out. The body was then washed and packed with bandages soaked in resin and bags of fragrant spices. After that it was bandaged and adorned with jewels and amulets for protection. A painted mask was placed over the face, which was rebandaged. Finally, the mummy was placed in a human-shaped inner coffin, which was often fitted inside two others. The coffin was deposited in a tomb and surrounded by burial objects to aid the deceased in the afterlife. Tombs were usually sealed with stones faced with plaster; however, this often did not prevent robbers from rifling them for precious burial objects.

Coffins were made of wood and plastered and painted on the inside and outside with magical texts to protect the deceased, as can be seen (BELOW) on the double anthropoid coffins of Nespamai, a priest from Akhmin in Upper Egypt.

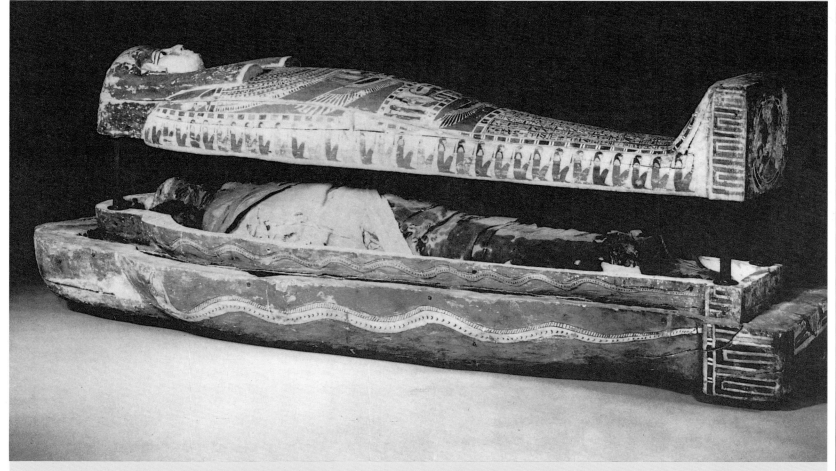

THE LAST EGYPTIAN KINGS

gypt's division into a number of small states in the north and a theocracy of Amun's high priests at Thebes in the south had left Nubia independent. During the eighth century B.C., the dynasty that emerged at the Nubian city of Napata worshipped Amun and was on good terms with the priests at Thebes. The Nubians increasingly involved themselves in Egypt's affairs; and, in the mid-eighth century, under their ruler Piankhy, they marched to Thebes and shortly afterward subdued the whole of Egypt. Piankhy shrewdly forced the "God's wife of Amun," who was now always the king's daughter and immensely powerful, to adopt his sister as her successor – thus assisting the Nubian claim to Egypt. In 715 B.C., Piankhy's brother Shabaka was installed on the throne as the first pharaoh of the Twenty-Fifth Dynasty.

For a time, Egypt was relatively peaceful under its new rulers; but soon they began to intrigue with the rulers of Palestine against powerful Assyria. In 701 B.C., the Egyptians escaped the wrath of Assyria only when the latter's forces were struck down by plague. Then, under the next Assyrian king, Egypt was attacked, and the pharaoh Taharqa was forced to flee from Memphis. Since the Assyrians left no army of occupation, Taharqa returned; but, under Ashurbanipal, the Assyrians attacked not only Memphis but also Thebes. The city was plundered and this was the end of its greatness and of the Nubian dynasty: the remnants returned to Nubia and established a new capital at Meroë, where they built pyramid-shaped tombs and continued to worship Egyptian gods and use the classical form of the Egyptian hieroglyphic script.

Although remains from the Twenty-First to the Twenty-Fifth Dynasties are relatively sparse, partly because the main cities were in the delta and have perished through flooding and silting, some fine works have been found, including beautiful

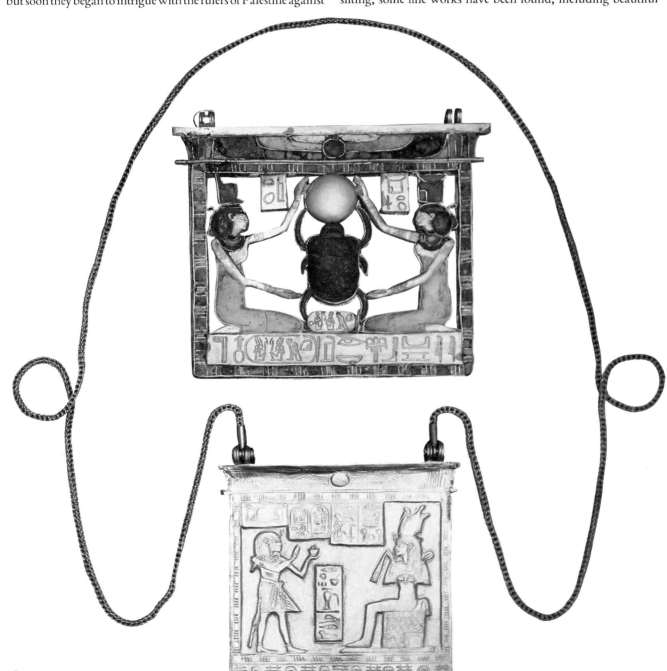

These pectorals, or chest ornaments, from the royal tombs at Tanis, form part of the funerary jewelry of King Amenophthis of the Twenty-First Dynasty. The upper piece, without the chain, is made of gold inlaid with lapis lazuli and is considered to be decayed. Because this was jewelry for the tomb, little care was taken over its execution. The design is in the form of a primeval shrine: Nephthys and Isis, supporting the scarab, are kneeling down on a podium on which are depicted the royal title and cartouche.

The lower pectoral is made of two sheets of gold, folded to an edging to form a thin box. The design is worked in repoussé and chased. The king is wearing the nemes headcloth, pectoral, kilt and bull's tail, and stands on the left before Osiris, to whom he offers incense.

The royal tombs at Tanis were excavated by Pierre Montet in 1939. The tombs of two Twenty-First Dynasty and four Twenty-Second Dynasty rulers were found; and although the tombs were disturbed in antiquity, a number of funerary jewels were found. Apart from these pieces, some of which were finely crafted, there is little surviving jewelry from this period, except for a few poor examples from provincial tombs.

jewelry. The burial mask of Psusenes I from Tanis and some fine statues show that the quality of craftsmanship was still high.

The Assyrian king appointed vassals loyal to himself over Egypt, but as Assyria's power declined, Egypt regained its independence under a dynasty of kings from Sais in the delta. The rule of these Twenty-Sixth Dynasty kings was a last great period of splendor in Egypt. There was an artistic renaissance and the kings encouraged a revival of earlier art forms. As a result, many beautiful pieces exist from the Saite era, as this period became known.

Egypt now became increasingly cosmopolitan, and Greek traders began to settle here. Work began on a canal to link the Red Sea with the Mediterranean. Psammetichus I and his successors built up a navy and merchant fleet with Phoenician help. And Pharaoh Necho (610–595 B.C.) sent an expedition under Phoenician sailors to circumnavigate Africa.

The Saite kings had established control over the Two Lands of Egypt, but their aspirations to become a great power again were crushed by the Babylonians, who defeated the Egyptians in battle in 605 B.C. Later, the fall of Babylon to the Persians in 539 B.C. brought a new neighbor and threat to Egypt. In 525 B.C., the Persians under Cambyses attacked and defeated Egypt. The country was now ruled as a Persian satrapy, or province, by a Persian satrap.

The Persians, however, administered Egypt efficiently, governing it mainly under its own laws and regularly collecting taxes. Nevertheless, there were several unsuccessful revolts. At one point, the Persians were driven out of the country, but they returned in 341 B.C. In the interim, native Egyptian dynasties, depending on Greek mercenaries, fought with each other and rendered their country increasingly unstable and poor. Then, nine years after the Persians returned, Alexander the Great of Macedon was welcomed by the Egyptians as their liberator.

This head of an unidentified king, made of green schist, dates from the Late Period – probably the time of the Thirtieth Dynasty (c.380–343 B.C.). Sculpted in the tradition of the earlier period of classical Egyptian art, it represents the ruler, who is wearing the royal nemes *headcloth, in an idealized manner.*

THE NUBIAN KINGS

The collapse of Egypt's empire in the early first millennium B.C. left a power vacuum in Nubia and Upper Egypt, and assisted the rapid rise of a Nubian dynasty at Napata. Nothing is known of the family's origins, but it seems likely that they were local chiefs who gave their support and protection to the priests of Amun at Jebel Barkal – the administrators of the region following the demise of pharaonic power. Their patronage of the Amun priesthood and command of the Nubian troops, on whom Egypt had long relied for protection, probably led to their being accepted by the priests as rulers at both Jebel Barkal and Karnak. In turn, the kings relied on the priests to sanction and legitimize their rule.

The first of these Nubian kings known by name was Kashta, who was sixth of the dynasty. It was he who first visited Thebes as the patron of Amun and defender of the faith. His son Piankhy succeeded him in about 751 B.C., and spent the first 20 years of his reign at Napata. When Thebes was threatened by one of the dynasts in the delta, Piankhy was asked to give his protection. He agreed, was victorious, and then returned to Napata, where he later died.

The succession to the throne usually passed to the deceased's surviving brothers and then reverted to his eldest son – a system that guaranteed adult kings. After Piankhy's death, his brother Shabaka succeeded him, followed by his son Shabataka. Although both ruled from Thebes, they were buried near Napata after their deaths. Taharqa, who became pharaoh around 689 B.C., had to cope with the problems created by his predecessors' involvement in Palestine. In spite of these difficulties, he built several temples in Egypt and Nubia. He, too, retired to Napata and appointed his nephew Tenutamon to rule the now diminished Egyptian territory. After the sack of Thebes by the Assyrians in about 667, the last king of the Twenty-Fifth Dynasty returned to his homeland. For the next 1,000 years, first at Napata and then farther south at Meroë, a centre of the iron industry, the Nubian kings ruled using the titles of the pharaohs.

Nubian pyramids, such as the one shown here at Meroë, the later capital of the Nubian kings, were smaller at the base and taller in proportion than Egyptian ones.

GREEK AND ROMAN RULE

THE ROSETTA STONE

In 1799, French soldiers of Napoleon Bonaparte's army, which had invaded Egypt, were digging fortifications in the delta town of Rosetta (Rashid) when they discovered a slab of black basalt (BELOW). On it was an inscription of a decree passed by a council of Egyptian priests in 196 B.C. expressed in two languages, Greek and Egyptian, and written in three scripts, Greek (BOTTOM REGISTER), Egyptian hieroglyphic (TOP REGISTER) and demotic, a late form of the Egyptian language, (MIDDLE REGISTER). The hieroglyphic script, hitherto untranslated, was deciphered by Jean François Champollion, a brilliant French scholar who published his discoveries in 1822.

Champollion's wide knowledge of ancient languages included both Coptic, a late form of Egyptian, and Greek, and from these he was able to identify the hieroglyphic characters of the name "PTOLMYS," or Ptolemy, which was written in a cartouche – the encircled name of the king. He then compared these hieroglyphic characters with a cartouche from another inscription, which had some of the same signs, namely P, L and O. He read this as "KLIOPADRA" – Cleopatra – which now gave him 12 characters. From this small number, he gradually built up a sign list from other royal names and titles, recognized by their surrounding cartouches. Although there was still much to be worked out, his pioneering work in unlocking the hieroglyphic script was an extraordinary feat.

In 332 B.C., the Persian satrap of Egypt surrendered to Alexander the Great (pp.114–15) without a struggle. Alexander was accepted as pharaoh and, on visiting the oracle of Amun at Siwa, was acclaimed as a god – the normal address to a pharaoh, but one which seems to have convinced him of his own divinity. The young Macedonian conqueror laid the foundations of Alexandria in the western delta and made plans for Egypt's administration. Native governors were appointed and arrangements made for tax collection.

After Alexander's death in 323 B.C., his general Ptolemy, son of Lagus, took the young king's body for burial to Alexandria, where a great tomb was built. In doing this, Ptolemy symbolically linked himself and his successors to the divine pharaoh and founder of the city. In 305 B.C., Ptolemy declared himself king of Egypt and became the first of a line that ruled Egypt until the end of the reign of Cleopatra VII when, in 30 B.C., the country was taken over by Rome. The Ptolemies took pharaonic titles and paid honor to the Egyptian gods, which gave them the support of the priests. Outwardly, Egyptian life was much as it had been in pharaonic times but, in fact, the interests of the local inhabitants were subordinated to those of their new masters.

The Ptolemaic period was a time of great contrasts. Alexandria was a great center of Hellenistic culture, having the world's first museum and the largest library of its time. Medicine, mathematics and geography flourished. The Egyptians, however, were subjected to heavy taxes and other conditions that resulted in increasing poverty. Farmers had to lease their land from the

CLEOPATRA'S CHARM

Perhaps the most famous woman of antiquity, Cleopatra VII, the last of the Ptolemaic rulers, was by all accounts a complex and charming woman, though not, it seems, a great beauty. The daughter of Ptolemy XII, she was born in 69 B.C. and became queen in 51, ruling jointly with her half-brother. In a court beset by intrigues, Cleopatra exploited the situation and emerged as supreme ruler. She captivated the hearts of the Romans Julius Caesar and Marc Antony, and her relationship with the latter has become one of the world's great love stories.

Her life was first written about by the Greek biographer Plutarch in the early second century A.D., and it was on this account that Shakespeare based his tragedy. Since then she has been the subject of numerous plays, poems and paintings, and, in recent times, films. In this medium, she has been portrayed as a great beauty by a series of screen goddesses, including Elizabeth Taylor and Claudette Colbert (RIGHT), who wears a headdress based on the symbol of the goddess Hathor. Cleopatra's reputed suicide by the bite of an asp in 30 B.C., depicted in a 17th-century German engraving (RIGHT ABOVE), happened after her defeat by the forces of Octavian at the battle of Actium.

CLAUDETTE COLBERT
in Paramount Pictures

state, which regulated the type and quantity of crops that they might grow each year. They had to maintain the canals, pay a tax in grain and allow the state to buy part of their crop at a fixed price. Industries also had to pay heavy taxes, and certain commodities were state monopolies. As time went by, strikes and flight from the land became quite common, and toward the end of the period, there was unrest and rural depopulation.

Under Roman rule, the country's administration was reorganized, and steps were rapidly taken to halt the agricultural decline. Egypt became the granary of Rome, and its importance is underlined by the fact that, unlike other Roman provinces, it was under the direct control of the emperor. Peace, security and efficient government brought a remarkable economic recovery, and agricultural production increased and commerce flourished. Nevertheless, this prosperity benefited Rome, not Egypt.

Little is known of the Egyptians themselves during the first two centuries of Roman rule. The ancient cults were maintained and temple building continued; but the temple lands were now owned by the state, and the priesthood was controlled by a Roman civil official. The hieroglyphic script, except for texts carved on the walls of the temples in Upper Egypt, was abandoned. By the end of the second century A.D., there were revolts and increasing lawlessness. The political, social and cultural decline of the Egyptians made them ready converts to Christianity. First brought to Alexandria, this new, universal religion spread rapidly. Several of the early church fathers were Egyptian, and it was here that monasticism first developed.

The distinctive art form of the Greco-Roman period can be seen in this statue of Anubis, the jackal-headed god of embalming. The god's traditional Egyptian form and dress have been replaced by a naturalistic human body, suitably dressed in a white toga.

From 1895 for some ten years, the British scholars Bernard Grenfell and Arthur Hunt excavated the ancient site of Oxyrhynchus in the Faiyum and found a huge number of papyri, such as the one shown here (LEFT). Most papyri were found as fragments in refuse deposits dating from the Greco-Roman period.

The Oxyrhynchus papyri have provided much information about life under the Ptolemies and Romans, for many are copies of edicts, petitions, receipts, contracts and letters. They also contain copies of lost works by classical authors and scholars, including Plato, Aristotle and Sophocles. In fact, a fragment from the latter's comic satyr play, the Ichneutae, or "Trackers," was used by the modern British writer Tony Harrison for his own conception of how Sophocles' original might have continued. Harrison's play included a chorus of satyrs, shown (BELOW RIGHT) in a performance at Delphi in Greece.

Oxyrhynchus

PERSIA

“ *Soft countries breed soft men. It is not the property of any one soil to produce fine fruits and good soldiers too.* **”**

WORDS ATTRIBUTED TO CYRUS THE GREAT (559–530 B.C.) BY THE GREEK HISTORIAN HERODOTUS

This drinking bowl *dates from the time of the Sasanian kings, the last Persian dynasty to rule before the coming of the Islamic Arab armies in the mid-seventh century A.D. It is silver and gilded, with applied repoussé, and possibly depicts King Shapur II dispatching a stag.*

For some 200 years from the late sixth century B.C., the Persian Empire of the Achaemenid dynasty, which embraced lands from central Asia to the Indus and from Egypt to the Mediterranean, was the largest and best organized empire hitherto in the ancient world. This achievement was all the more remarkable considering that the Achaemenids had been an obscure Iranian tribe just over a generation before. Cyrus the Great, the founder of this empire, unified for the first time the Iranian plateau, which became the new power center of the Near East.

Cyrus's capture of Babylon in 539 B.C. marked the beginning of the end of the old order, in which, for most of the preceding two and a half millennia, the region had been dominated culturally and politically by Mesopotamia and Egypt. This period also saw the beginning of close contact between the Near East and Europe, when the Greeks of Ionia in Asia Minor came under Persian control. In addition to the conflict between the Greeks and Persians, there was also an exchange of politicians, scholars, merchants and mercenaries whose journeys between these regions were facilitated by the magnificent Persian system of roads, including the Royal Road from Susa to Sardis.

The exploits of the Persian rulers from Cyrus to Xerxes are known from colorful Greek accounts, which also describe the wealth and splendor of the Achaemenid kings and their nobles. According to the Greek historian Herodotus, Persian generals went on campaign with furniture of gold and silver and with golden bowls and goblets. Superb examples of surviving gold and silver objects and the remains of Persian palaces at Persepolis, Susa and elsewhere bear out this image of opulence.

In Greek and biblical literature, a close association was made between the Persians and a related people known as the Medes—a linkage that reflected their actual political situation and their common Iranian tribal and linguistic background. It was the Greeks who first gave the name of Persia to the whole of Iran, taking it from Parsa, the regional homeland of the Achaemenids, now the modern province of Fars in the southwest. Iran, meaning "land of the Aryans," covered a far larger area than the present-day country and included parts of central Asia, Afghanistan and the Caucasus. The people of these regions, linked by their Iranian language and culture, were descended from the nomadic Indo-European Aryans, who migrated to the high plateau in the second millennium B.C.

Relatively little is known of the various groups who inhabited the land before the Iranian migrations. The lack of written

evidence means that their history is virtually limited to that of the kingdom of Elam in the southwest. Here, there was continuous contact with neighboring Mesopotamia, and the relationship between these lands is an enduring theme in Elam's history. Susa, the best known and most excavated Elamite city, was later adorned with beautiful buildings by Darius, under whom it became the main administrative center of the Persian Empire.

Achaemenid civilization is often criticized for the extent to which it drew on the cultural traditions of others. Nevertheless, the fusion of peoples and cultures which took place under the Achaemenids did create Iranian unity, one of the dynasty's lasting achievements. Alexander the Great's defeat of Darius III in 331 B.C. (pp. 114–15) brought Iran under Hellenistic control for a century and a half. But Hellenism did not spread much beyond the cities, and Persian culture and the Zoroastrian religion survived Seleucid rule (pp.116–17). The Iranian Parthian dynasty, which ruled from about 170 B.C. to A.D. 224, adopted Achaemenid traditions, as did their Sasanian successors. Both supported the Zoroastrian faith and legitimized their rule by claiming descent from the Achaemenid kings.

These Persian archers are part of a polychrome glazed brick frieze from the palace of the Achaemenid king Darius (522–486 B.C.) at Susa. Depicted with great poise and dignity, they were known as the immortals and formed the king's bodyguard.

ELAM AND EARLY IRAN

The great plateau of central Iran lies east of Mesopotamia, from which it is divided by the Zagros Mountains. Some of the world's earliest farming communities settled the western Zagros region; and farther south, reaching from the southwest flanks of the mountains to the Gulf, lay Elam, home of the earliest urban civilization in Persia. In the center and east of the plateau, uninhabitable salt deserts were bounded on their northern and southern sides by trade routes linking east and west. To the north, mountain chains separate the plateau from the Caspian Sea and central Asia.

In this land of diverse climate and geography, farming and settled village life expanded in those regions with suitable conditions. Archaeological evidence indicates that there were a

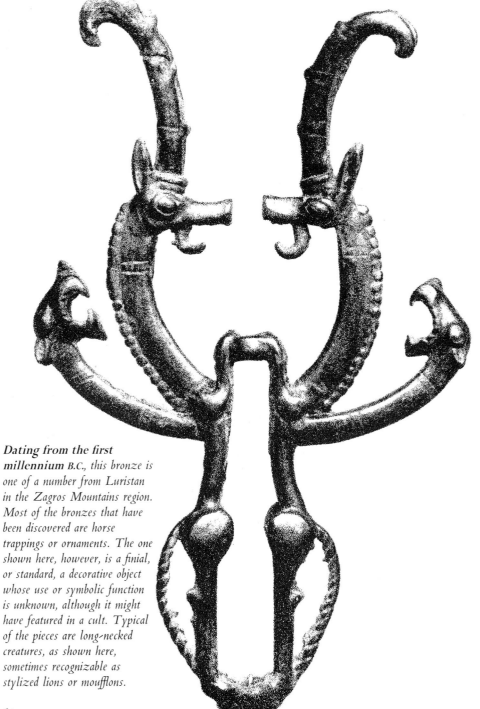

Dating from the first millennium B.C., this bronze is one of a number from Luristan in the Zagros Mountains region. Most of the bronzes that have been discovered are horse trappings or ornaments. The one shown here, however, is a finial, or standard, a decorative object whose use or symbolic function is unknown, although it might have featured in a cult. Typical of the pieces are long-necked creatures, as shown here, sometimes recognizable as stylized lions or moufflons.

number of cultures in this huge area from about 6000 B.C., suggesting that Iran was occupied by several groups with different traditions. A particular feature of the period to about 3000 B.C. is the remarkable pottery that was found at many sites. By the fourth millennium, it was being made on the wheel and many of the designs portray animals.

Late in the same millennium, some urban centers were using a pictographic writing system. Clay tablets written in a script known as proto-Elamite have been found at several sites, including Susa in Elam and Shahr-i Sokhteh near the modern Afghan border. By the third millennium, this town was a center of the lapis lazuli trade. The large quantities of this semiprecious stone found at sites of this period, such as Ur in Mesopotamia, probably came from mines in Afghanistan, along a route that passed through centers such as Shahr-i Sokhteh. Large quantities of lapis lazuli have also been found at Tepe Hissar on the northern trade route.

The Kerman area in southeast Iran seems to have been the center of a civilization with connections with Elam in the west and Afghanistan in the east. The metalwork of these people was outstanding, but after about 1900 B.C. there is little archaeological material from this region. The ancient kingdom of Elam in the southwest, now Khuzistan, was also an early center of copper and bronze metallurgy, and Elamite metalworkers were particularly skilled. Elam was partly a region of highlands, rich in minerals, stones and timber, with which it supplied the Sumerians. This area was less open to external influences than lowland Elam, or Susiana, an extension of the Mesopotamian plain and at times dominated by states of that region. Such contact influenced its culture, and in the first half of the second millennium, administrative texts of local rulers were still written in Akkadian and Sumerian, some time after the region had ceased to be controlled by Akkad and the Third Dynasty of Ur.

Carved rock reliefs, an Elamite tradition, date from the second millennium B.C., although they are more numerous at a later date. Indeed, monumental carved reliefs were also a feature of the Old Persian, Parthian and Sasanian periods and were even emulated by the Qajar rulers of the 19th century A.D. But the most distinctive and finest examples of this people's art date from the Middle Elamite period (1450–1100 B.C.). During this time, superb bronzes and objects of gold and silver were fashioned, and terra-cotta figurines were made from molds.

Susa, the best known of the Elamite sites, was only one of several important centers; others included Anshan, west of Persepolis in Fars. Haft Tepe south of Susa has been identified as Kabnak, built in the 14th century B.C. by the King of Susa and Anshan. Southeast of Susa at Choga Zanbil are the ruins of the capital built by King Untash-Napirisha (c.1260–1235 B.C.).

The inscriptions of this period were written in Elamite, which is not related to any known language and is only partially understood. In 1168 B.C., the Elamites attacked Babylon and took to Susa the Law Code of Hammurabi and other monuments, which were discovered in the 19th century. Around 1100 B.C., defeat by the Babylonians brought this phase of Elamite history to an end. A brief revival in the eighth and seventh centuries B.C. ended in the mid 640s when Elam was totally defeated and laid waste by the Assyrians. One result of this devastation was that Persian tribes moved into Elam.

Nomadic pastoralists of the Bakhtiari tribe in the Zagros region still practice transhumance — taking their animals to different pastures according to the season. Their way of life is probably similar to their Iranian ancestors of the first millennium B.C.

This map shows the principal sites of ancient Persia from prehistory through to the Achaemenid period and the Sasanian dynasty.

This bowl (BELOW) *and beaker* (RIGHT) *from Susa date from the late fourth millennium. Fine decorated pottery was common in Iran at this time.*

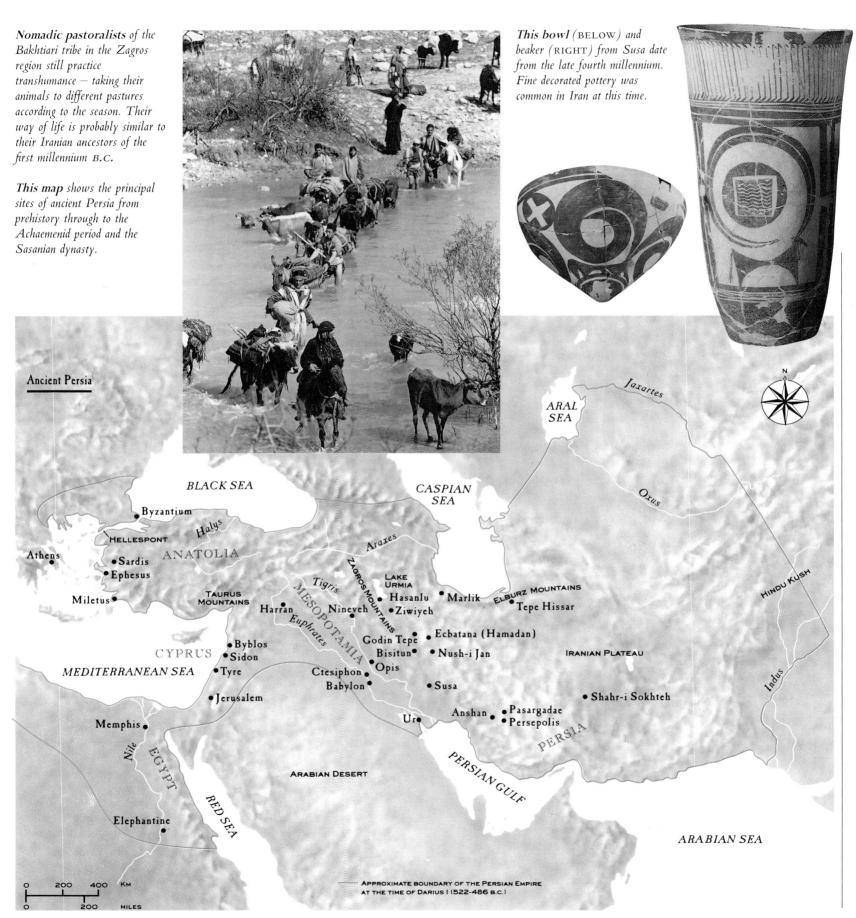

Ancient Persia

BLACK SEA

CASPIAN SEA

ARAL SEA

Jaxartes

Byzantium

Halys

HELLESPONT

ANATOLIA

Athens

Sardis

Ephesus

Araxes

Oxus

Miletus

TAURUS MOUNTAINS

ZAGROS MOUNTAINS

Tigris

LAKE URMIA

Hasanlu

Marlik

ELBURZ MOUNTAINS

Harran

Nineveh

Ziwiyeh

Tepe Hissar

HINDU KUSH

CYPRUS

Byblos

Sidon

Euphrates

MESOPOTAMIA

Godin Tepe

Bisitun

Ecbatana (Hamadan)

Nush-i Jan

IRANIAN PLATEAU

MEDITERRANEAN SEA

Tyre

Ctesiphon

Opis

Jerusalem

Babylon

Susa

Shahr-i Sokhteh

Indus

Ur

Anshan

Pasargadae

Persepolis

PERSIA

Memphis

EGYPT

Nile

ARABIAN DESERT

PERSIAN GULF

RED SEA

Elephantine

ARABIAN SEA

0 200 400 KM

0 200 MILES

APPROXIMATE BOUNDARY OF THE PERSIAN EMPIRE AT THE TIME OF DARIUS I (522–486 B.C.)

Medes and Persians first appear historically in Assyrian texts of the mid-ninth century, by which time they were settled in western Iran. When these Iranian peoples arrived in this region or where they came from is still a matter for scholarly debate. Groups of Indo-European Aryans are thought to have entered Iran from their supposed homeland in the plains of southern Russia around 1300 B.C., when archaeology shows evidence of a major cultural break. However, a mid-ninth century date is also possible.

Some time after 1400 B.C., a new type of pottery known as gray ware appears at sites in northwestern Iran and seems to derive from earlier Late Bronze Age gray ware, found southeast of the Caspian Sea. In turn, this style is related to pottery dating back to the late third millennium B.C. and found in Soviet Turkmenistan. Thus, if gray ware signifies the presence of Iranians, then it may be possible to trace the migration of these forebears of the Medes and Persians from Turkmenistan to southeast of the Caspian Sea and finally western Iran.

Gray ware has also been found in graves dating from about 1400 to 1000 B.C. at Marlik, between the Elburz Mountains and the Caspian Sea. And late gray ware (c.1100–800 B.C.) has been discovered at the citadel of Hasanlu, southwest of Lake Urmia. The buildings here were destroyed by fire, thought to have been the result of an attack by an army from Urartu in about 800 B.C. The rich finds at Hasanlu include iron weapons, bronze helmets, glazed tiles, and vessels of gold, silver and bronze. Some pieces show evidence of north Syrian and Assyrian influence, which is not surprising given Assyria's proximity to Hasanlu.

Assyrian influence in western Iran is also evident from a few stelae (carved rock slabs) and rock engravings found between the Zagros and the region of Hamadan, capital of the Medes. Some objects in the Assyrian style have also been found at Ziwiyeh in Kurdistan, a site thought to have been occupied by an indigenous people, the Manneans, known from Assyrian texts.

Luristan in the central Zagros region was also probably inhabited by indigenous people when gray ware appeared in other parts of western Iran. This area, in which a remarkable series of bronzes has been found, seems from Assyrian sources to be Ellipi, an independent kingdom of the early first millennium. Most of the bronzes date from this time, and the industry was at its height between the ninth and seventh centuries B.C., when the earliest iron objects were also made. Many of the bronzes are weapons or horse-pieces and were possibly made for an aristocracy of nomadic pastoralists.

The region's bronze production declined in the late seventh century, perhaps as a result of increased Median and Persian unity, which would have blocked access to the mines of the north and east. Also, the pastoralists would have suffered economically from the arrival of Iranian tribes. After 650 B.C., there is widespread evidence of an Iranian presence throughout the Zagros, doubtless related to the rapid rise of the Medes at about that time.

Although their precise origins are not known, the Medes were probably at first a loose confederation of tribes. By the seventh century B.C., possibly in response to repeated Urartian and Assyrian raids, they were united and in control of a wide area around their fortified capital Ecbatana (modern Hamadan). Little is known of the culture of the Medes, apart from their impressive fortress at Godin, built over a sheer drop of 80 feet, and evidence from Nush-i Jan. By about 650 B.C., their authority extended over the Persians, who had settled in Fars, and toward the end of the century they were attacking Assyrian cities. In 615, the Median ruler Cyaxares (625–585 B.C., known as Umakishtar in the cuneiform texts) made an alliance with the Babylonian king Nabopolassar against Assyria; and three years later, the Assyrian city of Nineveh fell to this alliance.

The victors divided the spoils, with the Medes acquiring the uplands into central Anatolia, where they came into conflict with the Lydians. Peace was made in 585 B.C., and the Halys River was established as the boundary between them. Beyond legend, little is known of the reign of the last Median king, Astyages (585–550 B.C.), who was overthrown by his grandson, Cyrus II, King of Anshan.

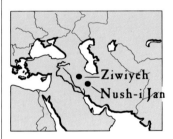

Situated in northwestern Iran, the modern village of Ziwiyeh nestles below the Kurdistan mountains. The ancient site, from where this photograph was taken, was built on a hill and surrounded by massive walls. It was here that a number of gold and other objects were claimed to have been found. However, because of looting from the late 1940s onward, it is difficult to trace the objects to their original places of discovery.

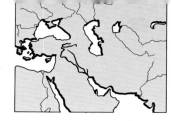

TREASURES FROM ZIWIYEH AND NUSH-I JAN

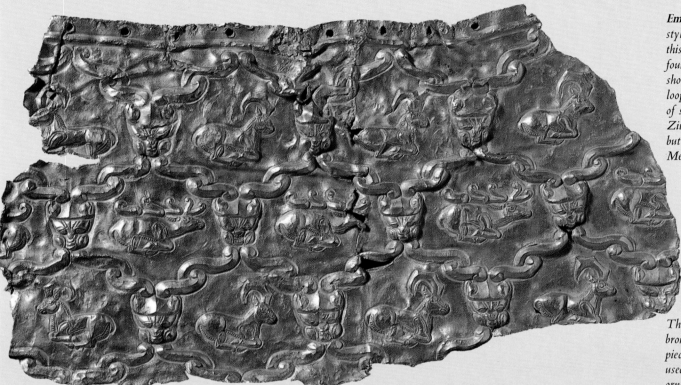

Embossed and chased in a style resembling Scythian work, this gold sheet was allegedly found at Ziwiyeh. The pattern shows lions' masks linked by looped tendrils enclosing figures of stags and goats. Objects from Ziwiyeh are of various styles, but there is no indication of Median influence.

The silver hoard from Nush-i Jan, some of which is shown here (BELOW), consists of bar ingots, pieces of silver, spiral beads or pendants, an earring, a bracelet and rings. They had been packed into a bronze bowl and buried. The pieces would probably have been used as money rather than as ornaments.

This gold sheet, reputedly from Ziwiyeh in northwestern Iran, and the pieces of silver (RIGHT) from a hoard found at Nush-i Jan in the Luristan region date from the period when the Medes were in the ascendant. Up to the present, virtually no objects other than pottery have been found that are of a distinctively Median style. The silver hoard was probably hidden in the sixth century B.C., but some of the pieces are of a much earlier period; for example, the spiral pendants resemble a type known from the late third or early second millennium B.C. As a result, there is not much evidence available for the characteristics of Median metalwork. Before the invention of coinage, the economic function of jewelry was particularly important, and it is probable that these silver pieces were used in business transactions as tokens of exchange.

Ziwiyeh was probably inhabited by a people known as the Manneans, an Iranian people whose territory lay southwest of the Caspian Sea and southeast of Lake Urmia. Their art was influenced by their neighbors, the Urartians, the Assyrians and the Scythians. This gold sheet, for example, shows elements of Scythian art. It is thought to have been part of a belt and would have been sewn onto a cloth or leather backing. Ziwiyeh has been looted during the last 40 years, so archaeologists are not sure whether objects reputed to have been found at the site really did originate there. Those that seem genuine include a number of carved ivories, strips of gold decorated with lions and birds of prey, a silver horse ornament, and a gold breastplate with mythological motifs.

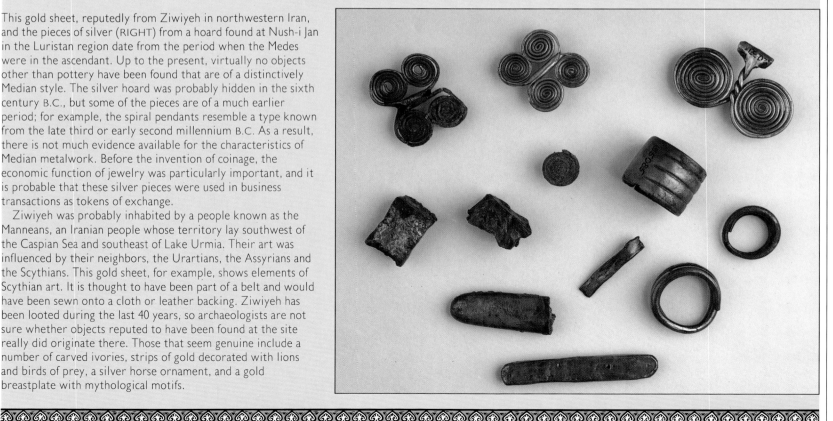

THE RISE OF THE ACHAEMENIDS

The painting on this Greek vase shows Croesus of Lydia on a pyre, about to be burned to death on the orders of Cyrus of Persia, making his final offering of wine. A servant kindles the blaze. There are varying accounts of the fate of Croesus after his capture by Cyrus.

Cyrus II, or Cyrus the Great as he was later known, was a member of the ruling Achaemenid dynasty of Persia (Fars), who traced their ancestry back to a certain Achaemenes, the founder of their line. Cyrus came to the Achaemenid throne in 559 B.C., succeeding his father Cambyses I, and united several Persian and Iranian groups. He also began diplomatic exchanges with Babylon and then rebelled against the Medes, who held sway over the Persians. In 549, he defeated the Median king Astyages and entered Ecbatana and established himself as the undisputed king of the Medes and the Persians. As such, he was ruler of already extensive territories even before he set out on the conquests that would create an empire reaching from eastern Afghanistan to the borders of Egypt.

Cyrus was said to be half-Mede through his mother Mandane, who was supposedly the daughter of Astyages. If this was so, the dynastic link would certainly have helped to give him authority in the eyes of the Medes. However, Cyrus's Median blood is not absolutely certain. In Greek records there are several different accounts of Cyrus's origins and rise to kingship. The most interesting feature of these stories is not so much their historical accuracy, but their resemblance to other Near Eastern traditions that tell of the rise of great men from obscure beginnings to kingship.

The new ruler of the Medes and Persians first turned his attention to Anatolia, where his Lydian neighbor, the immensely rich king Croesus, sought to expand his domains to the lands beyond the Halys River. The source of Croesus's fabled wealth was gold from the Pactolus River that ran through Sardis, the Lydian capital. By all accounts – borne out by archaeology – Croesus gave generously of his wealth to various Greek oracles. In return for this and other munificence, the oracle priests (pp.102–3) were naturally expected to provide helpful answers to the questioners. This is doubtless why they seem to have perfected the technique of providing enigmatic prophecies that were open to interpretation.

It was such a prophecy from Apollo's oracle at Delphi that helped to bring the kingdom of Lydia to an end. Before the conflict with Cyrus, Croesus asked the advice of this, the most famous of Greek oracles, and was told somewhat ambiguously that if he crossed the Halys a great empire would fall. Taking this to mean the empire of Cyrus, Croesus crossed the Halys in 547 B.C. After an inconclusive battle, the Lydians returned to Sardis and, because it was the end of the campaigning season, the levied soldiers were disbanded. Cyrus, however, advanced to Sardis and captured it in 546 B.C.

Following this success, Cyrus returned to Iran, leaving his general Harpagus to complete the conquest of Anatolia. Over the next two or three years, Lycia, Caria and the Greek city-states of Ionia were added to the new empire. Cyrus's activities in the seven years between the war with Lydia and the conquest of Babylon are not easy to trace, but it was probably during this time that he campaigned in the east as far as Bactria and Sogdiana and up to the River Jaxartes (modern Syr Darya). It is not known either to what extent he was consolidating existing territories or conquering new areas, but he probably penetrated territories as far as Gandhara in the east. By the time he returned from the east and took the road to Babylon, Cyrus had been the ruler of the Medes and Persians for just ten years.

THE PHRYGIANS AND LYDIANS

The kingdom of Phrygia, associated in Greek legend with the names of Midas and Gordius, lay toward the west of central Anatolia in territory that was formerly part of the Hittite Empire. The Phrygians have been linked to the Gaska people mentioned in Hittite texts and are found in the region after about 1200 B.C., when the Hittite Empire had disappeared. In the latter half of the eighth century B.C., the Phrygians became very powerful, and their capital city Gordion, on the banks of the Sakarya River, was heavily fortified. The families of kings and nobles were buried with plentiful grave goods in chambers constructed of timber, over which stones and earth were placed to create a mound or tumulus. After invasions by the Cimmerian people at the beginning of the seventh century B.C., the Phrygians declined in power and eventually came under the control of the Lydians.

Lydia, in the west of Asia Minor, came into conflict with the Medes following the demise of Phrygia. After five years of intermittent warfare, the Halys River was established as the boundary between them in 585 B.C. Lydia's wealth came from the gold of the Pactolus River and, lying astride two of the main routes from the coast to the interior of Asia Minor, the country became an entrepôt for trade. Their language indicates that the Lydians were an indigenous Anatolian people; however, their art and culture reveal they were receptive to influence from their Greek neighbors. The Lydians invented coined money and, according to the Greeks, they were innovators in music.

Although Croesus, the last king of Lydia, subjugated the Greek cities on the coast, his relations with them seem not to have been unfriendly. He contributed to the rebuilding of the Temple of Artemis at Ephesus and made offerings to Delphi and other Greek shrines. Croesus's erroneous interpretation of the Delphic oracle encouraged him to go to war against Cyrus, who had united the Medes and Persians, and was now his eastern neighbor. In 546 B.C., Croesus was defeated at Sardis, his capital, and Lydia became a Persian province.

This Phrygian bronze vessel in the shape of a ram's head was discovered in the Great Tumulus at Gordion and dates from the end of the eighth century B.C.

The Phrygians settled in *west-central Anatolia after the collapse of the Hittite Empire. Gordion was their capital and the site known as Midas City an important shrine. Lydia lay in western Anatolia, and its greatest city was Sardis.*

The tomb of Cyrus the **Great***, which was traditionally called the Tomb of the Mother of Solomon, is located at Pasargadae, just north of Persepolis. It is unique, for it is the only tomb of a Persian ruler to be a free-standing structure — other kings were buried in rock-cut tombs. Built of stone, it has a gabled roof and occupies a dominant position on a stepped mound.*

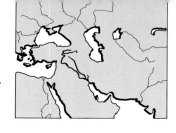

In October 539 B.C., the ancient city of Babylon was taken by the forces of Cyrus without a battle. The city first came under Persian control on the 12th, when Cyrus's general Ugbaru, governor of Gutium, an area to the east of Babylon, entered it — apparently without a fight. According to the cuneiform text on the Cyrus Cylinder, Cyrus and his troops approached Babylon later in the month — "their number like that of the water of a river could not be established."

On October 29, Cyrus (2), riding in his chariot, led his combined force (1) of Persians and Medes, wearing crownlike and rounded headgear, respectively, along the Processional Way that led to Babylon's Ishtar Gate (4). This magnificent 40-foot-high edifice, flanked by towers rising almost 100 feet in the sky, was faced with enameled bricks bearing the stylized figures of lions and bulls.

Watching Cyrus's arrival with a mixture of excitement and anticipation were cheering Babylonian citizens and a delegation of high-ranking Babylonian officials (3), flanked by Gutian soldiers. According to the Cyrus Cylinder, after his bloodless victory, Cyrus was fêted not only by the Babylonians but also by the "entire country of Sumer and Akkad, princes and governors."

After gaining control of Anatolia and expanding the empire's eastern domains, Cyrus turned his attention to Babylon and took advantage of the unpopularity of the Babylonian king Nabonidus. As elsewhere, Cyrus used a skilled propaganda campaign to extol his clemency and tolerance in religious matters. It seems that after the conquests of Media and Lydia, Cyrus had spared the lives of their respective kings, Astyages and Croesus — proof not only of clemency, but also of good diplomacy, for such a policy meant his new subjects would not be alienated.

By the time Nabonidus came to the throne in 555 B.C., Babylon was probably not as powerful as it had been under Nebuchadrezzar (pp.36–37). Even before the latter's death in 562, there seem to have been anxieties about the possibility of attack, perhaps from the Medes, since toward the end of his reign a defensive wall was constructed north of Babylon. And there is evidence of internal problems, since there were three kings and two rebellions in the seven years between the death of Nebuchadrezzar and the accession of Nabonidus.

Nabonidus was a devotee of the moon god Sin, whose temple at Harran he restored early in his reign. At Ur, he restored the ziggurat of Nana, the ancient Sumerian moon god, but at Babylon he neglected local affairs and religious rituals. These included the cult of Marduk, the city deity, and the New Year festival which renewed the fertility of the land. Only the king could perform this ritual, but for several years his absence at the oasis of Tema in Arabia prevented the performance of this important rite. He had also introduced administrative reforms that effectively gave control of temple finances to the Crown.

Thus there was cause for dissatisfaction among the Babylonians and, in particular, the temple scribes, who gave their support to Cyrus at the fall of Babylon and also compiled pro-Persian propaganda. Their accounts extol Cyrus and claim that Babylon fell without a struggle because Cyrus was welcomed by all. Nevertheless, there seems to have been a fierce struggle when the Persians attacked the Babylonians at Opis early in October 539 B.C. It is possible that it was in this battle that Belshazzar, the crown prince known from the Bible, died.

After this victory, Cyrus took Sippar. Then his Gutian troops under Ugbaru, possibly a Babylonian deserter, entered Babylon without a battle on October 12. Nabonidus, who had fled to Babylon from Opis, was captured, and Ugbaru's troops guarded the city peacefully until the arrival of Cyrus at the end of the month. During this time, all the proper religious rituals were observed, and when Cyrus entered the city, he was warmly welcomed: "All the inhabitants of Babylon . . . greeted him as a master through whose help they had come to life from death . . . and they worshipped his very name."

This conquest gave Cyrus not only Mesopotamia, but the entire Babylonian Empire, which reached to the borders of Egypt. Yet again he showed his clemency and repatriated various exiles, including, it seems from the Book of Ezra in the Bible, Jews who had been deported by Nebuchadrezzar. At some point, he returned to Iran and was killed while campaigning on the northeastern frontier in 530 B.C. His body was taken back to Pasargadae, the capital he had built for himself, reputedly at the site of his victory over Astyages. He was laid to rest in a magnificent stone tomb of great simplicity.

THE REIGN OF DARIUS

On the death of Cyrus the Great in 530 B.C., his son Cambyses came to the throne. He had clearly enjoyed his father's confidence and for a brief time had been the effective ruler of Babylon. Cambyses has been badly served by history, for the Greek historian Herodotus depicted him as a madman and vicious tyrant. There is certainly no evidence that he was. Four years after his accession, Cambyses marched to Egypt and advanced southward to beyond the First Cataract; he also took control of territory to the west, beyond Cyrene. So effective was Cambyses' consolidation of Persia's position in Egypt, that there was no rebellion there until the end of his successor's reign.

In 522 B.C., however, news reached him of a revolt in Persia, perhaps led by his brother Bardiya, or possibly by an imposter named Gaumata. While traveling from Syria to Persia, Cambyses was accidentally killed. Darius, an army officer who had been spearbearer to Cambyses and came from a branch of the Achaemenid family, continued the march to Persia and succeeded in crushing the rebellion.

As is the case with Cyrus, the details of Darius's reign that have passed to posterity are based on his version of events. For example, the account of his defeat of the rebels is contained in a great inscription that he had carved at Bisitun, high on a cliff face overlooking the Great Khorasan Road. The inscription not only relates how Darius crushed the revolt and came to power, but also proclaims his right to rule through his paternal ancestors. In reality, it seems that he gained the throne by leading the party of nobles who opposed the rebellion and by controlling much of the army. The revolt was widespread, and the restoration of peace took more than a year to achieve.

In the early years of his reign, Darius mounted an expedition to India, where he annexed the Sind and possibly the Punjab. Less successful was his campaign against the Scythians to the north of the Black Sea. In spite of this failure, it was under Darius that the Persian Empire reached its greatest extent, embracing lands that stretched from the Indus River in the east as far as Libya in the west.

Darius was a brilliant administrator and divided the empire into provinces, or satrapies. There were 20 of these, according to Herodotus, and each had its own governor, or satrap, usually a Persian noble or member of the royal family. A separate official, in charge of the army, was responsible for collecting the annual tribute, which was paid not only in gold or silver, but also in kind. The reliefs of the tribute bearers from Persepolis depict a wide range of products, including ivory from Ethiopia, incense from Arabia and even camels from Bactria.

Darius moved his capital from Pasargadae to Susa and made it the main administrative center, although the old capital continued to be used, probably for ceremonial purposes. The climate of Susa was warmer, and in the summer the court moved to the cooler heights of Ecbatana, the old Median capital. Darius's construction work at Susa was extensive and included an "apadana" – a columned audience hall – and a new palace. Both here and at Persepolis, craftsmen from all over the empire worked at the palaces he built. In the one adjoining the apadana at Susa, Babylonian craftsmen made panels of molded polychrome glazed tiles to decorate the walls. One showed a frieze of royal guards, the Ten Thousand Immortals, honored by the king in gratitude for their support.

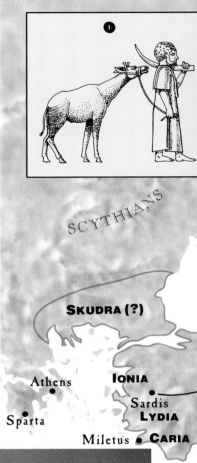

The palace complex built at Persepolis (RIGHT) by Darius and his successors reflects the wealth and majesty of Persia. On the stone facades of stairways were depicted tribute delegations from 23 lands, all wearing their native costumes.

The satrapies, provinces, of the Persian Empire are shown on the map (OPPOSITE PAGE), their names printed in extra bold. Less important regions are shown in ordinary bold. Some of the people paying homage to Persia with their gifts are shown above the map, based on the original reliefs at Persepolis. These are a Kushite (1) leading an okapi; a Lydian (2) holding precious vessels; an Indian (3) carrying pots probably containing gold dust; a Scythian (4) bringing a horse; and a Bactrian (5) offering a camel.

The satrapies of the Persian Empire

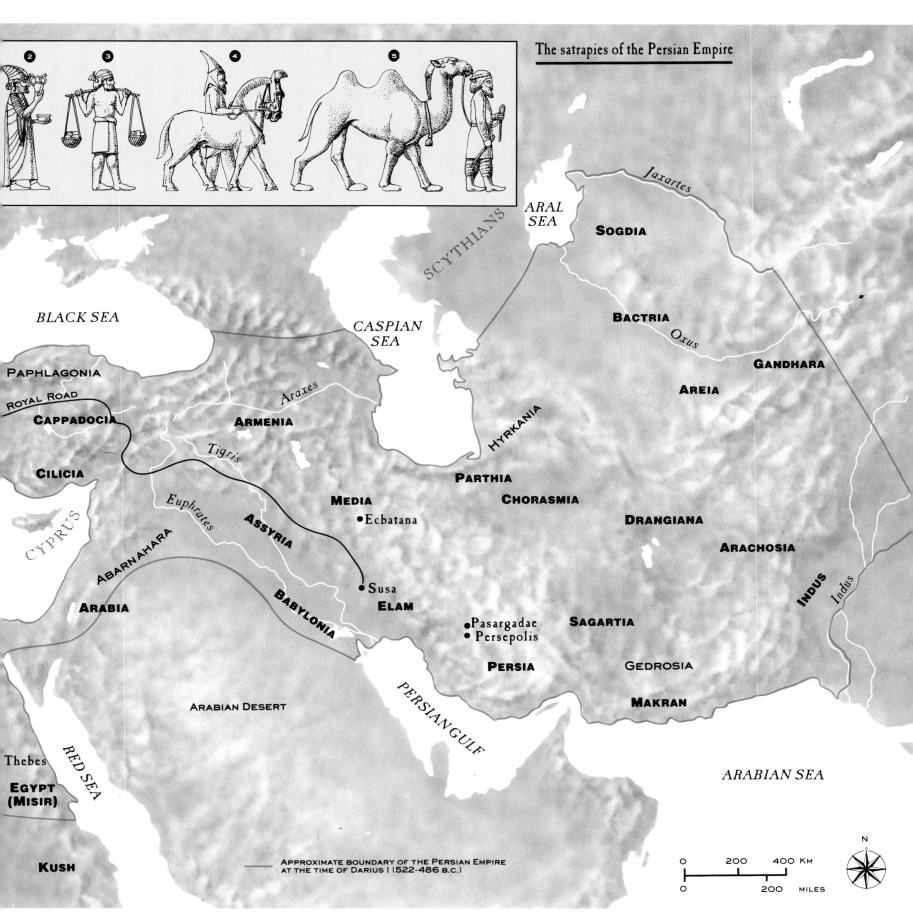

SCYTHIANS

ARAL
SEA

Jaxartes

SOGDIA

BACTRIA

Oxus

GANDHARA

CASPIAN
SEA

AREIA

BLACK SEA

PAPHLAGONIA

ROYAL ROAD

CAPPADOCIA

ARMENIA

Araxes

HYRKANIA

CILICIA

Tigris

PARTHIA

CHORASMIA

CYPRUS

MEDIA

ASSYRIA

Euphrates

• Ecbatana

DRANGIANA

ARACHOSIA

ABARNAHARA

BABYLONIA

• Susa

ELAM

SAGARTIA

INDUS

Indus

ARABIA

• Pasargadae
• Persepolis

PERSIA

GEDROSIA

Arabian Desert

PERSIAN GULF

MAKRAN

Thebes

RED SEA

EGYPT
(MISIR)

ARABIAN SEA

KUSH

—— APPROXIMATE BOUNDARY OF THE PERSIAN EMPIRE
AT THE TIME OF DARIUS I (522–486 B.C.)

0   200   400 KM

0   200 MILES

N

73

DECLINE AND FALL

RAWLINSON AT BISITUN

Henry Creswicke Rawlinson (RIGHT) succeeded in deciphering the Old Persian text of Darius's great trilingual cuneiform inscription at Bisitun (BELOW) near Kermanshah. This provided the key to understanding Akkadian and Elamite, the other languages of the inscription. Rawlinson was an officer in the British East India Company's service, who was sent to Persia in 1833 to assist in the reorganization of the Persian army. From 1835 to 1839, he was stationed at Kermanshah, where he was military adviser to the Shah of Persia's brother. During this time, he copied the first 200 lines of the inscription at Bisitun. This in itself was difficult, since the inscription is carved about 500 feet above the ground; he then translated this section.

The Afghan War, in which Rawlinson served with distinction, and other duties delayed further work until 1844, when he finished copying the text and completed his decipherment. Although other scholars, most notably the German Georg Grotefend, had worked on copies of Old Persian cuneiform inscriptions from Persepolis, these were mainly royal names and titles and were not long enough to decipher the language fully.

The long inscription at Bisitun provided sufficient material for a full decipherment, which Rawlinson was able to do because of his knowledge of Persian. He began with the characters that he had seen on other inscriptions and had tentatively concluded were royal names, known from Greek sources, and so built up a sign list. With this

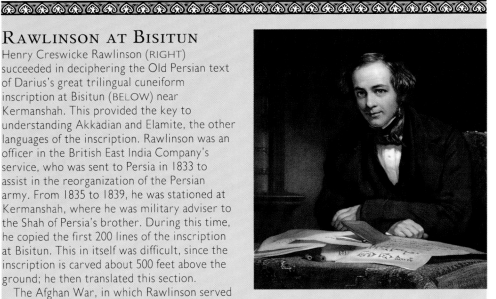

translation, it became possible to decipher the other languages in which the text was written.

The relief, surmounted by the symbol of the god Ahura Mazda, shows Darius with his foot on the body of the usurper Gaumata, facing nine captive rebel kings and accompanied by two attendants. The accompanying inscriptions detail his successful struggles for the kingship and his justification for his claim to this office.

The relief panel measures some 18 by 10 feet and was probably carved in stages in 520/19 B.C. on a smoothed rock face of Kuh-i Parau Mountain. This rises from the plain at Bisitun, along which runs the ancient road from Persepolis to Hamadan. It appears that this was the first inscription to be written in Old Persian, the language spoken by the Achaemenids.

The Bisitun relief, whose inscription was deciphered by Henry Rawlinson.

Toward the end of Darius's reign, the great conflict with the Greeks began (pp.102–3). Almost nothing of this encounter, made so famous by Herodotus, is known from Persian sources. Ten years after the revolt and suppression of the Greek cities of Ionia in Asia Minor, Darius sent a punitive expedition to Greece in 490 B.C. But the Persians were defeated at Marathon and forced to retreat. Darius died in 486 and was succeeded by his son Xerxes (486–465 B.C.). The new ruler crushed a rebellion in Egypt in 485, and three years later put down a revolt in Babylon. In both cases he followed his victory with a ruthlessness that was the reverse of traditional Persian tolerance. Then in 480, at the head of a 70,000-strong army, Xerxes led a grand invasion of Greece. However, despite initial success, the Persians were eventually defeated.

The latter part of Xerxes' reign was occupied with his building program at Persepolis and with harem intrigues, which led to his assassination in 465 B.C. During the reigns of the next three Persian kings, the Peloponnesian War (pp.108–9) was being fought between Athens and Sparta, with Persia giving assistance to whichever side would favor her interests. For example, by the Peace of Callias, Persia agreed to relinquish her interest in the Aegean, and in return Athens promised to stay out of Asia Minor.

From the late fifth century, the Persian Empire was beset with constant strife and rebellion. In 405 B.C., Egypt successfully revolted; and three years later, Cyrus the Younger, brother of the king Artaxerxes II (405–359 B.C.), hired 10,000 Greek mercenaries and marched east from Anatolia to take the throne, but was defeated in battle. The Greek mercenaries retired in good order and made their way home, as their leader Xenophon recorded in his *Anabasis*. This feat was a measure of the growing vulnerability of the empire. As if further proof of weakness was needed, Artaxerxes gave back provinces to satraps who had revolted in 373. The reigns of the last kings all began or ended with murders, and in 336, the manipulations of the eunuch Bagoas brought Darius III to the throne. Five years later, the empire was lost to Alexander of Macedon (pp.114–15) and for a time became part of the new Hellenistic world.

In its heyday, the Persian Empire had been ruled with relative tolerance. Conquered people retained their own customs and religions and even, to some extent, their own forms of government. The bureaucracy was administered efficiently, and each province had two law courts, one for local affairs, the other for matters that came under imperial or Persian law.

Trade and commerce were assisted by the system of roads, which gave access to larger markets, as well as by the imperial standardization of weights and measures, the use of coinage and the expansion of banking procedures. The economic decline of the last years was initially the result of the unstable political situation, which led to large sums being given in bribes and paid to foreign mercenaries. Rapid inflation and rising rates of interest caused economic hardship, which led in turn to political unrest.

The Greeks regarded the Persians as people who had become decadent and luxury-loving since the great days of Cyrus. Certainly, considerable wealth was expended on conspicuous display. Apart from using vessels of precious metals, aristocrats wore magnificent pieces of jewelry, and large bracelets were often awarded as a token of distinction.

THE OXUS TREASURE

In 1877, a hoard of gold and silver objects was found, reputedly on the north bank of the Oxus River. Three years later, these treasures were stolen while being transported overland by a group of Afghan merchants traveling from Kabul to Peshawar. However, a British political officer named Captain F.C. Burton caught up with the robbers and persuaded them to hand over most of the stolen goods.

The merchants rewarded Burton with a magnificent gold bracelet, similar to the one shown here (LEFT), and sold the rest of the objects in Rawalpindi, in what is now Pakistan. Here they were bought piecemeal by General Sir Alexander Cunningham, Director General of the Archaeological Survey of India, and from him they eventually found their way to the British Museum.

The Oxus Treasure, as it is now known, consists of about 170 pieces, dating largely from the fifth and fourth centuries B.C., the time of the Achaemenids. Their alleged place of discovery was well within the Achaemenid Empire, on the borders of Bactria and Sogdia. It is not certain, however, if all the pieces were found together or whether some were added to a core collection.

The great wealth and splendor of the Achaemenid kings and their nobles is evident from their magnificent jewelry and other objects, such as those of the Oxus Treasure. Perhaps the most spectacular pieces are a pair of massive gold armlets, one of which is shown here, with terminals of winged griffins. They were originally inlaid with semiprecious stones and colored glass. Persian kings are known to have given large bracelets as a mark of honor.

This gold model of a chariot drawn by four small horses or ponies is also from the Oxus Treasure. Both the driver and his companion are wearing Median-style garments. The fact that Median dress is evident here does not mean that the object predates the Achaemenids, since Median clothes were common in the Achaemenid period.

PARTHIANS AND SASANIANS

After the death of Alexander the Great in 323 B.C., his generals quarreled over the division of his conquests (pp.116–17). Seleucus emerged victorious in the east and, by 300 B.C., he controlled Iran, Mesopotamia and north Syria. Seleucid rule of Iran lasted for about 150 years. By the mid-third century B.C., its power was waning and the northeastern provinces of Bactria, Sogdiana and Parthia seceded.

In 247 B.C., Arsaces, an Iranian, founded the Arsacid or Parthian dynasty, which was to last for nearly 500 years. During the weak rule of the Seleucid king Antiochus IV, Phraates I began to expand Parthian territories, but it was his younger brother Mithridates I (171–138 B.C.) who was the true founder of the Parthian Empire. Advancing west, Mithridates took Media, probably by 148/47 B.C. He later went on to take control of Mesopotamia; and in 141, he entered the old Seleucid capital of Seleucia-on-the-Tigris.

On Mithridates' death, Parthia extended from Babylonia in the west to eastern Bactria. This region – after one more attempt by the Seleucids to recover their territories had failed – was controlled by the Parthians for three centuries. Under Mithridates II (124–87 B.C.), Parthia reached its greatest extent, with its western border at the Euphrates in Syria. Here the Parthians came into contact with the might of Rome, and in 53 B.C., at Carrhae (Harran) in northern Syria, the Parthian cavalry ignominiously defeated a force of Roman infantry.

For about a century, there was no serious challenge to Parthian domains. Then in A.D. 116, the Roman emperor Trajan captured Ctesiphon, the Parthian capital, and advanced to the Persian Gulf. Although he soon withdrew, Parthian power was now waning. There was internal dissension, and accession to the Parthian throne became marked by intrigue and murder within

the royal family. Also, before long, the Parthians had problems in the east, where a people known as the Kushans were an emerging force. Although her fortunes revived in the latter half of the second century A.D., Parthia was in terminal decline.

The Parthian kings increasingly looked upon themselves as the true successors to the Achaemenids. As early as the reign of Mithridates II, the Achaemenid title King of Kings was used on coins. This ruler also claimed that he was descended from Artaxerxes II (405–359 B.C.), thus linking himself back to the Old Persian dynasty. Reliefs of Parthian rulers not only echoed motifs of the ancient kings, but were even carved into the same cliffs, such as at Bisitun, and at Achaemenid tombs.

In about A.D. 226, the last Parthian king was toppled by Ardashir, a leading member of the Sasanian dynasty from Fars. His ancestors, who took their name from a certain Sasan, were connected with the Zoroastrian cult at Istakhr, a town that had

The head of Arsaces, founder of the Parthian dynasty in 247 B.C., can be seen on this contemporary silver coin. Practically no Parthian records exist to shed light on this dynasty's own history – most information comes from the subjective accounts of classical authors. However, inscriptions on coins and potsherds have helped to corroborate the finds of archaeology as well as Greek and Latin texts.

The Parthians, it seems, were originally a nomadic tribe from central Asia, who at some point entered Iran. Their influence in this region was at its peak at about the end of the second century B.C. Sandwiched between Rome in the west and China in the east, the Parthians were able to control part of the Silk Route and act as middlemen between these two great powers.

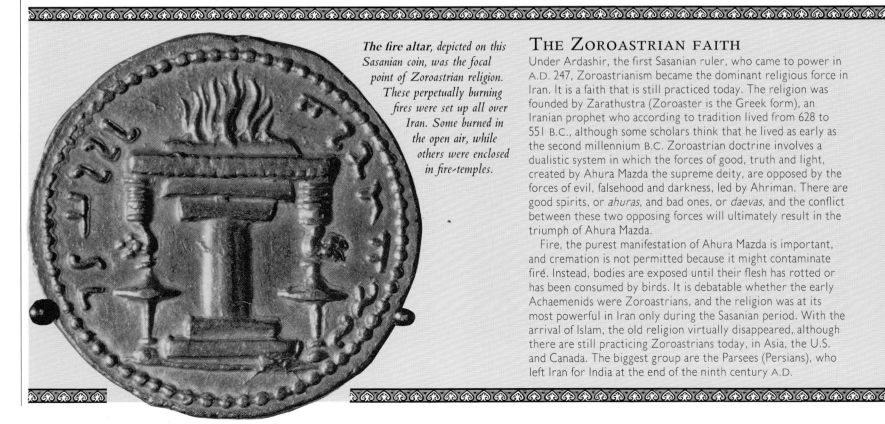

The fire altar, depicted on this Sasanian coin, was the focal point of Zoroastrian religion. These perpetually burning fires were set up all over Iran. Some burned in the open air, while others were enclosed in fire-temples.

THE ZOROASTRIAN FAITH

Under Ardashir, the first Sasanian ruler, who came to power in A.D. 247, Zoroastrianism became the dominant religious force in Iran. It is a faith that is still practiced today. The religion was founded by Zarathustra (Zoroaster is the Greek form), an Iranian prophet who according to tradition lived from 628 to 551 B.C., although some scholars think that he lived as early as the second millennium B.C. Zoroastrian doctrine involves a dualistic system in which the forces of good, truth and light, created by Ahura Mazda the supreme deity, are opposed by the forces of evil, falsehood and darkness, led by Ahriman. There are good spirits, or *ahuras*, and bad ones, or *daevas*, and the conflict between these two opposing forces will ultimately result in the triumph of Ahura Mazda.

Fire, the purest manifestation of Ahura Mazda is important, and cremation is not permitted because it might contaminate fire. Instead, bodies are exposed until their flesh has rotted or has been consumed by birds. It is debatable whether the early Achaemenids were Zoroastrians, and the religion was at its most powerful in Iran only during the Sasanian period. With the arrival of Islam, the old religion virtually disappeared, although there are still practicing Zoroastrians today, in Asia, the U.S. and Canada. The biggest group are the Parsees (Persians), who left Iran for India at the end of the ninth century A.D.

developed in the Persepolis area. This dynasty, with its origins in the ancient Achaemenid homeland, became strongly nationalistic and religious and ruled Iran for over 400 years. Surviving monumental rock reliefs, a tradition the Sasanians continued, show the Zoroastrian deity Ahura Mazda bestowing kingship on Sasanian rulers in various investiture scenes.

Ardashir's son Shapur I (A.D. 240–272) expanded the empire's borders to include all of modern Iran, parts of Afghanistan, Pakistan, central Asia, Iraq and the east coast of the Arabian peninsula. Shapur I defeated three Roman emperors, conquered Armenia and overran the Kushan Empire in central Asia. Shapur was also a tolerant ruler, allowing religious minorities to practice freely, unlike the three succeeding Sasanian kings, who persecuted those not of the Zoroastrian faith. The worst victims were the Manichaeans, followers of the prophet Mani, who practiced a religion that combined elements of Zoroastrianism, Buddhism and Christianity. However, this policy was abandoned in A.D. 293 by Bahram III, and once again Persian kings behaved with their traditional tolerance.

The reign of the strong ruler Shapur II (A.D. 309–379) was followed by almost constant warfare against nomadic groups on the northern and eastern frontiers. The Sasanians even had to pay a tribute to the Hepthalite Huns of central Asia. In the west, the traditional enemy was Rome, now the New Rome of Byzantium, with whom the Sasanians fought extensive wars. The last Sasanian king, Yazdigird III (A.D. 632–651), who had been placed on the throne by the nobility, was defeated by an Arab Islamic army. In 637, Ctesiphon fell, and within a few years, the Islamic conquest of Iran was completed. Nearly a thousand years after the last Achaemenid king, Darius III, was murdered as a fugitive, the last Sasanian met the same fate.

Carved out of marble, this Parthian statue shows a ruler of the city of Hatra, situated between the Tigris and Euphrates. Hatra was founded some time during the first century B.C. as a military outpost of the Parthian Empire, but was governed by local rulers. In time it achieved autonomy and became the capital of a small state called Araba. Because of its strategic riverside position, the city flourished from trade and became an important religious center. Hatra was later conquered by the Sasanian king Shapur I during the third century A.D.

The Parsees of India still practice the Zoroastrian faith, some 2,500 years after its appearance in Iran.

77

PREHISTORIC EUROPE

‹‹ *The entire race is bellicose, high-spirited and quick to fight, but otherwise simple and not uncouth.* **››**

GREEK HISTORIAN STRABO ON THE CELTS

Lying to the north of the Mediterranean civilizations of antiquity, the world of prehistoric Europe, an area stretching from the Atlantic seaboard eastward to the Russian steppes, was a long-neglected field of study. The term "barbarian," originally used by the Greeks to describe any people who were not of their own culture, gradually came to be applied to these nonliterate people of the north and acquired a pejorative meaning. Since the 19th century, however, archaeology has revealed the existence of many interesting and sometimes brilliant ancient cultures in this vast area. In the case of later peoples, such as the Celts and the Germanic tribes of the late first millennium B.C., material evidence is supplemented by accounts, albeit biased, of classical authors.

The use of radiocarbon dating has completely revolutionized the chronology of the prehistoric world. It has also altered the earlier archaeological framework constructed for Europe, which was based on the hypothesis that skills, such as building in stone and copper metallurgy, were acquired from the Near East. It is now known that these "primitive barbarians" were building great megalithic monuments a thousand years before the construction of the pyramids of Old Kingdom Egypt. From then until the early Christian era, a mosaic of original cultures succeeded each other in Europe.

In the lands of the Atlantic seaboard, late Neolithic people journeyed by sea and constructed the first megalithic tombs with the help of only polished stone tools. In addition to being skilled engineers, these people also developed distinctive art forms. For example, some of the most original statuary of the ancient world, idols with heads of fish-men, was being carved in the sixth millennium B.C. by the hunter-gatherers of Lepenski Vir, on the Danube in modern Yugoslavia.

With the discovery of copper metallurgy, which took place independently in the Balkans and Iberia, metalworking spread through Europe, and in the late Bronze Age during the early first millennium B.C., the technological development was remarkable. Similarly, the ironwork of the protohistorical people of Europe was outstanding, as was first realized with the discovery in 1824 of the rich burials at the village of Hallstatt – after which the early European Iron Age is named – in Upper Austria.

Farther east, the treasures found in the burial mound, or kurgan, of Kul Olba in southern Russia, in 1830, revealed the wealth of the Scythians of the first millennium B.C. These nomadic people of the Eurasian steppes were famous in antiquity for their horsemanship. In fact, the horse first appeared as a domesticated animal during the fourth millennium B.C. on the steppes of southern Russia and is represented on a silver vase from the tomb at Maikop in Kuban, southern Russia, that dates from about 2500 B.C. It is possible that horses were also domesticated very early in central Europe in the area of modern Hungary.

Since the early 18th century, Scythian objects have been deposited in the Kunstkamera, the Russian emperor's collection of curiosities in St. Petersburg (modern Leningrad). This interest in the indigenous culture of the region was echoed in western Europe during the 19th century, when the first archaeological museums were opened. As material from excavations increased, European interest in the heritage of their own countries became tied in with an upsurge of nationalism. Since the 19th century, there has been a vast increase in knowledge of the achievement of Europe's earlier inhabitants, from the Neolithic builders to the founders of the medieval world.

The Trundholm Sun Chariot (RIGHT ABOVE) *was discovered in a bog at Trundholm on Zealand, the largest of the islands that constitute the modern state of Denmark. Dating from about the middle of the second millennium B.C., the chariot consists of a wheeled model of a horse drawing a disk, ten inches in diameter, which is plated with gold on one of its sides. The entire model is about two feet long and made of bronze. It is believed that the disk probably symbolized the sun and the moon, with the horse drawing them across the skies.*

Multiple rows of standing stones, *or alignments, stretch into the distance near Carnac in Brittany, northwest France. More than 3,000 stones were raised in this area, probably some time during the second millennium B.C., representing the most extraordinary megalithic monument in Europe.*

The function of these stones is unknown, although according to folklore, they constitute the ranks of Roman soldiers who were literally petrified by a local saint. Some scholars believe that the stones were connected with astronomy — that they were set up as a sort of megalithic observatory to study the movements of celestial bodies.

EARLY FARMERS AND THE MEGALITHIC AGE

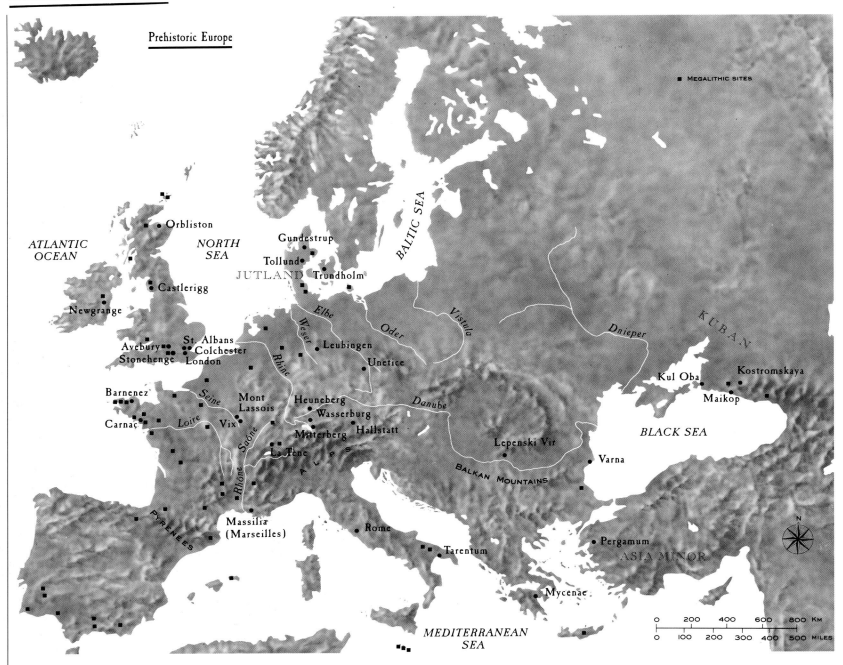

Prehistoric Europe

■ MEGALITHIC SITES

ATLANTIC OCEAN

NORTH SEA

BALTIC SEA

Orbliston

Castlerigg

Newgrange

Gundestrup

Tollund

JUTLAND   Trundholm

Elbe

Weser

Oder

Vistula

Dnieper

KUBAN

St. Albans

Avebury   Colchester

Stonehenge   London

Leubingen

Unetice

Rhine

Kul Oba

Kostromskaya

Maikop

Barnenez

Seine

Mont Lassois

Heuneberg

Carnac

Loire

Vix

Saône

Wasserburg

Mitterberg   Hallstatt

Danube

BLACK SEA

La Tène

Rhône

A L P S

Lepenski Vir

Varna

BALKAN MOUNTAINS

Massilia (Marseilles)

PYRENEES

Rome

Tarentum

Pergamum

ASIA MINOR

N

Mycenae

MEDITERRANEAN SEA

0   200   400   600   800 KM

0   100   200   300   400   500 MILES

The world of prehistoric Europe stretched from the Atlantic seaboard in the west to the Black Sea and beyond in the east. The many peoples who populated this region, from the first farmers of the seventh millennium to the barbarian tribes known to the Romans in the first millennium A.D., were preliterate. But their material remains, ranging from megalithic monuments, whose distribution is shown here (ABOVE), to golden jewels, are most impressive.

In the seventh millennium B.C., farming spread to southeastern Europe, probably from Anatolia. In this region, conditions for farming were similar to those of the Near East; but as farming techniques spread west and northward, crops and stock were adapted to the cooler and more temperate climate. The rich soil of central Europe was well suited to agriculture; and it was in this area of extensive forest that thatched, timber longhouses, some more than 130 feet in length, were built. Villages were arranged with houses built in groups, each with its own animal pens and refuse pits. Within a few hundred years, such longhouses were being raised from central Europe to the Netherlands. This early farming culture is named Bandkeramik after its pottery, first found in central Europe and later in the north and west.

Farther north, where there was an abundance of food that could be gathered, hunted or fished, farming was adopted later,

as natural food resources became insufficient. This transition occurred in western Europe from around 4500 B.C., and within a thousand years, large areas of forest had been cleared. With farming now well established, communities increased in size, trading links expanded and craft specialization developed.

While few settlements of the Neolithic farmers of Europe have survived, the great megalithic tombs in the lands bordering the Atlantic and North Sea still bear witness to their skills as builders. Carbon dating has shown that these large stone monuments, created centuries before the Great Pyramids of Egypt, are the earliest known stone monuments. The chamber tombs of Brittany in northwest France were built before 4000 B.C., and in both Britain and Denmark there were stone tombs raised before 3000 B.C. Such tombs are also found in Portugal, Spain, Ireland, Holland, Sweden and Germany.

Magnificently carved spirals (LEFT) decorate the huge stone, ten and a half feet long and four and a half feet high, that lies in front of the passage grave of Newgrange in Ireland. The monument consists of a mound, 250 feet in diameter, inside which a passage leads to a corbeled, cross-shaped chamber. This inner sanctuary is illuminated by the sun's rays only around the midwinter solstice, when light enters the mound via the "roof box," which can be seen above the entrance behind the spiral-decorated stone.

Stonehenge (BELOW) is the greatest megalithic monument in Britain. The site first consisted of a circular bank and ditch. But by the end of the second millennium B.C., a configuration of circles made from sarsen stones, quarried from nearby hills, and blue stones, which probably came from south Wales, encompassed a number of huge sarsen trilithons — two stones topped by a third — some 16 feet high. Stonehenge may have been a temple or a meeting place for rituals or festivals. The fact that the midsummer sunrise is aligned with its axis may suggest that it has an astronomical function.

Castlerigg Stone Circle (ABOVE) in northwest England is not as well known as Stonehenge, but its setting — on the crown of a hill within a bowl of scenic peaks — is one of the most delightful in Britain. Probably dating from the second millennium B.C., the 60 roughly hewn stones stand up to seven feet high. It has been claimed that there are purposeful alignments between the stones and the surrounding hills.

These structures, ranging from simple chambers covered with large stones to huge gallery graves or circular tombs, were all built of stone and are termed megalithic (from the Greek for "big stone"). Used for multiple burials on successive occasions, these tombs contained simple grave goods, such as pots and stone tools. Although some later burials contained copper weapons or ornaments, the megalithic tombs were built before metallurgy came to these areas.

Passage graves, such as the one at Newgrange in Ireland, consist of a stone-built central burial chamber set in the middle of a circular mound. This is entered by a long passage of upright stone slabs, roofed by horizontal slabs. In some tombs, the passage walls are made of smaller stones laid flat, and this dry-stone wall technique was also used for corbeled roofs. An example of the latter can be found at the Barnenez tomb in

Brittany, built before 4000 B.C., far earlier than the tholos, or beehive, tombs of the Aegean. At West Kennet in the west of England, the megalithic burial chambers of the longbarrow were used for over 1,000 years, from about 3600 B.C.

From about 3200 B.C., the people of Britain and northwest France began to build ritual monuments of standing stones. These include circles, exemplified by Stonehenge, the greatest of Britain's megalithic monuments; alignments (single or multiple rows of standing stones), such as the one at Carnac in France; and menhirs (single standing stones). There were also simple henges — circular ditch-and-bank enclosures. In Britain and Ireland, there are about 1,000 stone circles and 80 henges, while in northwest France, there are over 1,200 menhirs. Though little is known about the purpose of these monuments, it is thought that they were perhaps linked with the seasons and astronomy.

THE BRONZE AGE

Warriors of the late Bronze Age, such as the one depicted here, benefited from improvements in bronze working, which led to finely wrought weapons, particularly swords. The short dagger had become longer and was now a true sword, with a leaf-shaped blade which placed the weight at the point, allowing the warrior to fight by slashing. A long lance, with a metal point and butt, and a mace were also used.

A great novelty was defensive weaponry, for warriors now girded themselves with bronze. They wore crested or rimmed helmets and cuirasses made from sheet metal, with a front and back plate attached to each other. Bronze greaves were laced on the shins, and a round shield completed what was an impressive panoply.

In Europe, the first copper and gold objects were produced in the Balkans and date from about 5000 B.C. They were relatively simple and were made by hammering pure metals, found in areas of ore-bearing rocks. Later, from about 4500 B.C., larger objects, such as tools and weapons, were manufactured by the techniques of smelting and casting. Metalworking spread east, west and north from the Balkans, reaching most of Europe and southern Britain by the third millennium.

Before the Bronze Age began in about 2300 B.C., the Chalcolithic ("copper-stone") period marked the beginnings of hierarchical societies, controlled by wealthy elites. In burials of southeast and east-central Europe during the fifth and fourth millennia, poorer graves contained only pottery, stone objects or nothing at all, while richer graves included metal ornaments and weapons. A rich grave at Varna in Bulgaria, for example, contained bracelets, beads and an array of other golden objects.

As metal usage spread, skills in metalworking developed, and raw materials and worked objects were traded. Long-distance trading networks of the third millennium can be traced by the appearance in northern and western Europe of metalwork found with the distinctive pottery known as Beaker and Corded Ware originally made in central Europe. Farther east, in the Kuban region of southern Russia, richly furnished burials, such as at Maikop, dating from about 2500 B.C., contained gold and silver objects and copper tools made from local ores.

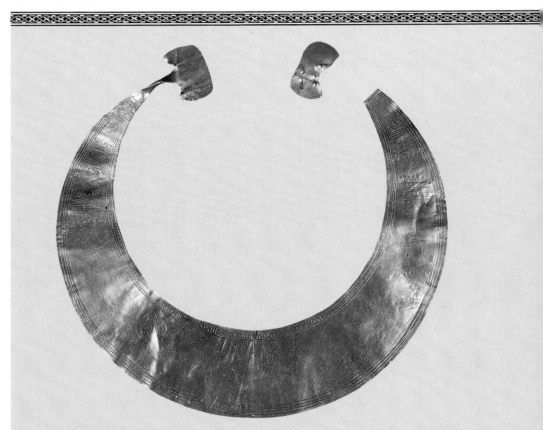

This collar, or lunula, of about 2250 B.C., comes from Orbliston in Scotland and is made of beaten sheet gold with incised decorations. Such pieces were exported in large quantities from Ireland to Britain and the European continent in the early Bronze Age. It is possible they were worn on ritual occasions.

From about 2300 B.C., the first bronze objects appear in the tombs and settlements of Europe. Bronze, which is harder than copper and so better for weapons and tools, is an alloy of copper and tin, which was found only in parts of western Britain and France, northwest Spain and north Italy. Large mining complexes, such as the Mitterberg copper mines in Austria, developed, and these, coupled with the long-distance trade in metals, led to the emergence of the Bronze Age in Europe.

In northern Europe at this time, around Jutland and the Baltic, amber – highly prized for beads – as well as probably furs and skins were traded in exchange for metals. As bronze became available to them, Scandinavian craftsmen also became expert metalworkers; one of the best examples of their work is a cast bronze wheeled model of a horse drawing an engraved gold-covered sun disk. It was found in the Trundholm Bog in Denmark and dates from about 1650 B.C. The lack of oxygen in this and other boggy ground has preserved many gold and bronze objects, including *lurer*, elegant bronze wind instruments shaped like horns.

In time, European Bronze Age society became increasingly stratified, as the burials of the wealthy elite reveal. By the early second millennium B.C., individuals were being interred under large mounds, or barrows, often set apart from the rest of the community and containing rich grave goods. At Leubingen in Germany, the center of such a mound held a huge timber mortuary structure containing the body of a man and a young girl, buried with much bronze and gold. Barrow burials, which required extensive labor for their construction, became widespread in southwest England and Brittany. As these were both areas with access to tin sources, it is possible that control of supplies led to the emergence of elite groups who were considerably wealthy and powerful.

From about 2000 B.C., settlements in eastern and central Europe were increasingly fortified. About 800 years later, this trend spread to western Europe, and hillforts and fortified lake settlements, such as at Wasserburg in southern Germany, were founded. At the same time, a new culture known as Urnfield, characterized by the dead being cremated and their ashes placed in urns that were deposited in large cemeteries, or urnfields, spread widely through Europe from the middle Danube area.

Bronze work was now advanced, and throughout Europe new types of bronze weapons and armor were used, including slashing swords, helmets, greaves, breastplates and shields. Late Bronze Age society had become militaristic, but although warfare was rife, it was still localized. Bronze had ceased to be a luxury article used only by the wealthy, and countless bronze tools and trinkets were made. This prolific bronze production suggests a time of prosperous trade, and it was in such conditions that the use of a new metal – iron – would begin to spread through Europe.

MAKING METALS

The first metals to be worked were surface and alluvial copper and gold nuggets, soft enough to be hammered and cut with stone tools. Such deposits, however, are fairly rare and rapidly depleted. Metallurgy began with the discovery that metal-bearing rocks, or ores, underwent chemical changes when heated, thus enabling pure metal to be extracted. After this process of smelting, the metal could be reheated until molten, then cast in molds to make artifacts. Smelting and casting seem to have arisen independently in different places: the techniques were being used in the Balkans around 6000 B.C., and from here they spread to much of Europe.

In the third millennium B.C., bronze, an alloy of copper and tin, was discovered. This much harder metal usually consisted of 10 percent tin and 90 percent copper. To extract copper, Bronze Age miners used bronze picks to excavate tunnels, and then fire and water to break up the ore and bring it to the surface. Smelting required temperatures of over 1,800 degrees Fahrenheit. In the late Bronze Age, new techniques, such as the making of high-quality sheet metal, were introduced and perfected. Another innovation in Britain and northern France was the addition of seven to ten percent lead. This made a copper-tin-lead alloy which produced a metal that was easier to pour and resulted in fewer faulty castings.

At a time when bronze production in Europe was transformed by new techniques, it was superseded by an even harder metal: iron. First smelted and forged in the Near East in the second millennium, iron became widespread there by the early first millennium B.C., when it spread to Europe; by the seventh century B.C., it had largely replaced bronze for many artifacts. Iron needs to be smelted with a mixture of carbon to 2,700 degrees Fahrenheit. Once iron smelting was perfected, it continued virtually unchanged until the Middle Ages.

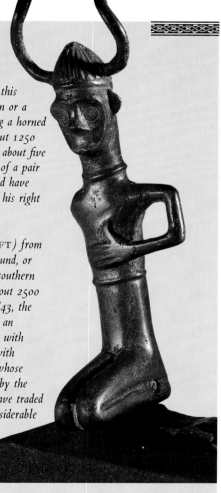

Discovered on Zealand, Denmark, this bronze figure of a man or a god (RIGHT) wearing a horned helmet dates from about 1250 B.C. Measuring only about five inches high, he is one of a pair of statuettes and would have been holding an ax in his right hand.

This gold bull (LEFT) from the Maikop burial mound, or kurgan, in Kuban in southern Russia, dates from about 2500 B.C. Excavated in 1843, the great mound contained an immensely rich burial, with metalwork decorated with animals. The people whose culture is exemplified by the grave goods seem to have traded in cattle, but their considerable wealth came from control of mineral deposits in the Caucasus.

European traders

This magnificently decorated archaic Greek bronze wine vessel, or crater (OPPOSITE PAGE), was one of the grave goods placed in a late sixth century B.C. tomb of a princess at the *oppidum* of Vix, near the site of Mont Lassois and the modern town of Chatillon-sur-Seine in France. The vessel came from either Greece or the Greek colony of Tarentum in southern Italy. Such vessels may have been used by the Greeks as diplomatic gifts, or as merchandise for new customers. An extraordinary quantity of Greek pottery has been found at Vix, almost certainly supplied by the Greeks of Massilia in the south of France. The Vix finds are clear evidence of the trade in wine and other luxuries from the Mediterranean to the Hallstatt Celts in exchange for slaves, skins, cattle and salt. It is possible that the Celts acted as middlemen in the trade in amber and furs from the Baltic and Scandinavia to the south.

There were several amber routes (RIGHT) in the first millennium B.C.: the main one from the Baltic went directly south to the Adriatic, while from Jutland there were two land routes, one through the Brenner Pass to the Adriatic and the other down the Rhône to the Mediterranean at Massilia; there was also a sea route to Britain. Tin, important for bronze production, was carried from Cornwall in the west of England across to France and then to the western Mediterranean and along the Brenner Pass amber route from Bohemia.

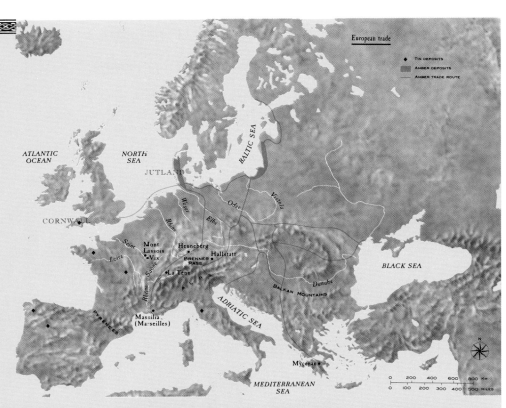

Greeks and Romans knew the Iron Age people of late pre-historic Europe as Celts (*Keltoi*) or Gauls (*Galli*). The Celts were not a single people with a shared history, nor were they migrants: Celtic Iron Age societies developed out of those of the late Bronze Age, and Celtic or Celtic-associated remains first appear in Austria and south Germany in about 800 B.C.

Ironworking spread to Europe from the Near East by an unknown route early in the first millennium B.C. Before the seventh century B.C., only a few iron pieces were found, since the new technique spread slowly through Europe. But when iron was fully adopted, it brought important changes to warfare, agriculture and craftsmanship. Some of the earliest iron objects found north of the Alps are from Hallstatt in Upper Austria. This site, with its rich burials containing iron weapons, has given its name to the earlier phase of the European Iron Age, which lasted from the eighth to the fifth centuries B.C.

The earliest burials at Hallstatt were of the late Bronze Age Urnfield culture, and it is clear that there was a considerable continuity during the transition from bronze to iron. Salt mined at Hallstatt was exported to central Europe and Italy. And trading contacts can be inferred from the rich grave goods, which include Italian bronzes. An aristocracy grown wealthy from trade became evident.

During the seventh and sixth centuries B.C., Hallstatt culture expanded and developed in southern Germany and eastern France. Hilltop fortresses were built, such as the Heuneburg on the Danube, probably the dwelling of a chieftain. Here, Mediterranean influence can be seen in part of the fortifications and in imported pottery and bronze wine vessels. Many such beautiful objects have been found in tombs of wealthy aristocrats, such as the one at Hochdorf in Germany. The deceased was typically buried in roofed wooden chambers under great mounds of earth, the body placed on a four-wheeled wagon with weapons, precious objects and horse equipment.

At Vix, in eastern France, the rich burial of a princess seems to confirm the tradition that aristocratic Celtic women had equal status with men. The burial also contained a huge wine vessel of Greek work – major sources of Greek and Etruscan luxuries were the Greek colonies of the Adriatic and Massilia, at the mouth of the Rhône. Exports to the classical world included salt and slaves, and the Celts also profited from being intermediaries in trade between the north and the Mediterranean.

At the village of Hallstatt in Upper Austria, shown in this 19th-century engraving, a settlement was found after which the earlier phase of the European Iron Age is named. The site was first occupied in the late Bronze Age, when the local salt mines began to be worked. The prosperity of this center came from exports of salt. The burials at Hallstatt show both the degree of continuity between the late Bronze and early Iron Age cultures and the emergence of an aristocratic elite.

In the mid-fifth century B.C., a new and more clearly defined Celtic culture emerged, known as La Tène after a site on Lake Neuchâtel in Switzerland. The remains of the La Tène Celts, especially their superb metalwork, are found widely dispersed across Europe. Their wheeled vehicles, which included a light two-wheeled chariot, were among the most advanced of the ancient world, as were their weapons. The quality of their ironworking was so high that some swords still spring back when bent; gold and silver were used for torques and brooches decorated with stylized forms of animals and religious motifs. The Celts did not write, but the Druids, their priests and lawgivers, memorized the rituals and laws.

These Celtic people were fierce warriors, as the classical world found to its cost: the Gauls sacked Rome in about 390 B.C. and Delphi in about 272 B.C. The Gauls moved into Asia Minor, where they were known as the Galatians, as well as into the Balkans and northern Italy, where they contributed to the demise of the Etruscans.

In the last centuries B.C., from Romania to Gaul, Celtic states emerged and large fortified settlements known as *oppida* were built. Some were of considerable size, with thatched and timber houses, barns, warehouses and workshops for producing weapons, tools, leather goods and textiles dyed with woad and other vegetable dyes. They were defended by large timber-framed ramparts held with vast quantities of iron nails. These states minted their own coins and increasingly imported wine vessels and tableware from Rome, now the great Mediterranean power. Although fearless in battle, the Celtic tribes were disunited, and the Romans gradually brought them within their empire; only in Ireland and Scotland did the Celtic way of life continue.

This wine vessel, or crater, from Vix in France, was discovered in the grave of a princess who is estimated to have been 30 to 35 years of age. The crater was shown to be of Greek manufacture and its sheer size suggests that it was used on ceremonial occasions. Both of the handles are in the form of gorgons — monstrous mythological figures — and a decorative frieze runs along the crater's neck.

Also found in the grave was a bronze Etruscan-style wine flagon, which prefigures the increase of Etruscan imports in central Europe during the fifth century.

REDISCOVERING ANCIENT EUROPE

From the late 18th century A.D., Europeans became increasingly interested in the distant past of their own lands. In part this was the result of the Romantic movement, which rejected those qualities – especially classicism – valued by the preceding Age of Reason in favor of that which was held to be "natural" and "primitive." Another reason was a growing nationalism: in northern Europe, from the British Isles to Scandinavia and Germany, people no longer looked for their origins in common classical and Christian culture, but sought their distinctive European roots.

In areas where history merged into legend, patriotic imagination ran freely, and in the 19th century the Vikings became a favorite subject. Ancient heroes and Dark Age knightly chivalry were used as themes in many poems; the ancient gods were reborn, and mythological painting drew its inspiration from other artistic sources. For example, *The Wild Hunt of Odin* by the painter Peter Nicolai Arbo evokes the barbaric power of the sky god and his horde of wild horsemen, collected by the Valkyries (choosers of the slain) from battlefields on earth. It was painted in 1872, a few years after the great German composer Richard Wagner wrote his opera *Die Walküre* (BELOW). Wagner himself drew freely on European mythology for inspiration.

While artists rendered their vision of the ancient north, scholars began to piece together historical evidence, working on ancient texts in Old Norse, Old High German and Anglo-Saxon, and editing and publishing the ancient sagas, such as the Anglo-Saxon epic *Beowulf*. Excavations were carried out, and, as finds increased, museums were founded. Denmark was particularly rich in remains, since many deposits in bogs had been well preserved. It was in Denmark in 1836 that the Danish scholar Christian Thomsen (1788–1865) formulated the three-age classification system (stone, bronze and iron) of prehistory on the basis of antiquities in the Copenhagen Museum. Since that time, his system has been widely used.

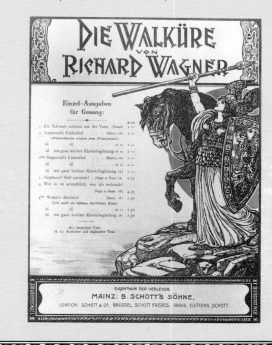

Scythian horses were dressed up — according to the wealth and nobility of the rider — with painted saddles, leather trappings adorned with appliqué and embroidery, and other ornaments. Deer masks (RIGHT) were also used.

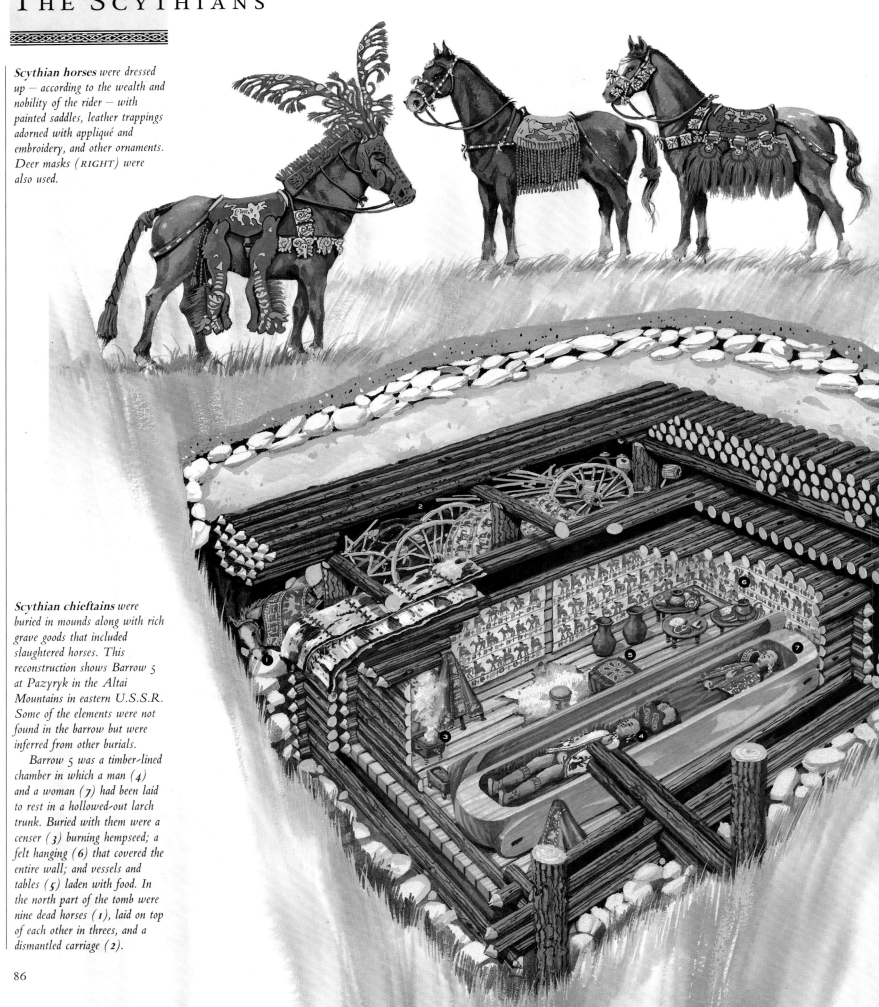

Scythian chieftains were buried in mounds along with rich grave goods that included slaughtered horses. This reconstruction shows Barrow 5 at Pazyryk in the Altai Mountains in eastern U.S.S.R. Some of the elements were not found in the barrow but were inferred from other burials.

Barrow 5 was a timber-lined chamber in which a man (4) and a woman (7) had been laid to rest in a hollowed-out larch trunk. Buried with them were a censer (3) burning hempseed; a felt hanging (6) that covered the entire wall; and vessels and tables (5) laden with food. In the north part of the tomb were nine dead horses (1), laid on top of each other in threes, and a dismantled carriage (2).

Among the objects found in Barrow 5 were these swans (RIGHT), a felt wall hanging (BELOW RIGHT) and a carriage (BOTTOM), all shown here restored. The swans were made from felt cut-outs and are Chinese in style. They were originally attached to the top of the carriage, which was found dismantled in the tomb. The wall hanging shows a rider approaching a seated figure, thought by some to be a goddess. Her long robe and tight-fitting cap suggest Chinese influence.

Scythian craftsmen excelled in making gold jewellery, such as this pectoral, 12 inches wide. The top frieze shows Scythians engaged in everyday activities, such as making a shirt and milking a sheep. The bottom frieze depicts animals fighting each other.

A nomadic people of the Asian steppes, the Scythians were driven westward in the eighth century B.C., some settling in Armenia and others between the Caspian and Aral seas. Many moved into south Russia, occupying the lands north of the Black Sea until they were eliminated by the Sarmatians in the second century A.D. Scythian tribes also invaded eastern and southeastern Europe in the fourth century B.C., and their tombs have been found from northern Germany to the Balkans.

An Indo-European people, speaking an Iranian language, the Scythians are known largely from their burials, some of which are well preserved, and from the records of the settled people with whom they came into contact. Evidence from the Near East suggests they were a warlike people; and Chinese, Persian and Greek accounts describe a tribal and hierarchical society of mounted warriors headed by chieftains.

At Pazyryk in the Altai Mountains of Siberia, Scythian tombs were accidentally sealed by a layer of ice shortly after the burials were placed there in the fifth century B.C.; as a result, all the organic materials that would normally have decayed were frozen and preserved. Among their contents were a complete, though dismantled, wooden wagon; various objects of leather and wood, including equipment for horses and a musical instrument; furs; textiles, notably carpets; embroidered silk and appliqué feltwork; and the tattooed bodies of the dead. The silk had come from China: since this was the period when silk appears in the Mediterranean and central Europe, it is possible that the Scythians acted as middlemen in this trade. Certainly, as many burials reveal, some Scythians were very wealthy.

The Scythians developed their own distinctive art style, often portraying highly stylized animals, such as the golden stag which is the centerpiece of a shield found at Kostromskaya in southern Russia. Here, as in other tombs in the region, there were also gold and bronze ornaments made either in the Greek cities of the Black Sea coast, or by Greek craftsmen working directly for Scythian chieftains. One of the most exquisite pieces in the Greek style, a quadruple golden torque, was found in the princely burial of the Tolstaia Mogila kurgan, farther north in the lower Dnieper Valley.

Only in southern Russia, where the sedentary western Scythians lived, are there remains of permanent settlements, such as the large fortified site at Kamenskoye, north of the Black Sea. Such settlements are relatively rare, since these nomadic people, who reared cattle, sheep and horses, and sometimes also hunted, traveled between pastures with the seasons, the men on horseback and the women and children in wagons. Their belongings were portable and they journeyed with their homes — tents furnished with hangings, rugs and cushions — and cooked in great bronze cauldrons.

The Scythians were famed horsemen, riding bareback on small swift horses, armed with bows and arrows. The Greek historian Herodotus, who wrote a detailed account of the Scythians, described their fierceness in battle and their custom of scalping enemies. They also practiced guerrilla tactics, harassing the enemy and swiftly retreating, burning crops as they withdrew. Both Persians and Greeks employed Scythian cavalry as mercenaries. Modern archaeology has confirmed some of Herodotus's description: in the Altai tombs, hemp has been found, together with implements for smoking it.

THE GERMANIC WORLD

BARBARIAN TRIBES

During the first centuries of the first millennium A.D., smaller barbarian tribes formed into larger, distinct groups and posed a potential threat to Rome and her provinces. In the fourth century, the westward advance of the Huns (pp. 144–45) pushed other tribes toward the borders of the empire, which, unable to withstand the pressure, eventually fell. The tribes listed below were the principal barbarian peoples involved in the upheavals during this time.

Ostrogoths and **Visigoths**: originally from eastern Germany, they finally founded kingdoms in Italy and southern France and Spain.
Vandals: originated from eastern Europe, but ended up settling in Spain and north Africa.
Jutes, Angles and **Saxons**: from the Jutland peninsula and north Holland, they invaded south and east Britain, where they settled in the fifth century.
Burgundians: migrated into the Rhine-Main area in about A.D. 400 and later established a kingdom; they subsequently settled on the Saône and the Rhône.
Alemanni: the second largest Germanic group, they established themselves on the Rhine.
Franks: by the fifth century they had moved from east of the Rhine to Gaul, where the Merovingian kingdom was formed.

In northern Europe, beyond the Celtic world, lay the lands of the Germanic peoples, first distinguished from their Celtic and Scythian neighbors in the lost *Histories* of the Syrian philosopher Poseidonius (*c*.135–51 B.C.). The term *Germani* was given to these barbarians beyond the Rhine by the Romans; it was not, as far as is known, used by these people to describe themselves. Nor can it be assumed that the various German tribes were conscious of any ethnic or cultural unity.

The Germanic world lasted roughly for more than 1,000 years from about 500 B.C., from which time its material culture can be traced. The Germanic peoples lived in what today forms most of Germany, Poland, southern Norway and Sweden, Denmark, northern Holland and part of Czechoslovakia. German expansion from this region was a long-drawn-out process; land shortage, the result of population increase, was the initial impetus. Another was the attraction of the wealth of Roman provinces. As events would show, the Roman historian Tacitus was mistaken when he wrote in his *Germania*: "We show our homes and our farms [to the Hermunduri] and they do not covet them."

The first known tribal movement was that of the east German Bastarnae, who threatened the Greek cities of the Black Sea coast in about 200 B.C. In the following century, there were large-scale migrations into Belgium and the Rhineland, and in 120 B.C., the Cimbri and Teutones migrated from Jutland; the Celts south of the Main now retreated to Switzerland. There were further

The silver cauldron from which this detail of a horned deity comes was found in 1891 in a bog at Gundestrup in Jutland, where it was deposited as a ritual offering. It dates from the first or second centuries B.C. and was possibly made in Romania or eastern Europe.

GODS OF THE GERMANS

An accurate account of Germanic religion is difficult to reconstruct because most of the information comes from classical sources. It seems, however, that there were a number of gods, among the most important of which were those connected with war and fertility. It is clear that people practiced human sacrifice to these deities, and prisoners of war are known to have been ritually slaughtered. Wodan, identified with the Norse god Odin, was one of the war gods, as well as a deity of storm and wind; but he was also concerned with trade and the protection of traders and played a part in leading the spirits of the dead to the underworld.

Another war god was Tiwaz (later Tiw or Tyr), associated with the battlefield and law and order. He, too, was offered human sacrifices, and there seems to have been an annual assembly in a sacred wood that was connected with his ritual. Donar, the predecessor of Thor, was a god of thunder and had strong associations with forest groves and especially oak woods. The youthful twins, the Alcis, were also worshipped, although little else is known about them. The fertility goddess Nerthus visited her devotees at special times in a sacred wagon, which only her priest might touch or look inside. Slaves washed her cult image and were later drowned.

The Germans made votive offerings to their gods in the form of deposits, such as the Gundestrup cauldron (LEFT), in bogs and marshes; these offerings seem to have included humans and animals. They had no temples, but many votive sites found by the bog deposits suggest that clans or families had their own sacred places. Divination was used, and auspices were taken from the flight of birds and birdsong, from the branches of fruit trees and from the actions of sacred white horses.

movements of Germanic tribes into areas formerly held by Celts on the Danube and west of the Rhine during the first century B.C.

In 61 B.C., the Suevi under Ariovistus allied with the Celtic Sequani and attacked the Celts of central Gaul, which led to the intervention of Julius Caesar. By the time of Augustus (pp. 134–35), Germans occupied most of the land between the Rivers Weser and Rhine. There was corresponding expansion in the east, as the German tribes advanced to the lower Elbe and the River Vistula.

In northern Europe, iron technology developed slowly because of the lack of the right type of ore deposits. However, by the third and fourth centuries A.D., there were many smelting sites in several regions producing a large amount of iron. The German barbarians were now skilled metalworkers, and the weapons they made help to explain the shift of the military initiative from Rome to the barbarians in the fourth century.

The German practice of depositing votive offerings in the bogs and marshes has preserved many vessels of precious metal as well as military equipment, perhaps offered to the gods after victories. Most of this evidence comes from Denmark, where the war equipment of one deposit included a warship, 150 wooden shields, 138 iron spearheads and 20 coats of mail. Later deposits in the early centuries A.D. often included Roman weapons. Some contained human bodies, most of which appear to have

been ritually murdered, either by hanging, decapitation or stabbing, or by strangulation, as in the case of the body found at Tollund in Denmark.

Until the end of the second century A.D., the German tribes had more or less been held in check by Roman forces along the Rhine and the Danube, partly by force and partly by diplomacy. Some 20 years of campaigns against the Marcomanni ended in 180, when the Roman emperor Commodus made peace with the tribes in return for subsidies. Rome's clear ascendancy over her northern neighbors had now ended, and pressure increased on the frontiers. Shortly after the mid-third century, there were massive German invasions into the Balkans and Gaul; then at the end of the century, the Goths moved into Dacia. The Roman policy of allowing tribes to settle on the borders and receive payment for protecting the frontiers is first heard of in 294; in the following century, many more were settled in this way.

The westward advance of the Huns (pp. 144–45) gave the impetus for the great migrations of the fourth century. By then, the Germanic world was changing, and the small tribes of earlier times were becoming larger political groupings, such as the Franks and Goths. Within a century Rome had fallen, and the medieval world would grow out of the kingdoms of these former tribes.

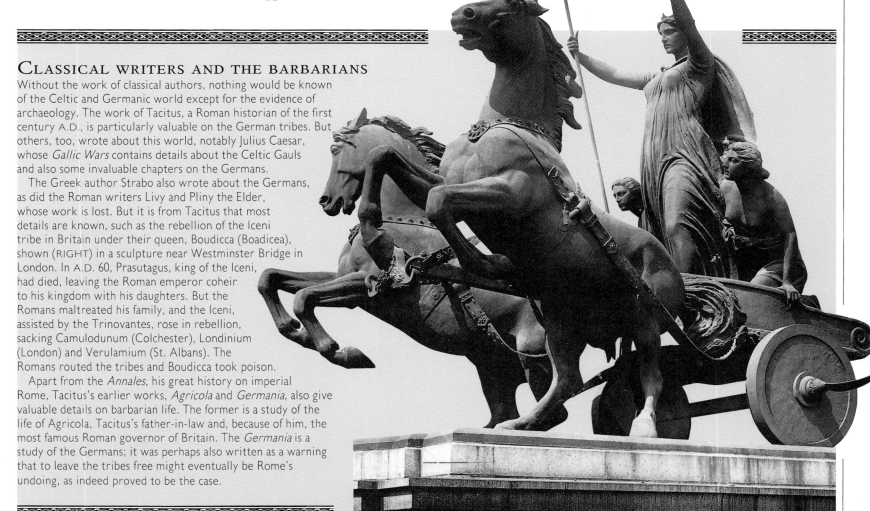

CLASSICAL WRITERS AND THE BARBARIANS

Without the work of classical authors, nothing would be known of the Celtic and Germanic world except for the evidence of archaeology. The work of Tacitus, a Roman historian of the first century A.D., is particularly valuable on the German tribes. But others, too, wrote about this world, notably Julius Caesar, whose *Gallic Wars* contains details about the Celtic Gauls and also some invaluable chapters on the Germans.

The Greek author Strabo also wrote about the Germans, as did the Roman writers Livy and Pliny the Elder, whose work is lost. But it is from Tacitus that most details are known, such as the rebellion of the Iceni tribe in Britain under their queen, Boudicca (Boadicea), shown (RIGHT) in a sculpture near Westminster Bridge in London. In A.D. 60, Prasutagus, king of the Iceni, had died, leaving the Roman emperor coheir to his kingdom with his daughters. But the Romans maltreated his family, and the Iceni, assisted by the Trinovantes, rose in rebellion, sacking Camulodunum (Colchester), Londinium (London) and Verulamium (St. Albans). The Romans routed the tribes and Boudicca took poison.

Apart from the *Annales*, his great history on imperial Rome, Tacitus's earlier works, *Agricola* and *Germania*, also give valuable details on barbarian life. The former is a study of the life of Agricola, Tacitus's father-in-law and, because of him, the most famous Roman governor of Britain. The *Germania* is a study of the Germans; it was perhaps also written as a warning that to leave the tribes free might eventually be Rome's undoing, as indeed proved to be the case.

GREECE AND THE AEGEAN

"Future generations will marvel at us, as the present age marvels at us now. . . ."

ATHENIAN STATESMAN PERICLES (*c.*495–429 B.C.)

If an Athenian of the fifth century B.C. had witnessed the revolutionary movements in Eastern Europe and China in recent years, during which placards proclaimed the potent word "Democracy," he would have understood these turbulent eruptions in a way no other representative of the ancient world could have done. For democracy, rule by the *dēmos*, or people, is one of the most significant gifts the ancient Greeks have bequeathed to civilization.

In the fifth century B.C., government by democracy created in Athens an unprecedented degree of social justice and sense of

The head of the famous Bronze Charioteer of Delphi is used on this modern Greek poster to advertise an international festival of ancient Greek drama at Delphi. The lifesize statue, now housed in the Delphi museum, was excavated in 1896 and would have stood in a chariot drawn by horses. To the right of the image are the names of the countries and their entries, including Euripides' Bacchi by a Dutch company and Sophocles' Ajax by a French one.

responsibility among its citizens, whose votes in the Assembly were crucial to the city's decision-making and welfare. This vibrant atmosphere of *glasnost* and accountability helped to turn Athens into an intellectual and cultural hothouse and lay the foundations of western civilization. Herodotus and Thucydides, for example, are still considered models of the historical method. The western philosophical tradition that has developed over the last 2,000 years or more has been described as mere footnotes to the brilliant works of Plato.

In the arts, the great tragedies of Aeschylus, Sophocles and Euripides are still performed. Palaces, museums, banks and other municipal and corporate buildings around the world display features derived from Greek temples. Even in sports, the greatest athletics event in the world today, the Olympic Games, is held in commemoration of the first such contest in 776 B.C. at Olympia, in the Peloponnese.

Ancient Greece was never at any time a unified country with a central government and a capital city. Until the rise of Philip of Macedon in the middle of the fourth century B.C., when a semblance of Hellenic unity emerged, Greece was in reality a collection of independent city-states, each with its own government, laws and sphere of influence.

The earliest Aegean civilization was that of the Minoans on the island of Crete, which lasted from about 2200 B.C. for several hundred years. In about 1450 B.C., most of the Minoan palaces of Crete were destroyed, and there is evidence that Mycenaeans from mainland Greece invaded the island. But the dominance of Mycenae over the Greek world crumbled before the onslaught of Dorian invaders from the north in about 1250 B.C. or later. This ushered in a Dark Age which lasted until the gradual rise of the city-states in the ninth and eighth centuries. At this time, the first Greek colonists left their home towns to found settlements and, after the conquests of Alexander the Great of Macedon in the fourth century B.C., it was possible to travel from southern France to India and communicate only in Greek.

Alexander died in 323 B.C. and, almost immediately, his Greek empire fragmented. Soon the city-states, which had lost their independence under the Macedonian kings, would come under the heel of Rome. But even divorced from a political base, Greek culture – prized and absorbed by the Romans, and later assimilated into Christian theology and thought – has continued as the intellectual and artistic lifeblood of the western world.

An elegant Mycenaean lady (RIGHT) *holds a carved ivory box in this restored fresco. The Mycenaeans of mainland Greece replaced the Minoans of Crete as the dominant power in the Aegean in about 1450 B.C..*

This head of a bronze statue (FAR RIGHT), *found in the sea off Cape Artemision in 1928, is believed to be of Poseidon, the Greek god of earthquakes and later of the sea. One of the Olympian gods, Poseidon was the son of Kronos and brother of Zeus and Hades. He was believed to live beneath the Aegean Sea in a palace, from which he rode out in a chariot drawn by sea horses.*

The temple of Poseidon (RIGHT) *on Cape Sunium is said to have evoked the same sort of emotion in ancient Athenian sailors returning home as the Statue of Liberty and the White Cliffs of Dover were later to inspire in American and British mariners. It was this temple, built in the late fifth century B.C., that stirred the British Romantic poet Lord Byron to write: "Place me on Sunium's marbled steep,/Where nothing save the waves and I/ May hear our mutual murmurs sweep,/There swan-like there let me sing and die."*

THE MINOANS (I)

The first major civilization of the Aegean was created by the Minoans of Crete and flourished between about 2200 and 1450 B.C. This Bronze Age civilization is named after the legendary King Minos, and until excavations by the British archaeologist Sir Arthur Evans less than a century ago, its existence was unknown. Between 1899 and 1935, Evans worked at Knossos, the greatest of the Minoan palaces on Crete, and partially restored it. It is possible that the building's complex floor plan, with its numerous corridors, lay behind the myth of Minos's labyrinth, which housed the Minotaur, a creature with the body of a man and the head of a bull. This monster, the offspring of Pasiphaë, wife of King Minos, and a bull, was eventually killed by the Athenian hero Theseus.

The archaeological evidence suggests that this lost world of the Minoans is partly preserved in myth as well as in the legendary accounts of Crete in the works of the great epic poet Homer, who describes the island as being well populated and wealthy. Later, the Greeks of classical and Hellenistic times regarded Crete as a source of ancient religious traditions and long-lost social systems. The philosopher Aristotle (384–322 B.C.), in his discussion of the caste system, remarked that it was not new and that it had been introduced in Crete by Minos. In the fifth century B.C., the historians Herodotus and Thucydides both accepted that Crete had once been ruled by Minos and that the Cretan navy had dominated the seas.

According to Homer in his *Odyssey*, "Out in the dark blue sea there lies a land called Crete, a rich and lovely land, washed by the waves on every side, densely populated . . . ." The island measures only about 170 miles from east to west, while its longest north-south axis is just 35 miles. But within this relatively small

The first great civilization of the Aegean world was that of a people known as the Minoans on the island of Crete. After their demise in about the mid-15th century B.C., power resided in the people of the mainland, where the mountainous terrain helped to give rise to independent city-states. From about 1000 B.C. onward, Greek colonists set off to found new cities abroad, especially on the coast of Asia Minor and around the Black Sea.

Greece and the Aegean

0   50   100   150   KM

0   20   40   60   80   100   MILES

area agriculture flourished in the fertile plains and valleys. Crete is roughly equidistant from Greece and Libya, and from earliest times, its many sandy bays provided anchorage for voyagers from north Africa, Asia and Europe. Although it was receptive to external influences, these were not dominant, and the Cretan Bronze Age civilization developed gradually from the island's Neolithic culture.

The first palaces began to be built in about 2200 B.C., notably at Knossos in the north, at Phaistos in the south, and probably at Mallia on the northeast coast. It is not certain whether the palace of Zakro on the island's east coast existed at this time. Nor is it clear whether each palace was the center of an independent kingdom, with Knossos the largest. The similar styles and types of objects found at the different sites suggest it is more likely that Knossos was the principal palace of a centralized power. And it

is probable that these palaces were not merely royal residences, but also served as economic and religious centers, containing substantial communities.

Shortly after the first palaces were built, writing came into use, probably for administrative purposes. The earliest Cretan script, in use from about 2000 to 1600 B.C., was pictographic, and has been found mainly on seal-stones, but also on clay tablets. From this system developed the script known as Linear A, in use between about 1900 and 1450 B.C. and found on clay tablets from Knossos and elsewhere. Neither of these scripts has been deciphered, although the 75 signs of Linear A seem to represent syllables. Its ideograms resemble those of Linear B, which was used at Knossos between 1450 and 1400 B.C. and later at sites on the Greek mainland. At present, all that can be said is that the Minoans did not speak Greek.

Portuguese youths test their bravery against a bull in a sport which might be construed as a modern equivalent of the Minoan bull-leaping ritual, shown in the fresco (BELOW). That the bull held a special place in Minoan life is also suggested by the myth of the Minotaur, depicted in an etching (LEFT) by the modern artist Michael Ayrton. This half-human, half-bull monster was kept by King Minos in a labyrinth and fed on young sacrificial victims.

THE BULL IN ANCIENT CRETE

In a remarkable fresco (BELOW LEFT) from Knossos, a boy somersaults over a bull's back while a girl waits to catch him; at the same time, another girl grasps the bull's horns and prepares to leap. Similar scenes of bulls and bull-leapers have been depicted on Minoan seal-stones, bronzes and ivories. And there are also many other images of the bull in Cretan art. The significance of this sport in Minoan culture is not understood, although it may have been part of a religious ritual, at the end of which the bull was sacrificed. There is no evidence of bull worship or a bull god in Minoan society. However, in Near Eastern religions, the different forms of the sky god are frequently represented as, or linked to, bulls, for example by being shown standing on bulls or with bull's horns.

Whether the notion of the bull as a sacred animal came to Crete from the Near East is not known, but it might be possible. The later Greek deity Zeus was a sky god, and although he was associated with Mount Olympus on mainland Greece, there is also a tradition of a Cretan Zeus, whose characteristics are not unlike those of Dionysus, a deity connected with the bull. Moreover, there is the myth of Europa, who was abducted from Tyre by Zeus, who had adopted the form of a bull. He took her to Crete, where she bore him three sons, including Minos.

Finally, the bull-leapers call to mind the legend of the Minotaur, the monster to whom youths and maidens were sacrificed. According to the legend, King Minos was married to Pasiphaë, who developed an unnatural passion for a bull. The offspring of this union was the Minotaur, which was kept in a labyrinth. Each year, Minos's Athenian subjects were required to send seven youths and seven maidens to be fed to the Minotaur. Then Theseus, prince of Athens, went with the chosen victims to Crete; and, with the help of Minos's daughter Ariadne, who helped him find his way out of the labyrinth by means of a ball of thread, he killed the Minotaur. Theseus escaped with Ariadne, but abandoned her on Naxos, where she married Dionysus.

It has been claimed that this tale reflects in mythical form Athenian subjection to, and emancipation from, Cretan overlordship in the Bronze Age. However, all bull representations from Crete are of actual bulls, not creatures such as the Minotaur, and it may be that the legend refers to an early ceremony which was later forgotten.

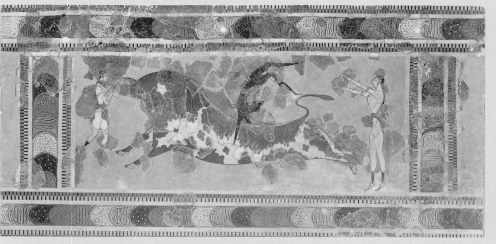

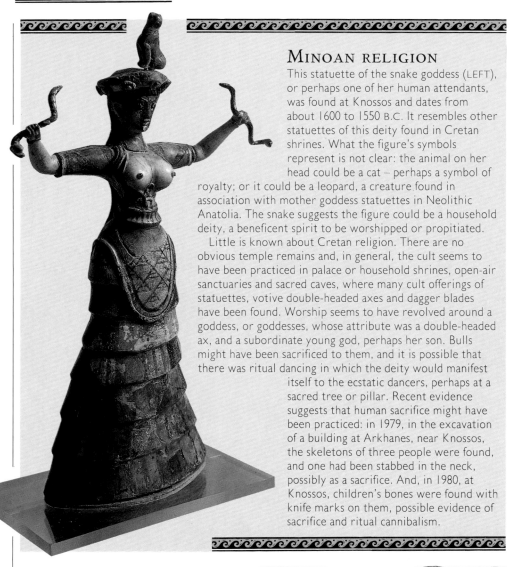

MINOAN RELIGION

This statuette of the snake goddess (LEFT), or perhaps one of her human attendants, was found at Knossos and dates from about 1600 to 1550 B.C. It resembles other statuettes of this deity found in Cretan shrines. What the figure's symbols represent is not clear: the animal on her head could be a cat – perhaps a symbol of royalty; or it could be a leopard, a creature found in association with mother goddess statuettes in Neolithic Anatolia. The snake suggests the figure could be a household deity, a beneficent spirit to be worshipped or propitiated.

Little is known about Cretan religion. There are no obvious temple remains and, in general, the cult seems to have been practiced in palace or household shrines, open-air sanctuaries and sacred caves, where many cult offerings of statuettes, votive double-headed axes and dagger blades have been found. Worship seems to have revolved around a goddess, or goddesses, whose attribute was a double-headed ax, and a subordinate young god, perhaps her son. Bulls might have been sacrificed to them, and it is possible that there was ritual dancing in which the deity would manifest itself to the ecstatic dancers, perhaps at a sacred tree or pillar. Recent evidence suggests that human sacrifice might have been practiced: in 1979, in the excavation of a building at Arkhanes, near Knossos, the skeletons of three people were found, and one had been stabbed in the neck, possibly as a sacrifice. And, in 1980, at Knossos, children's bones were found with knife marks on them, possible evidence of sacrifice and ritual cannibalism.

Discovered at the Minoan site of Akrotiri on the island of Thera (Santorini), this fresco of ships and dolphins shows the exuberance of the Minoan artist and provides circumstantial evidence for the Minoans' reputation as a seafaring people.

Early Minoan palaces suffered damage, perhaps from earthquakes, around 1700 B.C., and new ones were built on an even grander scale. Crete appears to have become more populous at this time, and communities flourished all over the island, including in the west. Small towns such as Gournia and Mochlos now expanded, although the palaces remained the main economic and social centers. Large country houses, similar to those found near the palaces, were also built.

It is the Knossos of the late stage of this phase that can be seen today. This extensive palace, which had no defenses, covers about three acres, with numerous rooms set around a central courtyard. On the west side lay a room used for cultic practices and the Throne Room. To the west of the cultic area were many storage rooms, some of which contained huge storage jars, or *pithoi*, in which oil and wine were kept. Other rooms probably stored grain or products such as honey, textiles and metals.

A huge monumental staircase linked the various levels. The walls of many rooms were decorated with lively and naturalistic frescoes of plant and animal life and depictions of slender-waisted men in kilts and elegantly dressed women with exposed breasts and elaborately curled hair. The artistic Minoans also produced exquisite jewelry and engraved seal-stones, and their carving of ivory and various gemstones was excellent. Pottery, faience and metalwork were also widely produced.

Some of the paintings at Knossos and elsewhere depict young men and women leaping over charging bulls in what may have been a religious ritual. Certainly the bull is found in various forms in Minoan art, including bronzes and ivories of bulls and bull leapers, and vessels in the form of a bull's head. And it is possible that bull games took place in the courtyard of the palace.

Little is known about Minoan religion. There are no temple remains, although ritual offerings have been found at various shrines, including the cult room in the basement at Knossos, a position that suggests that it was dedicated to an earth deity. Also, from the Neolithic period until late antiquity, the caves on the island were used as cult centers. According to the later Cretan myth of the birth and infancy of Zeus, the god was hidden from his father Kronos in a cave and fed by animals. The Cretan Zeus, a vegetation deity who died and was born again annually, differs from the traditional Zeus of the later Greek pantheon and resembles Dionysus, also a dying god and connected with the bull. There also seems to have been an earth or mother-goddess, whose name is not known. Human sacrifice may have been practiced in times of extreme crisis, but this is not certain.

The Minoans, as the marine motifs on their pottery suggest, were great seafarers. They traded with lands of the east Mediterranean and were known to the Egyptians as the Kheftiu. There is also evidence of a Minoan presence on Aegean islands, including Thera (Santorini). Here, in about 1500 B.C., the settlement at Akrotiri was destroyed by an earthquake and the island was abandoned. This quake was followed by a massive volcanic explosion, which was perhaps linked to the destruction of the Cretan palaces and settlements that happened in about 1450 B.C. The palaces, apart from Knossos which survived sufficiently to be repaired, were now abandoned forever. In the wake of this disaster, Knossos was occupied by Mycenaeans from mainland Greece until about 1400 B.C., when the palace was burned down and never rebuilt.

Knossos

Housing up to 80,000 people, the palace of Knossos was at least twice the size of any other Cretan palace. The lack of fortifications — an unusual feature shared by other Minoan palaces on Crete — may indicate Knossos's strength as a naval power. This reconstruction shows the palace as it was after being rebuilt in about 1700 B.C.

The palace was raised on the side of a hill and had a number of different levels. The focal point was the Central Court (*3*), where rituals involving bulls may have taken place. Off to the west was the Throne Room (*6*), with its carved gypsum "throne," a shrine (*4*) and the Stepped Porch (*5*) leading to the first floor.

To the east of the court were the royal apartments and the Grand Staircase (*8*), with its light well. Situated behind the staircase was the principal reception room of the palace, the Hall of the Double Axes (*9*). Adjacent to this was the Queen's Hall (*10*), decorated with a fresco of dolphins. Other notable features of the palace include the Procession Corridor (*1*), the West Court (*2*) and an area (*7*) which may have been used for ceremonies.

Sir Arthur Evans, the British archaeologist, was the first person to uncover the brilliant Bronze Age civilization of Crete, which he named Minoan after the island's legendary King Minos. Evans devoted almost half his 91 years to excavating Knossos. He died in 1941.

First built during the 20th century B.C., Knossos, as the ground plan (ABOVE) shows, was a vast complex of corridors, porticoes and innumerable rooms for residence, workshops, storage and administration.

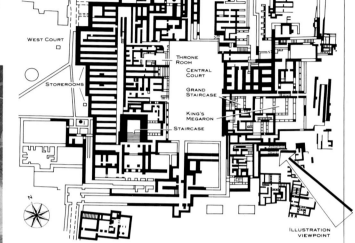

95

THE MYCENAEANS (I)

SCHLIEMANN AND MYCENAE

Born in Germany in 1822, Heinrich Schliemann (BELOW), the son of a poor pastor, was entranced as a child by the Homeric legends of Greek heroes and the siege of Troy. Later, unable to complete his classical studies because of poverty, Schliemann worked his way up from being a penniless errand boy to a very wealthy entrepreneur. A brilliant linguist, he mastered several languages, including Dutch,

Spanish, Italian and Portuguese, as well as Latin, English, French and Russian.

Determined to spend his fortune finding the Troy of Homer, Schliemann retired early, studied Greek and then identified the mound of Hissarlik in Turkey as Troy. In 1871, he began to excavate there and found what he termed King Priam's Treasure. In fact the material dated from about 2300 B.C., some 1,000 years before the likely date of Homer's Troy. In 1991, it was announced in the press that Schliemann's finds from Troy, which had disappeared from Berlin during World War II, had been discovered in the U.S.S.R., where they had been taken by Russian soldiers.

In 1874, Schliemann turned his attention to Mycenae, convinced that here lay the graves of Agamemnon and his family. Again he uncovered evidence of a formerly unknown age, though one that predated the age of the Homeric heroes by some 400 years. He meticulously excavated the site and published his findings. He died in 1890.

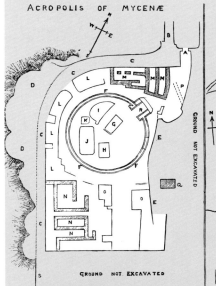

Schliemann's excavations at *Mycenae, are shown here in the contemporary engraving* (RIGHT) *and on his own site plan* (ABOVE). *The tinted area shows the location of the shaft-graves, whose treasures probably belonged to Mycenaean royalty of the early 16th century B.C.*

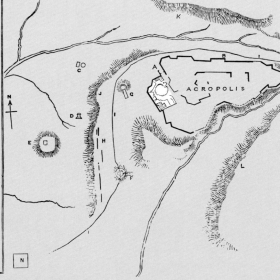

In about 1450 B.C., the Mycenaeans replaced the Minoans as the dominant power in the Aegean. These people had been the strongest power on mainland Greece from about 1600, and they continued to rule the region from their citadel cities until about 1200 to 1100 B.C. Among the most important of their centers were Mycenae, Tiryns and Pylos in the Peloponnese; Athens; and Iolkos on the coast of Thessaly. Although some sites, notably Mycenae, appear to have been much wealthier than others, it is unlikely that any one ruler controlled the entire Greek mainland during this period.

Mycenae was first excavated between 1876 and 1878 by the German Heinrich Schliemann, discoverer of the city of Troy. Schliemann found a series of rich burials in shaft-graves, which bore out Homer's epithet that Mycenae was "rich in gold." Although he believed that he had uncovered the graves of Agamemnon, the legendary king who led the Greek expedition to Troy, and his contemporaries, these finds were later shown to be too early, dating from about 1600 B.C. They do, however, give the first evidence of the Greek Bronze Age civilization, to which the name "Mycenaean" has been given. The extent to which the Homeric poems, and in particular the *Iliad*, preserve memories of this Mycenaean world is difficult to assess. But some elements of the poems, written down in their final form in the eighth century B.C., shed light on the Bronze Age, as do the shaft-graves.

How Mycenaean civilization emerged is not clear. It was not simply a direct continuation of the earlier "Helladic" culture (1900–1600 B.C.) that preceded it in the region, but seems to have fused both Helladic and Minoan cultural elements. Apart from archaeological evidence and the cautious use of Homeric texts, there are also contemporary documents that help to provide a picture of the Mycenaean Palace Age of the 14th and 13th centuries B.C. These come in the form of clay tablets, written in a script known as Linear B, which have been found at the final stratigraphic level of Knossos and on the Greek mainland at Pylos. A few tablets have also been found at Thebes and Mycenae, as well as fragments at Tiryns. This script, deciphered in 1952, represents an early form of Greek and developed from the undeciphered script known as Minoan Linear A.

Mycenaean cities, which started as hillside villages, were massively fortified, with walls made of huge irregular blocks. These constructions were later called "Cyclopean" by the Greeks because they appeared to have been the work of the Cyclopes, mythological one-eyed giants. Those at Tiryns are particularly big and support Homer's reference to "great walled Tiryns." Only at Pylos and other smaller settlements have no traces of such walls been found.

Mycenaean builders tended to choose a low hill site for both walled cities and unfortified towns and adapted the layout of houses and other buildings to the local terrain. The great fortified citadels were crowned by the local ruler's palace, which was typically much simpler than those of Crete. The palace's most important feature was a large hall known as a megaron, which resembled earlier Helladic models. The megaron formed the centerpiece of the building and had a central circular hearth flanked by two columns, as well as a vestibule and an anteroom. There were other rooms arranged around courtyards, with floors and walls that were plastered. The walls were decorated with frescoes, an art form clearly borrowed from the Minoans.

MICHAEL VENTRIS AND LINEAR B

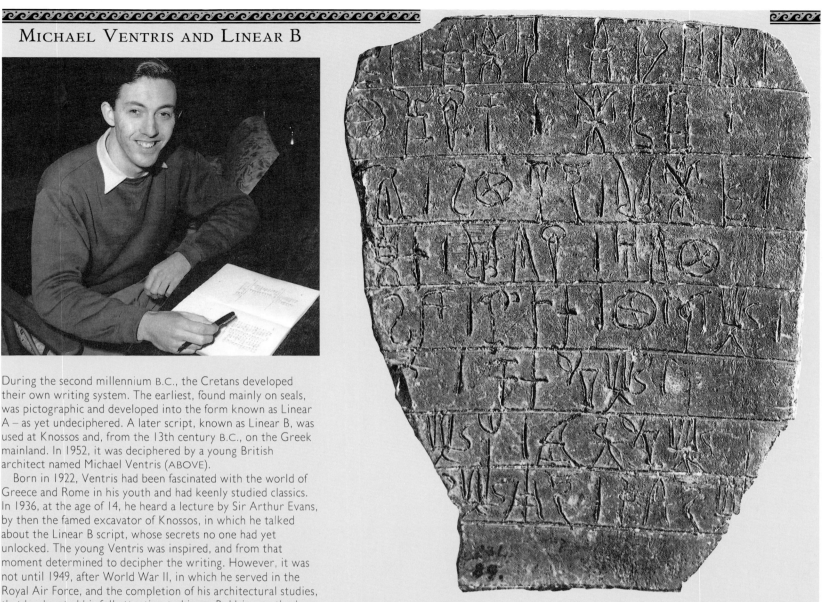

During the second millennium B.C., the Cretans developed their own writing system. The earliest, found mainly on seals, was pictographic and developed into the form known as Linear A – as yet undeciphered. A later script, known as Linear B, was used at Knossos and, from the 13th century B.C., on the Greek mainland. In 1952, it was deciphered by a young British architect named Michael Ventris (ABOVE).

Born in 1922, Ventris had been fascinated with the world of Greece and Rome in his youth and had keenly studied classics. In 1936, at the age of 14, he heard a lecture by Sir Arthur Evans, by then the famed excavator of Knossos, in which he talked about the Linear B script, whose secrets no one had yet unlocked. The young Ventris was inspired, and from that moment determined to decipher the writing. However, it was not until 1949, after World War II, in which he served in the Royal Air Force, and the completion of his architectural studies, that he devoted his full attention to Linear B. Using methods employed to crack enemy codes during the war, Ventris studied numerous clay tablets inscribed with the script, making a careful note of repeated signs. At length he was able to construct a grid of a number of consonants and vowels, though he was still no wiser as to what language he was dealing with. In the end, he experimented with the notion that the script might have been an archaic form of Greek and, to his surprise, he found that the tablets made sense.

Linear B *was inscribed on clay tablets, such as the one (*ABOVE*) found at Knossos, and is written from left to right. It consists of three elements: a group of about 90 signs that represent syllables; ideograms (idea signs); and a numerical* *system based on decimals. The content of the tablets consists largely of administrative and economic data, for example lists of different types of produce.*

Soon after his results had been made known, Ventris's claim that Linear B was an old *form of Greek was confirmed by Carl Blegen, an American archaeologist. Blegen used a tablet (*BELOW*), one of 400 found at Pylos, to test Ventris's syllabary and found that it worked: the inscription was an inventory of pots.*

THE MYCENAEANS (2)

Quantities of gold and other precious objects that were found in the shaft-graves at Mycenae reveal the immense wealth of the Mycenaean aristocracy. The considerable personal riches, the large numbers of weapons and the tall strong figures of the skeletons all indicate that this was a society with a warrior elite. Warfare was clearly an important element: engraved seal-stones, ivories and metalwork depict scenes of fighting, and there are daggers worked with hunting scenes; wall paintings and pottery also portray soldiers with spears and swords. Although the style of many of these objects is Minoan, or shows Minoan influence, the content is purely Mycenaean.

The Mycenaeans used chariots for hunting, but there is no pictorial or other evidence of their use in warfare. The warriors appear to have worn helmets – one made of boars' tusks, as described by the epic poet Homer, has been found – and carried either large body shields or a smaller type in the shape of a figure of eight. These shields were later superseded by smaller round ones, and it is possible that body armor now began to be worn. Stock Mycenaean weapons were spears, swords and daggers.

In about 1450 B.C., the Mycenaeans took the city of Knossos in the wake of the great destructions on Crete (pp. 94–95). The end of Minoan control of the sea allowed the Mycenaeans to expand their power and, from this time, their distinctive pottery appears in Syria, Palestine, Egypt and elsewhere. From the Cretans they learned to write and to organize a bureaucratic system based on written records.

These records bear out the archaeological evidence, which indicates that Mycenaean palaces were centers of political and economic control. The archive from Pylos reveals a complex economic system, with a considerable degree of specialization, central control and regular inspections. There are tablets that relate to land, grain, animals and metals; there is one that lists quantities of bronze to be given by officials to the palace for the making of weapons; while another contains details of bronze

The most important site of the Mycenaean world is Mycenae itself, situated in the northeast of the Peloponnese. Also impressive is nearby Tiryns, with its imposing palace. Mycenaean pottery and tholos tombs (shaped like beehives) are the best available evidence for the spread of Mycenaean trade and culture, which reached as far as Asia Minor, Crete and even the Levant, Sicily and southern Italy. Among the goods imported into the Greek mainland at this time were ivory from Syria and copper from the island of Cyprus.

Clytemnestra, shown here in the British National Theatre's production of the Oresteia by Aeschylus, was the wife of Agamemnon. During the latter's absence in Troy, she took a lover named Aegisthus, and then murdered her husband on his return. Clytemnestra paid for her crime by being killed by her son Orestes.

The Mycenaean world

AEGEAN SEA

given to smiths for working. Mycenaean rulers not only had control of vast areas of land with extensive crops and numerous flocks, but also seem to have overseen the production and trade of certain commodities such as metals. The texts also indicate that the Mycenaeans were served by large numbers of slaves and that they worshipped many of the gods and goddesses known from later Greek religion. The Pylos texts record offerings which were brought to these deities at their shrines, the remains of which have been found, along with cult statues. The offerings were received on the deities' behalf by a priest or priestess.

The end of the Mycenaean world was sudden: by the late 12th century B.C., all the palaces and towns had been destroyed or abandoned. Why such a rich and powerful civilization should have ended so suddenly is still a mystery. It is possible that there was an internal disturbance – perhaps a revolution – or that the Mycenaeans were overwhelmed by invaders, known as the Dorians, from the north. More probably, there was a combination of factors.

However, the fact that Mycenaeans settled on Cyprus suggests that there was a disruption in the Mycenaean world at about this time. Also, Mycenaean-style pottery is found in the regions that were settled by some of the wandering Sea Peoples (pp.28–29). Whether the end of the Mycenaean world is linked to the disturbances farther east at the end of the Bronze Age is not known either. But, whatever the cause, Greece entered a Dark Age, and little is known about its history until about 800 B.C.

THE FACE OF AGAMEMNON?

On December 6, 1876, Heinrich Schliemann noted in his journal the discovery of the first shaft-grave of Circle A at Mycenae. Eventually, he found five graves, in which there were 15 skeletons, and in Shaft Grave V, a gold funerary mask which Schliemann called the "mask of Agamemnon." Following this sensational discovery, Schliemann cabled the king of Greece: "It is with extraordinary pleasure that I announce to Your Majesty my discovery of the graves which, according to tradition, are those of Agamemnon, Cassandra, Eurymedon and their comrades, all killed during the banquet by Clytemnestra and her lover Aegisthus." However, the golden face mask and other jewellery and weapons have been dated to about the late 16th century B.C., too early to be the image of Homer's Agamemnon or any other Achaean combatant of the legendary Trojan War, which, if it occurred, would date to about 1200 B.C.

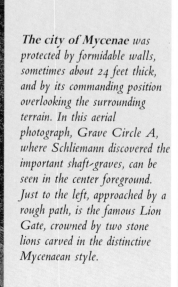

This gold death mask was declared by Heinrich Schliemann to be the face of Agamemnon, the king of Mycenae who led the Greek forces at the legendary siege of Troy. In fact, the mask predates the Trojan War – if it ever happened – by several hundred years. The story of the war and Agamemnon's part in it is described in Homer's Iliad.

The city of Mycenae was protected by formidable walls, sometimes about 24 feet thick, and by its commanding position overlooking the surrounding terrain. In this aerial photograph, Grave Circle A, where Schliemann discovered the important shaft-graves, can be seen in the center foreground. Just to the left, approached by a rough path, is the famous Lion Gate, crowned by two stone lions carved in the distinctive Mycenaean style.

99

EMERGENCE FROM THE DARK AGE

After the fall of the Mycenaean world in about 1200 to 1100 B.C., Greece entered a Dark Age of some three to four centuries about which there is little information. People known as the Dorians, who spoke a form of Greek, moved into central and southern Greece. The art of writing was lost, and the population declined, perhaps to one-tenth of what it had been in Mycenaean times. The absence of fine buildings and other material wealth is reflected in the paucity of archaeological evidence for the period up to about 800 B.C.

During this time, migrations from the Greek mainland to the coast of Asia Minor and the eastern Aegean islands occurred, as people, doubtless driven by poverty, sought out new farming land. These population movements began around 1000 B.C. and continued for about 200 years. They are known from later local traditions, and also the different Greek dialects spoken in the new areas give clues to their speakers' places of origin.

The Greeks who emigrated to Asia Minor, and particularly Ionia, were later to produce some of the greatest writers and artists of the Greek world. By tradition, Homer, the giant of Greek literature to whom are attributed the *Iliad* and the *Odyssey*, was an Ionian from Smyrna. These epic poems were written down probably during the eighth century; but their origins date back to the Dark Age, when the Greeks were illiterate. The *Iliad* tells of the siege of Troy by the Greeks under the leadership of Agamemnon of Mycenae and is a heroic tale of war, death and honor. The *Odyssey* is the story of the Greek hero Odysseus's ten-year voyage from Troy to his island home of Ithaca after the war.

The *Iliad* and the *Odyssey* were probably formed over many centuries and passed down orally by illiterate poets who recited the verses to the accompaniment of music. These bards would have added their own lines to the received body of verses. Sometime during the eighth century, the poems were written

The expansion of Greek trade and colonization, shown on the map (BELOW), began during the eighth century B.C., a period which is reflected in the Odyssey, *the epic poem that tells the story of the Greek hero Odysseus's voyage home to Ithaca from Troy. This Roman mosaic shows Odysseus bound to the mast of his ship in order to resist the Sirens, creatures who lured sailors onto rocks.*

COLONIZATION AND TRADE

The Greeks began to colonize largely as a result of poverty. The coast of Asia Minor and the islands off it were settled at the beginning of the Iron Age at about the start of the first millennium B.C. However, the greatest period of colonization occurred between about the middle of the eighth century to 500 B.C. During this Archaic period, Greek cities spread along the coasts of the Black Sea and the Mediterranean. Much of this period is undocumented, but from accounts of the Greek historians Herodotus and Thucydides and other, much later authors, such as the geographer Strabo, there is some information to supplement archaeological evidence. Politics and geography determined the regions selected so, with few exceptions, there was no settlement in areas such as Egypt or the Levant. There were, however, occasional trading colonies

Greek colonies and trade routes

down, with Homer attributed as the author. But the question of Homer's identity and the exact compilation of the poems is still a matter of scholarly debate. The poems contain details of the distantly remembered world of "Golden Mycenae," of golden drinking vessels and "tower-tall" shields – objects uncovered by archaeology. The *Odyssey* also contains images that seem to relate to the late Dark Age.

The other important figure of early Greek literature was the Boeotian poet Hesiod, writing at the end of the eighth century, who described the hard lot of the farmer. Greece was clearly still poor, and Hesiod suggested that one way to get rich was to go to sea and trade, which, increasingly, his kinsmen were doing. From this time, Greeks gradually began to trade with the Near Eastern countries of the Mediterranean, and it was probably through contacts with Phoenician traders that the Greeks borrowed and adapted the Phoenician alphabetic script.

Another movement of Greek emigrants occurred from about 700 B.C. onward, and colonies were founded from the Black Sea coast to Spain. Corinth founded both Syracuse and Corcyra (Corfu), and Massilia (Marseilles) was also established at this time. Miletus, an Ionian city founded on the coast of Asia Minor during the early migrations, now set up numerous colonies near the Black Sea. Trade began to expand: olive oil, wine and pottery were important commodities, and timber for shipbuilding and grain were exported from lands north of the Black Sea to much of the Aegean. From Carthage and the older Phoenician cities came salted fish, purple dye and textiles, while papyrus, in demand as a writing material, was imported from Egypt.

established by invitation, such as Naucratis in Egypt and Posideum (Al Minah) at the mouth of the Orontes River.

In general, colonists sought areas with a similar climate to Greece, so southern Italy (Magna Graecia, Great Greece) and Sicily were the first major areas of settlement. Corinth founded Syracuse in 733 B.C., while Tarentum was founded by Sparta in 706. The Euboean cities founded several cities in southern Italy, including Cumae and Rhegium. At the same time there was settlement of the Thracian coast, and a little later the cities of

the Black Sea coast were started, including Apollonia and Odessus. Cyrene on the coast of Africa was founded in 630 and Massilia (Marseilles) in 600. They were largely farming communities, as land shortage in Greece was the main reason for their existence. Some, however, called "emporia," were founded for the specific purpose of conducting trade, particularly in the Black Sea region.

A colony normally formed a new city-state, but it also maintained real or symbolic links with the mother-city. These colonies became islands of Greek culture, or Hellenism, on the edge of barbarian territory, although relations between Greeks and natives seem to have been more often friendly than hostile. In time, some colonies exported their produce; and from the Black Sea region, grain exports became important, as did timber for shipbuilding. Ceramics, notably the black- and red-figure pottery of Corinth and Athens, were sought after and have been widely found, especially in Etruria (pp.120–21).

Wine and olive oil were also traded, as were honey and dried fish. In return, the Greeks received papyrus from Egypt, as well as faience, which was also produced in the Levant. Glass, ivory, purple dye from Tyre and textiles were also widely traded. Apart from being traders, the Greeks acted as middlemen, a function for which they competed with the Phoenicians, also prolific merchants, at an earlier period.

Although Greek colonists preferred the temperate climate of southern Italy to that of Egypt, Greeks were invited by the Egyptians to found a colony at Naucratis in the western delta. Contacts such as this one with foreign countries had an effect on the Greek art of this period. For example, the sphinx (LEFT) discovered at Delphi and dating to about 575 B.C. shows Egyptian influence.

Found at the French town of Auxerre, southeast of Paris, this Greek statue of the Archaic period shows the extent of Greek trading contacts. It is likely that the statue, which is thought to depict a goddess, reached its destination via the Greek colony of Massilia, now the French port of Marseilles. From Massilia, it would have been taken up the Rhône valley and from there to Auxerre.

It was during the eighth century B.C. that the Greek city-state, or *polis* – the distinctive social and political unit of Greek society – emerged. Greece's mountainous terrain, with its small plains and valleys, encouraged the formation of numerous small states, rather than a few larger ones. Each city-state usually consisted of a walled town center or city surrounded by farmland. A sense of community was engendered by the citizens' involvement in their city's legal and political procedures, although different cities had different forms of government. Citizens were also bonded by their ties to the city's particular protective deity.

Originally, most city-states were dominated by a few aristocratic families, but during the eighth century this control was gradually undermined. As literacy spread, citizens could read and question the publicly displayed laws that aristocrats had formerly decided on. Also, as new colonies were founded with new laws and criteria for land distribution, the way in which wealth and power were shared out in the older cities was now

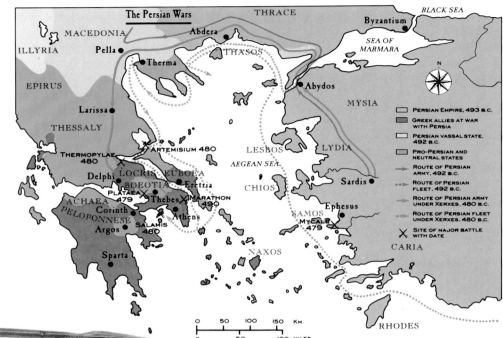

The Persian Wars

Greek hoplites (heavily armed infantrymen), such as this one, were instrumental in defeating the more numerous, but more lightly armed, Persians. As the Athenians showed at Marathon, a determined and coordinated charge by lines of hoplites was almost irresistible. Each soldier was protected by a bronze helmet, which covered most of the face, a sturdy cuirass made of layers of linen, bronze greaves for the legs, and a large, round wooden shield edged with bronze. The principal weapon was a long spear used for thrusting rather than throwing.

Perched on the side of a mountain overlooking a canyon of olive trees, Delphi, home of the famous oracle, was the most sacred site of Greece. The view (ABOVE) taken from the modern town of Delphi shows the Gulf of Corinth and the site of Delphi's ancient port. The tholos (RIGHT) is a circular building lying to the east of the main shrine. It dates back to the early fourth century; its function is unknown.

The Persian Wars were fought in two main phases. The first ended in 490 B.C. when the Persian king Darius was defeated at Marathon. The second involved a full-scale invasion of Greece by Xerxes, ten years after Darius's failure. In 480, the Greeks met the Persians at Thermopylae where, in a narrow pass, 300 Spartans and their allies fought bravely but were eventually outflanked. The Athenians then left their city to the enemy and forced a naval battle at Salamis, which they won. Xerxes returned home, leaving behind a large force. In 479 at Plataea, the Persians were again beaten, and after the defeat of the Persian fleet at Mycale, the threat to mainland Greece was over.

questioned. The introduction of armor and tactics suited to infantrymen known as hoplites meant that fighting was no longer confined to an aristocratic cavalry, and this gave ordinary people a sense of their own power. Finally, soil erosion had made the land less fertile, and as crop yields decreased, many people became indebted to land-owning aristocrats, whom they increasingly resented.

In some cities, new laws began to restrict the power of nobles, and in others, aristocratic rule was replaced by that of tyrants, who sometimes seized power with the help of hoplites. Many tyrants were initially popular because they ended misrule, cancelled peoples' debts to the nobles and sometimes shared out their estates. In some cities, the nobles were replaced by small groups of wealthy people, who ruled as oligarchies (rule by "the few").

During the Archaic period, from about 750 to 500 B.C., Athens and Sparta, which developed in very different ways, became increasingly powerful. Sparta was ruled by a system of two kings and controlled much of the Peloponnese. Most of its population was tied to the land as serfs, known as helots, and its citizens, trained as warriors from childhood, lived almost permanently under arms.

Athens took the first steps toward democracy when its laws were reformed by Solon in 594 B.C. However, there was still discontent in the city and, later, Peisistratus became tyrant from 540 to 527 B.C. The tyranny was maintained by his two sons until one was killed and the other fled the city. With the end of the Peisistratid regime in about 510, far-reaching democratic reforms were introduced by Cleisthenes. Athens grew wealthy from trade and from her silver mines at Laureion. A new vein found in 482 proved to be of singular importance; the general Themistocles persuaded the Athenians to use the extra silver to build a fleet, which, in 480 B.C., defeated the Persians at Salamis.

In fact, the threat to mainland Greece from Persia had begun in the 490s, when Greek cities in Asia Minor, under Persian control, revolted with aid from Athens. The rebellion was crushed; and in 492, a Persian expedition subdued Macedonia, though the accompanying Persian fleet was destroyed in a storm off the northern coast of Greece. Then, in 490, the Persian ruler Darius sent a force to Greece to punish the Athenians. On the plain of Marathon, a determined charge by the Athenian infantry routed the Persians. (From a later story of the runner who carried news of the victory to Athens came the tradition of the modern marathon race.) However, ten years later, a bigger Persian force, under Xerxes, would return to fight at Thermopylae and Salamis and, a year later, Plataea — battles that would decide the fate of Greece and, ultimately, the western world.

DELPHI AND ORACLES

Oracles played an important part in the life of the ancient world. They were shrines where prophecies or advice were given by a god to a questioner, via a human intermediary. At various times, certain oracles were more important than others; but the oracle of the god Apollo at Delphi retained its primacy (despite the fact that it advised the Greeks not to resist the Persian invasion under Xerxes) until the Hellenistic period. At Delphi, the responses were given by the Pythia, a priestess who entered a frenzy, perhaps induced by chewing bay leaves. Her utterances were interpreted by priests who rendered them in verse for the petitioners.

Oracles pronounced on a variety of problems, including matters of cult and individual morality. Political prophecies were also made, and in this respect Delphi had the greatest authority, having come to prominence during the period of colonization. At this time, potential colonists would seek its advice on the choosing of a suitable site or patron deity. Later, the oracle seems to have been able to answer questions requiring a sound understanding of current affairs, perhaps implying the active involvement of its priesthood. Replies could often be ambiguous, as in the case of the Lydian king Croesus, who was told that if he attacked the Persians a great empire would fall – which turned out to be his own.

Where religion was concerned, the oracular method of learning the will of the gods was of particular importance to the Greeks because in general they had no sacred books. Apollo was most esteemed as an oracle and had several shrines apart from Delphi, notably at Thebes and, until the end of the sixth century, at Delos; Didyma in Asia Minor was also important during the Hellenistic era. Other popular oracles included those of Zeus and Asclepius at Dodona and Epidauros, respectively.

THE RISE OF ATHENS

The Persian Wars, in which the Greeks defeated a numerically superior enemy, later came to be seen in the Greek tradition as an epoch-making conflict between Greek and Barbarian, west and east. The threat of Persia, albeit reduced, became a rallying cry for politicians wanting the cooperation between Athens and Sparta to continue, or, indeed, for any cause for which the specter of the Persian menace could be exploited. However, the Greek historian Herodotus, in his *Histories*, does not dismiss the Persians as barbarians. For, as he explains, his account of the war was written "so that the memory of the past may not be blotted out from among men by time, and that great and marvelous deeds done by Greeks and foreigners and especially the reason why they warred against each other may not lack renown."

Although the threat to the Greek mainland was removed, the Greeks of Ionia in Asia Minor, still under Persian control, wanted to continue the struggle. It was now that Athens, benefiting from the prestige she had gained from the war, replaced Sparta as leader of the eastern Greeks, who formed an alliance under her leadership. Created in 478 B.C., this Delian

THE SCIENCE OF POLITICS

The Greek city-state or *polis* (from which derives the word "politics") was more than just a particular city surrounded by a certain amount of territory. It was a self-governing state, and under democratic rule its citizens acted in concert, bound by their laws and their involvement in making political decisions. There were a number of different forms of government, including local variations which were practiced by the city-states – indeed, Aristotle's school of political science gathered accounts of 158 different Greek constitutions. However, the development of a typical Greek state usually followed the same general pattern. A monarchy was followed, successively, by an aristocracy (rule by "the best," i.e. the nobility), a tyranny (dictatorship), an oligarchy (rule by "the few," i.e. an elite, such as the wealthy) and finally a democracy (rule by the *dēmos*, the common people).

Tyranny, or autocratic rule, originally had none of the pejorative connotations in ancient Greece that it later accrued. Plato describes the tyrant as being more akin to a wolf than a man: he deals ruthlessly with political opponents and resorts to foreign wars to distract his people from their misery. Eventually, Plato writes, the tyrant is seen for the monster he is. Plato's comments could equally apply to modern tyrants, such as Adolf Hitler (LEFT).

Pieces of pottery, such as this one on which the names Aristeides and Lysimachus have been scratched, were used as votes in ostracisms, a political procedure by which prominent citizens were temporarily exiled.

President John F. Kennedy, until his tragic death in 1963, seemed to embody the ideals of modern western democracies. The greater size and complexities of modern nations militate against the full involvement of citizens which occurred in Greek democratic city-states. But the basic concept of citizen participation in government through voting is common to both.

League met on the island of Delos, with each member paying a contribution. Its aim was to expel the Persians from the Greek territories they still held. It was not long before it expanded to include most of the Aegean islands and many of the northern and eastern coastal cities.

In 450 B.C., fighting between the Greeks and Persians eventually ceased and was ratified by the signing of the Peace of Callias a year later. However, despite the end of hostilities, the league remained intact, with Athens increasingly dominating the other members. Indeed, four years before, the league's treasury had been moved from Delos to Athens, giving the latter control of the alliance's funds.

During this period Athens's democratic development came to fruition. The city's sovereign authority was the Assembly (*ekklēsia*) in which all citizens had the right to vote. However, this meant, in effect, only adult men, since neither women nor slaves were full citizens. The Assembly met several times a month, and any citizen could propose a motion, which, if it received a majority of votes, normally became law. Only another meeting of the Assembly or the Athenian courts could overrule a law.

The power of the citizens was considerable and included ostracism, a procedure by which citizens could be sent into exile, or ostracized. Each year, a vote was held in the Assembly as to whether an ostracism should be held. If it was successful, citizens then had to write the name of the person they wanted to exile on an "ostrakon" — a piece of broken pottery. If a person collected 6,000 or more votes, he was duly ostracized for ten years.

Since the Assembly was large and unwieldy, a council, or *boule*, of 500 men chosen by lot helped to supervise its administration, prepare its agenda and take minor decisions. The council's members changed annually, and no one could serve in it for more than two years. After 487 B.C., the archons, the once powerful chief magistrates, were chosen by lot, thus reducing their political influence.

Citizen power also extended to the law courts, where ordinary people, not professional lawyers, presented their own cases, which were heard by juries chosen by lot. Some government positions were decided by election, including military commanders, who were elected annually. The Areopagus, the ancient council recruited from former archons, was stripped of its more important powers in 462/61 B.C. This was brought about by the prominent citizens Ephialtes and Pericles (who would soon become famous); it removed any residual aristocratic influence and gave the citizens full control of all the institutions.

The rate of political development varied, so some states could still be monarchies as late as the fourth century B.C.; and there might also be dramatic changes of government, for example from democracy to oligarchy. Tyranny could be moderate and enlightened, but it was usually autocratic and unconstitutional. Democracy, now thought to be one of the greatest legacies of ancient Greece to modern civilized society, was in fact disapproved of by the great philosophers Plato (429–347 B.C.) and Aristotle (384–322 B.C.), whose works mark the beginning of political theory. In Plato's *Republic* and Aristotle's *Politics*, political systems were analyzed and theories of government formulated, and it was from this legacy that political science developed in the western world.

It was not so much the actual example of ancient democracy, but the writings of later philosophers and political theorists, such as Thomas Hobbes and John Locke in Britain and Jean-Jacques Rousseau in France, that ultimately gave rise to modern democratic institutions. Crucial differences, such as slavery, remain between the latter and ancient Greek democracies. However, both share certain basic principles – for example, the right to vote, free speech and the belief that the state exists for the sake of the individual, and not vice versa.

Election posters *on the walls of a Cretan village proclaim the merits of PASOK, the modern Greek socialist party, and its leader Andreas Papandreou in 1989. Democracy was restored in Greece in 1974 after the collapse of the seven-year dictatorship of a group of army colonels. The two principal parties in Greek politics are currently PASOK and the conservative New Democracy.*

RECORDING HISTORY

The two finest historians of ancient Greece, Herodotus (c.490/80–425 B.C.) and Thucydides (c.460–400), were also the first. Both men chose great contemporary conflicts (the Persian and Peloponnesian wars, respectively) as the central theme of their works; but more important, each sought to uncover the reasons men behave as they do and to explain what they fought each other for. Herodotus, who was born in the Ionian city of Halicarnassus in Asia Minor, has been called the Father of History. He inherited the scientific spirit of inquiry for which Ionia was famous, the fruits of which can be read in his digressions on geography and anthropology which punctuate his classic account of the struggle between Greece and Persia.

Thucydides was an Athenian who took part in the early stages of the Peloponnesian War, which was fought between Athens and Sparta and their allies (pp.108–9). His account focuses on the causes and conduct of the war, including the political background. But, as with Herodotus, Thucydides goes beyond a mechanical narration of the conflict and seeks to understand the nature of man and his behavior.

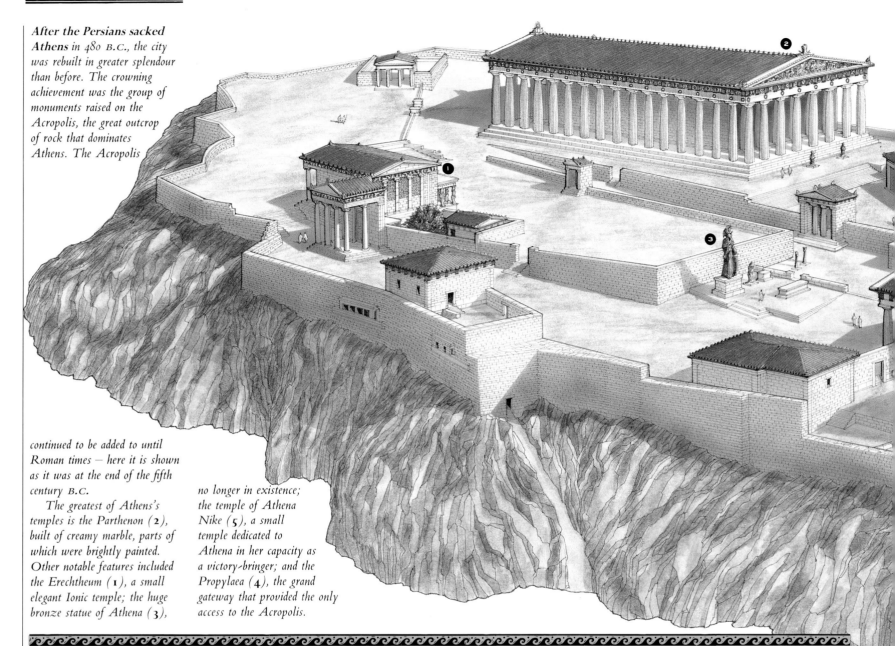

After the Persians sacked Athens in 480 B.C., the city was rebuilt in greater splendour than before. The crowning achievement was the group of monuments raised on the Acropolis, the great outcrop of rock that dominates Athens. The Acropolis continued to be added to until Roman times — here it is shown as it was at the end of the fifth century B.C.

The greatest of Athens's temples is the Parthenon (2), built of creamy marble, parts of which were brightly painted. Other notable features included the Erechtheum (1), a small elegant Ionic temple; the huge bronze statue of Athena (3), *no longer in existence; the temple of Athena Nike (5), a small temple dedicated to Athena in her capacity as a victory-bringer; and the Propylaea (4), the grand gateway that provided the only access to the Acropolis.*

THE ELGIN MARBLES

The frieze and sculpture from the pediments of the Parthenon, the temple dedicated to Athena, were taken from the Acropolis to England in 1806 by the British aristocrat Thomas Bruce, 7th Earl of Elgin. These sculptures, carved by the mastercraftsman Pheidias, are known as the Elgin Marbles and reside in the British Museum. Lord Elgin has been much maligned for this act and at the time was labeled a vandal by Lord Byron and others. In 1983, the Greek government demanded the return of the marbles, a request which the British Museum has refused.

The removal of the sculptures, however, should be seen in the context of the time. In 1795, Elgin engaged Thomas Harrison, a rising young architect,

to build a new mansion, Broom Hall, for his bride. Elgin agreed that Harrison could build it in the classical style. In 1799, Elgin was appointed ambassador to Constantinople, the capital of the Ottoman Turks, and Harrison asked him for copies and casts of Greek art and architecture, newly fashionable in Britain.

Elgin placed his secretary in charge of this request, and the latter engaged a painter and craftsmen to record, measure and make casts of ancient Greek monuments, including parts of the Parthenon. The task was made harder by the fact that the Turks, who were in control of Greece, were using the Acropolis as a fortress, and many of

the structures were badly damaged. While Elgin's men were engaged in their work, the British Embassy chaplain at Constantinople, who was visiting Athens, wrote to Elgin and urged him to obtain permission from the Turks to allow his men to remove the sculptures. They were then shipped off as prospective ornaments for Broom Hall. (Except for one brief visit, Elgin was not present.)

Elgin left Constantinople in 1803, but his return home was delayed by his detention in France. When he reached England, he found that his wife had left him, and the marbles were the subject of bitter controversy. Badly in need of money, he sold them at considerable loss to the British government.

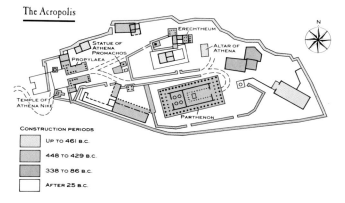

The Parthenon, Nashville, Tennessee, is a lifesize copy — the only one in the world — of the original in Athens. Built of granite in 1931, it houses replicas of the Elgin Marbles.

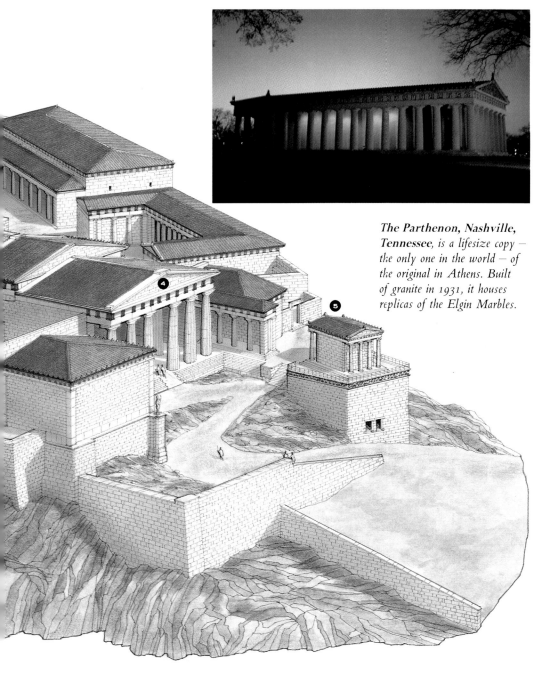

The Acropolis

CONSTRUCTION PERIODS

Up to 461 b.c.

448 to 429 b.c.

338 to 86 b.c.

After 25 b.c.

The transfer of the Delian League's treasury from Delos to Athens in 454 b.c. meant that Athens had financial, as well as political, control over the alliance. In effect, the league had become an Athenian empire. Even before this happened, some allies had been forced to continue payments to the alliance and maintain hostilities against Persia. In 471 b.c., the island of Naxos attempted to break away from the league, as did Thasos in 465. Athens sent warships against these and other disaffected allies, and forced them to continue their contributions, which in effect amounted to tribute money. Later, Samos, in 440, and Mytilene, in 427, also suspended payment and were crushed.

Athens was at its most prosperous and powerful. With the alliance's funds at its disposal, it used some of them to rebuild the temples and beautify the city. Athenian warships — also built with alliance funds — escorted merchant ships bringing grain from the Black Sea area and prevented other states from buying grain. As a result, food was cheap and more plentiful.

After 462 b.c., when he had helped to pass measures reducing the political status of the Areopagus, the statesman and orator Pericles took an increasingly important part in the making of Athenian policies. He was a greatnephew of Cleisthenes, who had initiated many democratic reforms after the end of the Peisistratid tyranny in about 510. From 443, Pericles headed the board of ten generals chosen by direct popular vote. From this position, to which he was elected annually almost continually until his death in 429, Pericles was able to steer the ship of state through its golden years of intellectual and artistic achievement.

This era found the most enduring reminder of its splendor in the construction, begun in 448/47, of the Parthenon, the magnificent Doric temple on the Acropolis, dedicated to the city's patron goddess, Athena. This imposing marble structure, measuring 100 by 230 feet, could be seen for miles around and was a fitting symbol of Athens's imperial pretensions.

The superb sculptures on the Parthenon, executed by the sculptor Pheidias, included scenes of the birth of Athena and her creation of the olive tree, sacred to the city. The frieze running around the building depicted the battle of the centaurs, while the frieze of the inner section showed the Panathenaia, the great procession in honor of Athena. The sculptures were painted and the bridles of the horses in the procession were made of bronze. The interior of the temple was dominated by the great statue of Athena the Virgin, also created by Pheidias. Constructed on a wooden framework, the statue was overlaid with ivory for the flesh and gold for the clothes. However, it has not survived — nor has the great bronze statue of Athena the Defender, which stood outside the temple.

The great gateway to the Acropolis, the Propylaia, was started in 437, when the Parthenon was completed. Although there was criticism of Pericles and the Athenians for their lavish building and use of alliance funds, the project did benefit the ordinary people and craftsmen of the city, as well as the supporters of Pericles, by providing them with work.

Much of the menial labor in Athens and other Greek cities was done by slaves, of whom there were thousands. Some were captives, and others had been born into slavery. The silver mines were worked by slaves, and conditions for them were so terrible that many attempted escape. However, some slaves grew rich and were able to buy their freedom.

THE GREEKS DIVIDED

RELIGION AND THE
GODS OF OLYMPUS

Greek religion was polytheistic, and its gods took the shape of humans. By classical times, there were established 12 great gods, some of whom are shown in the detail from a pot (ABOVE), who were believed to dwell on Mount Olympus (BELOW), the highest mountain in Greece. In some regions, the composition of these deities differed, and some gods had more than one personality or set of attributes. Each city-state had its own patron deity, and different groups of people revered different gods. There were also innumerable minor deities and some important ones, such as Dionysus, the god of wine, who never joined the Olympians.

Rituals to the gods were carried out at open-air altars and not in the temples, which were the gods' sanctuaries. Altars might be situated outside temples, at places of assembly or in the home. There

Mt. Olympus

were also religious festivals, games and processions, when a particular god was celebrated and actually seen, in the form of a statue brought from the temple. There was no separate class or caste of priests; instead, there were laymen, servants of the state, who operated under the same rules as other officials. In Athens, the highest cult official, whose title was "the king," reflecting a much earlier situation, was one of the nine annually elected magistrates, known as archons. In Sparta, the two kings were the chief religious officials. Even at the sacred shrine of Eleusis, the cult of the goddess Demeter was taken care of not by priests, but by members of two aristocratic families.

The Olympians
Zeus: The supreme deity; a sky god who wielded the thunderbolt; dispenser of justice.
Hera: Wife of Zeus, of whom she was violently jealous; Hera's cult spread all over Greece.
Apollo: Youthful god of music, of ritual purity and oracles; as the god Phoebus Apollo, he is associated with the sun.

Artemis: The huntress, sister of Apollo, she was a nature deity associated with the moon; also, as Hecate, she was a deity of death and of childbirth.
Athena: A goddess of war and crafts; she was also the patron deity of Athens.
Ares: A war god; he is less frequently found than the other deities.
Aphrodite: Goddess of love and beauty; a pre-Olympian deity, she was born from the sea, traditionally at Paphos.
Demeter: Goddess of grain, whose mourning for Persephone brought the winter, and with whose return from the underworld came the spring; she was linked to death and rebirth and to the mystery cult at Eleusis.
Hephaestus: The blacksmith deity, also connected with crafts.
Poseidon: Lord of the sea and of earthquakes; he was also the god of horses.
Hermes: The messenger of the gods and the carrier of souls to the underworld; he was also the god of shepherds and herdsmen.
Hestia: An ancient goddess of the hearth.

By the latter part of the fifth century B.C., Athens's power was resented by many Greek cities, including several in its own empire. Sparta, in particular, was hostile to Athens and its support of democracies, and probably feared losing control of its own allies in the Peloponnese. A head-on collision became inevitable, and the result was the Peloponnesian War, which lasted almost continuously between 431 and 404 B.C.

In 433 B.C., a two-year quarrel between Corinth and her colony Corcyra, which had gained the support of Athens, ended in a naval battle in which Athenian intervention narrowly robbed Corinth of victory. In the following year, Potidaea in the Chalcidic peninsula revolted from the Athenian alliance and Corinth unofficially sent help. Later that year, exhorted by Corinthian delegates, Sparta and her allies of the Peloponnesian League voted for war against Athens.

In 431, the Spartans invaded Attica, the area around Athens, met no enemy and so ravaged the land for a month and then retired. Pericles had persuaded the Athenians not to give battle, but to desert their land and withdraw behind the Long Walls, which connected Athens with her ports and made the city an isolated fortress that could be provisioned by sea. This strategy was designed to combat Athenian weakness on land while exploiting her great strength at sea. The first year, everything went according to plan, and Athens remained undamaged.

Spartan invasions of Attica continued over the next six years. During this time, a plague that had broken out in 430 raged in Athens, and more than a quarter of the city's population died. Among those who perished was Pericles, but the Athenians kept to his strategy of not engaging the powerful Spartans on land and also managed to win several naval victories. Eventually, the Spartans sued for peace, which, at the insistence of the demagogue Cleon, the Athenians refused. But, after more losses and victories on both sides, peace was made in 421 B.C.

Six years later, however, Athens made the serious mistake of attempting to conquer Sicily, which then appealed for Spartan help. At the same time, Athens's most talented leader, Alcibiades, implicated in a religious scandal, fled to Sparta and gave his old enemies strategic advice. Sparta sent a general to the aid of the Sicilians in 414 and, the following year, the great Athenian fleet that had nearly captured the city of Syracuse was trapped and destroyed. Sparta now went on the offensive in Greece, strengthened, in 412, by Persia's agreement to finance her fleet in return for recognition of Persia's claim to Ionia. Within Athens, there was a brief period of nondemocratic rule in 411, but she fought on, in spite of all the difficulties and the loss of her empire, as states in the alliance threw off Athenian rule.

In April 404 B.C., a year after the Spartan fleet had captured Athens's navy and cut off the grain ships supplying the city, the Athenians were starved into capitulation. Sparta's victory was complete; and, under a pro-Spartan oligarchy known as the Thirty Tyrants, led by a man named Critias, the Athenians were subjected to a brief reign of terror before democracy was restored in 403. Although there was an amnesty for all but the leaders of the oligarchs, revenge was taken on those who had made attacks on democracy with the trial of the philosopher Socrates. In 399 B.C., Socrates was sentenced to death for allegedly corrupting the youth of Athens. In fact, Socrates was probably paying the penalty of being an associate of both Critias and Alcibiades.

THE ART OF PAINTING POTS

From the tenth century B.C., well-shaped protogeometric pottery painted with wavy lines and circular motifs was made in Athens. Over the next two centuries, geometric designs were used to cover the entire surface of pots; gradually, figures were introduced, at first in isolation, but later in panels.

By the eighth century, the influence of Near Eastern contacts on Greek pots is evident, with lions and stylized animals, including the sphinx and phoenix, as well as flowers and other eastern motifs, being used for decoration. Potters at Corinth now produced what became known as black-figure ware, in which figures were drawn in silhouette and details were incised to show the clay beneath.

By the end of the seventh century, this technique was being used in Athens. Also, narrative scenes increasingly took precedence over animal friezes, which in time disappeared; and a large range of tableware was now made, with ever-improving standards of painting. Near the end of the sixth century, a new technique was introduced by which the background was blacked out, and the painting was left the color of the clay. Within a couple of decades, this red-figure ware took over completely. However, two centuries later, vase painting declined because of the development of mural and panel painting.

The different shapes of Greek vases, bowls, pitchers and cups are functional, but their decoration is simply to please. The wide range of subjects depicted is a major source for details of Greek life, as well as mythology.

The inside of the kylix (ABOVE), a two-handled drinking vessel, shows the god Dionysus sailing in a boat with grapevines, a common motif in Greek art. The small vase (RIGHT) from Attica depicts Apollo and his muses. Both the kylix and the vase are examples of black-figure ware, in which the subject matter was painted with a liquid clay that turned black when fired. The background and the incised details reveal the vessels' original color.

FESTIVAL GAMES

Sport was highly regarded by the Greeks, especially as a training for warfare, and it also played an important part in religion. The oldest athletic festival was held at the sanctuary of Zeus at Olympia, by tradition in 776 B.C.; and at Delphi, the important Pythian games were held in honor of Apollo. Both festivals were held every four years, and there were others, including the annual Panhellenic games. Originally, games were held at funerals, but by the fifth century B.C., their ritual meaning had effectively been lost. Success at the festivals was of great importance, since it brought honor, visible in the form of a wreath, to the victor, as well as to his family and city. Events included running, jumping, discus and javelin throwing, wrestling and boxing. In addition to these, there were also horse and chariot races.

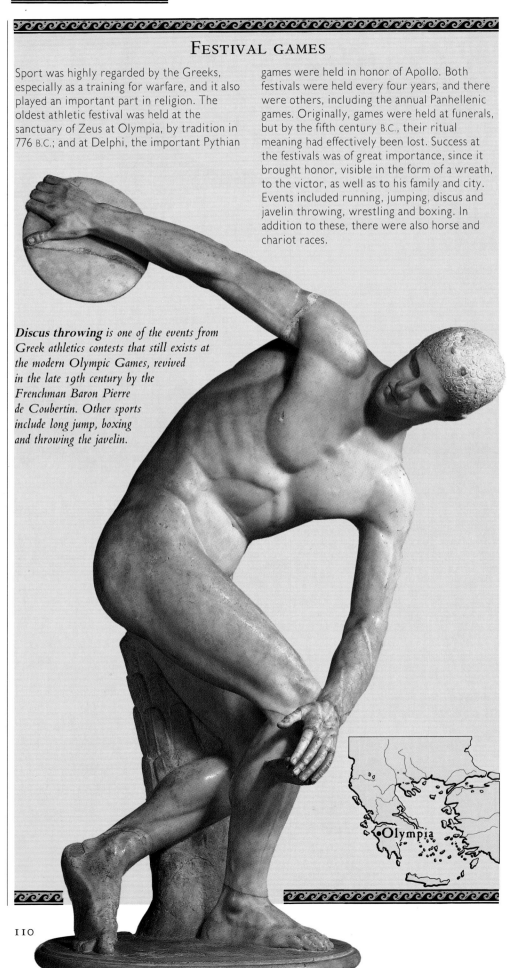

Discus throwing is one of the events from Greek athletics contests that still exists at the modern Olympic Games, revived in the late 19th century by the Frenchman Baron Pierre de Coubertin. Other sports include long jump, boxing and throwing the javelin.

Athens's defeat by Sparta in the Peloponnesian War did not bring peace to Greece. Under the restored democracy, Athens gradually regained her strength, although never to the level it had been before the long war. From 404 B.C. for the next 30 years, Sparta abused the power she had gained by her victory. The former dependencies of Athens effectively became tribute-paying subject states in a Spartan empire. Even her allies in the Spartan alliance, which were, in theory, sovereign states, were offended by Sparta's imperialistic and harsh policies.

Nor was it long before the Spartans fell out with the Persians who, in return for recognition of their claim to Ionia, had helped finance Sparta's war effort. By 401 B.C., Sparta was unofficially at war with them, because of her assistance to Cyrus the Younger in his revolt against his brother, the Persian king. Following the fall of Cyrus at Cunaxa, near Babylon, his Greek mercenaries made their way through Persian territory to the Black Sea, an epic journey which has been immortalized in the *Anabasis* of Xenophon, who led the march. However, open conflict between Sparta and Persia came in 400, when the Spartans sent a force to protect Ionia; and, in 396, the Spartan king Agesilaus was sent to lead the Greek forces in Asia Minor.

In this campaign, the Spartans received no support from the other main cities of Greece. Indeed, their former allies Corinth and Thebes, and old enemies Athens and Argos, formed a coalition supported by Persian money and, in 395, declared war on Sparta. Agesilaus was recalled and, in a battle near Thebes, the Spartans defeated the allies. The Greek states continued to feud until, in 387, they signed under the direction of the king of Persia a fragile peace treaty, known as the King's Peace.

But this treaty failed to stop the aggression, notably that of Sparta, which captured Thebes by stealth in 382. The Thebans recovered their city three years later and gradually grew in power. Their great moment came in 371, when a Theban army under Epaminondas defeated the much-feared Spartan troops at Leuctra. Sparta failed to recover, largely because of the gradual breakdown of its social and economic system. Nor did Thebes long maintain its strength. In 362, the Thebans defeated a coalition that included Sparta and Athens at the battle of Mantinea, but Epaminondas was killed, and with him crumbled Theban domination.

Within four decades of her victory over Athens, Sparta had been humbled, her power gone forever; and all the other Greek states were weak and divided among themselves. Xenophon's *Hellenica*, the only surviving account of these troubled years, carries on the history of the conflict between the Greek states from where Thucydides' *History* breaks off. Xenophon, like Thucydides, had lived through the years about which he wrote and had taken part in many of the events.

During this turbulent period, the practice began of writing down speeches for circulation. The Greeks had a strong interest in oratory as an art form, and many of these speeches are fine literary pieces. Those of Lysias, who left Athens during the year of the Thirty Tyrants, display the delight that the Greeks took in good argument. Isocrates, too, began his orations shortly after the Peloponnesian War, although it is for his later speeches addressed to Philip of Macedon (pp.112–13) that he is better known. Prose, it seems, rather than poetry, was the main type of literature in the troubled times of the fourth century B.C.

DRAMA AND DRAMATISTS

The focal point of a Greek theater was the orchestra, a circular dance-floor where the chorus danced and sang. It probably had its origins in the threshing floor, still used in rural Greece for dancing. During the Roman period, the orchestra changed, but at Epidaurus (ABOVE), the best preserved Greek theater, there is still a circular one. Above the orchestra, cut out of the hillside, were rows of seats that formed the semicircular auditorium. It is said that the acoustics at Epidaurus are so good that a match struck at ground level can be heard in the topmost row of the auditorium.

The plays of the Greek tragedians are still performed worldwide. The legend of Agamemnon — shown (RIGHT) in a still from a modern Greek film — his sacrifice of his daughter Iphigenia and his murder by his wife provided a rich thematic source for both Aeschylus and Euripides.

In ancient Greece, drama was an important part of certain religious festivals. At Athens, for example, a festival was held every spring in honor of Dionysus, with a drama competition lasting three days, at the end of which prizes were awarded. At the City Dionysia festival, also in Athens, three poets entered four plays each, three tragedies and a satyr play – a farce in which the actors wore the costumes of satyrs, half-human mythological creatures. Comedies were also staged, and here, as in tragedy, the chorus of dancers and singers was an important element. However, in tragedy, the chorus gradually became smaller, and innovations were made by the great playwrights: Aeschylus introduced a second actor and Sophocles a third, while Euripides in some of his plays virtually reduced the chorus from its central role to simply an interlude.

The origins of tragedy are not clear, but it perhaps emerged from a combination of lyric poetry and Dionysiac ritual. However, although it retained a religious link in its association with the Dionysus festival, it was not ritual drama. The greatest dramatists, Aeschylus, Sophocles and Euripides, were all

Athenians and spanned the fifth century. Of the 300 plays they wrote, only about a tenth survive; no plays by the other 150 known writers of tragedy have been found. The great creative period of this genre was partly the result of the situation in fifth-century Athens; for all its faults, the Athenian political system created a world in which the dramatist could write free of constraints except for those imposed by the medium itself.

Tragedies explored the human soul and were often concerned with moral issues related to the affairs of the city-state. In *The Persians* by Aeschylus, presented only 10 years after the Greco-Persian war, the central theme is the establishment of Athenian liberty. More profound is the same playwright's Oresteian trilogy. He takes as his starting point the murder of Agamemnon (pp.98–99) by his wife Clytemnestra and traces the consequent blood feud and its final resolution through the introduction of law. Themes such as this are universal, and it is hardly surprising that the tragedies of Aeschylus and his succesors, Sophocles and Euripides, continue to be produced more than 2,000 years after they were written.

THE RISE OF MACEDON

This reconstruction of Philip II of Macedon was made from clay, plaster of Paris, wax and hair by the British scientist Richard Neave, who based it on fragments of his skull from Vergina (p.115) and known images of him. Philip's right eye was hit by an arrow in battle in 354 B.C.

By about the mid-fourth century B.C., the weakness of the Greek states encouraged Macedon, a previously backward kingdom in northeastern Greece, to attempt to take control of the whole of Greece. In 359 B.C., Philip II became king and immediately began to reorganize his army, using his experience of three years spent as a hostage in Thebes to train his infantry along Theban lines. Philip's kingdom had considerable resources, including gold, silver, copper and iron mines, great stands of timber for shipbuilding, and large areas of pasture and extensive farming lands.

Early in his reign, Philip conquered the lands of the Illyrians, Paeonians and Thracians, and also took the Greek cities on the coast nearest to him. By 339 B.C., his Balkan empire extended from the lower Danube to the Aegean coast, and from the Adriatic coast to the Black Sea and the Dardanelles. He founded new towns with mixed populations and encouraged agriculture and trade, leaving local people, as far as possible, to administer themselves. Within his own territories, he subjugated any Greek city that opposed him.

In Greece, Philip won the alliance of Thessaly, to the south of Macedon, and in 346 B.C. brought to an end a war between the Greek states for control of the sacred site of Delphi. He used a combination of force and diplomacy, but did not succeed in winning the favor of Athens, where the brilliant orator Demosthenes led the opposition against him.

Many Greeks genuinely regarded Macedonia as a backwater of barbaric tribesmen, and they also disliked its system of kingship, which they had long abandoned. It was certainly true that many Macedonians had been hillsmen and shepherds until Philip's victories had provided them with other forms of occupation, including soldiering. However, Philip himself was a patron of Greek art and culture, although the rich grave goods and style of royal Macedonian burials, which included horses, is more akin to the heroic age of the Mycenaeans than to fourth-century Athens.

Philip achieved a final victory over the Greek opposition, which included Athens and Thebes, at Chaeronea in 338 B.C. He proposed the creation of a self-governing league of Greek states and put forward a daring plan that would weld together the disparate city-states of this Panhellenic union: an invasion of Persia. Except for Sparta, all the mainland cities agreed. But Philip did not live to carry out his grand plan – he was assassinated at his daughter's wedding party in 336 B.C.

Philip was succeeded by his 20-year-old son Alexander, already a seasoned soldier and a veteran of Chaeronea, who continued with his father's campaign. It is not certain whether at the outset Alexander planned to conquer the entire Persian Empire, but as time went by, this clearly became his aim. By all accounts Alexander was a brave, inspirational commander, personally leading his troops into battle. According to a popular story, when he was only 12 years old, he tamed the fiery horse Bucephalus, which no one else could ride. For 20 years, until Bucephalus died, this was his favorite horse.

In 334, with 32,000 infantry and 5,000 cavalry – half of them Macedonian, the rest Greek, including mercenaries – Alexander crossed the Dardanelles into Asia Minor. In the same year, after holding games at Troy, at which he dedicated his shield to Athena, Troy's patron goddess, he engaged the forces of the western Persian provinces at the River Granicus and defeated them. In this battle, Alexander used only his Macedonian troops, the Thessalian cavalry and the mercenaries. It was an auspicious start, but his greatest triumphs were yet to come.

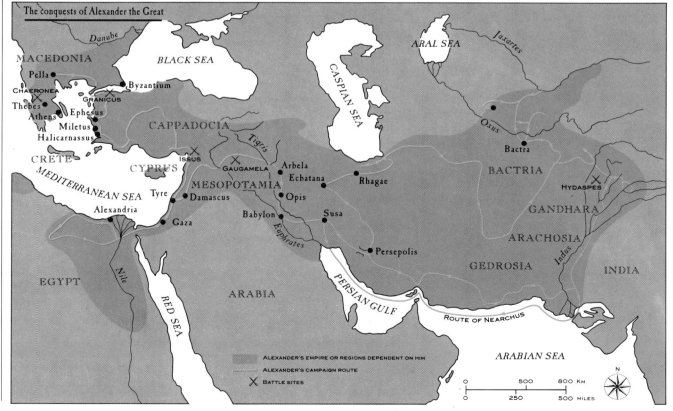

The conquests of Alexander the Great

In 334 B.C., Alexander the Great crossed with his army from Thrace into Asia Minor: his object was the destruction of the Persian Empire. Over the next three years, Alexander inflicted heavy defeats on the Persians at Granicus, Issus and Gaugamela. He then took Darius's great cities of Babylon and Susa, and in 330, captured Ecbatana. He resumed his eastward march and defeated the Indian king Poros at the battle of Hydaspes. But now his army was becoming weary of war and rebelled, forcing Alexander to return home.

The young Macedonian turned westward and crossed the Gedrosian Desert, while his admiral Nearchus sailed back along the coast to the Persian Gulf. Alexander died at Babylon, probably of a fever, in 323, at the age of 33.

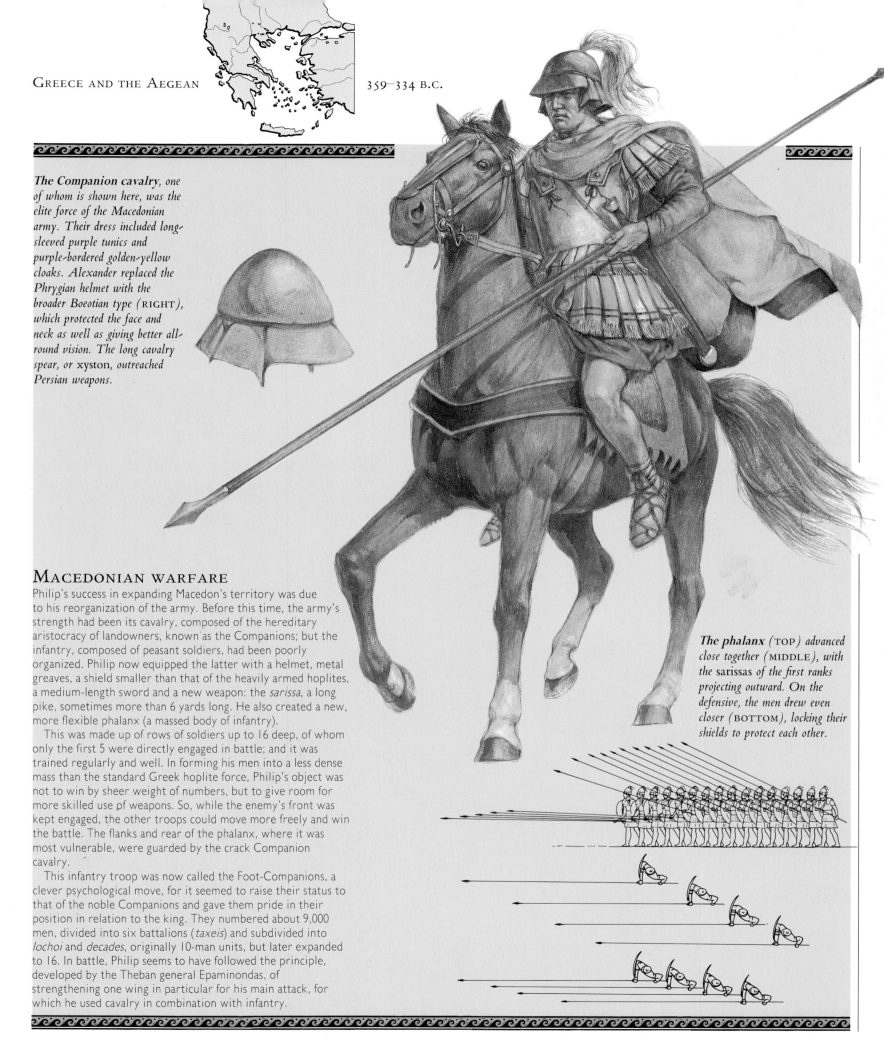

The Companion cavalry, one of whom is shown here, was the elite force of the Macedonian army. Their dress included long-sleeved purple tunics and purple-bordered golden-yellow cloaks. Alexander replaced the Phrygian helmet with the broader Boeotian type (RIGHT), which protected the face and neck as well as giving better all-round vision. The long cavalry spear, or xyston, outreached Persian weapons.

MACEDONIAN WARFARE

Philip's success in expanding Macedon's territory was due to his reorganization of the army. Before this time, the army's strength had been its cavalry, composed of the hereditary aristocracy of landowners, known as the Companions; but the infantry, composed of peasant soldiers, had been poorly organized. Philip now equipped the latter with a helmet, metal greaves, a shield smaller than that of the heavily armed hoplites, a medium-length sword and a new weapon: the *sarissa*, a long pike, sometimes more than 6 yards long. He also created a new, more flexible phalanx (a massed body of infantry).

This was made up of rows of soldiers up to 16 deep, of whom only the first 5 were directly engaged in battle; and it was trained regularly and well. In forming his men into a less dense mass than the standard Greek hoplite force, Philip's object was not to win by sheer weight of numbers, but to give room for more skilled use of weapons. So, while the enemy's front was kept engaged, the other troops could move more freely and win the battle. The flanks and rear of the phalanx, where it was most vulnerable, were guarded by the crack Companion cavalry.

This infantry troop was now called the Foot-Companions, a clever psychological move, for it seemed to raise their status to that of the noble Companions and gave them pride in their position in relation to the king. They numbered about 9,000 men, divided into six battalions (*taxeis*) and subdivided into *lochoi* and *decades*, originally 10-man units, but later expanded to 16. In battle, Philip seems to have followed the principle, developed by the Theban general Epaminondas, of strengthening one wing in particular for his main attack, for which he used cavalry in combination with infantry.

The phalanx (TOP) advanced close together (MIDDLE), with the sarissas of the first ranks projecting outward. On the defensive, the men drew even closer (BOTTOM), locking their shields to protect each other.

113

ALEXANDER THE GREAT

After his victory over the Persians at Granicus in 334 B.C., Alexander advanced through Asia Minor, setting free the Greek cities and establishing democracies. Miletus and Halicarnassus resisted and were duly besieged and taken. He then moved south to Lycia and Pamphylia, before turning north to winter at Gordium, where he cut the Gordian knot. (According to legend, whoever undid this complicated knot would have control of Asia: Alexander simply cut it with his sword.)

Moving south through Cilicia, he reached Issus near the north Syrian coast in 333. Here, he met a large army led by the king of Persia, Darius III Codomanus. Alexander won a brilliant victory, but did not give chase to the fleeing Persian king. Instead, after the difficult siege of Tyre, he entered Egypt in 332, where he was welcomed. He then founded the city of Alexandria and also visited the oracle of Amun at the Siwa oasis, where he was proclaimed a god by the priests. This was the normal form of address for an Egyptian ruler, but Alexander seems to have taken it quite seriously.

In 331, at Gaugamela in northern Iraq, Darius III made his last stand and was defeated. Darius, the last of the Achaemenid dynasty, fled north and was later killed by his own nobles, thus making Alexander Darius's successor by right of conquest. Alexander occupied Babylon and then moved west to Susa, and from there to Persepolis. Here, in the magnificent palace, a great conflagration broke out – perhaps as a result of arson.

Alexander then traveled north and east by way of Ecbatana, the ancient capital of the Medes. Bactria and Sogdia were conquered, and here he met the Sogdian princess Roxanne, who became his wife. As he progressed farther from Greece, he began to make use of Persian soldiers and appoint Persian nobles to positions of authority – actions that were resented by his Macedonian soldiers. Finally, he reached the Indus, and there defeated the Indian king Poros.

But now, at the Beas River, his weary troops refused to go any farther and so, at last, in 324 B.C., the conqueror turned back west and crossed the Gedrosian Desert. At the same time, Nearchus, his admiral, took the sea route back to the Persian Gulf. Alexander eventually rejoined Nearchus and proceeded to Susa. Then, at Opis, he faced a mutiny of the Macedonians, which he managed to resolve. Not long after this, his closest friend and

THE IMAGE OF ALEXANDER

After Alexander's death, tales of his exploits began to circulate, and a cycle of stories developed. Many had their origin in Alexandria in Egypt, and in time romantic fables of Alexander were known in many languages from northern Europe to China. In these, no task seemed impossible for this idealized Alexander, who journeyed in glass submarines or flew the skies in a basket, assisted by griffins. In the east, he was known as Iskandar, and among other achievements, he visited China in disguise and exchanged riddles with its ruler; he then returned to Iran and there built a great wall against the barbarians. Even now in remote areas of the east, fair children or those with red hair or blue eyes are said to be descended from Iskandar.

An idealized Alexander receives the family of Darius, in a painting (ABOVE) by Paolo Veronese, and enters the sea in a glass diving bell, in an Islamic miniature (RIGHT).

companion, Hephaestion, died. And in 323, Alexander, a great warrior who had survived countless battles, succumbed to illness at the city of Babylon and died on June 10.

In ten years Alexander had created an empire that reached from the Indus River to Greece, and it was possible that before his death he was planning a campaign to Arabia and then to the lands of the western Mediterranean. Perhaps the most lasting of his innovations were the new towns, many called Alexandria. In these the first settlers comprised Greeks, Macedonians and Asians and were self-governing, although subject to edicts of the king. In time, the character of these cities changed and their Greekness was lost, but of the cities themselves, some, such as Tashkent, Karachi, Kandahar and Alexandria, still survive.

Alexander had increasingly adopted Persian forms and dress, and it would seem that he was trying to create a joint partnership of Greeks and Persians. An example of this were the numerous marriages he instigated between the Greeks and daughters of the Persian aristocracy. He needed the help of the Persians to run the eastern parts of such a widespread empire – a sound policy which might have succeeded had he lived.

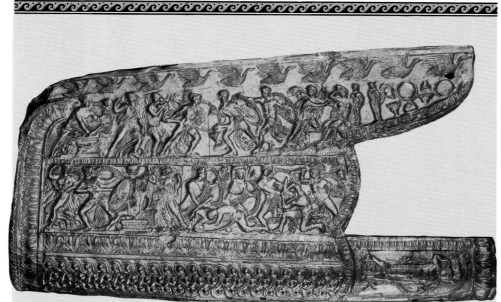

This exquisitely decorated gorytas, *a Scythian-style bow case, from Vergina has an exact parallel in a Scythian burial of the same period northeast of Macedon. This provides a link with Philip II because it is known that he campaigned in this region and had dealings with a Scythian king. The gorytas was found in the king's tomb and its embossed and chased detail depicts fierce fighting.*

THE VERGINA TREASURE

In November 1977, the Greek archaeologist Manolis Andronikos excavated two tombs in the Great Mound near the village of Vergina (ancient Aigai) in northern Greece. Four years later, three more tombs were opened up. The excavations seem to show that the tombs belonged to Macedonian royalty, including the family of Philip II, the father of Alexander the Great. The contents are quite extraordinary, both in richness and beauty. Such burials, in terms of the quantity and wealth of grave goods, are more akin to a heroic age – for example, the Mycenaean burials discovered by Schliemann (pp.96–97) – than to the more austere contemporary Greek burials.

The tombs themselves were made of marble and finely decorated, and were well protected by the enormous mound of earth under which they lay. The contents of the king's tomb included a pair of greaves, one of which, just over an inch shorter than the other, was made for a slightly lame man, as Philip is known to have been. There was also a helmet made of iron, whose curved crest resembled a Phrygian cap, and a sponge that still retained some of its suppleness.

On the floor of the king's tomb were also found several small ivory heads, which were probably ornaments of a funerary couch. They are tiny, some only an inch or so high, and are examples of superb workmanship; one closely resembles known portraits of Philip on coins and another would seem to be of Alexander. There were also a gold-plated silver diadem, adjustable for the king's head, and two finely made golden caskets containing the remains of the royal cremations.

In one of these caskets, found in the tomb's antechamber, the ashes of the dead person had been covered in a fabric whose intricate floral motifs, woven in purple on a gold background, were still clearly discernible after their consignment to more than 2,000 years of darkness. In addition, the tombs held silver vessels and cups, a gold funerary wreath and objects of bronze, including a shield cover.

THE HELLENISTIC WORLD

After Alexander's death in 323 B.C., his empire soon disintegrated as his generals, the Successors, fought among themselves for control of the various regions. Alexander's wife, his posthumously born son, his simple minded half-brother and his mother were all murdered. Finally, by 278/77 B.C., there were three great Hellenistic kingdoms: in Egypt, a line founded by Ptolemy, son of Lagus, ruled; Babylonia, Syria and lands farther east belonged to the Seleucids, named after Seleucus I; and the descendants of Antigonus II Gonatas controlled Macedonia.

From these kingdoms, Greek culture spread from the Mediterranean to India. This Hellenistic (from Hellas, Greece) world lasted for some three centuries, from the death of Alexander until the gradual absorption of these kingdoms into the empires of Rome and, to a lesser extent, Parthia (pp.76–77). Macedonia and Greece, for example, continued until their annexation by Rome in 146 B.C., while Egypt held out until A.D. 30.

These kingdoms varied greatly, but common to them all was the Greek language, even where Aramaic was widely spoken. Common too was kingship, a form of government not seen in Greece – Sparta excepted – for over 500 years. In both Egypt and Asia, local concepts of absolute monarchy and the divine nature of royal authority produced monarchies similar to the pharaohs and the Achaemenids. In Macedonia, the monarchy had been, in a limited way, elective, and the king had ruled with the consent of the people and, in particular, the army. The Antigonid dynasty retained this idea – their monarchy was more similar to Macedonian kingship prior to Alexander's conquests. But everywhere in the Hellenistic world, Alexander was honored as a god, and all kings claimed descent from him.

The Ptolemaic kingdom consisted of Egypt and some coastal territories of the eastern Mediterranean. Its population was the least rebellious, and this, together with geographic unity and ancient tradition, rendered it the most manageable. It also had the most effective navy and, until Ptolemaic policy encouraged people to abandon the land, the most productive agriculture.

In the Greek peninsula, the Antigonids ruled Macedonia securely, but their control over the traditionally independent and often democratic city-states of southern Greece was less secure. To the east, the Seleucid domains spread over a huge area and included many peoples. Much of their original territory became independent ethnic kingdoms, ruled by local or mixed Greek and local dynasties, among them Bactria, Armenia, Bithynia and Pontus. The Seleucids ruled as the Achaemenids had before them, with local governors, or satraps.

THE SPREAD OF HELLENISM

With the establishment of the Hellenistic kingdoms in the Near East and Egypt, Greek culture became widespread, although the extent to which it was adopted by conquered peoples varied in different places. In general, Hellenization was greater nearer the Mediterranean. Rural communities farther east were probably little influenced, and although *koine* Greek, the common Greek tongue, was widely spoken, so too was Aramaic. It was largely the conquered aristocracy that embraced Hellenism, for this gave them access to the otherwise closed world of the Greek ruling class.

The main centers of Hellenism in the Seleucid and Ptolemaic domains were recently founded Greek cities. Both these dynasties ruled from new capitals – not from the old cities of Babylon or Memphis. In Egypt, Alexandria, the capital, was the greatest of all the Hellenistic cities, founded by Alexander himself. In Mesopotamia, the Seleucids moved to their new city Seleucia-on-the-Tigris (setting a precedent for future capitals, for both Ctesiphon and Baghdad were set on this river and not, as for millennia, on the Euphrates). Later they founded Seleucia and Antioch in Syria. In Mesopotamia, the influence of Hellenism is clearly evident in early Parthian art (pp.76–77), although it

The Dying Gaul, *a Roman copy of a statue from Pergamum in Asia Minor, shows clear Hellenistic influence in its realism. During the third and second centuries B.C., Pergamum became a great city in which the arts flourished. The statue commemorates the repulse of an invasion by Gauls, who then settled in Galatia in central Anatolia, an area that was named after them.*

In Pontus and Commagene, in southern Anatolia, native dynasties adopted Hellenism, resulting in perhaps the most visible evidence of the transplanting of Greek culture in Asia. This is epitomized by the tombs of the Pontic kings, but even more so by the monuments (RIGHT) of Antiochus I at Nemrut Dağ in modern Turkey.

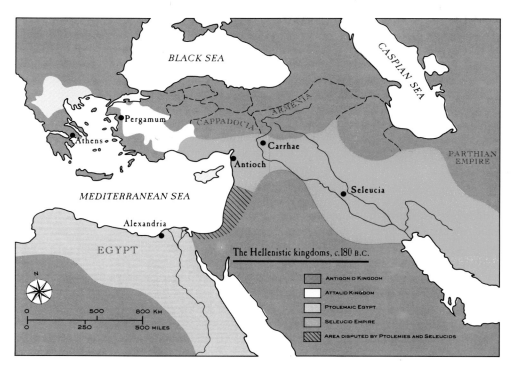

The Hellenistic kingdoms, c.180 B.C.

- ANTIGONID KINGDOM
- ATTALID KINGDOM
- PTOLEMAIC EGYPT
- SELEUCID EMPIRE
- AREA DISPUTED BY PTOLEMIES AND SELEUCIDS

The Attalid kings, named after King Attalus I Soter (241–197 B.C.) of Pergamum in Asia Minor, transformed the city from a Seleucid fortress into an independent state. Then, with the defeat of the invading Galatian tribes by Attalus's son Eumenes II (197–159 B.C.), Pergamum became one of the strongest of the Hellenistic kingdoms.

Far to the east, in the most easterly parts of present-day Iran, Afghanistan and northwest India, a series of Indo-Greek kings founded kingdoms in what had been Seleucid territories. They produced beautiful coins, from which their names, but little more, are known. The Hellenistic legacy in the east is not immediately evident, but can be seen in the art of Gandhara (pp.158–59) and in the Parthian world. This region fell to invading tribes, and gradually the visible influence of the Greek world disappeared.

But that Greek culture endured for centuries, even in isolation, is clear from the discovery of a Greek city at the site of Ai Khanum, near what is now Afghanistan's border with the U.S.S.R. Here, in distant Bactria, Greeks could visit the theater to watch the plays of Aeschylus and Sophocles. It is clear that the city maintained its Greek buildings and institutions more than 200 years after the death of Alexander the Great.

was not lasting – indeed, it was consciously rejected later.

The archaeological evidence from Susa, the former Achaemenid administrative center, shows Hellenistic influence, but, in general, outside the towns Iran seems to have been little affected by its period of exposure to Hellenism. Nevertheless, the excavations at a Greek city on the Oxus, at the site of Ai Khanum, seem to bear out the statement of the late Greek traveler Plutarch that because of Alexander "Homer became widely read [in Asia] . . . the Gedrosians sang the tragedies of Euripides." For here, on the borders of Afghanistan and Russia, is a small foundation, where in the third century B.C., the famous Delphic maxim "Know Thyself" was inscribed on a pillar in the city's gymnasium.

But, in spite of all the possible Hellenistic influences on the art of Gandhara or the formation of short-lived Indo-Greek kingdoms and the continued existence of Alexandrian foundations at Kandahar and Samarkand, it was in Asia Minor and not in the east that Hellenism flowered and took root. In the splendid city of Pergamum, center of the Attalid dynasty, the library rivaled that of Alexandria. Parchment was created for its books, in response to the Ptolemies' refusal to sell papyrus to the Pergamenes. On its lofty hill, the city grew from a garrison fort with the funds of Lysimachus's treasury and was adorned with the most spectacular theater of antiquity and with splendid buildings. Fame and wealth came from the defeat of the Galatians, to whom tribute had formerly been paid. The Great Altar of Zeus dedicated in thanksgiving was decorated with sculptures that epitomize the full-blown realism of the Hellenistic Baroque. Even after Pergamum became Roman territory, bequeathed to Rome by the last Attalid, it remained prosperous and retained a quality of cultured cosmopolitanism.

When the Romans took control of Egypt in 30 B.C., they inherited the Hellenistic culture that had taken root in the country for some 300 years under the Ptolemies. This coffin of the Roman period (RIGHT) from the Faiyum district shows its classical influence in the lifelike portrait of a young man named Artemidorus, who died, aged 19 to 21, probably during the early part of the second century A.D.

THE ROMAN WORLD

❝While stands the Coliseum, Rome shall stand;
When falls the Coliseum, Rome shall fall;
And when Rome falls — the World.❞

BRITISH POET LORD BYRON (1788–1824), QUOTING A TRADITIONAL LATIN PROVERB

The Roman triumphal arch, such as the one shown here (LEFT) dedicated to Emperor Constantine in A.D. 316, was built to commemorate Roman victories. The arch has been copied in later ages — examples include Marble Arch in London, Washington Square Arch in New York City and the Arc de Triomphe (BELOW), built in Paris in 1836 to a design by Jean Chalgrin.

The story of Rome, the village that grew to be an empire ruling much of the western world, has never lost its fascination. The city was founded, according to tradition, by a Latin prince named Romulus on April 21, 753 B.C. From the start, the Roman people showed an aptitude for soldiering which resulted in the conquest of the Italian peninsula and, later, an empire that at its height reached from the North Sea to the Atlas Mountains and from the Atlantic coast to the Euphrates River. It embraced lands that today form all, or part of, more than 25 countries, some so different in character that there is little common ground for intercommunication. Although separated by only a few hours' flight, the people of Damascus in Syria and Lyons in France, or Bath in England and Antalya in Turkey, now seem farther from each other than did their counterparts living in the same cities under Roman rule.

Rome and its imperial tradition has had a compelling relevance in the 20th century. When the Italian dictator Benito Mussolini came to power, he claimed he had "restored the *fasces*," the Roman symbol of power, and was thereby attempting to underpin his regime by associating it with his country's glorious past. Centuries before Il Duce in A.D. 800, Charlemagne, the king of the Franks, was crowned Holy Roman Emperor and resuscitated the dormant Roman Empire, even making the journey to the now holy city to be crowned and anointed. Later, like Charlemagne, Napoleon Bonaparte also dreamed of a universal empire and made the symbolic pilgrimage to Rome. Napoleon's background was not dissimilar to that of important Roman families, and his military prowess was in the grand tradition of great Roman generals.

Rome's rise to power was founded on discipline and simple peasant virtues: *pietas* (dutiful behavior), *frugalitas* and *simplicitas* were highly regarded — all the more so when they were seen to be practiced by wealthy senators. But when Hellenistic culture and practices, with their "unmanly" sensual pleasures, were later introduced into the city, the statesman Cato (239–148 B.C.)

and others of the old school tried in vain to stem this corrupting tide. Times were changing, however, and the virtues of earlier heroes, like Cincinnatus, who had returned to his farm after saving his country, became hallowed as model qualities.

As the city grew to become the capital of an empire, it became increasingly cosmopolitan and violent, as the suicides and proscriptions of the dying republic bear witness. But with the establishment of the empire, and the peace it brought, Rome entered its golden age, of which the British historian Edward Gibbon wrote: "In the second century of the Christian Era, the empire of Rome comprehended the fairest part of the earth, and the most civilized portion of mankind."

Rome eventually fell to invading barbarians: with the deposition of the prophetically named Romulus Augustus by the German chieftain Odoacer in A.D. 476, the western empire came to an end. But the influence of Rome has continued down to the present, for the fabric of western civilization is interwoven with threads of Roman culture. Rome's political system, her legal code, language, engineering and architecture can all be traced in their modern equivalents. Perhaps the most far-reaching legacy was Rome's adoption of Christianity as the state religion in the fourth century. As a result, Christianity was transformed from a persecuted minority sect to the established faith of the empire; and, centuries later, it would become a major world religion.

The legendary hero Hercules, dressed in a leopard skin, and the god Bacchus, the Roman equivalent to the Greek Dionysus, engage in a drinking contest in this Roman mosaic. Made of small cubes of stone, glass and terra-cotta, mosaics often copied paintings and were used to decorate walls and floors. In Italy, floor mosaics were frequently black and white.

THE ETRUSCANS

From about 800 to 300 B.C., Etruscan civilization flourished in the region that still reflects its ancient heritage – Tuscany, bounded by the Rivers Arno and Tiber and the Apennine Mountains. Known as *Tusci* or *Etrusci* in Latin, the Etruscans called themselves *Rasenna*, while the Greeks knew them as *Tyrrhenoi*, from which derives the Tyrrhenian Sea. Etruscan culture strongly influenced early Rome in such matters as religious cults, including the Capitoline triad of Jupiter, Juno and Minerva; divination, for example in the form of interpreting the flight of birds or reading the entrails of slaughtered animals; the processional triumph after a military victory; the royal insignia, notably the *fasces* (pp.124–25); and public games.

There has been speculation about the origins of the Etruscans since antiquity. The Greek historian Herodotus believed that they came from Lydia in Asia Minor and eventually settled "among the Umbrians, founding the cities they still live in." According to Dionysius of Halicarnassus, who wrote at the time of Emperor Augustus, they were indigenous to the region. There is evidence to support both theories, although the latter is one that is becoming increasingly popular among modern scholars. But whatever their origins, it is clear that Etruscan civilization took shape in northern Italy, and that by the end of the seventh century B.C., the Etruscans had become a single people, with a common language and a uniform culture.

Most Etruscan towns were built on hilltops, and the oldest – for example Veii, Caere and Tarquinii – lay within easy reach of the coast. Only Populonia opposite the island of Elba was a coastal city. Farther east, important Etruscan cities, such as Clusium and Arretium, developed at a later period. The Etruscan people consisted of a loose confederation of politically independent cities, with a religious center at Volsinii. The cities were ruled by kings, although in some cases they were later replaced by elected magistrates. There was a wealthy upper class and, at the other extreme, a class of rural serfs.

Situated in a well-watered region, with fertile volcanic soil, several towns of Etruria depended on agriculture for their wealth. Rich deposits of copper and iron, particularly in the region between Volaterrae and Vetulonia, were mined until the first century B.C. The iron ore mined on Elba was processed at Populonia, where there was also copper. The large areas of forest provided fuel for the smelting furnaces of the mining industry.

The Etruscans were at their most powerful around 500 B.C., at which time they controlled a considerable area, from the Po to central Campania. But Etruscan expansion, which was linked to trade, was short-lived; in the north, their power was broken by invading Celts at the end of the fifth century B.C., and in the south, they were defeated by the Greeks at Cumae in 474 B.C. By the mid-fifth century B.C., the Samnite people had pushed them

The world of ancient Rome covered an area that corresponds to most of present-day Europe, plus parts of Asia Minor and northern Africa. The city of Rome itself, which grew into a vast metropolis of about one million people, was the hub of this extensive empire, well situated to receive goods by land and sea. The map shows the principal cities of the Roman Empire, some of which are still important European centers. These include Londinium (London), Lugdunum (Lyons), Nemausus (Nîmes), and Augusta Treverorum (Trier).

The Roman world

THE ROMAN EMPIRE AT ITS GREATEST EXTENT IN A.D. 117

out of Campania. In the next century, the great city of Veii was destroyed by the Romans, and by the end of the third, Rome had defeated or absorbed all the cities of Etruria.

The Etruscan language is not yet fully understood, although it can be read. As the many brief funerary inscriptions provide little material beyond names, knowledge of the Etruscan civilization comes largely from the tombs and grave goods of the wealthy aristocracy. The superb tomb paintings at Tarquinii and elsewhere, with their scenes of feasting, music and dancing, hunting and wrestling, give a picture of the lives of these people. Etruscan jewelry was of outstanding quality, as was its bronze work, ranging from household goods and furniture to large cast pieces. Greek models inspired Etruscan vase painting, and both the ceramics in the Greek style and the Etruscan *bucchero* ware were exceptional.

The Etruscans were strongly influenced by Greek culture, as can be seen, for example, in the architecture of the reconstructed Etruscan temple of Veii (BELOW LEFT). However, they developed their own highly original artistic traditions and are noted for their bronzework.

Painted terra-cotta sculptures decorated the superstructures of temples, but their skill in this medium is best illustrated by life-size figures. These include the statue of the god Apollo from Veii (RIGHT), made by the famous sculptor Vulca, and the sixth-century sarcophagus (BELOW) from Caere, showing a reclining couple.

The Etruscans were also outstanding architects and engineers, building temples which were used by the Romans as models, and constructing drainage systems, including the Cloaca Maxima which drained the Forum at Rome.

EARLY ROME

According to legend, Rome was founded in 753 B.C. and named after Romulus, a Latin prince from Alba Longa, who, after killing his twin brother Remus, chose the site for the city on the banks of the Tiber. In addition to the literary tradition, knowledge about early Rome comes from archaeological, religious and linguistic evidence. Excavation has shown that among the earliest sites on the plain of Latium, dating from about 1000 B.C., were villages on the Palatine and neighboring hills. By the eighth century B.C., these Latin farming villages had developed into larger, more diverse, communities, in contact with the Greeks in the south of the Italian peninsula, as well as with the Etruscans.

By the mid-seventh century B.C., Rome had expanded considerably to include the valley of the Forum. The town was well situated at the lowest crossing of the Tiber and controlled the routes north and south, as well as the river, at the mouth of which were lucrative salt pans. Throughout the century, Rome enlarged its territory with the conquest of Alba Longa and, later, by the incorporation of Ficana and other settlements, which took the boundaries to the coast.

This phase of expansion took place under Tullus Hostilius and Ancus Marcius, the third and fourth kings after Romulus and Numa Pompilius. These early rulers were men of Latin or Sabine extraction, and this, along with Sabine influences in the Latin language, suggests that there was a significant Sabine element in the population of early Rome.

Toward the end of the seventh century, there is evidence of considerable change, as Rome began to develop into a sizable city. The center was drained and given a focal point by the creation of a central market place, the Forum, which was paved. The first public buildings were constructed, including the shrine of Vesta, goddess of the hearth, and the royal palace, the Regia. Temples, such as that of the supreme god Jupiter on the Capitoline, and cult statues were set up. In parts of the city, huts were replaced by much more robust timber-framed houses with stone foundations and tiled roofs.

The transformation of the city in the sixth century B.C. began during the reign of Tarquinius Priscus (616–579 B.C.). A wealthy Etruscan who had migrated to Rome, where he was accepted in influential circles, Tarquinius was chosen as king by popular vote after the death of Ancus Marcius. It seems that several Etruscan families took up residence in Rome, and their names are later found among consuls of the early republic. Evidence suggests that in early Rome and in some Etruscan cities, individuals or groups could freely move from one community to another and be accepted, even at the highest levels.

As a result of the Etruscan presence, their civilization, with its advanced technologies and developed artistic traditions, had a strong influence on the cultural life of Rome. But although of Etruscan origin, Tarquinius and his successors were kings of an independent city and not, as is sometimes suggested, a foreign regime imposing Etruscan domination. When the Tarquins

The second longest river in Italy, the Tiber flows through the city of Rome and enters the Tyrrhenian Sea near the ancient port of Ostia. The small Tiberina Island (BELOW) is joined to the mainland by the Fabricio Bridge, on the right of the picture. Built in 62 B.C. by the consul L. Fabricio, the bridge is the oldest in Rome.

According to ancient sources, the Tiber was originally known as Albula because of its supposedly white water, but it was renamed after Tiberinus, a king of Alba Longa who is said to have drowned in it.

were overthrown, it was not as a reaction against Etruscan power, but against a tyrannical regime.

Tarquinius Priscus had enrolled new men into the governing body of elders known as the Senate, which until then was drawn from the heads of the leading families. His successor, Servius Tullius, was credited with introducing reforms that created a new assembly (pp.124–25). Both he and his successor, Tarquinius Superbus, ruled without the vote of the original assembly, the *comitia curiata*. The rule of Tarquinius Superbus proved intolerably despotic, and in 509 B.C. a group of aristocrats expelled him from the city and established a republican government that would last some 500 years.

Tarquinius Superbus, *Tarquin the Proud, on the far left of the picture, founds the temple of Jupiter at Rome in a painting by the 15th-century Italian artist Perin del Vaga. Tarquinius was the seventh and last king of Rome, whose reign of terror ended in a revolt led by a group of senators.*

Romulus and Remus are *suckled by a she-wolf in this archaic bronze statue. According to tradition, the twins were the progeny of the daughter of the king of Alba Longa and Mars, the god of war. As infants, they were cast into the Tiber by their mother's uncle, but were saved by a shepherd named Faustulus, who found them being fed by the wolf. He reared them as his own until they were adults, when they returned to found the city of Rome. In a dispute about seniority, however, Romulus killed his brother before becoming king and reigning for 40 years.*

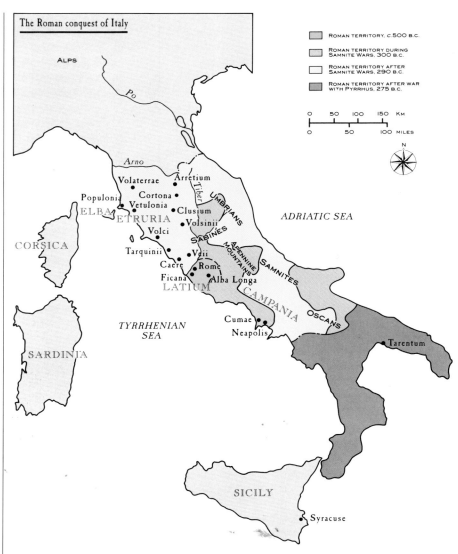

The Roman conquest of Italy

ALPS

ROMAN TERRITORY, c.500 B.C.

ROMAN TERRITORY DURING
SAMNITE WARS, 300 B.C.

ROMAN TERRITORY AFTER
SAMNITE WARS, 290 B.C.

ROMAN TERRITORY AFTER WAR
WITH PYRRHUS, 275 B.C.

Po

Arno

Volaterrae · Arretium
Populonia · Cortona
Vetulonia · Clusium · UMBRIANS
ELBA · ETRURIA · Volsinii
Volci · SABINES · ADRIATIC SEA
Tarquinii · APENNINE MOUNTAINS
Caere · Veii · SAMNITES
Ficana · Rome · OSCANS
Alba Longa
LATIUM · CAMPANIA
Cumae · Tarentum
Neapolis
TYRRHENIAN
SEA

CORSICA

SARDINIA

SICILY

Syracuse

Extensive territory and a strong army were combined in the new republic of Rome. It soon dominated the other Latin-speaking towns in the area and had trading and diplomatic links with the Etruscans and with the Greeks of the south, as well as with Carthage in north Africa, later to become Rome's great enemy. Nevertheless, Rome's military authority was not invulnerable, and the history of the republic's first years is a confused picture of turmoil and disorder. To the north, the Celts who had crossed the Alps were disrupting Etruscan cities; in the south, Apennine hill people were pressing down on to the coastal plains. In Latium itself, Rome had to fight to remain supreme. In about 499 B.C., the Latins were defeated at the epic battle of Lake Regillus, and the treaty that followed set the pattern for all subsequent Roman foreign relations.

Disturbances were also caused by roving private armies, such as that of Lars Porsenna of Clusium, who came to the aid of the exiled Tarquinius Superbus and probably captured Rome in about 507 B.C. The migration to Rome about three years later of the Sabine leader Attius Clausus with 5,000 clients and dependants is another such example. It seems that with the end of the monarchy there was no strong central authority, and powerful aristocrats with private armies could pursue their interests free of

At the start of the republic *in about 500 B.C., Roman territory consisted merely of the city itself and the area of the plain of Latium. In a little over 200 years, however, Rome had gained almost the entire Italian peninsula. In 325 B.C., war broke out between the Romans and the Samnites, a bellicose hill people, and lasted, with interruptions, until 290. Rome's victory gave her possession of central Italy, an area that was later increased after the war with Pyrrhus of Epirus (pp.126–27).*

THE CONSTITUTION OF THE REPUBLIC

The republican system of government underwent several changes from the time of its inception in 509 B.C. The monarchy was replaced by two chief magistrates, the consuls, who held supreme power, or *imperium*. In times of emergency, the consuls could appoint a dictator with total power for six months. Assisting the consuls were: praetors to look after legal cases; censors to guide public morals and investment in property; curulian aediles to supervise markets, festivals and temples; and quaestors to take charge of public finance. The old advisory council, the Senate, was drawn from the heads of clans (*patres*) and former consuls and served to advise the magistrates and authorize popular decisions.

The magistrates and Senate were complemented by four public assemblies, with different functions, whose members voted in groups and spoke at the invitation of the presiding magistrate. These assemblies were: the *comitia curiata*, the original assembly dating from the regal period which became less important later; the *concilium plebis*, the assembly of the plebeians who elected tribunes as their representatives and whose decrees came to be binding on all; the *comitia tributa*, which was virtually the same as the plebeian assembly, but with the addition of a small number of patricians; and the *comitia centuriata*, whose members met in army units, with the better armed, namely the wealthy, voting first.

The **fasces** *consisted of a bundle of rods enclosing an ax and symbolized the power of the consul. The rods suggested the consul's right to beat a person, and the ax his right to award the death penalty. The fasces were carried by minor officials known as* **lictors**.

Diagram labels

SENATE — ADVISES → MAGISTRATES

CONSULS — APPOINT → DICTATOR

PRAETORS

CENSORS

CURULIAN AEDILES

QUAESTORS

ELECTS

TRIBUNES

ELECTS

ELECTS

ELECTS

PUBLIC ASSEMBLIES

COMITIA CURIATA — COMITIA TRIBUTA — COMITIA CENTURIATA — CONCILIUM PLEBIS

ROMAN PEOPLE

The rape of the Sabine women — an episode narrated by the Roman writer Livy (59 B.C.–A.D. 17) — is shown in this sculpture by Giovanni da Bologna (1579–83). According to Livy, after Rome had been built the Romans were short of women, so they invited the Sabines and other neighbors to a festival and, at a given point, seized the Sabine women. It seems likely that the story was intended to explain the arrival in Latium of early settlers such as the Sabines during the early expansion of the republic.

state control. The economy declined and debt became widespread among the common people, the plebeians. This period ended when the plebeians began to challenge the aristocrats.

The downfall of the monarchy had resulted from the aristocrats' reaction to kings who had challenged their power and privileges. With the foundation of the republic, measures were therefore taken to prevent a recurrence of monarchism. An official was appointed to take care of the king's former religious responsibilities, and in the political and military sphere, the king was replaced by two magistrates, or consuls, who ruled the city and commanded the army.

In short, the government of the republic was the collective rule of an aristocracy, dependent in theory – and to a varying degree in practice – on the will of a popular assembly. At first, senatorial and official posts were held by patricians, a hereditary elite, who formed a small minority of the city's total population. Thus in the early years of the republic, this small group had acquired a virtual monopoly of political power. The patricians were able to control the state only because, as patrons, they received support from their hereditary clients. This ancient institution of clientship was not a legal, but a moral, bond and was an important element of aristocratic power throughout the republic's history.

The plebeian challenge to patrician control began a conflict that dominated the domestic history of Rome for a little over two centuries. It began in 494 B.C. when the debt-ridden plebeians organized themselves and withdrew from the city to the Sacred Mount, located about 14 miles northeast of Rome. This was the first of three secessions, and it resulted in the plebeians being able to secure their own officials, the tribunes, and shortly afterward their own assembly. Not all plebeians were poor, and in the fourth century, wealthy citizens representing them obtained access to high office. Finally, in 287 B.C., the plebeians were given the right to pass laws in their assemblies, a measure which succeeded in ending the conflict.

Beyond the city, the treaty with the Latins in about 493 B.C. had provided the base for a Latin league. Although it was a treaty between equals, with military cooperation and other mutual rights, Rome played a dominant part, and the allied army was under a Roman commander. To the north, Rome's great adversary was the Etruscan city of Veii. The conflict perhaps arose from the attempts of each city to control the salt trade, and there was a series of wars between them during the fifth century. Finally, following a long siege by Rome and her allies, Veii fell in 396 B.C., and Roman territory was doubled.

Following the destruction of the Etruscan city of Veii in 396 B.C., Rome's position seemed to be secure. Yet within six years disaster struck, when the city was captured and sacked by the Gauls from the north. A few years after this trauma, new city walls were built, and the land won from Veii was colonized. North of this new territory lay the Etruscan city of Caere, which now befriended Rome and thus secured her northern border.

Based on a third-century B.C. statue, this Roman army officer, either a consul or a legate, wears the style of armor that was common throughout the time of the republic. The panoply included a plumed helmet with cheek guards, bronze greaves and open sandals, and a cuirass around which was tied a sash, indicative of rank.

The Romans were an earthy, pragmatic, disciplined people with great organizational skills. But it was their stern martial qualities that helped them to establish themselves in Latium and which later made them masters of Italy and, in time, the Mediterranean.

At first, the Roman army consisted of a citizen militia. The basic unit was the century, or 100 men, of which there were about 200, divided into classes determined by wealth. The standard formation was the Greek phalanx (pp.112–13) until this proved to be ineffective in the rocky terrain over which much of the fighting against the Samnites was conducted. By about the end of the fourth century B.C., a more flexible formation of three lines split into small groups of 120 men, or maniples ("handfuls"), had come into being.

After the Gallic sack, the Latin alliance had ceased to function, and the Apennine hill people now returned to their attacks, but were defeated. Rome reasserted her control over the Latins, and the alliance was renewed. In 338 B.C., Rome defeated a coalition of Latins and Italians, and some of the defeated Latin cities now became part of the Roman state and their people became Roman citizens. This peace settlement set the pattern for the future expansion of Rome in Italy. Conquered people became allies and had to fight alongside Rome in subsequent wars.

In the years following the Latin War, Rome established her position by founding the first of many colonies. This policy greatly assisted the consolidation and eventual unification of Roman Italy. But it also led to war with the Samnites, a hill people who had begun to encroach on Campania. For the next 40 years, from 327 B.C., Rome intermittently fought with the Samnites before defeating them. During these years, Roman territory was extended by alliances, conquests and colonization. With the defeat of the Samnites in 290 B.C., Roman territory was extended to the Adriatic coast. Soon afterward, the Etruscans and Umbrians were compelled to become allies.

During the third century B.C., Rome became involved in the affairs of Greek cities of Italy. Tarentum, the strongest of these cities, concerned about Rome's growing power, sought help from Pyrrhus, king of Epirus in the northwest of the Greek mainland. In 280 B.C., Pyrrhus landed in Italy with a large army and 20 elephants. He fought several battles against the Romans, but although he won costly Pyrrhic victories, he returned home after his defeat in 275.

The whole peninsula was now under Rome's control. During the wars, there had been massacres; territory had been confiscated and captives enslaved. Yet the settlement imposed on the vanquished was enlightened: communities that were not extended full or half-citizenship were bound by alliance and, apart from foreign policy, were left to run their own affairs. Rome imposed no taxes or tribute, and although land had been confiscated, some was used for colonies, whose settlers came from both Rome and the allied states. In this way, a partnership was created by which the allies helped Rome in return for a share of the profits, which included booty, slaves and land. Another factor that guaranteed the loyalty of Rome's allies was the Senate's support for local aristocracies.

In the longer term, the people of Italy became assimilated as full Roman citizenship was extended, beginning with the Sabines in 268 B.C.; Latin became widely spoken, and the Roman way of life was gradually adopted. The great system of roads, although built primarily for strategic purposes, improved communications and led to the further spread of Roman culture.

Rome itself was transformed during these wars. A new ruling elite had formed after the consulship was opened to plebeians and this patricio-plebeian nobility became a dominant group in the Senate; the expansion of the nobility now intensified the competition for senior office. Because of the voting system in Roman assemblies, those who owned most property had the most rights, so wealth based on land was the key to political power and office. Roman wealth, notably in land, increased as a result of the conquests. Even the less well-off benefited with the foundation of colonies. The spoils of victory financed the building of temples and public works, including aqueducts for the expanded city.

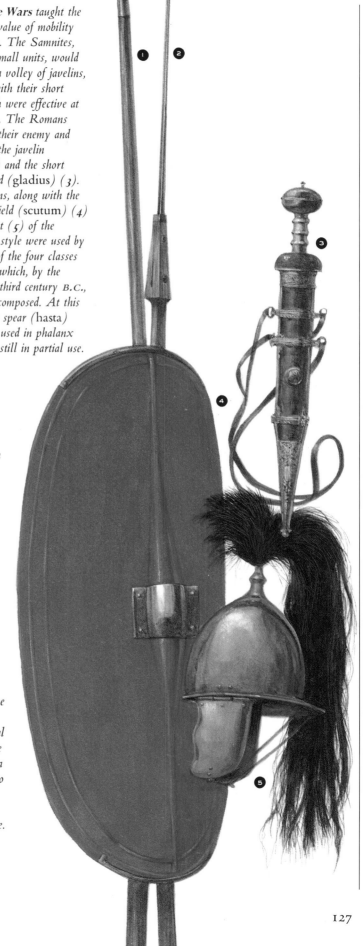

Made in the sixth or fifth century B.C., *this bronze statue represents a Samnite warrior wearing full armor — a cuirass and belt, a short leather tunic, greaves for the shins and a helmet whose plume is missing. The Samnites were an Oscan-speaking hill people who fought a series of three, ultimately unsuccessful, wars against the Romans, from 343 to 341, 316 to 304 and 298 to 290 B.C.*

Their greatest moment came with the destruction of a Roman force under the consuls Veturius and Postumus in 321. The Romans were caught in a narrow defile, blocked by the Samnites at each end, and were starved into surrender. Hostages were taken and the remainder of the army was made to pass through a makeshift archway of spears as a mark of disgrace before being allowed to return to the city of Rome.

The Samnite Wars *taught the Romans the value of mobility and flexibility. The Samnites, operating in small units, would first unleash a volley of javelins, then charge with their short swords, which were effective at close quarters. The Romans learned from their enemy and soon adopted the javelin (pilum) (2) and the short stabbing sword (gladius) (3). These weapons, along with the large, oval shield (scutum) (4) and the helmet (5) of the Montefortino style were used by hastati, one of the four classes of soldiers of which, by the middle of the third century B.C., a legion was composed. At this time, the long spear (hasta) (1) formerly used in phalanx warfare, was still in partial use.*

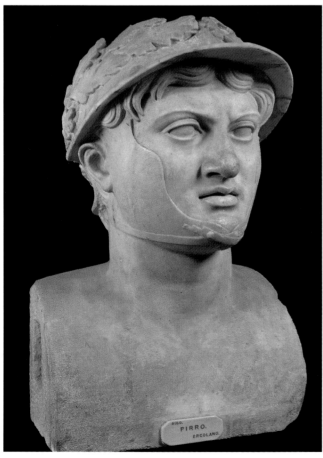

King Pyrrhus of Epirus *in northwestern Greece was asked by the people of Tarentum in 281 B.C. to help them prevent further Roman expansion in Greek territory in the south of Italy. With his large army of about 25,000 men and several war elephants, Pyrrhus landed in Italy and in 280 won an expensive victory against the Romans. After another costly victory in the following year, Pyrrhus crossed to Sicily in 278 and conquered most of the territory held by the Carthaginians. His tyrannical regime, however, alienated the Sicilian Greeks and, within a couple of years, he returned to Italy. There, in 275, he was defeated by the Romans and compelled to return to Greece.*

ROME AND THE MEDITERRANEAN

CHRONOLOGY OF THE PUNIC WARS

First Punic War, 264–241 B.C.

264: Rome and Carthage are drawn into a war between Messana and Syracuse on the island of Sicily. Following the initial Roman victory against Carthage and Syracuse, the latter changes sides.

261: The Romans conquer Sicily as far as Agrigentum.

260: The Romans win the naval battle of Mylae using new ships built on a Punic design.

256: After a victory at Cape Ecnomus, the Romans land in Africa and advance to Carthage.

255: The Carthaginians defeat the Romans at Tunis and the Roman survivors are shipwrecked on their way back to Sicily.

254: The Romans win a victory at Panormus on Sicily, but fail to make further progress.

241: At the battle of the Aegates Islands off Sicily, the Romans destroy the Carthaginian fleet, effectively ending the war.

Second Punic War, 218–201 B.C.

218: The Carthaginian general Hannibal reaches northern Italy, having crossed the Pyrenees and Alps with an invasion force of 50,000 men, 9,000 cavalry and 37 elephants.

217: The Romans are defeated at Lake Trasimene.

216: At the battle of Cannae, Hannibal inflicts defeat on Rome – the worst in her history.

210: After the death of Hiero of Syracuse, his successor allies with Carthage and the Romans capture and sack the city. Meanwhile, the Roman general Publius Scipio lands in Spain.

208: The Carthaginian general Hasdrubal is defeated by Scipio at Baecula.

206: Scipio's victory at Ilipa forces the Carthaginians out of Spain.

204: Scipio lands in Africa; in the following year, Hannibal returns home from Italy.

202: The Carthaginian army is destroyed at Zama. The war ends a year later with harsh peace terms imposed on Carthage.

Third Punic War, 149–146 B.C.

151: Carthage engages in a war with Numidia and thereby breaks her treaty with Rome.

149: A Roman army sets out for Africa.

146: Carthage falls after a long siege. The city is razed and its people sold into slavery.

The Carthaginian general Hannibal Barca (ABOVE RIGHT) was one of the great military leaders of all time. His invasion of Italy with war elephants, such as the one shown on the Punic coin (ABOVE) minted at the time of the Second Punic War, resulted in crushing defeats for Rome, even though Hannibal was unable to achieve final victory. After the war, under pressure from Rome, Hannibal went into voluntary exile to Syria and, later, Bithynia. In 182/83, he committed suicide rather than face capture by the Romans.

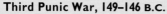

The Punic Wars

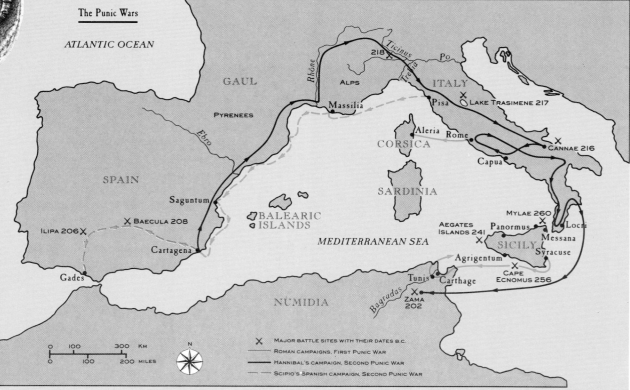

Shortly after the Romans had completed the conquest of Italy, they became involved in a major war: in 264 B.C., they challenged Carthage, a Phoenician colony in northern Africa and the major power of the western Mediterranean, for control of Sicily. What began as a small incident changed the balance of power in the Mediterranean world. In less than a century, Rome reduced Carthage to impotence; and by the end of the Punic (the Roman word for "Phoenician") Wars in 146 B.C., Carthage had been eliminated, and Rome was an imperial power.

Before the wars, Carthage had had a monopoly of regional trade and was backed by a strong navy. She had also originally been friendly with Rome, since there had been no conflict of interest. They first clashed when, on the island of Sicily, the people of Syracuse attacked Messana, which was controlled by Italian mercenaries known as the Mamertines. Rome and Carthage were drawn into the affair on opposite sides, and a long war ensued, lasting from 264 to 241 B.C. Because the Massanians had expelled the Carthaginian garrison that had been installed in their city, Carthage allied itself with Syracuse. But, after initial Roman successes, Syracuse changed sides.

Rome was unable to establish her superiority until she built a powerful fleet. Eventually, however, the Carthaginians were defeated and ejected from Sicily, which became the first Roman province. Carthage was obliged to pay a large indemnity, which left her in a weak position, unable to prevent Rome from seizing Sardinia and Corsica.

A second war between Rome and Carthage began in 218 B.C. The Carthaginian general Hannibal, who, when he was young, had been made to swear eternal hostility to Rome, invaded Italy with a large army and several elephants after an epic crossing of the Alps. Despite brilliant victories at Trasimene and Cannae, Hannibal failed to foment rebellion in Rome's Italian allies. Instead, over the next few years, he was gradually worn down by tactics devised by Quintus Fabius Maximus.

In 203, he returned to Africa and there, a year later, was defeated by Scipio Africanus at Zama. As a result, Rome gained further provinces from former Carthaginian possessions in Spain and received another huge indemnity. The third war (149–146 B.C.) was deliberately provoked by Rome: the city of Carthage was obliterated, and the survivors were sold into slavery; the territory of Carthage now became the Roman province of Africa.

In the meantime, Rome had been drawn into the affairs of the Hellenistic world. Rome's earlier success against Hannibal's ally Philip V of Macedon caused Pergamum in Asia Minor and others to ask her for help when Philip began a series of conquests in the eastern Mediterranean. Philip was duly defeated and forced to give up control of Greece. The Romans proclaimed Greece free – no territory was annexed, but a precedent of intervention had been set, and Rome was to become involved in the disputes of the Greek world. In the first decades of the second century B.C., the Romans decisively defeated the major Hellenistic kingdoms of Greece and Asia Minor, and by 167 B.C., Rome was mistress of the eastern Mediterranean. In 146 B.C., Greece became a province; and in 133 B.C., Pergamum was bequeathed to Rome and became the Roman province of Asia.

These overseas successes vastly increased the Roman nobility's power and wealth. Booty from a successful campaign could be enormous, and these financial gains were invested in large landed estates, worked by enslaved prisoners of war. Slave labor replaced the small peasant farmers who were the backbone of the Roman army. Extended military service in distant lands made it increasingly difficult for peasants to maintain their farms. In this way, many were driven off their land into a life of poverty. One of the results of this was that recruiting soldiers became difficult because the law required a property qualification for military service. Also, social tensions began to develop.

The carving out of an empire meant a greater scope for industry and commerce. This had little interest for Roman aristocrats, but it did enhance the importance of wealthy businessmen, who grew even richer. Slavery increased in private households. There were more public games, and the city was adorned with new public buildings. During the wars, many Romans had been exposed to Greek culture, which became pervasive as Romans imitated the style of the great centers of the Hellenistic world. Some nobles were ardent philhellenes and adopted luxurious and increasingly sophisticated habits. Greek philosophers lectured in Rome, and the earliest Roman historians wrote in Greek. In art and architecture, religion and literature, too, Greek influences prevailed.

This relief of a Roman warship shows the type of vessel that was built to fight the Carthaginians. Up to the First Punic War, Rome had possessed few warships. But, by a stroke of good fortune, a shipwrecked Punic quinquereme (a vessel with five tiers of rowers) fell into Roman hands and was used as a model by Roman shipwrights.

The Romans modified the design by fitting their ships with a movable gangway which, at a suitable distance, could be lowered onto an enemy vessel. A spike, or corvus ("crowsbill"), at the head of the gangway secured it to the enemy vessel's deck, allowing Roman marines to storm across and put their superior hand-to-hand fighting skills into effect.

SOCIAL CONFLICT AND CIVIL WAR

The widening gulf between Rome's rich and poor eventually resulted in social conflict and political breakdown. One of the main problems was the plight of the Italians, who did not have the benefits of Roman citizenship, but had to carry the burdens. Many were evicted from their lands to make way for ex-soldiers or for the large estates of the nobles. In 133 B.C., a tribune of the people named Tiberius Gracchus proposed a land reform to redistribute among the poor the state-owned land that had been taken by the rich. This proposal was strongly opposed by those with vested interests, and Gracchus was murdered. Ten years later, his brother Gaius attempted to introduce wide-ranging popular reforms. He too was killed, and his death spelled a victory for the reactionary party.

Toward the end of the second century B.C., Rome was faced with military threats in several parts of the empire, including a revolt by the Italian allies. The incompetence of the ruling order in dealing with these crises was overcome only by permitting able and ambitious individuals to take control of the government and by creating a professional army from the proletariat by means of voluntary enlistment.

One such individual was an outstanding general named Gaius Marius, who became popular when, in Africa, he defeated the Numidians under their king Jugurtha after the Senate had failed in its conduct of the war. Marius held repeated consulships and defeated various tribes that were threatening the country. As consul, he carried out the reform that created the professional army. Although this solved Rome's military problem, it had dangerous political consequences, for it gave ambitious nobles the chance to gain power by armed force.

Two factions now dominated the politics of Rome: the *Populares*, or Popular Movement, whose leaders had the support of the Popular Assembly, and the *Optimates* ("the Best People"), the reactionary and aristocratic faction which sought to preserve the powers of the Senate against that of the Popular Assembly. It was the *Optimates* to which the general Lucius Cornelius Sulla belonged. He bitterly opposed Marius, the people's champion, and the result was civil war, with Sulla eventually emerging the winner. In 81 B.C., Sulla became dictator and tried to change the political system; however, his reforms did not long survive his retirement in 79.

But now a destructive political pattern had been set. Dominant individuals, helped by their supporters, struggled with each other for power and to maintain their prestige. Another problem during this turbulent period was that of the administration of Rome's many provinces. The institutions of a city-state were not well suited to government of an empire. The various attempts

THE ART OF FARMING

The basis of the Roman economy was farming. This was originally on a small scale with family units working on a few acres; later, however, many smallholdings were replaced by large estates with absentee owners, who used slaves to work them. The highest standard of ancient cultivation was reached on these efficiently run estates, whose main cash crops were grain, grapes and olives. Cato's work *De agricultura*, written in about 160 B.C., dealt with the running of an estate of this type. He considered that the most profitable crops and resources for a farm of 100 *iugera* (about 430 acres) were vines, vegetables for market, a willow plantation, an olive orchard, pasture land, arable land, then timber and thickets.

Cato and the scholar Varro, who wrote *De re rustica*, published in 37 B.C., produced their works as practical aids to farm-owners of their own class. Owning land gave social distinction that other ways of earning income did not; according to the orator and statesman Cicero, "Of all gainful occupations . . . nothing better becomes a well-bred man than agriculture."

This traditional attachment to the land was given expression in poetry, notably by Virgil, whose 2,000-line *Georgics* was completed in 29 B.C. The illustration (LEFT), from a fifth-century A.D. manuscript, accompanying the third of the four books, shows a stock bucolic scene with a shepherd playing his pipe while another, leaning on his staff, listens. The second book ends with lines praising the simplicity of rural life, as opposed to urban luxury and formality. Virgil recognized the hard existence of farmers, yet this was still the best way to live. He did not expect his educated readers to labor in the fields; but he hoped that in remembering this ancient Roman way of life, from which the city had grown great, Romans might set aside greed and ambition and see the virtues of hard work.

made to modify them were not successful and the standard of provincial administration deteriorated. Some governors were driven by a desire for power, and others plundered their provinces for private gain. The Greek cities of the east were a favorite destination of avaricious Romans. Caius Verres, the governor of Sicily from 73 to 71 B.C., was the most notorious.

During the 70s, Rome had to deal with a series of military crises. These included a conflict in Spain; a war against Mithridates of Pontus, a kingdom on the Black Sea; and a slave uprising under a Thracian gladiator named Spartacus. During this time, much of the Mediterranean came under the control of pirates, who even captured two high-ranking Roman officials. The pirates became so strong that it was difficult for Roman armies to sail between Italy and Greece. But those who suffered most were the Roman businessmen, whose trading activities virtually ceased, and the poor, whose corn supplies were scarce.

In 67 B.C., the Popular Assembly gave command to the general and statesman Pompey against the pirates, and within a few months he swept them out of the Mediterranean. In the following year, Pompey defeated Mithridates and settled matters in the east, where he reorganized the client-kingdoms and promoted the urbanization of Asia Minor. He also established Syria as a Roman province.

Pompey returned to Rome only to find that the other nobles were not prepared to accept his undoubted preeminence. The result was a compromise, and in 60 B.C., with Licinius Crassus, the richest man in Rome, and Julius Caesar, soon to rise to preeminence, an informal arrangement of power-sharing, known as the First Triumvirate, was established.

Marcus Porcius Cato, or Cato the Elder, shown here with his wife Portia, was an inveterate opponent of Hellenism whose name became a byword for austerity and high moral ideals. Born in 234 B.C., Cato fought in the Second Punic War and later became a censor in 184, in which position he passed laws taxing luxury.

THE INFLUENCE OF HELLENISM

Rome had long been exposed to Greek influences, at first indirectly through the Etruscans (pp.120–21), and later through contact with the Greek cities in the south of Italy. But it was with the Roman conquest of the Greek world that Hellenization made its impact on Rome. As the historians Livy and Polybius both noted, the Roman sack of Syracuse in 212 B.C. during the Second Punic War marked the beginning of the Romans' admiration of Greek art. Thereafter, culminating with the sack of Corinth in 146 B.C., countless works of Greek art were taken to Rome.

By the mid-first century B.C., the taste for interior decoration had become widespread, and the Hellenistic influence can be seen at the suburban villa of P. Fannius Sinistor at Boscoreale, a mural from which is shown (ABOVE). As Roman taste became more sophisticated and the sources of Greek art were gradually exhausted, Greek artists began working for Roman patrons. Although many earlier pieces were copied, a new Greco-Roman style of sculpture developed.

The contents of several great Hellenistic libraries came to Rome, and Greek influence on the development of Latin literature was immense. The Greek epic poem, the *Odyssey*, was translated into Latin, which was now used for poems and plays based on Greek works. Comedies in the style of the Greek comic playwright Menanader were written in Latin by Terence and Plautus. The first Roman histories were written in Greek, but after Ennius's historical epic about Rome, Latin became the language for Roman historians.

Cato the Elder, who wrote a history of Rome entitled *Origines*, as well as a work on agriculture, was critical of the influence of Hellenism on young men who aped Greek manners, had affairs with boys and courtesans, and gave extravagant banquets. Nevertheless, he recognized the value of certain Greek literary forms and was one of the first to use Greek techniques of oratory. Finally, it was the spread of Greek methods of education that made the deepest impression on Roman life.

Coins, such as this one, were issued to commemorate the murder of Julius Caesar on the Ides of March, 44 B.C. The coin shows two daggers and the pileus, a cap worn by freed slaves. It bears the legend EID MAR – the Ides of March.

Julius Caesar (c.100–44 B.C.), the great Roman soldier and statesman, became dictator of Rome in 48 B.C. and continued in this position until his assassination. He was a brilliant general and orator, but his antirepublican stance and autocratic behavior offended Roman traditionalists and led to his murder.

In 59 B.C., Julius Caesar became consul, and immediately legislation was introduced that furthered the ambitions of Pompey and Crassus, the other members of the triumvirate, as well as Caesar himself. The triumvirate was a formidable partnership, for it allied Pompey's popular appeal to the wealth and connections of Crassus and the political skills of Caesar. The alliance was renewed in 56 B.C. and lasted a total of six years, ending with the death of Crassus during a battle against the Parthians at Carrhae in 53.

Pompey's plans for reorganizing Rome's eastern territories were now confirmed and land was given to his veterans as well as destitute people, many of whom had suffered from the civil strife of previous years. A law that reduced the price that taxmen, or *publicani*, had to pay for lucrative contracts to collect taxes in Asia probably benefited Crassus financially. And Caesar gained a special command in Gaul (the greater part of modern France) for a period of five years.

Caesar took most of Gaul in three years. He twice crossed the Rhine and also made two expeditions to England. In 52, a revolt broke out in Gaul under Vercingetorix, but later that year, Caesar besieged and captured him at the fortress of Alesia in Burgundy. By 51, Gaul was completely subjugated.

The year before, Pompey was elected consul, without the usual colleague, to restore order to Rome, where anarchy reigned. The death of his wife Julia, who was also Caesar's daughter, had severed the bond between the two men. Also, Pompey began to fear Caesar, whose power had increased as a result of his Gallic victories and whose term in Gaul was nearing its end. As a result, Pompey formed an alliance with the *Optimates* – the reactionary faction that had formerly opposed him. The Senate tried to end Caesar's command, to stop him from passing directly into a second consulship, and in January 49, they formally gave Pompey the responsibility of defending the republic against Caesar.

Meanwhile, Caesar, with his legions, crossed the Rubicon River, knowing that by doing so he would be declaring his aggressive intentions. His forces proved irresistible, and Rome and Italy fell, with Pompey and part of the Senate fleeing to Greece. After taking Spain, Caesar crossed to Epirus, in northwestern Greece, and in 48, at Pharsalus, Caesar defeated Pompey, who escaped to Egypt, where he was murdered.

Shortly afterward, Caesar arrived at Alexandria. He made Cleopatra (pp.60–61) his mistress and installed her on the Egyptian throne. In Asia, he put down a revolt by Pharnaces of Pontus, crushing him at Zela. He then defeated the republicans in Africa and finally in Spain.

In 46, Caesar became dictator for ten years, a time span that was changed two years later to in perpetuity. He then set about implementing a vast program of reform: debts were reduced, veterans were settled in Italy and the provinces, the corn dole was regulated, Roman citizenship was extended, a new forum was built, and a remodeled calendar – which is still used in the west – was introduced. He ruled as king in all but name, wore a purple toga, placed his statue with those of the kings on the Capitol, and issued coins bearing his portrait. These and other actions caused grave offence to those who felt the republic was being destroyed; consequently, on the famous Ides of March (the 15th), 44 B.C., Caesar was murdered as a result of a senatorial conspiracy which was engineered by Cassius and Brutus.

Mithras *was an ancient Persian god of light and truth, the enemy of Ahriman, the force of evil. In Persian tradition, his titles included Warrior and Victorious — attributes that made him especially popular among Roman soldiers, who helped to spread Mithraism through the Roman world. In its Roman form, Mithraism was a "mystery" cult with secret rites for its initiates.*

Mithras was also a creative god, symbolized by the **tauroctony,** *the sacrifice of the bull (*LEFT*), whose blood was seen as the source of life. Mithraic temples were artificial caves, sometimes partly subterranean, and recalled the cave where Mithras caught and slew the mystic bull.*

This ancestral shrine, or lararium, *was discovered in the house of the Vetii at Pompeii. Roman homes usually contained shrines to the gods of the household, the Lares, Penates and Vesta. The Lares were the spirits of the ancestors and were bound up with the family's respect for its forebears. The Penates guarded the family larder, while the goddess Vesta tended the hearth.*

This shrine has been painted with representations of the household deities. In the middle is the genius, the spirit of the paterfamilias, *the father of the family, holding a libation bowl and a box of offerings. On either side are the Lares, each holding a drinking horn and ritual bucket. Below is a snake, about to take an offering. The* lararium *was normally in the atrium in the center of the house.*

THE RELIGION OF ROME

In the traditional religion of Rome, ritual was of great importance, for it established right relations with the gods. There were innumerable deities, and among the greatest were the Capitoline triad: Jupiter, a sky deity and king of the gods; Juno, his wife; and Minerva, goddess of wisdom. Mars, another major deity and the god of battle, was once a god of the fields, for the farmers of Rome were also its soldiers.

The family cult involved the propitiation of the gods of the household – Vesta (the hearth), the Lares (ancestral spirits) and Penates (the larder); it also formed the basis of the state cult, which was carried out on behalf of the people by the chief priests and magistrates. The priests were members of the aristocracy and were organized in colleges to conduct the rituals and arrange the festivals. These were agricultural to begin with, although new ones were added. The chief college of priests, that of the *pontifices,* took care of the records and accumulated lore; the augurs were responsible for divination; and the Vestal Virgins tended the hearth fires of the state.

The Romans also adopted the gods and cults of other people, particularly the Greeks, and sometimes identified local gods with their own. Abstract concepts, such as Victory or Fortune, were represented as gods and had also been adopted from the Greeks. One of the earliest foreign cults to come to Rome, in 204 B.C., was that of the Phrygian fertility goddess Cybele. But the orgiastic rites so shocked the Senate that for a time Romans were forbidden to take part in them. The cult of Mithras was popular with soldiers, and the worship of the Egyptian goddess Isis and the god Serapis also became widespread.

Since 60 B.C., the republic had been effectively dead, and the murder of Julius Caesar in 44 B.C. would not bring it back. The period immediately after Caesar's death was marked by confusion, then a power struggle and further civil war. Marcus Antonius, or Marc Antony, the surviving consul, reached an agreement with Cicero, leader of the conservative faction, and also with Brutus and Cassius, Caesar's murderers, who were allowed to leave Rome. Marc Antony, who had the support of the army in Italy, seemed to be gaining control in the country.

But with the publication of Caesar's will, a new factor emerged; for his heir was Gaius Octavius, his sister's grandson, whom he had adopted. The 19-year-old student returned from Greece to claim his inheritance. Cicero now attempted to use Octavius, or Octavian (he became Gaius Julius Caesar Octavianus), against Antony. But Octavian and Antony settled their differences, and with Lepidus, the Master of the Horse, they were legally appointed as a triumvirate for five years in 43 B.C.

This period began with a reign of terror, and 300 senators, including Cicero, received a death warrrant. Antony and Octavian then advanced to crush the only challenge to their power — Brutus and Cassius, who, after their defeat at the battle of Philippi in Greece in 42, committed suicide. Two years later, the triumvirate partitioned the empire among themselves, with Antony receiving the east, Octavian the west, and Lepidus the unimportant province of Africa.

Antony campaigned unsuccessfully against the Parthians, who were threatening Asia Minor and the Levant. Then, having sent his wife Octavia, the sister of Octavian, back to Rome, he married Cleopatra, who had been Caesar's mistress, in 36. He provocatively proclaimed Cleopatra's son Caesarion the legitimate heir of Julius Caesar, and apportioned parts of the eastern empire to the Egyptian queen and Caesarion, and to his children by her. Antony's behavior was too much for Octavian, and a war between them became inevitable. In 31, at the naval battle of Actium, Octavian defeated Antony and Cleopatra, who fled to Egypt and later committed suicide. Octavian was now sole ruler of the entire empire.

Octavian managed to retain the loyalty of his army and, for three years after Actium, establish a position of supreme power that did not offend republican sentiment. His great achievement was in finding a lasting solution to these conflicting requirements. Then, in 27, he surrendered his supremacy and formally restored government to the Senate and people. This act was reciprocated by special powers being granted him, and he was also bestowed with the name Augustus, an honorary title meaning "revered." Later he took other powers, but he made certain that they were voted to him. His authority was helped by his personal prestige, influence, wealth and political skills.

The new regime, which brought peace, prosperity and stability, was welcomed by the upper and middle classes and wealthy provincials. Augustus was hailed as a savior and benefactor, and formal cults of the emperor were established, becoming a focus for his subjects' loyalty. Augustus sought to restore traditions, including the Roman state religion, and festivals. His long reign also became a golden age of art and literature. Horace, Propertius and Virgil were the greatest of the Augustan poets, who all praised the new order. Ovid, however, whose erotic poems were disliked by Augustus, was banished.

The Colosseum, or Flavian Amphitheatre — it was called the Colosseum in the Middle Ages after a large statue of Nero which once stood near it — was begun by the Emperor Vespasian and dedicated by his son Titus in A.D. 80. This remarkable structure measured about 200 by 170 yards and could seat up to 50,000 people. Built of concrete and faced with stone, it had three arcaded storys that concealed a network of corridors (5). Seating was in the first three tiers, with the lowest section (2) reserved for the upper classes. To protect the spectators from the elements, a velarium, or canopy, was drawn across the top of the stadium by a team of sailors and supported on poles (1).

The arena (3) consisted of a wooden floor covered with sand — which is what the Latin word arena means — and could be flooded for displays of mock naval battles. Beneath it was a warren of rooms and cages (4) in which were kept wild animals and mechanical elevators that could raise specially designed props for the fighting.

The games began with a procession, with the combatants dressed in purple and gold riding in chariots into the arena. Before the fighting, the gladiators addressed the emperor with the words: "Ave Imperator, morituri te salutamus" — "Hail Emperor, we who are about to die salute you." The gladiators were usually prisoners of war, condemned criminals and slaves, and were divided into four categories, depending on their armor and weapons.

The fight was to the death, but an appeal could be made to the emperor for mercy. When a gladiator was dead or fatally wounded, an official dressed as Charon the ferryman — an underworld figure — hit him on the head with a wooden mallet.

Wild beasts, such as those shown in this Roman mosaic, added an exotic flavor to the games. Sometimes there were mock hunts in which the animals were killed by gladiators known as bestiarii. Events involving animals were known as munera and at one time had a religious significance. It is said that at the munera held by the Emperor Titus to celebrate the opening of the Colosseum, some 5,000 creatures were slaughtered in a single day.

SABATI S

During his reign, Augustus extended the frontiers of the empire: Galatia in Asia Minor became a province in 25 B.C. and Judaea in A.D. 6. In the north, the frontier was advanced to the Danube River and the Balkans were protected by a chain of provinces. The frontiers were now secure, and there was strong, stable and efficient government.

On August 19, A.D. 14, Augustus died peacefully, and the Senate decreed that he should be accepted among the gods of the state. Outside his mausoleum, bronze tablets inscribed with his *res gestae* ("things done") were set up. He was succeeded by his stepson Tiberius (A.D. 14–37), who was an able and experienced administrator. The provinces of Cappadocia and Commagene were established in Asia Minor, and the campaign against the German tribes was discontinued because of excessive

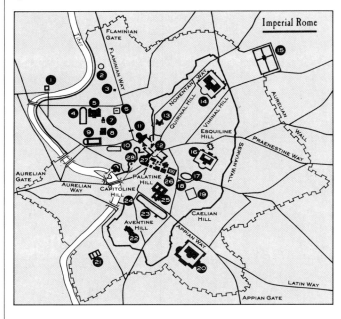

Since Etruscan times, Rome had gradually been beautified with temples and public buildings. The map shows the city as it was at the height of the empire. During the early imperial period, marble was widely used, and Augustus's claim that he had found a city of brick and left one of marble is at least partially true.

With the building of aqueducts, increased water supplies came to the city, and old Etruscan sewers were extended. The city contained a huge circus for racing, as well as the Colosseum, numerous statues and columns commemorating events, and a new Roman feature — the triumphal arch, erected to celebrate a victory.

Imperial Rome's monuments:

1 Tomb of Hadrian
2 Tomb of Augustus
3 Altar of Peace (Ara Pacis)
4 Stadium of Domitian
5 Baths of Nero
6 Temple of Hadrian
7 The Pantheon
8 Baths of Agrippa
9 Theater of Pompey
10 Circus Flaminius
11 Arch of Diocletian
12 Imperial forums
13 Baths of Constantine
14 Baths of Diocletian
15 Praetorian camp
16 Baths of Trajan
17 Colosseum
18 Arch of Constantine
19 Temple of Claudius
20 Baths of Caracalla
21 Granaries of Galba
22 Baths of Decius
23 Circus Maximus
24 Forum Boarium
25 Imperial Palace
26 Arch of Titus
27 Roman Forum
28 Temple of Jupiter

costs. His long reign was marred by conflicts with the Senate, treason trials and palace conspiracies. These resulted from the excessive confidence Tiberius had placed in Sejanus, the Prefect of the Praetorian Guard, which acted as the imperial bodyguard.

A remote and difficult man, Tiberius had done little to make himself popular, and his death in 37 was not greatly mourned. The reign of his successor Gaius Caesar (A.D. 37–41), known as Caligula, meaning Baby Boots, started well but degenerated into tyranny. He seems to have gone mad after a serious illness, and became cruel and capricious. He was eventually murdered by members of the Guard, who then installed Claudius (A.D. 41–54), Tiberius's nephew, on the throne.

Claudius, whose stammer, undignified appearance and scholarly interests made him a figure of fun, was in fact an effective emperor: during his reign, southern Britain was conquered in 47, a harbor was built at Ostia, Roman citizenship was extended, and he solved a number of other administrative problems. He was finally murdered by his scheming wife Agrippina, which thus enabled Nero (A.D. 54–68), Agrippina's son by a previous marriage, to come to power.

In the first years of Nero's reign, the empire was well ruled, but with the murders of his mother, wife and brother-in-law, and his shameless public appearances in the guise of a singer or charioteer, he lost the respect of most of the upper class. To make matters worse, there were revolts in Gaul, Spain, Palestine and north Africa. Finally, the Senate and the guard deserted him and, in 68, he killed himself.

With Nero's suicide, the Julio-Claudian dynasty was now extinct, and the legions were no longer held by dynastic loyalty. The following year, 68–69, was the year of the four emperors. First, Galba, the governor of Spain, was recognized as emperor. He was murdered by the Praetorian Guard, who backed Otho, the governor of Lusitania. Otho was defeated by Vitellius, backed by the Rhine legions, who in turn lost out to Vespasian (A.D. 69–79), who had the support of the legions in the east.

Vespasian restored the imperial finances, placed Italians and provincials in the depleted Senate, and founded more colonies for soldiers. Also, it was now seen that the emperor did not have to come from the Roman nobility. He was succeeded by his son Titus (79–81) and then by Domitian (81–96), the last of this dynasty. The new emperor's initially benign rule deteriorated into despotism, which eventually led to his murder in 96.

The Julio-Claudian dynasty — the four successors of the Emperor Augustus — were indirectly descended from Julius Caesar (of the Julia gens, or tribe) and the Claudia gens.

In A.D. 14, Augustus was succeeded by Tiberius, the most able of the dynasty. His efficiency was marred by the severity of the latter part of his reign. He spent much of his later years at Capri, but his supposed sexual appetite was a later literary invention.

Caligula was famous for his caprices and outbursts of cruelty, seemingly due to mental illness. He was followed by Claudius, whose much-derided personal habits and unfortunate appearance belied the effectiveness of his rule.

Nero, the last of the dynasty, was perhaps the most notorious. His reign was marked by systematic murders, and, according to rumor, it was Nero who started the great fire of 64, which he tried to blame on the Christians. After the fire, he built his famous Golden House, which overlooked a lake. It later became the site for the Colosseum. Before he committed suicide in 68, he is reported to have said: "Qualis artifex pereo" — "What an artist dies in me."

The Altar of Peace *(Ara Pacis) of Augustus symbolized the emperor's achievement as a peacemaker. Dedicated in 9 B.C., the altar is covered with reliefs showing aspects of the new age brought in by Augustus's reign. The sculptured relief includes a sacrificial procession and members of the imperial family.*

The Julio-Claudians

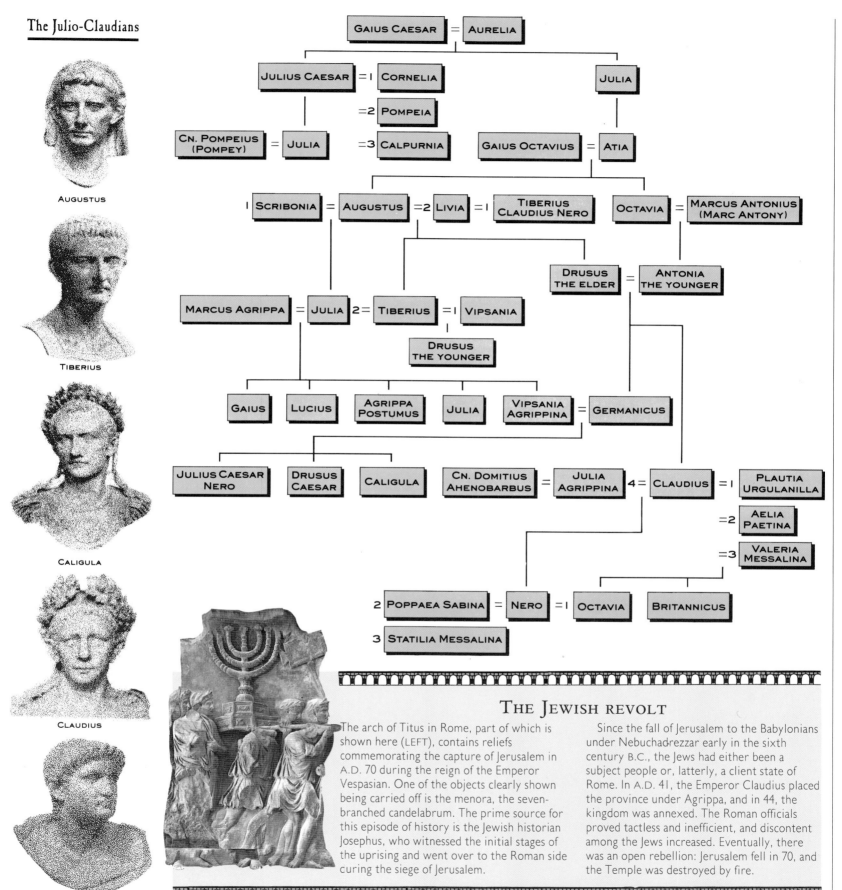

AUGUSTUS

TIBERIUS

CALIGULA

CLAUDIUS

NERO

THE JEWISH REVOLT

The arch of Titus in Rome, part of which is shown here (LEFT), contains reliefs commemorating the capture of Jerusalem in A.D. 70 during the reign of the Emperor Vespasian. One of the objects clearly shown being carried off is the menora, the seven-branched candelabrum. The prime source for this episode of history is the Jewish historian Josephus, who witnessed the initial stages of the uprising and went over to the Roman side during the siege of Jerusalem.

Since the fall of Jerusalem to the Babylonians under Nebuchadrezzar early in the sixth century B.C., the Jews had either been a subject people or, latterly, a client state of Rome. In A.D. 41, the Emperor Claudius placed the province under Agrippa, and in 44, the kingdom was annexed. The Roman officials proved tactless and inefficient, and discontent among the Jews increased. Eventually, there was an open rebellion: Jerusalem fell in 70, and the Temple was destroyed by fire.

After Domitian's death in A.D. 96, the Senate proclaimed the weak and ineffectual Nerva (96–98) the new emperor. The possibility of renewed civil war was averted only by Nerva's adopting as his successor the popular general Trajan (98–117), the commander of Upper Germany and its armies. Trajan came from Spain and was the first emperor to have a provincial background. Under him, the empire reached its greatest extent. He conquered Dacia (modern Romania) and established it as a province in 106. Roman occupation of Numidia was strengthened, and the vassal kingdom of the Nabataeans became the Roman province of Arabia, also in 106. And, after a campaign against the Parthians, he took Mesopotamia in 115, but in the next year, a revolt compelled him to install a client king.

The treasures won in the wars were used to finance public works and buildings. Measures were also taken to ameliorate the condition of the poor. The *alimenta*, an allowance for sustenance to poor children, was introduced, and free grain distribution continued. The provision by the emperors of "bread and circuses" in Rome was both a manifestation of civic munificence and a way of reducing social problems. However, the urban poor became so used to state food handouts and entertainment that to discontinue this largesse could fatally undermine the emperor.

In Rome, new baths and the splendid Forum of Trajan, designed by the architect Apollodorus of Damascus, were built. New roads and bridges were constructed both in Italy and abroad – such works being carried out by the army, which kept noncombatant legions occupied and so reduced any potential danger presented by an inactive professional army.

Trajan's firm and humane administration was also extended to the provinces. The governors were carefully chosen and administrators were put in charge of finance. He sent the experienced Pliny the Younger to Bithynia and Pontus to supervise the finances of the cities there. The official letters between Pliny and Trajan about various problems show the sensible judgment of both, and that the emperor personally directed the administration and was strict and just to all. This correspondence, in which Christians are mentioned by name, also illustrates the increasing imperial influence on municipal affairs.

Trajan managed to restore much of the lost prestige of the imperial office, and the title *Optimus Princeps*, Best of Emperors, was accorded him in 114. Not since the time of Augustus had the emperor been held in such high esteem. After his death in 117, Trajan was succeeded by Hadrian (117–138), a relative by marriage who, like his predecessor, came from Spain. Hadrian put down disruptions in Judaea, Egypt and Cyrenaica, and made peace with the Parthians. And, following a second Jewish revolt, this time led by Bar Kochba, he destroyed Jerusalem and in its place established a legionary camp.

Hadrian traveled ceaselessly through the empire, inspecting armies and reorganizing frontier defense. In the remotest reaches of Britain, Hadrian's Wall defined the northern frontier of the empire. Many of the legions were now recruited locally and were less mobile, and detachments, rather than whole legions, were usually sent to deal with crises. An intellectual and a connoisseur, with a deep love of Greek culture, Hadrian had a keen amateur interest in architecture. During his journeys through the empire, he erected several buildings, including a library at Athens. In Rome, he restored the temple of the Pantheon, the shrine of all the gods, and his mausoleum, now Castel San Angelo, still recalls his taste as patron of architecture.

Sunlight streams into the Pantheon's interior from an opening at the top of the dome.

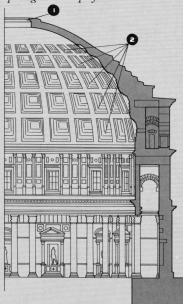

A TEMPLE FOR THE GODS

The Pantheon, "a shrine of all the gods," was initially built as a conventionally shaped temple – rectangular, surrounded by columns, with a gabled roof – by Marcus Agrippa in 27 B.C. However, it was totally restructured by the Emperor Hadrian in about A.D. 120. Its most striking feature is its magnificent dome, the largest in antiquity, which measures 142 feet in diameter and 71 feet from its top to its base.

The porch, with its grand row of Corinthian columns, is conventional in style, but the main building, which is lit by a circular opening (1), or oculus, at its peak, marks a radical departure in ancient architecture. Although the building's exterior is relatively austere, the interior is faced with colored marble, and its walls have seven recesses fronted by double columns. The inside of the dome, which, like the rest of the structure, was made of concrete, was envisioned as symbolizing the firmament, with the oculus representing the sun. The dome was coffered (2), or cut with indentations, probably in the early third century under the Emperor Severus, and decorated with bronze rosettes. Later, in 609, the temple was dedicated as a Christian church, which is what it remains today.

THE DESTRUCTION OF POMPEII

Situated on a small hill some five miles southeast of the volcanic Mount Vesuvius, Pompeii was totally destroyed in A.D. 79 by a massive eruption of the volcano. A description of the events is given by Pliny the Younger, who was visiting his uncle's home at the time. The site of the city, as well as that of the nearby town of Herculaneum, also destroyed, were forgotten by the time of the Middle Ages, but later rediscovered in 1748. Since then, there has been continuous excavation and about four-fifths of Pompeii has been uncovered.

The city lay at the mouth of the River Sarnus and was the gateway to Campania. According to the Greek historian Strabo, it was occupied successively by Oscans, Etruscans, Pelasgians, Samnites and Romans, although from about the mid-sixth century B.C., the main influences were Greek.

In the second century B.C., the main forum was made into a dignified civic center. Nearby were a gymnasium and a large open-air theater. The city was affluent, and increasing numbers of Hellenistic-style buildings, such as the public baths, were constructed. The cult of Isis was introduced, and the style of the houses clearly shows the strong Hellenistic influence, both in the wall paintings and in design, where a Greek peristyle – a series of columns – is often found added to the Roman atrium, or internal court. Unlike the wealthy who had beautifully decorated houses and gardens, the poor lived in their shops or in tiny apartments.

The numerous mosaics, often copies of great paintings such as that of the Battle of Issus between Darius III and Alexander, artifacts and paintings give a picture of the luxurious domestic lives of these people. The forum was also a flourishing industrial center, and cloth-making and fulling were major activities. There is also evidence that various crafts flourished, and many different shops (*tabernae*) opened directly onto the streets.

The ruins of Pompeii were so well preserved by the cocooning layers of volcanic ash and mud that from the air its street plan and structure (RIGHT) could almost be mistaken for those of a modern town. In the 17th century, the excavation of Pompeii caused great excitement in Europe, and the site became an important stop for travelers embarking on the European Grand Tour. And the city's buildings and brightly painted frescoes were a source of inspiration to architects, potters and artists, including the British painter John Martin (1789–1854) whose depiction of the eruption of Vesuvius is shown here (ABOVE). More recently, Pompeiian style and elegance can be seen in the architecture of the Paul Getty Museum (ABOVE RIGHT) in California.

THE ANTONINE AND SEVERAN EMPERORS

In 138, the Emperor Hadrian died of a wasting disease. His successor, Antoninus Pius (138–61), famed for his integrity, was not a military man and, by contrast with Hadrian and Trajan, seems never to have set foot out of Italy. His policy was mildly progressive, and although he was on good terms with the Senate, he conceded no new powers to them. For the last years of his reign, he ruled jointly with his nephew Marcus Aurelius. On his death, Antoninus was, by universal accord, deified, and the succession was peaceful.

Marcus Aurelius (161–80) ruled as joint emperor with his adoptive brother Lucius Verus until 169, when Verus died. From 177 until his death, Marcus ruled with son Commodus. One of the most admired emperors, Marcus Aurelius was a follower of Stoic philosophy – a doctrine that advocated austere self-sufficiency, but also humaneness – and his fame has rested partly on his contemplative work, the *Meditations*. In his reign, the tensions that were to affect the empire and change the structure of its government can first be seen. From now on, campaigns would be fought not for expansion but for defense against mounting pressure on the Danube frontier.

The death of Marcus in Vienna marked the end of a golden age. During this time, Roman citizenship had been extended in the provinces and the social base of the governing class had widened. Prosperity and a tradition of civic pride and public duty among wealthy provincial benefactors enhanced the cities, which were graced with numerous buildings and public works.

Commodus (180–92) hastily settled with the barbarians against whom his father had defended the boundaries. Whereas Marcus had had to contend with war throughout his reign, the morally dissolute Commodus preferred to control the tribes by treaties and subsidies from the safety of Rome.

The death of Commodus was followed by a period of civil war, until peace was restored by Septimius Severus (193–211), commander of the armies of Pannonia and a native of Leptis Magna in Africa. Severus campaigned against Parthia and annexed northern Mesopotamia, taking the Roman frontier to the Tigris River. During his reign, there were extensive building projects, particularly at Rome and his native city.

Severus died while he was in Britain, and his son Caracalla (211–17) succeeded him, killing his brother Geta in the following year. As his father had, he raised the soldiers' pay and conferred Roman citizenship on all the inhabitants of the empire. While on a campaign in Parthia, he was assassinated, and Macrinus, the Praetorian Prefect, was made the new emperor.

After Macrinus (217–18), conspiracy and murder brought to power Elagabalus (218–22) and then Alexander (222–35), Syrian relatives of Julia Domna, wife of Septimius Severus. Alexander was murdered by the army, and a new emperor, Gaius Julius Maximinus, was proclaimed. Alexander's murder had been prompted by his inability to meet the military crisis facing the empire, and the accession of Maximinus (235–38), a general, marks the beginning of a new phase of Roman history.

The early empire had brought prolonged peace to the Mediterranean world. Imperial officials and veterans had helped to romanize the west, particularly its upper classes. Up to the end of this period, the Roman world had seemed to be flourishing, but the death of Alexander, the last Severan emperor, was to be followed by 50 years of internal instability and foreign invasions.

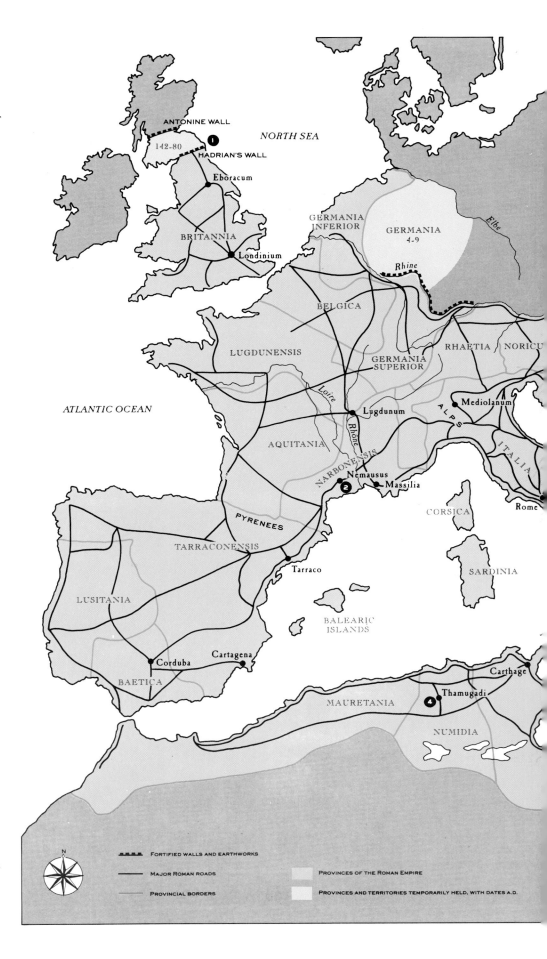

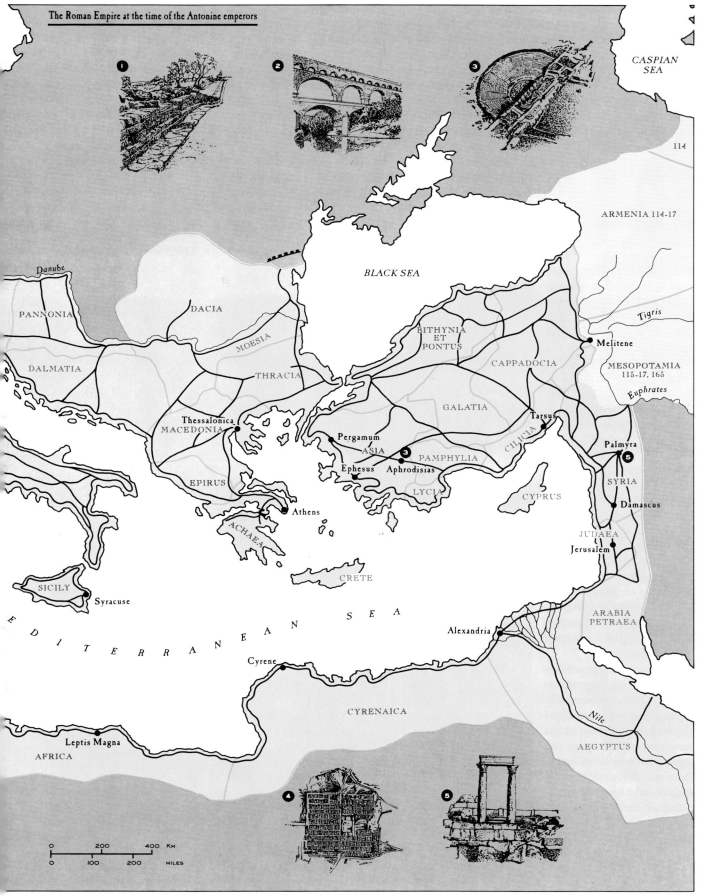

The Roman Empire at the time of the Antonine emperors

The Roman Empire *was at its most prosperous from about the early second to the late third centuries* A.D. *The north European and Mediterranean worlds were assimilated in one political system. At this time, a Roman citizen could make the long journey from Britain to Africa or the east along well-made roads and bridges, speaking Latin everywhere, and, in the east, Greek, and needing neither a passport nor different currencies.*

This map shows the provinces of the Roman Empire during this period, the major roads, and illustrations of five notable structures and towns.

*Hadrian's Wall (**1**), in England, was completed in* A.D. *126 as a bulwark against the Celtic tribes in the north. The wall was punctuated by turrets every 540 yards and by small forts, manned by patrols, every 1,620 yards.*

*At Nemausus (Nimes, France) stands a magnificent aqueduct (**2**) known as the Pont-du-Gard. Water was delivered to a central distribution point where ducts carried it off for various civic purposes.*

*At Thamugadi (Timgad, Algeria) (**4**) a veterans' colony was founded in* A.D. *100 and built on a strict grid plan, as this aerial view shows. It became a successful city with 14 public baths, a theater and a library.*

*Palmyra (**5**), in Syria, was an ancient trading city annexed by the Romans in about* A.D. *18. It maintained a measure of independence and had its own militia for policing the desert.*

*Aphrodisias (**3**), in present-day Turkey, was particularly favored by Roman emperors and was adorned with numerous statues and public buildings. It was also an important supplier of marble, and Aphrodisian sculptors are known to have worked in Rome.*

*This head of a gigantic
statue* of Constantine comes
from his basilica in Rome and
symbolizes the might and
strength of the sole ruler of the
Roman Empire. His military
and financial reforms and his
ability as an administrator made
him one of the best of the later
emperors.

During the disasters of the mid-third century, which
included civil war, economic breakdown and foreign
invasions, Rome's political system collapsed, and one emperor
after another succumbed to assassination or revolt by the army. In
the 50 years between the end of the Severan dynasty and the
accession of Diocletian in 284, some 20 emperors were proclaimed by armies in different regions of the empire.

Pressure from the German tribes beyond the Rhine and
Danube, already evident in the reign of Marcus Aurelius, now
became intense, as Gaul and Germany were ravaged by the
Alemanni and Franks. Here, as elsewhere, one of the problems
was the absence of client states on the border to act as buffers. On
the lower Danube, the Goths pressed hard on the Balkan
provinces and raided Greece and northern Turkey by sea.

In the east, the formerly weak Parthian state had now become
the domain of the powerful Sasanians (pp.76–77). The eastern
provinces were frequently attacked, and in 260 Syria was overrun and the Emperor Valerian taken captive. Constant wars
made increasing demands on the empire's finances. As a result,
the government depreciated the currency, which in turn led to
rampant inflation. By the 250s, the empire's money system had
broken down: payments to soldiers and officials were made in
kind, as indeed were taxes. The land was deserted, bandits took
over, and famines and epidemics reduced the population.

The tide began to turn with a series of military successes in the
270s. The economy recovered slightly, and under Diocletian
(284–305), political stability returned. He divided the empire
into two, taking charge of the east himself and choosing Maximian as his colleague in the west. Each emperor, known as

+SCS BALTHASSAR +SCS MELCHIOR +SCS GASPAR .

Augustus, took an assistant and designated successor, who had the title of Caesar. This tetrarchy (rule of four) was planned as a permanent institution, and when Diocletian and Maximian abdicated in 305, their Caesars, Constantius and Galerius, became Augusti in the west and east respectively.

However, Diocletian's system of succession soon failed, resulting in a power struggle and civil war. In 312, Constantine, the son of Constantius, emerged victorious in the west. In 324, he defeated Licinius, the eastern emperor, and reunited the empire under his sole rule, which lasted until his death in 337. His new capital Constantinople (modern Istanbul), the new Rome, was dedicated at the site of ancient Byzantium.

The empire and its finances were completely reorganized by Diocletian and Constantine. Diocletian reformed the tax system and introduced an annual budget. The provinces were divided into smaller units, and their governors no longer had any military command. The army was enlarged and divided into a permanent frontier force and a mobile field army stationed in fortified cities and ready for combat. In this way, order was restored; but the central government was oppressive and a huge, inefficient bureaucracy developed.

Since its beginnings in the early first century A.D., Christianity had spread. Although state persecution of the religion had intensified under Diocletian, in 313, Constantine issued an edict of toleration, marking the end of the hostility. Constantine himself was baptized on his deathbed and almost every subsequent emperor was nominally Christian. The new city of Constantinople was from the beginning a Christian center, and it was here that power now rested.

Personifying Rome and Constantinople, these two silver gilt furniture ornaments (FAR LEFT and RIGHT) are from the Esquiline Treasure, which was found on the Esquiline Hill in Rome in 1793.

On May 11, 330, the foundation of Constantinople was celebrated, and the city gradually gained preeminence, although Rome still remained important, with Constantine himself endowing it with fine buildings. These ornaments, dating from the first half of the fourth century, are in the form of Tyches, the female personification of fortune used in the classical world to symbolize the city. Rome is here shown as an embattled figure resting on her shield with a lance in one hand, while Constantinople (RIGHT) holds a cornucopia, symbol of plenty.

THE EARLY CHURCH

In about A.D. 28, Jesus of Nazareth, an itinerant Jewish teacher in Palestine, gathered about him a group of disciples who came to regard him as the long-awaited Messiah, who would usher in a period of peace and harmony on earth. Jesus was seen by the Romans as a potentially subversive leader and put to death. Jesus's passion, crucifixion, resurrection and the imminence of the Last Judgment were the earliest themes of Christianity (from *Christos*, the Greek for "Messiah," "Anointed One").

Originally limited to Judaea, the new faith spread when Paul the Apostle was converted and preached to non-Jews. Christianity spread rapidly around the Roman Empire for a number of reasons, not least because it was an actively proselytizing religion that excluded no one. Indeed, the earliest converts included many women and slaves. To the poor, the dispossessed and unprivileged groups, it offered hope of salvation, if not in this world, then in the next.

The instability of the empire in the mid-third century A.D. may have shaken the faith of many in the powers of Rome's gods and in the various local divinities. The bravery of Christian martyrs and the Christian ethic may also have given inspiration. Eventually, Constantine's various actions, such as the Edict of Toleration in 313, his material support to the Church and the founding of Constantinople, where pagan temples were conspicuously absent, marked the transition of Christianity to its future role as the established religion of Rome.

The fish, shown on this early epitaph, is said to have been a Christian symbol because the Greek for fish, ichthus, is an acrostic for Ieous Christos Theou Uios Soter — Jesus Christ, God's Son, Savior.

The Magi (LEFT) adorn a wall of the church of Sant' Apollinare Nuovo, Ravenna. The city became the imperial capital in the west during the fifth century.

Although Constantine had reversed Diocletian's division of the empire, it was from the Greek east and the Christian city of Constantinople that he ruled, a move that symbolized the declining importance of Rome and the growing separation of the eastern and western halves of the empire. The empire was solvent, and Constantine introduced a stable gold coinage, largely financed by temple treasures confiscated late in his reign.

After Constantine's death in 337, there were conflicts over the succession until Constantius, the late emperor's last surviving son, emerged as sole ruler. He was followed by his nephew Julian, known as the Apostate, who was a committed pagan. Julian does not seem to have understood the great changes that had occurred in Roman society since the time of Marcus Aurelius, whom he greatly admired. The very group upon whose support the empire depended, the cultured urban upper classes, had largely become Christian, and it was impossible for Julian to turn back the clock. Julian died in 363 while on campaign in Persia, and his successor, Jovian, made peace with the Sasanians, ceding much land. There was peace on the eastern front, but barbarian migrations to the north created problems elsewhere in the empire.

Attila (c.404–53), *King of the Huns.*

CODIFYING THE LAW

Soon after becoming emperor in A.D. 527, Justinian, shown (RIGHT) in a mosaic from Ravenna, began the reorganization and codification of Roman law, which is one of Rome's most impressive legacies to posterity. The earliest Roman code of laws was the Twelve Tables, drawn up by a special commission of ten men in 451–450 B.C. It contained rules from all areas of law, private and criminal, public and sacred. These tables were never abolished, but many of them became obsolete; some, however, remained operative until Justinian.

Prior to Justinian, in A.D. 429, the Emperor Theodosius II appointed a commission to codify all laws made since 312. This attempt to reform the law failed, but in 435 a second commission carried out the task, and in 438, the Theodosian Code was promulgated in both the western and eastern halves of the empire. The code contained general enactments from the time of Constantine.

Six months after his accession, Justinian ordered another commission to make a new compilation. Whereas Theodosius had made a compilation of imperial edicts, Justinian aimed to produce a new code, which made sure there was nothing incompatible with the teachings of Christianity. Justinian's code was ready within 14 months and came into force in April 529. A fuller edition which included the emperor's own laws appeared five years later.

In 530, a second commission, under the direction of a jurist named Tribonian, was appointed to codify the work of classical jurists. Known as the *Digest*, this was published in 533 as 50 books, with each book subdivided into titles. In the same year, the *Institutes* was published. Based on an earlier classical textbook and including Justinian's changes, the *Institutes* was intended to give an outline of legal institutions for law students. Justinian's last legal work, the *Novellae*, consisted of collections of new laws implemented by the emperor from 534 to 565. All these works, except for the *Novellae*, were written in Latin, which is still the language of law in the west.

The fourth and fifth centuries A.D. *were a period of turmoil. In about 370, the Huns arrived in southern Russia; in the next century Attila, shown on the coin (*LEFT*), became their king, but his advance into the empire was halted by defeat at the Campi Catalaunii.*

In 376, the Visigoths were admitted into the empire. Under Alaric, they moved west and sacked Rome. Later, they founded a kingdom in southern France. The Vandals, pushed aside by the Visigoths, moved first to Gaul then, in the early fifth century, to northern Africa.

The Ostrogoths, forced westward in the fifth century, founded a kingdom in Italy centered on Ravenna. In the same century, the Angles, Jutes and Saxons invaded Britain.

The destruction of the Ostrogothic kingdom in southern Russia by the Huns in about 375 pushed the Goths and various Germanic tribes westward to attack Gaul and Britain. However, they were resisted by the Emperor Valentinian (364–75), and the Rhine was restored as a frontier, as was Hadrian's Wall in Britain. In the east, Goths who had been granted permission to settle on imperial land got out of control as they crossed the Danube, compelling the Romans to face them in a battle in which Valens (375–78), the eastern emperor, died.

Under Theodosius I (379–95), the Goths were allowed to settle in the Balkans as federates under their own leaders. And similar agreements with other Germanic groups turned the armed attackers into "peaceful invaders" who increasingly helped to man the Roman army. Theodosius was a devoted Christian who suppressed pagan worship: ancient temples were closed, their properties confiscated and sacrifice was abolished. In 391, Christianity became the state religion.

In his final year, Theodosius was sole ruler; but on his death, the empire was partitioned between his young sons Arcadius (395–408) and Honorius (395–423), who reigned in the east and west respectively. From then on, the eastern empire followed its own course; and the western empire, with its capital at Ravenna after 404, although threatened by barbarians and ruled by weak emperors, existed for another 80 years.

At the beginning of the fifth century, the Visigoths under Alaric arrived in Italy and, in 410, captured and sacked Rome. During these years, the Rhine frontier collapsed, and Gaul was invaded by German tribes and then settled by Goths, although some moved on to Spain and Africa. In 407, there were revolts in Britain, and the province was formally renounced by Rome in 410. Meanwhile, the Huns moved into eastern Europe and invaded Thrace. Although repulsed, they later forced the eastern empire to pay them tribute in 430. Four years later, this was doubled at the demand of Attila, the new Hun king. Under Attila, the Huns attacked Gaul in 451 and, four years later, invaded Italy. But after negotiations, Attila withdrew.

There was now total disintegration in the west, and in August 476, the soldiers proclaimed the German Odoacer as their king, who then deposed the young emperor Romulus Augustus. With Romulus's deposition, the western empire ended. Few at the time had, it seems, noticed its passing, since barbarians had long manned the Roman armies, their generals had controlled the last western emperors, and Rome itself had ceased to be the imperial residence. The western empire had fallen because of barbarian pressure on the frontiers which built up during the third century and became too severe to withstand in the fifth. Although there were other factors, such as shortage of soldiers and excessive taxation, these were symptoms, not the cause.

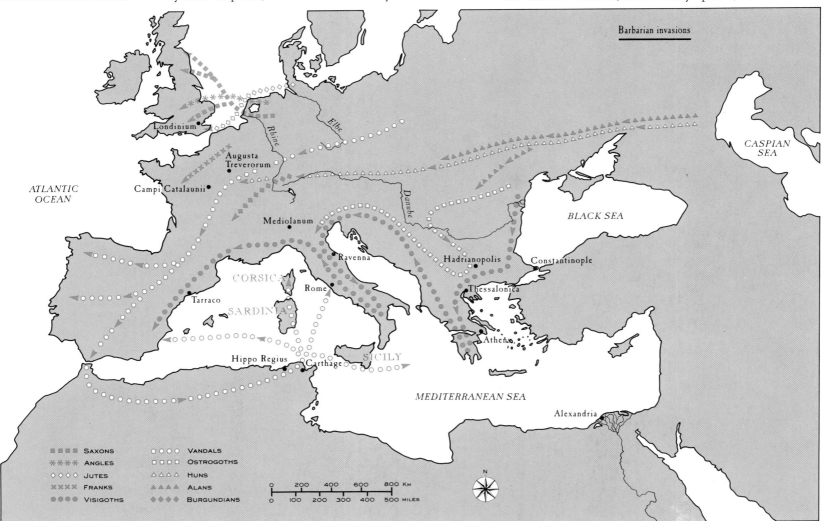

INDIA

"I have had banyan trees planted to give shade to man and beast; groves of mango trees I have had planted . . . ."

EDICT OF THE EMPEROR ASHOKA (*c.*272–232 B.C.)

This modern Indian temple dancer (BELOW RIGHT) *strikes the "seeing" pose of the Bharatanatyam style of dance. Dance formed part of the ancient Hindu temple ritual and has a long tradition within the religion. The figurine* (BELOW) *from the Indus Valley dates from 2300 to 1750 B.C. and is thought by some scholars to portray a female dancer.*

From the Himalayas to its southernmost tip, India is a land that encompasses desert, alpine pastures and tropical forest, and in which there is considerable ethnic, linguistic and cultural variety. The use of English as India's official language reflects the fact that its huge population is not homogenous. Similarly, the various regions, still in the process of becoming integrated, are a reminder of a time when many different social and political units existed side by side; for instance, the civilized empire of the Mauryans in the third century B.C. was contemporaneous with the Neolithic people of the south.

The historical map of ancient India is like an unfinished puzzle with gaps that have yet to be filled in. But although many details of the country's history may be missing, her past can still be seen in the present – far more than in most other areas of the world. For example, the daily prayers and rituals of the Hindus are a living reminder of forms that have lasted for some 4,000 years.

Throughout India's history, the northwest has been a gateway for numerous invaders. Although material evidence bears witness to the arrival of several of these newcomers, there is as yet no visible trace of the Aryans, who played so large a part in shaping India. Only a thousand years after their estimated arrival in 1500 B.C. is there evidence of settlement at places associated with legends written in Sanskrit, the language of the Aryans.

However, something of this uncharted millennium can be glimpsed in the great body of sacred literature known as Vedic which, though not strictly historical, does contain details that can be interpreted in the light of more recent scholarship. The legacy of the Aryans' literature and religion has survived every change that India has undergone, including domination by Islamic and Christian rulers.

In addition to being the home of Hinduism, India was also the birthplace of Buddhism, one of the world's great religions. Although Buddhism has virtually disappeared within India, it was one of the country's great bequests to central and southeastern Asia, where it is still extensively practiced. Indian merchants carried it abroad, and in the third century B.C., the Buddhist Mauryan emperor Ashoka sent his son to Sri Lanka to convert the king.

In fact, the very name of Ashoka, the greatest of India's ancient rulers, had been forgotten until it was recovered in the 19th century, when his inscriptions carved on rocks and pillars in Brahmi and Kharoshthi scripts were deciphered. (It is the image of one of Ashoka's pillar edicts that adorns the flag of the modern republic of India.) The decipherment was the work of the British scholar James Prinsep, who, while Assay Master of the Mint in Benares, became interested in India's antiquities. Subsequently he was Secretary of the Royal Asiatic Society of Bengal, an institution founded in 1784 by Sir William Jones, the person who first showed that Sanskrit was related to Latin and Greek. The contributions of the Asiatic Society and, later, the Archaeological Survey of India to the recovery of India's past have been immeasurable. Under the aegis of the latter, the civilization of the Indus Valley was discovered – the finds at Mohenjo-daro, Harappa and other sites revealed the world's largest known Bronze Age civilization.

Discovered at Mohenjo-daro in the Indus Valley, this steatite bust of a man dates from 2000 to 1750 B.C. His powerful features, carefully trimmed beard and trifoliate-patterned robe suggest that he might have been a person of some authority, possibly a priest.

Saffron-robed Buddhist monks congregate at the holy shrine of Bodh Gaya in northeastern India. It was here, in the latter part of the sixth century B.C., that the 35-year-old Siddhartha Gautama reached enlightenment, or Buddhahood. Seated under a fig tree (later known as the Bodhi, or Bo, tree — the Tree of Awakening), Gautama entered a state of profound meditation at the end of which he had achieved Nirvana, a blissful state of being, free from mortal desires.

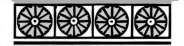

THE INDUS CIVILIZATION (I)

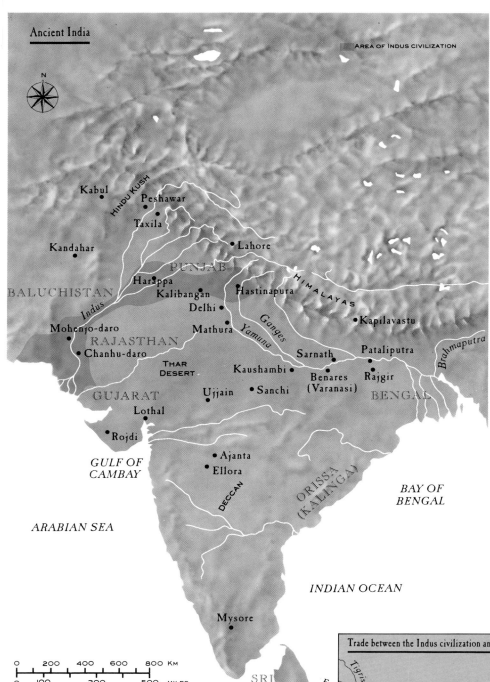

Ancient India

AREA OF INDUS CIVILIZATION

Kabul

HINDU KUSH

Peshawar

Taxila

Kandahar

Lahore

PUNJAB

Harappa

HIMALAYAS

BALUCHISTAN

Kalibangan

Hastinapura

Indus

Delhi

Kapilavastu

Mohenjo-daro

Mathura

Yamuna

Ganges

RAJASTHAN

Chanhu-daro

THAR

Sarnath

Pataliputra

Brahmaputra

DESERT

Kaushambi

Rajgir

Ujjain

Sanchi

Benares

(Varanasi)

BENGAL

GUJARAT

Lothal

Ajanta

Rojdi

Ellora

GULF OF

CAMBAY

DECCAN

ORISSA

(KALINGA)

BAY OF

BENGAL

ARABIAN SEA

INDIAN OCEAN

Mysore

0   200   400   600   800 KM

0   100   300   500 MILES

SRI

LANKA

Named after the great river system on which many of its towns and cities were centered, the Indus civilization (c.2500–1750 B.C.) extended over a region larger than either ancient Egypt or Mesopotamia. Known also as the Harappan civilization or culture, after one of the most important sites, it covered a roughly triangular area of about half a million square miles. Most of the 150 known sites of this Bronze Age culture are in present-day Pakistan. The two largest, Mohenjo-daro in Sind and Harappa in Punjab, appear to have been the main centers.

The Indus civilization remained unknown until the 1920s, when the first excavations were carried out at Mohenjo-daro and Harappa. In fact, the latter was first discovered in the 19th century, but its importance was not understood, and it was heavily plundered for ballast when the railroad to Lahore was being constructed. In 1931, another city was excavated at Chanhu-daro, closer to the mouth of the Indus. Since then, further sites have been uncovered, including Kalibangan in northern Rajasthan, Lothal and Rojdi in the Cambay area and Sutkagen Dor, once on the Makran coast. There has also been renewed excavation of Mohenjo-daro and Harappa.

This extensive urban civilization is thought to have developed from the earlier Neolithic cultures of Afghanistan and Baluchistan to the west. By 4000 B.C., their agriculture had become more diversified, and a network of towns and villages appeared in the areas bordering the Indus Valley, as well as a few in the flood plain. The subsequent increase in population prob-

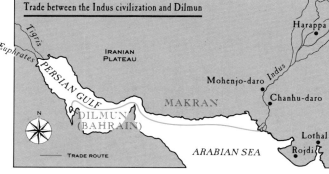

The civilization of ancient India spanned more than 3,000 years, from the Indus Valley culture (c.2500 B.C.) to the Gupta kings — the last great Indian dynasty, whose power ended in the sixth century A.D. The major sites of this period are shown on the map (ABOVE). India was protected on its western, eastern and southern flanks by water and in the north by the Himalayas. The most accessible passage for invaders was through mountain passes in the northwest.

Trade between the Indus civilization and Dilmun

Tigris

Euphrates

IRANIAN

PLATEAU

PERSIAN GULF

Harappa

Mohenjo-daro

Indus

Chanhu-daro

MAKRAN

DILMUN

(BAHRAIN)

Lothal

Rojdi

ARABIAN SEA

TRADE ROUTE

A modern Indian dhow, or trading vessel, unloads at the port of Bahrain in the Persian Gulf, continuing an ancient trading link (shown on the inset map) that is thought to have occurred at least 3,000 years ago. Bahrain, known as Dilmun in ancient times, had rich copper deposits and is mentioned in Mesopotamian texts of this period, as are Magan, thought to be the Makran coast, and Meluhha, probably the Indus area itself.

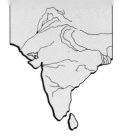

ably encouraged further settlement of the region, and by 3500 B.C., or earlier, there were several villages in the fertile alluvium.

Over the next thousand years, walled towns, specialized crafts and trading networks developed. By about 2500 B.C., this formative phase, known as the Early Indus period (also Early or pre-Harappan) culminated in the mature Indus civilization. It has been maintained in the past that this civilization appeared suddenly in its developed form, but more recently it has become clear that the material culture of the early phase represents an important element in its subsequent development.

At present, it is not possible to relate a history of the Indus people. Although a hieroglyphic script was used, it has not yet been deciphered. The inscriptions, which are beautifully en-graved – usually with animal motifs – on seals, are short, and it is unlikely that their decipherment would yield much historical information. Indus scribes probably wrote mostly on perishable material such as wood, which has long since decayed. Instead, material evidence comes from archaeology, and only the barest historical outline can be reconstructed.

Seals used for securing bales of merchandise have been found along with other Indus objects at Mesopotamian sites, which can be dated fairly accurately. Thus these finds have been able to provide some absolute dates for the Indus civilization. Also, they show evidence of trading links – although not necessarily of direct contact – between these two regions until about 1900 B.C., a date which corresponds to the decline of the Indus people.

One of the most notable features of the Indus civilization is its uniformity, all the more remarkable given the vast area it covered. Equally striking is the fact that throughout the several hundred years that the Indus cities were at their zenith, there appear to have been no great changes. Nothing is known of the social and political system, but the cultural unity displayed at all the sites suggests a rigid, authoritarian political system. The evidence, however, is ambiguous and open to other interpretations.

This engraved steatite seal from Mohenjo-daro depicts a Brahmani bull, a type recognizable from its neck folds and hump and held sacred in modern India. Thousands of similar seals have been found at Indus Valley sites. When the carving had been done, the seals were covered with an alkali solution and fired to produce a lustrous white finish.

Mohenjo-daro was one of the two great cities of the Indus civilization. The site, which began to be excavated in the 1920s, consists of two mounds. The higher of the two, shown here (BELOW), was the so-called citadel, which housed a number of public buildings and which later became the site for a Buddhist stupa.

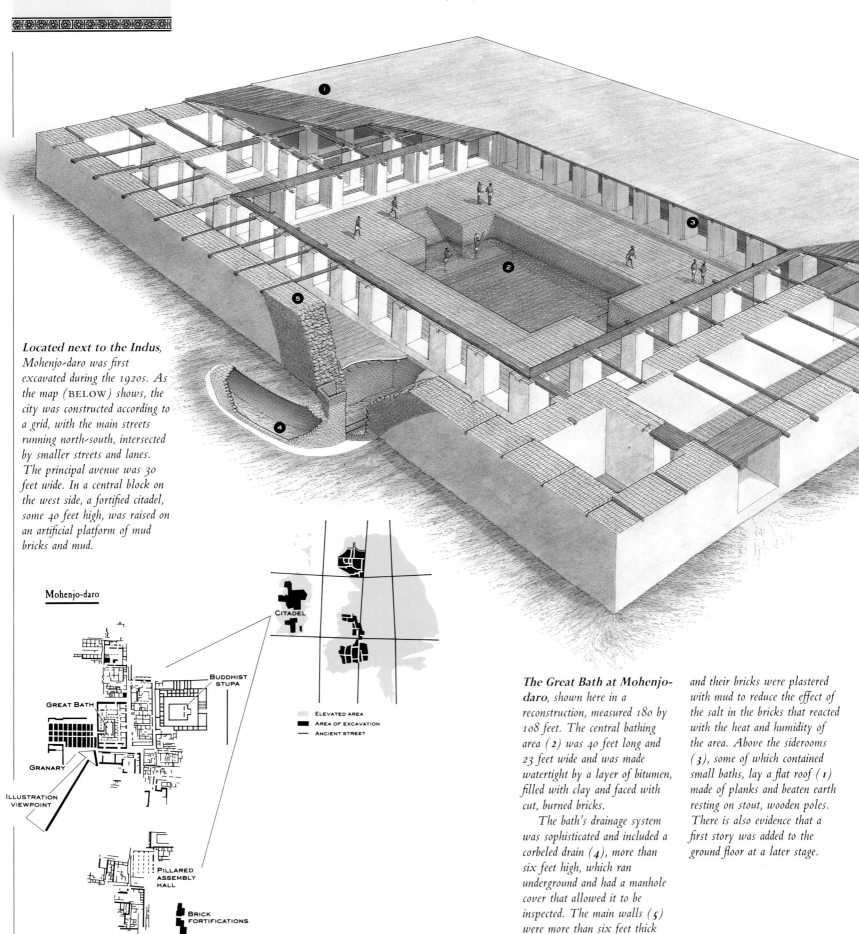

Located next to the Indus, Mohenjo-daro was first excavated during the 1920s. As the map (BELOW) shows, the city was constructed according to a grid, with the main streets running north-south, intersected by smaller streets and lanes. The principal avenue was 30 feet wide. In a central block on the west side, a fortified citadel, some 40 feet high, was raised on an artificial platform of mud bricks and mud.

Mohenjo-daro

BUDDHIST STUPA

GREAT BATH

GRANARY

ILLUSTRATION VIEWPOINT

PILLARED ASSEMBLY HALL

BRICK FORTIFICATIONS

CITADEL

ELEVATED AREA
AREA OF EXCAVATION
ANCIENT STREET

The Great Bath at Mohenjo-daro, shown here in a reconstruction, measured 180 by 108 feet. The central bathing area (2) was 40 feet long and 23 feet wide and was made watertight by a layer of bitumen, filled with clay and faced with cut, burned bricks.

The bath's drainage system was sophisticated and included a corbeled drain (4), more than six feet high, which ran underground and had a manhole cover that allowed it to be inspected. The main walls (5) were more than six feet thick and their bricks were plastered with mud to reduce the effect of the salt in the bricks that reacted with the heat and humidity of the area. Above the siderooms (3), some of which contained small baths, lay a flat roof (1) made of planks and beaten earth resting on stout, wooden poles. There is also evidence that a first story was added to the ground floor at a later stage.

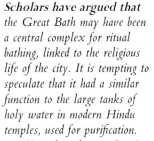

Of the many known Indus sites, Mohenjo-daro and Harappa suggest through their much greater size that they were perhaps capital cities. Both these centers, which each covered more than 245 acres, and the smaller towns, mostly about 25 acres in area, had a number of similar features which possibly indicate that they were carefully planned. They were laid out on a regular grid of straight streets intersected by small lanes. The size of the building bricks was identical, with baked brick being widely used; also, there were highly organized drainage systems. At Harappa, Mohenjo-daro and elsewhere, a high mound or citadel, usually situated to the west, looked over the lower town. And at Lothal, there is an interesting structure which is thought to have been a harbor.

Mohenjo-daro, the best known of the excavated sites, lies beside the Indus River. It was first examined in 1920 by R.D. Banerji, whose excavations two years later were continued under Sir John Marshall until 1931. In the 1950s, the site was re-examined by Sir Mortimer Wheeler. The city seems to have had a nearly square plan, divided into rectangular blocks.

There were a number of important buildings on the citadel. The names used for these structures were given to them by the excavators and were suggested by their appearance and possible function. On the west lay the Granary, the remains of which consist of solid blocks of brickwork divided by passages. This surviving podium originally supported a timber superstructure and the layout of the passages between the blocks meant that air could circulate beneath the building. Grain was probably brought here from the countryside for storage. It has been suggested that this grain was perhaps a form of state tax and that it was probably distributed as wages to government workers, but it

might simply have been stored centrally for convenience, perhaps as a reserve supply against the possibility of famine.

East of the Granary was the Great Bath, possibly used for ritual bathing. But the purpose of the other buildings on the citadel – the so-called college and the assembly hall – is not understood. In the lower town, several of the houses were spacious and well appointed, with bathrooms, toilets, proper drainage and water supplies from their own wells, and hearths for fires. The larger ones were built around a courtyard and had stairs up to a flat roof. The less wealthy lived in cramped conditions in houses with one or two rooms. Most buildings were of baked brick, and the streets had drains covered in brick, with holes for inspection.

Also in this part of town were workshops of many craftsmen. They included metalworkers, beadmakers, potters, masons and textile manufacturers. In fact, cotton cloth found here and at Lothal is the earliest evidence of cotton cultivation in the world. Many stone weights have been discovered, and it is clear that a standard system of weights and measures was used.

Sometime around 1700 B.C., the Indus civilization came to an end. Environmental changes were probably a contributing factor, since during the late Harappan period, there was a tectonic shift of the earth's plates along the coast of the Indus delta. This created long-lasting floods and accumulations of silt, and several cities that were once on the coast are now inland sites. Mohenjo-daro slowly became a city in a marshy lake, and there was constant rebuilding to raise the structures ever higher. There was a gradual deterioration in building standards and in the maintenance of the city. The decline of this culture probably occurred over a period of time rather than suddenly.

Scholars have argued that the Great Bath may have been a central complex for ritual bathing, linked to the religious life of the city. It is tempting to speculate that it had a similar function to the large tanks of holy water in modern Hindu temples, used for purification.

Water has always played an important part in religious rituals. In ancient Greece, pilgrims at the Delphi oracle had to purify themselves in the nearby Castalian spring before they were allowed to approach the oracle priestess. And water is used for ritual ablutions in Islam and for Christian baptism. In modern India, the waters of the Ganges are held sacred, especially at Benares (Varanasi) (RIGHT). Here, the water is held to be so holy that it can purify the soul, releasing it from the cycle of rebirth once and for all.

FROM THE ARYANS TO THE BUDDHA (I)

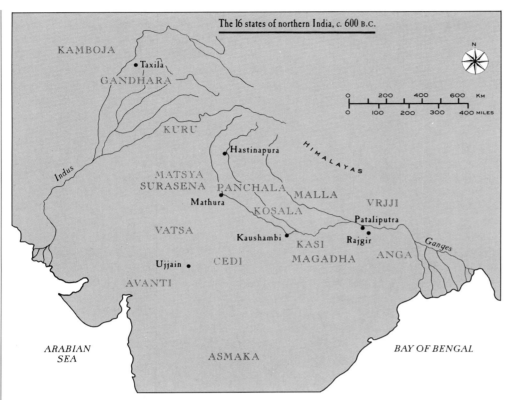

The 16 states of northern India, c. 600 B.C.

Sometime in the second millennium B.C., probably about 1500, a new group of people known as Aryans arrived in the northwest of India. Whether or not these people, who came through the passes of the Hindu Kush, were linked to the final demise of the Indus civilization is not known. Apart from archaeological evidence, of which there is very little, information about the millennium that followed the arrival of the Aryans comes from literature.

The earliest source is a collection of hymns known as the *Rig-Veda*, parts of which were composed before 1000 B.C. and which was passed down from generation to generation orally. The hymns are written in Sanskrit, the language of the Aryans and the basis of north Indian languages spoken today. The oldest known manuscript of the *Rig-Veda* was written in about the 15th century A.D., over 2,500 years after its estimated date of composition. Consequently, it is hazardous to reconstruct Aryan life from the *Rig-Veda* – although archaeological evidence, albeit scarce, and surviving traditions do seem to reflect some elements of the world depicted in the hymns.

The early Vedic literature – that which relates to the *Rig-Veda* and other early sacred writings – depicts the Aryans as warriors driving horse-drawn chariots, who subdued the dark-skinned *Dasas*, the pre-Aryan inhabitants. The Aryans had at first been nomadic pastoralists whose wealth was counted in cattle. It may be that the great economic value of the cow made it especially

Indra (RIGHT) *was the war god of the Aryans, who invaded India during the second millennium B.C. In the sacred Vedic hymns, he is depicted in heroic terms, riding a golden chariot drawn by two powerful horses — an image sometimes construed as a symbol of the sun. Indra's weapon is the thunderbolt, which he carries in his right hand and uses to destroy or revive those who have fallen in battle.*

Indra won his early ascendancy in the Hindu pantheon by slaying Vitra, the serpent of drought, who had swallowed the cosmic waters and lay in coils enveloping the mountains. Indra's thunderbolt split the serpent's stomach, releasing the waters, generating life, and liberating the dawn.

By about the fifth century B.C. Indra had fallen to the second rank of deities. He was demoted to a god of paradise, and his life-sustaining functions on earth were assumed by Vishnu.

THE ORIGINS OF CASTE

The word "caste," used to describe the system of social groups in modern India, comes from the Portuguese and was not used before the 16th century A.D. The Sanskrit word for caste, *varna*, used from Vedic times, means "color," and its usage probably reflects the formation of a new social group following the subjugation of the dark-skinned indigenous *Dasas* by the light-skinned Aryans. When the latter first came to India, they were divided into three social classes, the *kshatriyas* (warriors or aristocracy), the *brahmans* (priests), and the *vaishyas* (cultivators). There were no castes, but these divisions probably facilitated the social and economic organization of the tribes.

The treatment of the *Dasas*, perhaps stemming from the Aryans' fear of assimilation, was the first step taken in the direction of caste, a system of hierarchical ranking, based on religious rules of ritual purity. The *Dasas* and those of mixed Aryan and *Dasa* origin, and thus impure, became the lowest caste, the *shudras*. The subsequent elevation of the *brahmans* to the highest caste, above the *kshatriyas*, was linked to the emergence of divine kingship. According to the *brahmans*, only by their priestly authority could divinity be transmitted to the king. This change also gave religious sanction to caste, which became hereditary and increasingly rigid, with prohibitions forbidding contact between castes. With the formation of a wealthy merchant class, there was a further modification, as this group became the *vaishyas*. The cultivators, or ordinary people, were moved down to become the fourth caste of the *shudras*, which in turn relegated the former *shudras* to a casteless group known as the "untouchables."

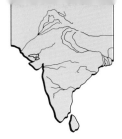

venerated and that this was the origin of its later sacred status. As pastoralists, the Aryans ate meat, but beef later became taboo except on specific occasions. The horse was also important, since it drew the chariots of warriors and gods.

For a time, cattle-rearing remained important, but gradually the Aryans adopted agriculture and settled in farming communities with the original inhabitants, whom they dominated. As they became settled farmers in villages, specialist craftsmen emerged, and as elsewhere, differences in land ownership and wealth arose. Then, with the formation of wealthier land-owning groups and the development of artisan and trading communities, towns began to emerge.

The centuries during which the Aryans expanded eastward, formed their petty kingdoms and fought between themselves are reflected in the epic poems the *Ramayana* and the *Mahabharata*, which were first written down in about 1300 A.D., but seem to be set between about 1000 and 700 B.C. By about 600 B.C., some 16 states (OPPOSITE PAGE) had emerged in northern India, from Gandhara in the northwest to Anga on the lower Ganges, and some of their cities, known from the epics, have been excavated.

These include Hastinapura, the starting place of the *Mahabharata*; Kaushambi, with its splendid palace partly roofed by stone vaults; and Rajgir, the capital of Magadha, later to emerge as the most powerful monarchy in the Ganges plain. In the late sixth century B.C., Gandhara became part of the Persian Empire and its capital Taxila became an intellectual center of both Vedic and Iranian learning. In time, the impact of Persian ideas was to be felt in various spheres of Indian life.

Between the arrival of the Aryans and the births of the great religious reformers, Mahavira the Jain and Gautama the Buddha in the sixth century B.C., immense changes had occurred in northern India. Society had become detribalized, states had been formed and certain religious and social institutions that have Aryan roots, such as Hinduism and the caste system, were firmly established. Sanskrit had become the language of the educated upper castes and remained so for many centuries. As iron technology spread, much of the land was cleared for large-scale agriculture, and rice was widely cultivated in the lower Ganges Valley. With the emergence of urban life, there came rapid social and economic change.

THE RELIGION OF NON-VIOLENCE

Jainism was founded in northeastern India by an ascetic named Vardhamana (c.540–468 B.C.), whose followers called him Mahavira ("Great Hero") and Jina ("Victor"), after which title they took their name *Jainas*. According to Jainism, the purpose of life is to purify the soul so that when it leaves the body, it achieves release from the endless cycle of birth and rebirth. Purity of soul can be gained by living a balanced life in accordance with Jain tenets. These are exemplified by the 24 great Jain saints, the *Tirthankaras* (Mahavira was the last), who achieved release of their souls by complete purification of their minds and bodies. Thus death by starvation is considered meritorious. Jains believe that the universe is a living organism and that everything in it, material or otherwise, has a soul. The concept of *ahimsa*, or non-violence, originates from this belief in the sacredness of all life, even that which is too small to be seen. Jain monks and nuns can be seen in India, wearing gauze masks over the mouth and nose to prevent them from inhaling living organisms; they also carry brushes to sweep any minute insects from their paths. Because of their aversion to the taking of any life, they are also strict vegetarians. This ascetic religion places great emphasis on frugality and personal austerity. Some Jains have regarded wearing clothes as a sign of worldly involvement and have remained naked. In Jain monasteries, this extreme degree of asceticism is still observed by some monks.

A devotee of Jainism makes his way using a broomstick to sweep his path clear of small creatures and wearing a mask to prevent him from swallowing insects. Because strict Jains take care not to destroy animal life, they have become established in trade and commerce rather than farming.

Statues of Jain saints adorn the 15th-century A.D. fortress of Gwalior near Agra in northern India. Jainism first took root in the Ganges Valley, the area where Mahavira first preached.

FROM THE ARYANS TO THE BUDDHA (2)

By the sixth century B.C., two forms of politically organized states had emerged from the earlier tribal system of the Aryans. In the republics, which were in effect oligarchies (rule by an elite), the ancient tribal tradition of a representative assembly and elected officials was retained. In the monarchies, the influence of the priests, or Brahmans, was immensely powerful, for their sacrifices and rituals were necessary to bestow divinity on the king. The mutual interdependence of king and priest had developed with the emergence of divine, hereditary kingship; and in these states the ancient Vedic traditions were strictly imposed by the Brahmans.

During this century, trade expanded – doubtless helped by the use of coinage, which spread from the Persian-held territories. It was probably by the same route that writing was reintroduced to India, for the Kharoshthi script, derived from Aramaic, was widely used in northern India, and in time other scripts evolved elsewhere. In the growing towns, the artisan class expanded and wealthy trading communities emerged. It was a period of social conflict in which the aspirations of the newly rising urban groups came into conflict with established orthodoxy. There had long been a tradition of revered sages and ascetics living contemplative, solitary lives. But now a wide variety of sects and philosophies emerged in response to those sections of society for whom the existing theology was no longer satisfactory.

Of all these sects, only Jainism and Buddhism, both of which drew on earlier reforming ideas, were to become independent religions. Their founders were contemporaries and of *kshatriya* origin. Each rejected caste and the Brahmans' emphasis on ritual, particularly the use of sacrifices as a means to salvation.

The religion founded by Gautama the Buddha (the Enlightened One) was to become one of the great world religions. Born in about 566 B.C., near the Himalayan foothills, Siddhartha Gautama lived the life of a rich young nobleman until he was about 29 years old. Becoming increasingly dissatisfied with his life of luxury, he left his family and spent six years as an ascetic. Rejecting this as a means to salvation, he embarked on a 49-day meditation and achieved enlightenment, or Buddhahood.

The Buddha preached his first sermon at Sarnath, where he gathered his first disciples. Into this sermon he compressed the essence of Buddhist teaching. It was a simple philosophy; *Nirvana*, or enlightenment, could be achieved by following a life of good conduct, known as the Middle Way. For the remaining 40 or so years of his life, he traveled the Ganges Valley, preaching to and converting people, regardless of their caste. He founded refuges and communities of monks and, occasionally, of nuns. The establishment of the monasteries accelerated education and made it available to people of all classes.

Buddhism spread rapidly, for the strength of its teaching lay in its humanity and the breadth of its appeal. It was not excessively ascetic, but it offered salvation to all who chose the path of good conduct. Since it did not directly challenge prevailing tradition, it was able to attract Brahmans to its fold, and, by rejecting caste, it appealed to the oppressed and those of low caste, although many followers were the Buddha's peers. Buddhism was to undergo many changes, both in India, where it later almost totally disappeared, and in the Asian countries to which it spread. Theravada, the earliest surviving form of Buddhism, is still predominant in Sri Lanka and Southeast Asia.

THE BEGINNING OF BUDDHISM

The founder of Buddhism, Siddhartha Gautama, who came to be known as the Buddha (the Enlightened One), was born into a prominent *kshatriya* family in about 566 B.C. There are various legendary stories about his early life, ranging from his wondrous birth to his princely rank. But given the family's status, his youthful life would have been that of a rich and well-born young nobleman; he was probably quite sheltered, for he grew up on an estate near the town of Kapilavastu in the Himalayan foothills. Accordingly, he was shocked and troubled, it is said, when, outside his home, he encountered the hardships afflicting the lives of ordinary people. So at the age of 29, he left

his young wife and child and set out to seek a solution to human suffering. He became an ascetic, but after six years, he realized that this would not solve the problem of understanding suffering. He then began a long meditation, traditionally beneath a tree that became known as the Bodhi, or Bo, tree, and reached enlightenment and an understanding of the causes of suffering in this world. Now, as the Buddha, he preached his first sermon, called the Turning of the Wheel of the Law, near the town of Benares and gave a lucid exposition of his teaching, which required no grasp of complex metaphysical thought for it to be understood.

The nucleus of the Buddha's teaching was the Four Noble Truths, which state that: existence is suffering; the cause of suffering is human desire; by overcoming desire, there is an end to suffering, a state known as *Nirvana*, or total extinction; and *Nirvana* can be attained through following the Eight-Fold Path. This consists of eight principles: right views, resolves, speech, conduct, effort, livelihood, recollection and meditation, which, combined, are described as the Middle Way. *Nirvana* brings freedom from the endless cycle of birth, death and rebirth. Only those who attain this state can transcend *karma*, a natural law of moral cause and effect, according to which all actions determine later destiny, so man's state in this life results from actions in past incarnations. A development of the idea of the

The mural of the Buddha (BELOW LEFT) *from Ajanta dates from the second century B.C. and is one of the earliest surviving works of Indian art.*

The stupa at Sarnath (BELOW) *near Benares marks the site of the Buddha's first sermon. Stupas contain relics of the Buddha and Buddhist saints.*

A Tibetan Buddhist (RIGHT) *uses a prayer wheel to make his devotions. Buddhism is now more popular in Tibet and other parts of Asia than in India.*

transmigration of souls, *karma* also has roots in Aryan traditions, in which life after death was envisaged in terms of punishment or reward for conduct during life. The Buddha rejected the Brahmans' insistence on ritual, and in the early pure form of the religion, it was almost entirely eliminated. Buddhism spread widely in Asia after it was adopted by the Mauryan emperor Ashoka (pp.156–57), who encouraged missionaries to spread the faith. It has undergone many changes from its earlier, more austere form, where the ideal was the *arhat*, or perfected saint, purified of all desires. Eventually two main forms of Buddhism emerged. In Mahayana Buddhism, the central concept is the innate Buddahood of all people, and the ideal being is the *bodhisattva*, the perfected one who postpones entry into *Nirvana* to help others become enlightened. The Theravada sect is the earlier, more pure form of Buddhism and was taken to Sri Lanka by one of Ashoka's sons.

THE MAURYAN EMPIRE

By the late fourth century B.C., the kingdom of Magadha was the most powerful north Indian state and controlled much of the Ganges basin. It was ruled by a king of the Nanda dynasty from their capital Pataliputra (modern Patna). Little is known of the Nandas, who had usurped the throne earlier in the century and who, according to a later source, were hated by their subjects.

The rise of Magadha had begun during the reign of Bimbisara, a contemporary of the Buddha, and continued under his son, Ajatashatru (*c.*493–461 B.C.). The conquest of territories to the southeast, north and west brought economic benefits to Magadha, which now controlled the routes to the seaports of the Ganges delta and those to the south. Magadha's power and efficiency were based on a centralized bureaucracy, a standing army paid out of taxation and a network of roads.

Meanwhile, northwest of the Ganges region, in modern Pakistan, there were several small kingdoms and tribal republics, as well as the Persian satrapies of Gandhara and Hindush (Sind). Alexander the Great entered India in 327 B.C. and temporarily occupied the Punjab and Sind. On his return to Babylon, Alexander left governors and a few garrisons in the conquered provinces, but in the years of strife that followed his death in 323 B.C., the Greeks departed.

Then, sometime between 324 and 317 B.C., a young adventurer named Chandragupta Maurya defeated the last king of the

Nandas and gained the throne of Magadha. He then moved northwest to exploit the power vacuum created by Alexander's departure, conquered the territories up to the Indus and advanced to central India. Subsequently he returned to the northwest and in 302 B.C. defeated the Seleucid king (pp.116–17) Seleucus Nicator, and as a result gained eastern Afghanistan.

Chandragupta's empire now reached from Kandahar in the west to the mouth of the Ganges in the east. Despite the conflict with the Seleucids, relations between them and the Mauryans

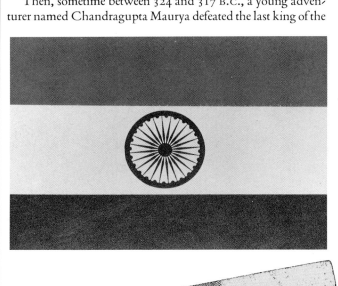

The lion-headed capital (RIGHT) *comes from one of the edict pillars of the emperor Ashoka. These polished stone columns, more than 50 feet high, were inscribed with proclamations of Ashoka's policies and put up at places associated with the Buddha's life. There is a well-preserved standing column in the state of Bihar, but the finest of the capitals is this one from Sarnath. On a fluted bell, resembling an inverted lotus, are carved four spoked wheels and four royal animals, surmounted by four lions — all of which are non-figurative representations of the Buddha.*

*The Sarnath capital has been chosen as the emblem for the modern state of India and appears on currency (*BELOW LEFT*). And the wheel, which derives from the idea of the wheel of* dharma, *or the universal law, forms part of India's flag (*LEFT*).*

were friendly, and there was a regular exchange of envoys and gifts. Seleucus's ambassador Megasthenes lived at Pataliputra (the site of the modern city of Patna) for many years and left a description of the city with its timber-built houses and great palace surrounded by extensive city walls.

Toward the end of his life, Chandragupta is said to have converted to Jainism and abdicated, before ending his life in the traditional Jain way – by deliberate starvation. His son Bindisura (c.297–272 B.C.) extended Mauryan control as far south as Mysore. Following his death, there was a dynastic dispute, and the throne was seized by his son Ashoka, reputedly a tyrant at the outset of his reign.

Eight years after his accession, Ashoka campaigned in Kalinga (Orissa), where, in his own words, "a hundred and fifty thousand people were deported, a hundred thousand were killed, and many times that number perished. . . ." Filled with remorse, he went through a spiritual crisis and became a convert to Buddhism. This eventually led him to forswear war.

Buddhism did not become a state religion, but because of Ashoka's support, the movement grew rapidly. The emperor sent missionaries abroad to the Hellenistic rulers, urging them to abandon aggression, and to Sri Lanka, where he also sent his son Mahinda, and possibly to Nepal. Many stupas, sacred dome-shaped structures containing relics of the Buddha or a saint, were set up, including the inner core of the Great Stupa at Sanchi. Ashoka's policies did not survive him, and on his death in about 232 B.C., the great empire began to disintegrate.

INDIA REDISCOVERED

Unlike some civilizations that have now vanished, India's ancient culture has never been totally lost. What is missing is accurate information about her early history. Although an extensive literature was passed down orally and to some extent in written form, any historical facts that it contains are obscured by accretions of legend and fantasy. From the 16th century A.D., however, European missionaries and merchants visiting India became interested in her languages and customs.

In the 17th century, a French physician named François Bernier took to Europe a Persian copy of a sacred text known as the *Upanishads*, whose translation provided a stimulus for Indian studies. Also, several officials of the British East India Company contributed to this recovery of India's history, which began in earnest with the founding of the Asiatic Society of Bengal in 1784.

More than 50 years later, in 1837, James Prinsep, secretary of the society, deciphered Ashoka's inscriptions written in Bramhi. Later, other inscriptions by Ashoka were found in the northwest and reveal the extent of his power. Since then, the study of Indian texts and coins and other sources has helped to map out India's history.

Discovered by a British army officer named Colonel James Tod in 1822, the Rock of Girnar in the province of Gujarat in western India was inscribed with one of the longest of Ashoka's inscriptions. It was later used by James Prinsep, Secretary of the Asiatic Society of Bengal, to decipher Ashoka's script.

After the emperor Ashoka's death in about 232 B.C., the provinces of his empire soon broke away. In 185 B.C., the last Mauryan emperor was killed by one of his Brahman generals, who became the first ruler of the Shunga dynasty. During the 112-year rule over what was effectively the earlier state of Magadha, Buddhism ceased to be the imperial religion, and there was a Brahman revival.

During the reign of Ashoka, two new powers had appeared in the northwest, having revolted against their Seleucid overlords. In Iran, the Parthians (pp.76–77) took control in the east. And Bactria, the Greek colony founded by Alexander, became independent under its governor Diodotus. With the decline of the Mauryans, the Bactrian Greeks crossed the Hindu Kush in about 200 B.C. and established themselves in the Kabul Valley and the Punjab. In this extensive region, they split into a number of small kingdoms.

The best known of the Indo-Greek rulers was Menander (c.155–130 B.C.), who ruled extensive domains reaching from Afghanistan through the northwest frontier region to Lahore. His fame, under the name of Milinda, has been preserved in a Buddhist text which relates his conversion to Buddhism. He

INDIAN ELEPHANTS

The elephant has played a prominent part in Indian society since the earliest times. Images of the animal have been found on seals of the Indus civilization, and several hundred years later, they were being used in warfare. These potentially terrifying beasts were encountered by Alexander the Great during his Indian campaign and thereafter played an important part in the wars of his Successors (pp.116–17).

In the Hindu religion, reverence for elephants is thought to promote rainfall and an abundance of crops. Also, the elephant-headed god Ganesha (ABOVE) is believed to remove obstacles to success and dispense wisdom. He is propitiated at the beginning of any important enterprise or business transaction. Ganesha is usually represented as a short, yellow, pot-bellied man. He has four hands and an elephant's head, and is sometimes shown riding on a rat, or attended by one. Ganesha is the son of Parvati and Shiva, and acts as the guardian at the gate of his mother's house. He is the counterpart of the Greek god Hermes and the Roman deity Mercury.

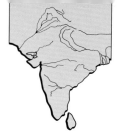

attempted to conquer the Ganges Valley, but according to tradition, he was recalled because of a Scythian threat in the rear of his forces and died in battle.

Divided into small kingdoms, the Indo-Greeks slowly gave way to the Sakas, formerly central Asian nomads, known also as Scythians (pp.86–87). Around 90 B.C., Gandhara and its capital Taxila fell to the Sakas; and by 40 to 30 B.C., the remaining Indo-Greek kingdoms had been overrun. Beyond the Punjab, the Sakas occupied the Indus Valley and Gujarat and advanced to Mathura and to Ujjain, where they established a prosperous kingdom that would remain in existence until the end of the fourth century A.D. In the first century A.D., Gandhara came under control of the Eastern Parthians.

The Sakas had earlier been driven south from Bactria by the nomadic Yueh-chih, who had themselves been pushed westward from China's border. In the first century B.C., one of the Yueh-chih tribes, the Kushans, conquered the other four and consolidated them into a single people. From Bactria they advanced to Gandhara, probably early in the first century A.D., and then moved into the Punjab. The Kushan chronology is uncertain, but the accession of Kanishka, their third and greatest king, is generally placed somewhere between A.D. 78 and 144.

Kanishka's realm extended from west of Kabul, south to Sanchi and east to Benares (Varanasi). His capital was Peshawar near the Khyber Pass, and Mathura to the south seems to have been another. Kushan wealth came from control of the trade routes crossing their territory, including the Silk Route from China. Forming a bridge between east and west, the Kushans were contemporary with the Roman Empire at the height of its wealth, when its demand for spices, ivory and other luxuries was great. Apart from the land routes, trade also crossed the Indian Ocean, thus creating wealth in western India, as reflected by the Buddhist monuments at Sanchi and at other sites in the area.

Kanishka was remembered by followers of Mahayana (Great Vehicle) Buddhism as a great patron. This less austere form of Buddhism advanced farther in India and was introduced, through Kushan territory, into northern Asia and China. After Kanishka died, the Kushans lost the Ganges Valley. The Sakas of Gujarat and Ujjain became independent and, with the rise of the Sasanians (pp.76–77) in Iran, the Kushans of the Punjab and Afghanistan became Persian vassals.

THE ART OF THE INDO-GREEKS

At Gandhara and Mathura, the first human images of the Buddha, such as the bust (LEFT) from Gandhara, were made for Buddhist chapels, shrines and monasteries. These sculptures came about as a response to the liberal doctrine of the Mahayana form of Buddhism, which permitted the representation of images. Until the time of the Kushan king Kanishka, in whose reign the rules of Mahayana were established, the Buddha had been shown in symbolic form, for example as a wheel or empty throne. Because Mahayana Buddhism could accommodate saints and gods, there were, in addition to the carvings of the Buddha image, reliefs about his life which often included depictions of the saintly *bodhisattvas*.

The Buddha is usually portrayed as an anthropomorphic deity with particular attributes. The *ushnishna*, or bump on the head, may have originated in Gandhara from the topknot worn beneath a turban. He is usually shown sitting in the cross-legged lotus position, often with his right hand raised, palm outward, although there are variants and later developments. There has been much debate on the stylistic origins of these sculptures, because they display certain western classical elements – largely of dress, the portrayal of the attendant figures and the architectural features. Also, jewelry, such as the bracelet and necklace (RIGHT) discovered at Taxila, the capital of Gandhara, shows a similar mixture of western and Indian styles.

It was first thought that the origins of this hybrid art could be traced to the Bactrian Greeks; but later scholarship has indicated that objects in this style date from the time of the Kushans, who were in regular touch with the Roman world and from whom such influences would have been received. However, the discovery of a Greek Bactrian city at Ai Khanum in what is now Afghanistan in the 1960s has finally proved the existence of Greco-Bactrian art and thus the possibility of such an influence on northwestern India.

THE GUPTAS

THE HINDU RELIGION

The religion of the majority of Indians, Hinduism originated from a synthesis of Aryan religion and that of the indigenous people in regions of Aryan expansion. Later it evolved in conjunction with local cults and beliefs. It is difficult to separate social and religious aspects of Hindu life, for closely bound up with Hindu belief and practice is the caste system (pp.152–53). Hindus accept the ancient Vedic literature, which includes prayers, hymns, magic spells and mystical writings, as their sacred scriptures. The authority of the priests, or Brahmans, in ritual and interpretation is still considerable. Like the Buddhists and Jains, Hindus believe in the continuous cycle of birth, death and rebirth, and the ultimate objective is liberation from rebirth and suffering. Hinduism is polytheistic, with a hierarchy of universal major and minor gods, as well as many local gods, spirits and demons. Some have similar attributes, and certain gods are worshipped in various manifestations. The major gods are Brahma, the creator; Vishnu, the preserver, who has ten avatars, or manifestations; and Shiva, the destroyer. Shiva personifies the forces of destruction, and in this aspect he is said to haunt cemeteries, wearing serpents around his head and skulls around his neck. He is attended by a host of demons, terrifying in their lust for power. Other gods include Rama and Krishna, the flute-playing cowherd, both avatars of Vishnu.

The Hindu god Vishnu, shown here in a sculpture from the Gupta period, has risen to an almost supreme position in the Hindu pantheon. The root of his name, vish, means "to pervade," and he is regarded as a presence that permeates everything. He is believed to have had ten chief incarnations, or descents (avatara) in this world, in a variety of forms. An avatar is said to appear whenever there is an urgent need to counter some great evil influence in the world. The avatars of Vishnu include Matsya the fish, Kurma the turtle, Naramsimha the man-lion, Varaha the boar, Vamana the dwarf and the Buddha.

During the fourth century A.D., the formerly obscure Gupta dynasty, based in Magadha, grew in power and importance until it dominated all of north central India. This expansion began under Chandra Gupta I (c.A.D. 320–335), who extended his control to the borders of Bengal. His son Samudra Gupta (c.335–376) made further conquests; and under Chandra Gupta II (376–414), who defeated the Sakas of Ujjain, Gupta rule reached its greatest extent, with hegemony across the whole of northern India from the Arabian Sea to the Bay of Bengal.

In emulation of the ancient Mauryans, the Guptas established their capital at Pataliputra. They also used the old Mauryan administration as a model, provided essential public works and regulated trade. But there was considerable local control over administration and even policy, so the Gupta system of government was not strictly imperial. Although they themselves practiced Hinduism, the Guptas were tolerant in religious matters, and many of their advisers were Buddhists. The Gupta kings, who married into pre-Aryan families and employed foreign women in their households, ignored caste. In such a climate, the various religions and their sects coexisted, and it was a time of scholarly discussion and debate.

The Gupta period was remarkable for its cultural activity. Kalidasa, one of the greatest Indian poets and dramatists, is said to have been the court poet of Chandra Gupta II. Kalidasa's poetry was admired by Goethe, and his play *Shakuntala*, drawn from the *Mahabharata* epic, was translated into English by William Jones, the great Sanskrit scholar, in 1789. It was also during this time that the *Mahabharata* and the other great epic, the *Ramayana*, attained their definitive Sanskrit form.

The classical period of Indian art also belongs to the Gupta period. Gupta sculpture seems to have developed from Kushan art, which had survived at Mathura despite the upheavals of the third century. Not only sculpted stone, but also the quality of Gupta bronze and copper casting was exceptional and is well illustrated by a remarkable bronze Buddha that is over seven and a half feet high. It was during this time that some of the earliest surviving examples of Indian painting were created, on the walls of the Buddhist caves at Ajanta.

The peace and prosperity that fostered such work continued under Kumara Gupta (c.A.D. 414–454), but toward the end of his life, there were attacks from the Hunas, or White Huns, known in the Byzantine world as Hepthalites. These Asian nomads had occupied Bactria in the late fourth century and had then gained control of Afghanistan and the Punjab, before advancing into Gupta territory. Skanda Gupta (454–467) was able to expel the Huns, but after his death there were dynastic disputes, followed by the reign of Budha Gupta (c.475–495).

Already the Gupta provincial governors had begun to take royal titles as vassal kings of the dynasty. By 500, when the Huns attacked again, the Gupta dynasty effectively controlled only the area that had once been the kingdom of Chandra Gupta I. Although the Huns were eventually driven out, there were now many local kings who did not give their allegiance to the Guptas. Some were descended from Gupta officials, and others were from the ruling families of earlier small kingdoms; but whatever their origins, they carved out little territories for themselves. The end of the Guptas meant the last of the great Indian rulers of large states, for no later king matched their achievement.

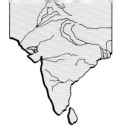

BUDDHISM ABROAD

The decline of Buddhism in India, the country of its origin, was evident to Chinese visitors of the seventh century A.D. As Indians turned to Hinduism, Buddhism spread rapidly to the countries of central and southeastern Asia. In fact, propagation of this religion had started in the third century A.D. under the Mauryan emperor Ashoka, whose son is reputed to have taken the religion to Sri Lanka, where it took root and flourished. The Theravada school of Sri Lanka is generally regarded as the oldest form of Buddhism (pp.154–55). In the fifth and sixth centuries A.D., there were Theravada centers on the southeast coast, and from here the sect spread to Burma. This form eventually reached Thailand, Laos and Cambodia, where it is still practiced. The development of the Mahayana doctrine occurred during the reign of the Kushan king Kanishka (pp.158–59) at a council held in Kashmir. Less severe than the more puristic Theravada school, Mahayana accommodated popular beliefs and permitted a pantheon and sainthood. And whereas before the strict dress code for monks had deterred their traveling in cold climates, the less stringent discipline of Mahayana now allowed them to be suitably attired for their journeys.

Mahayana Buddhism spread along the trade routes to China and central Asia. It is not certain precisely when Buddhism reached China, but, by A.D. 65, there was a community of Buddhist monks in China; and, by the second century, a Buddhist community existed in Luoyang, where sacred works were being translated into Chinese. At about the same time, there were Buddhist shrines and cave temples along the Silk Route. From China, Buddhism spread to Korea in the fourth century and to Japan in the sixth. Later, it spread to Tibet, where a distinctive form emerged.

Buddhism, in its Theravada form, reached Burma in about the middle of the first millennium A.D. The Shwedagon pagoda in the Burmese capital of Rangoon is known to have been an important Buddhist center as early as the 11th century. Covering an area of 14 acres, the pagoda is a complex of glittering structures dominated by a giant bell-shaped golden stupa (RIGHT) that rises more than 300 feet.

Framed against an icy peak, the shrine (RIGHT ABOVE) is one of many scattered in isolated places among the mountains of Nepal. Nepalese Buddhism has been influenced by both Tibet and India. By the eighth century A.D., Nepal had become increasingly affected by Tibetan culture, and the current use of prayer wheels and flags are evidence of this earlier contact.

CHINA

" *The best of all rulers is but a shadowy presence to his subjects.* "

CHINESE SAGE LAOZI

Once forming the knob and lid of a painted Yangshao pottery vessel, this masklike face from Gansu Province dates from about 2500 B.C. and is one of the earliest intact prehistoric images. It is possible that the face is that of a shaman — suggested by the snake, often a creature symbolic of the underworld, that crawls across the back of the head. Pottery such as this would have been used for rituals and burials rather than for daily life.

China's distinctive civilization – the world's oldest living culture – developed in isolation from other ancient centers. So geographically remote was China, that it was not until the late second century B.C. that the Chinese learned that there were other civilized people who lived beyond their borders. Until then, the only foreigners with whom they had come into contact were the nomadic tribes of the steppes to the north and northeast and the culturally less-developed peoples to the south.

China's civilization first developed in the area of the Huang He (Yellow River), where deep deposits of loess, highly fertile when watered, supported the early farmers and the first cities of the northern plain. Here, under the Shang, bronze technology developed in the second millennium and provided the weapons used by this clan-based militaristic society under whom the boundaries of the early Huang He heartland were first expanded.

From the earliest Neolithic villages in the sixth millennium until the demise of the Han dynasty in the second century A.D., the northern plain was the dominant region of China.

The first writing and the earliest cities were found here. Until the beginning of this century, little was known of ancient China, but with the discoveries of the cities and burials of the earliest dynasties, the roots of China's rich culture can now be seen. Arts and crafts such as jade and other stone carving, lacquerware, fine ceramics, cast bronze, silkmaking, painting and calligraphy have been practiced for thousands of years and continue to be.

More than in any culture, writing and scholarship have held long-standing primacy. Indeed, for the Chinese, the essence of civilization was the art of writing, and calligraphy was the most highly regarded art form, even more than the paintings which it adorned. The Chinese scholar had a status unequaled elsewhere, and it was the scholar-officials of the bureaucracy rather than soldiers or merchants who formed the elite.

Under the Han dynasty, which was contemporary with the Roman Empire, the bureaucracy which lasted until the end of the imperial era at the beginning of this century became highly developed. Run by men educated in the Confucian classics and selected on merit by examination, the imperial civil service was a remarkable institution and was a major factor in the continuity of Chinese civilization, both culturally and politically. The bureaucracy generated an enormous quantity of paperwork, and these documents, preserved in the official archives, provided the material that was from time to time incorporated into the official or dynastic histories.

Chinese society was strongly rooted in the countryside, and cities were mainly administrative centers. Although the scholar-officials spent much of their time in cities, they continued to regard the villages of their ancestors as their real homes. The imperial service was closed to merchants and their sons, and officials often invested in farms and became rural landlords. In this way the elite, of scholar-official and rural landlord or gentleman farmer, was extremely cohesive and able to remain dominant.

With the demise of the Han dynasty in the third century A.D., the north gradually succumbed to the barbarians and parts became grazing land. After the fall of the ancient capitals Chang'an and Luoyang to the barbarians, Danyang (Nanjing) on the Chang Jiang (Yangtze River) became the imperial center, and it was here that earlier traditions were preserved.

The Great Wall of China stretches for some 1,500 miles across mountainous terrain, from Liaoning Province in the east to central Asia in the west. It was once said that it was the only man-made construction visible on the earth from the moon. However, this has turned out to be untrue; nevertheless, the wall is one of the largest building projects ever undertaken.

The wall originated as a series of defensive walls constructed during the Warring States period (453–221 B.C.). Under Shi Huangdi, the first emperor of the Qin dynasty in 221 B.C., the walls were consolidated and extended, and the foundations of the wall as it is today were laid. Most of the present structure dates from the Ming period (1368–1644).

The cost of building the wall was great in human suffering, with thousands dying in the severe northern winters and as a result of maltreatment by their masters. The wall itself was originally built of masonry and earth, faced, in some parts, with bricks. Although there are variations, the structure is usually about 30 feet high.

EARLY FARMERS AND POTTERS

China divides naturally into two major areas: the north plain dominated by the Huang He (Yellow River) and the south by the Chang Jiang (Yangtze River). In this land of fertile river valleys, a distinctive Chinese culture developed that owed little to contacts with other ancient centers, from which China was geographically isolated. To the east lay the sea and to the west rose high mountains; southward there were forests and to the north lay desert and steppe.

Several early centers of Chinese civilization are found in the area of the middle Huang He, a region in which there are deep deposits of loess – a fine yellow dust blown from the central Asian desert. This soft soil, easy to work and rich in minerals, is fertile when watered, and from around 6000 B.C. it supported agriculture. In many Neolithic settlements of this region, such as Banpo in Shaanxi Province, millet was cultivated, and remains of other plants, including cabbage, have been found. Farming was at first intermittent, as the hunter-gatherers graduated from a

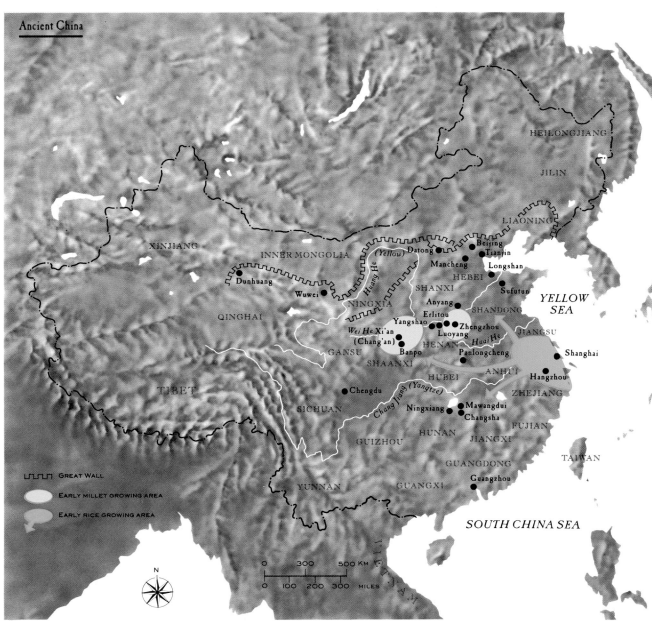

Ancient China

GREAT WALL

EARLY MILLET GROWING AREA

EARLY RICE GROWING AREA

The village of Banpo, shown in the drawing (LEFT), was used for several separate occupations from around 5000 B.C. The excavated area contains 24 houses and 160 storage pits, as well as the foundations of a large communal longhouse, shown here, which was built in a later phase.

The partly subterranean houses had low wattle and daub walls over which conical reed roofs were supported by wooden posts; the floors of beaten earth were usually plastered and had a central fire pit. The dwelling area of the settlement was surrounded by a ditch, beyond which were pottery kilns and a cemetery. The latter contained only adults, as children were buried in pottery urns deposited between the houses.

The principal sites of China's early centers are shown on this map along with areas of early rice and millet growing and present-day provinces. Names have been transliterated according to the Pinyin system. From the early sites of the Huang He (Yellow River) and the east and northeast, Chinese civilization expanded to extend over much of modern Inner China by the late first millennium B.C.

semi-settled to a fully settled life. Pigs and dogs were domesticated, and the diet was supplemented by hunting and fishing, for which fine bone hooks were used. On the eastern seaboard, rice was being farmed by the fifth millennium B.C.

In the northwest, the Neolithic culture is known as Yangshao, after the site at which it was first identified. The houses of Yangshao settlements were square or circular and partly subterranean, with thatched roofs. Tombs were set apart from the dwelling area, and men and women were buried separately; the presence of grave goods suggests a belief in an afterlife.

Yangshao potters made a fine-grained, lightly burnished painted ware, decorated with fish designs and faces of humans and animals, which was used mainly for burials; there was also a coarser earthenware for daily use. The pottery kilns, like the tombs, were some distance from the houses. The presence of stone whorls, which probably served as primitive spindles, suggests that cloth was made, and the remains of cut silkworm cocoons indicate that sericulture was known.

In the east and northeast, there was a separate Neolithic group known as Longshan, after the site in Shandong Province where rectangular ramparts of rammed earth and other distinctive features were discovered. This site probably represents a highly developed late phase of the culture, if – as seems likely – it developed from an earlier, separate eastern tradition, rather than as a later evolution of Yangshao.

Longshan pottery seems to have been finished on the wheel, and this thin-walled, highly burnished black ware was made in a wide variety of shapes, presumably for ceremonial functions. Other features of the Longshan group were jade carving, divination by scapulimancy – the interpretation of markings made by a hot implement on animal bones – and burial in the confines of the settlement.

From the fourth millennium B.C., there is increasing evidence of contact between the Yangshao and the Longshan Neolithic groups. In the east, the appearance of rich burials around 3000 B.C. suggests the rise of a hierarchical society, and this more advanced Longshan culture expanded westward, becoming widespread in the third millennium. In Henan and Shaanxi provinces, a new tradition containing elements of both cultures emerged, from which a distinctive Bronze Age culture developed. However, the late Neolithic period of northern China was not uniform: at some sites, a sequence of the three cultures, Yangshao, Longshan and mixed, is found, while at others one or the other may be absent.

According to later Chinese tradition, the Bronze Age Shang dynasty (pp.166–77) was preceded by the Xia dynasty, said to be founded by Yu the Great (2205–2197 B.C.). As yet, no trace of this dynasty has been found. However, it is mentioned in ancient Chinese records, and since they have proved to be accurate in other cases, the 500-year Xia reign cannot be discounted. It is possible that one of the late Neolithic groups, or one contemporary with the early Shang, will be found to be the Xia.

The Huang He (Yellow River) (BELOW) was the home of early Chinese civilization. On its course through the loess plain it carries increasing quantities of silt, from which channels have to be kept free. This picture shows a water wheel being used to raise water for irrigation.

The engraving (BOTTOM) represents Yu, the legendary founder of the Xia dynasty, directing irrigation works. According to later tradition, Yu spent 13 years digging channels and keeping the dikes low.

Dating from about 2000 B.C., this Neolithic vessel, which was used as a burial urn, was discovered in Gansu Province. On similar urns, the swirling lines and geometric motifs were combined with depictions of animals. At this time the paintbrush had not been invented, and the decoration was painted, it is thought, with the frayed end of a piece of bamboo or other type of wood.

This early pottery's harmony of shape and decoration continued down the centuries and should be seen as the first stage of a constantly evolving tradition which maintains a unifying sense of esthetics.

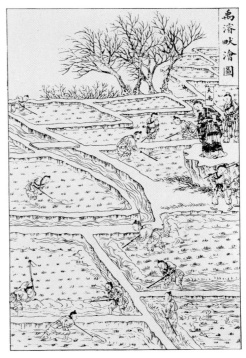

The Shang bronze cauldron, or fang ding, (BELOW) was discovered in Honan and dates from the 14th to 12th centuries B.C. The human face may indicate that this ritual vessel was used in human sacrifice, although the inscription "large grain" has been found on the vessel.

Chinese bronze working involved a complicated casting process: the metal was first melted in pottery crucibles and then poured into molds made of many clay parts fitted together. The Shang period was famous for its bronze pieces, thousands of which have been found.

North China was dominated by the Shang dynasty from about 1750 to 1050 B.C., dates which are only approximate since there are conflicting chronologies for this period. The center of Shang power was in the middle reaches of the Huang He (Yellow River), although at its height, Shang influence extended to Mongolia in the north, Gansu in the northwest and the Chang Jiang (Yangtze River) valley in the south.

Evidence for the Shang, whose rediscovery began only in 1903, comes from archaeology, the records of divinations on oracle bones and traditional histories. The rise of the Shang marks the end of prehistory and the beginning of the Bronze Age in China. Certain features of the Shang period had their origins in the eastern Longshan culture, a legacy which included traditional divination, jade working, rammed-earth walls and burial in stepped pits.

Bronze working seems to have first been known in Gansu Province in the west, where early bronzes of crude workmanship dating probably from the 18th century B.C. have been found. Bronze, an alloy of copper and tin, was used for ritual vessels and for weapons and armor. The principal weapons used by the Shang warrior aristocrats were the Chinese halberd or "dagger ax," the bow and arrow and spears, both with bronze heads;

PRODUCING POTS

By the end of the Neolithic period, the pottery wheel had come into use and a wide variety of shapes was being made by Longshan potters. Although the Shang and Zhou periods were dominated by bronze production, there were important developments in the making of pottery. The design of kilns was improved, perhaps as a result of sophisticated bronze technology, and a white-bodied pottery made from kaolinic clay was now produced.

Earlier, in the Yangshao, white clays had been used, but only as a slip coating or for simple surface decoration. Now, however, the white kaolinic clay, which was free of impurities such as iron, was used for thick handmade vessels. These are not unlike bronzes in their shape and decoration. Before completely hardening, the white ware was carved with decoration, such as on the *lei* jar (ABOVE). The firing temperature of white ware seems to have been between 1,900 and 2,100 degrees Fahrenheit.

Kaolinic clay lacks plasticity and could only be worked to produce thick-sided vessels. Nevertheless, the clay is reasonably brittle and perhaps for this reason seems not to have been worked after the end of the Shang period. The earliest wares which have glazes have been found at the site of Anyang; this important step, which renders the pots waterproof, took many centuries to develop fully.

bronze armor and helmets were also worn. Such weapons guaranteed the Shang aristocrats' dominance over their own people and their neighbors. Success in warfare, frequently engaged in by Shang kings, brought profitable plunder and tribute, as well as captives, who were enslaved or sacrificed.

Although the power and wealth of the Shang was in large part due to their control of bronze, their culture rested on an agricultural base that was still essentially Neolithic, even though new agricultural methods had been introduced. These included the expansion of rice cultivation and the taming of the water buffalo. Irrigation was certainly practiced, as the remains of ditches and the growing of rice show, and it is likely that the state was involved in production, as harvests were kept in the royal granaries. However, wood, bone and stone tools were still used by farmers and craftsmen.

Other distinguishing features of this period were a writing system, walled cities with palaces, large-scale tomb building, an administrative structure, a system of measurement and a calendar, kingship, organized ancestor worship and the practice of human sacrifice. Shang society, modern scholars consider, was probably clan-based, with each clan in the various localities dominated by its warrior nobility.

At the center was the royal clan, whose chief member, the king, was said to be descended from Shangdi, the lord of heaven and the ancestral founder of the Shang. On his death, a king went to heaven to join his great ancestor; the throne passed to one of the deceased king's brothers, then from the youngest brother to the son. In heaven, the dead could intercede on behalf of their descendants; hence Shang court rituals involved almost constant sacrifices, and it was for this that magnificent ceremonial bronze vessels were made.

Ancestral spirits were asked for their advice on warfare, hunting, the harvest and other matters by means of divination by oracle bones. It is these questions and answers, inscribed on the bones, that provide much detail about Shang life. The inscriptions and those on bronze ritual vessels of the late Shang period are the direct forerunners of later Chinese written characters. No Shang bureaucratic records have been found, but it seems extremely likely that they would have been kept and that they have long since perished.

The Shang capital was moved several times, and some of these sites have been excavated, notably Zhengzhou and Anyang, thought to be the last Shang capital. Of the sites found so far, the earliest is at Erlitou, identified by some as the first capital Bo, the seat of Tang, the dynastic founder. Even if it is not Bo, it was certainly an important early Shang center. Both Zhengzhou and Anyang have a rammed-earth platform on which stood palaces surrounded by houses, workshops and suburbs. Farther south, in the Chang Jiang basin, a large settlement has been excavated at Panlongcheng. Here, there were also ceremonial buildings and elaborate tombs. This center seems to have declined after the middle Shang; during the late period, Shang control appears to have been less widespread.

The last Shang king, Di Xin, was defeated in battle in the 11th century B.C. by the rebellious Zhou. However, the Shang had laid the foundations of later Chinese civilization and, in spite of their demise, many of their traditions continued.

ORACLE BONES

The earliest known Chinese writing is found on animal bones or tortoise shells used for divination. Scapulimancy (using bones) and plastomancy (using tortoise shells) were both practiced by Shang priests, who prepared the animals' shoulder blades and the shells by drilling holes in them. Questions were then written upon them, and a heated point was applied to the holes. As a result, cracks appeared, and these "answers" from the spirits or gods were given interpretations by the priests, who wrote them directly on the bone with ink and brush. The questions and answers were then incised with a sharp instrument and became a permanent record, as can be seen on the tortoise shell (RIGHT).

No important decisions – either royal or otherwise – could be made without prior consultation of the bones. The latter have provided a great deal of knowledge about the Shang period since the first decipherment was made in 1903. Most of the oracle bones have come from the vicinity of Anyang, the last Shang capital.

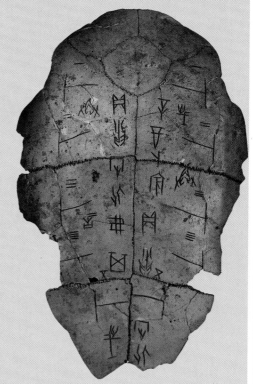

The Shang tomb at Sufutun

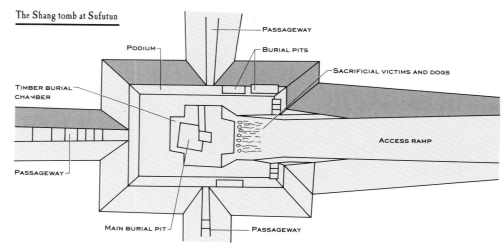

The late Shang dynasty tomb at Sufutun, Shandong Province, is the largest to be discovered outside the Shang capital of Anyang. The tomb, a plan of which is shown here (ABOVE), contained 47 human and 5 dog sacrificial victims, all found at the tomb's entrance. In addition, there are single human and dog burials in adjoining pits.

Most of the grave goods were stolen long ago, but the surviving pieces include fine bronzes, jade, and cowrie shells used for currency. The two bronze battle-axes in the outer trenches were usually symbolic of kingship. This factor and the size of the tomb, which had ramps 145 feet long, suggest that this was a burial of a local ruler.

Founded by Wu after his defeat of the Shang in the 11th century B.C., the Zhou dynasty became the longest-lasting and most revered of China's early ruling houses. The first two centuries were later regarded as a golden age of prosperity and good rule. In fact, central authority collapsed in the eighth century, and the removal of the capital to Luoyang in 770 B.C. marks the end of the period known as the Western Zhou.

During the three centuries of this era, there was considerable continuity of culture from the Shang. Building techniques, tombs, bronze vessels and the writing system remained unchanged. However, reflecting the later reputation of the early Zhou rulers as just, restrained and civilized, the excesses of

This bronze statue *from the Warring States period shows a young Mongolian figure with two birds made of jade. During this time, Mongolian nomads in the north were making their presence felt, and some states built walls as a protection against them.*

Shang human sacrifices and great hunting expeditions were curtailed. Also, oracles were no longer consulted extensively at court. Inscriptions on bronze vessels, which record the grants of land to vassals in exchange for allegiance, provide evidence of Zhou feudal organization. Fiefs were given to relatives of the ruler and those whose help was valued. Although these territories were theoretically the property of the king, in practice they became hereditary possessions.

The Zhou heartland was Shaanxi Province, but during the period of its supremacy, Zhou control extended to Hunan and Shandong. Zhou authority rested, in fact, on their superior organization, for metalworking was now becoming more widespread and available to the Zhou's adversaries. In theory, Zhou rule was based on the conception of the king, who was the "son of heaven," possessing the "Mandate of Heaven." According to this convenient theory, the whole world was his domain, which he had the right to rule, providing he did so with justice and concern for his people. If he did not, his mandate would be removed and given to another — as had happened to depraved and unworthy late Shang rulers.

By the eighth century B.C., the Zhou rulers had ceased to have effective power as the former fiefdoms emerged as rival states. In part, this changed situation was the result of the expansion of advanced technology to outlying regions. At the same time, the bonds between the dynasty and the feudal lords had gradually ceased to be those of kinship. The period between 770 and 481 B.C. is conventionally called the Spring and Autumn period (after the title of the annals of the state of Lu written by Confucius). In this world of small competing states, the earlier clan aristocratic culture changed to one that placed high value on chivalry, the correct observance of court ritual, courtesy as well as on similar forms of behavior.

Initially this was a world of small states, but ceaseless warfare led to the defeat and absorption of some by larger units, and by the fifth century seven kingdoms had emerged. During the following 250 years, they fought in turn with each other until one emerged supreme. This last period, from the fifth century to the unification of China in 221 B.C., is aptly known as the Warring States period.

However, in spite of the political fragmentation of what had been the Zhou state, the Spring and Autumn, or Eastern Zhou, was a period of innovation, development and intellectual activity. From the sixth century, iron began to be worked on a larger scale; and the application of casting techniques to iron resulted in advanced industry that produced tools as well as weapons, thus increasing agricultural productivity.

The standard of tomb furnishings also reveals the high level of craft skills. Lacquerware, wood carvings, silk painting and musical instruments are all found. The use of iron led to a decline in the use of stone tools for farming, although stone carvings continued. The Chang Jiang (Yangtze River) region now became the center of ceramic production: large quantities of pottery were made and decorated with paint, glaze and lacquer; and elaborately decorated roof tiles were now introduced.

By the time of the Warring States, the classical culture of China had been formed. A literature had begun to develop, which included the writings of the sages Laozi and, more famous in the west, Confucius.

Some early Chinese coins *were in the form of miniature implements, such as the hoe (ABOVE) and knife (BELOW), based on those actually used in barter. After the Qin period, coins were circular and pierced with a hole to allow them to be collected on strings.*

PURVEYORS OF WISDOM

During the Warring States period of turmoil and conflict, when long-established social and governmental systems proved to be inadequate, Chinese scholars and philosophers began to question the values on which their civilization was based. Early Chinese society was built on certain basic rules of conduct known as *li* – namely the proper observance of certain rituals and ceremonies, both in religion and everyday life. *Li* defined the social order, and Confucius in particular emphasized *li* and its associated rituals and forms in his belief that through the practice of external forms, inner qualities were developed. Confucius (*c.*551–479 B.C.) was born in the eastern state of Lu. He traveled widely and, before he began his teaching, held various public positions. His attempts by persuasion to curtail the corruption of contemporary feudal rulers failed, and in his last years he returned to his own province to complete his literary work, which included the *Spring and Autumn Annals*.

Confucius claimed no original thought, but believed that the anarchy of his own age could only be eliminated by a return to ancient values, based on good conduct. If this developed in people of high rank, they would be an example to others and would also guarantee a fair and just rule. In short, Confucius believed that society was ordered in a certain way and had to be accepted by people, who should obey their superiors and set an example to those below. It was a philosophy for life that did not encourage creativity or change. His teachings have been preserved in his *Analects* and are presented as a series of dialogues in which Confucius answers questions. Confucianism became deeply embedded in Chinese life, and the study of his work was the basis of entry into the civil service.

The other important and enduring school of thought, which also dates from this period, is Daoism, based on the philosophy of Laozi. Little is known of him, beyond the fact that he was born about 50 years before Confucius. According to Daoist belief, the *dao*, usually translated into English as "way," is an endless, ever-changing series of natural processes that sustain nature. People must be in harmony with the natural forces, living spontaneously and with purity.

Confucius, shown (LEFT) in an ivory statuette of the 16th century, was the greatest of Chinese thinkers, and his influence endures to the present day. His name is a latinization of the Chinese Kong fuzi – "venerable master Kong." Although he seems to have been indifferent to, rather than antagonistic toward, religion, it is for his humanistic ethical system that he is remembered. His ideal was not so much the noble warrior as the scholar gentleman, who was loyal, scrupulously honest and honorable.

A young girl makes an offering in a Daoist temple in present-day Guangdong Province. In contrast with Confucianism, Daoism urged aloofness from society and a life of simplicity at one with the rhythms of nature. However, as time passed, this initial tendency toward isolation, meditation and quietism changed, and Daoism gradually gained the trappings of a popular religion — complete with temples, priests, a pantheon and a host of mythological beliefs and superstitions.

THE FIRST EMPIRE

Dating from about 100 B.C., this superb jade burial suit (BELOW) was found in the tomb of Prince Liu Sheng, a Han nobleman of the royal family, and belonged to his wife, Princess Dou Wan. Their tombs were discovered in 1968 in Hebei Province and contained many valuable items. Dou Wan's suit consists of 2,160 plaques of jade combined with bits of iron wound with gold and silk. The plaques had holes drilled at each corner so that they could be wired together. The imperial family merited gold wire; for those of lesser rank, silver or copper was used.

From the late fifth to the late third centuries B.C., endless conflicts between China's warring feudal states inevitably resulted in the depletion of their resources. As these states grew weaker, the western state of Qin, despised by the others, who regarded its people as barbarians ruled by a family descended from horsedealers, grew in strength. The Qin were also held in contempt for their concern with material gain and seeming absence of ethical standards. According to one contemporary account: "Qin knows nothing about etiquette, proper relations and virtuous conduct, and if there be an opportunity for material gain, it will disregard its relatives as if they were animals."

In fact, part of the reason for Qin's rise to power was, ironically, its very "barbarism." The absence of a tradition of learning forced the Qin to employ learned Chinese advisers from outside the state. Most notable of these was Shang Yang, a member of the ruling house of Wei, who left his native state to serve the Qin in the mid-fourth century B.C. His reforms laid the foundations on which Qin would grow to become the most powerful state in China.

Shang Yang is credited with introducing a new economic and political structure, based on a strict system of rewards and punishment. The people were compelled to be highly productive, and a powerful military order was built. Shang's reforms in many respects were the antithesis of established traditions and were in complete disregard of the past.

As Qin gathered strength, the effect of Shang Yang's reforms became evident to its neighbors. By forming alliances and, later, by conquests, Qin gradually destroyed the power of the states around it. Within a century and a half, its numerous, if divided, rivals had been eliminated. The taking of Sichuan and, in 256 B.C., the area of Luoyang, both iron-working centers, greatly assisted Qin in its final conquests under the leader Qin Shi Huangdi. Following the defeat of Chu and Yan in 223 and 222, the last opposing state, Qi, was taken; and in 221, Shi Huangdi established himself as the first emperor of a unified China.

A man of ruthless determination, Shi Huangdi had come to the throne of Qin when only 13. His accession coincided with Qin's emergence as a major power in the region and one that already had considerable wealth. As emperor, Shi Huangdi began a thorough reorganization, introducing a bureaucratic form of government that became the model for future Chinese political administration. Shi Huangdi's reign was turbulent,

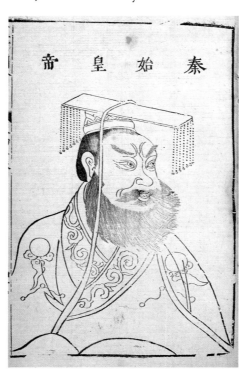

Shi Huangdi, shown here in a 17th-century engraving, was the first emperor of China, ruling from 221 to 210 B.C. During this time, China became a strongly centralized state. Weights, measures and coinage were standardized to regulate and control trade; and a single form of written Chinese was adopted for use by a burgeoning bureaucracy. He is best known today for the extraordinary army of life-size terra-cotta soldiers (RIGHT) found in huge pits near his tomb and now protected by a vast hangar.

and the dynasty was short-lived, ending four years after the emperor's sudden death in 210 B.C. Nevertheless, the Qin dynasty represents a turning point in Chinese history, not least because it marks the beginning of its existence as a unified state.

The emperor issued endless edicts aimed at controlling his subjects and strengthening the state. Feudal holdings were abolished, and noble families had to live in Xianyang, the capital. Peasant farmers were given more extensive rights, but had to pay taxes. Inspectors were appointed to audit accounts and check the administration of government and the law. Weights and measures were standardized, as was coinage. A network of roads and canals, constructed to improve supply for the army, which was now stationed in garrisons throughout the empire, improved communications.

During the Warring States period, frontier walls and ditches had been built by some of the northern China states. They served as protection both against each other and the "barbarians" of the north. Shi Huangdi now incorporated these walls into a Great Wall that extended from Liaoning Province in the east to Gansu Province in the west. This wall was maintained and rebuilt by subsequent dynasties and still stands.

Many of the emperor's innovations were criticized by the scholar-gentry. This section of society, much mistrusted by Shi Huangdi, remained attached to the ancient values and traditions. To remove the memory of the past and "to make the people ignorant," Shi Huangdi agreed to the burning of all books – only those books which dealt with the subjects of medicine, agriculture and divination were saved. The emperor was prompted in this action by Li Si, the Grand Councillor of Qin, "to prevent the use of the past to discredit the present." In 213 B.C., the notorious Burning of the Books took place, and in the following year there was a purge of scholars.

The emperor died two years later, aged 50. All the accounts of his life stress his fear of death and his constant search for the elixir of immortality. The construction of his tomb by 700,000 conscripts from the empire began shortly after the unification. The details of its structure and contents are known from ancient accounts, and his mausoleum still lies under a great burial mound of 130 feet. Nearby, an army of pottery soldiers was buried in pits, to guard and protect the entrance to the tomb. Their recent discovery and excavation have ensured that Shi Huangdi has achieved the immortality he so desired.

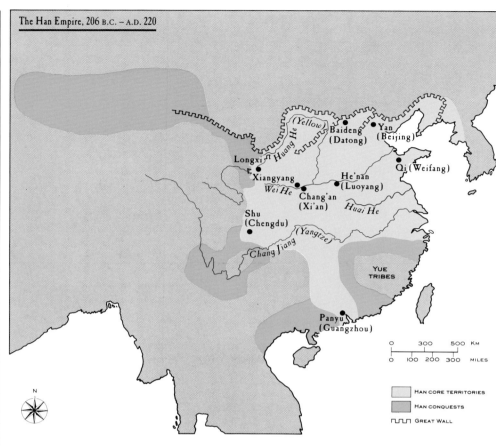

The Han Empire, 206 B.C. – A.D. 220

Aﬂter the death of the first emperor in 210 B.C., widespread revolts broke out, as people reacted to years of oppressive Qin rule. There were also intrigues at court, and a eunuch named Zhao Gao attempted to manipulate the succession – he even tried to claim it himself, but without success. Although this was the only time a eunuch tried to usurp the throne, a pattern later developed of eunuchs assuming great power at times when the emperor was weak.

A struggle between the various insurgent groups was won by a man named Liu Bang (249–195 B.C.), who came from a peasant background and was probably illiterate, but who was shrewd and a skillful military strategist. He became emperor under the name of Gao Zu and gave his dynasty the name of Han, after the region where he had first been recognized as a prince. Although the new emperor's origins were lowly, he understood the importance of a sound administration and the value of learned advisers. Much of the dynasty's early success was the result of the frugal policies of his prime minister Xiao He.

The Han dynasty, which was contemporary with the Roman Empire, lasted for some 400 years (206 B.C.–A.D. 220). During this long period, in which the "ancient traditions" of the Zhou were adopted and the oppression of the Qin mitigated, many forms and traditions were established that remained part of Chinese culture until the end of the empire in 1911.

Far more is known about the Han than earlier periods, as there is extensive documentary and archaeological evidence. The latter comes largely from tombs, whose contents are varied.

Core Han territories and *Han conquests are shown on this map (ABOVE LEFT), along with the principal Han centers. Modern names are given in brackets.*

The Great Wall, *shown in this photograph taken in the 1930s, came into being in the late third century B.C. when Shi Huangdi, the first emperor, linked up a number of existing walls that had been built as a defensive measure against the nomadic tribes of the north. The Han dynasty rulers continued to maintain and lengthen the wall, although important rebuilding took place later in the 15th and 16th centuries.*

Watchtowers were built at intervals, both as defensive measures in themselves and as communication points: signals could be sent to warn of an attack, either by smoke, during the day, or by fire, at night.

Apart from precious objects of jade, lacquer and bronze, there are earthenware models of buildings and stone tomb slabs and stamped bricks which are engraved with scenes of daily life.

In the case of written material, modern scholars have to evaluate the bias of different authors. For instance, there were the Modernists, seeking change and progress, as well as the Reformists, who looked back to a golden age and advocated traditional policies. These two schools of thought emerged against a background of debate on the ways and means of achieving a stable government. The protagonists in the debate were the officials of the bureaucratic organization, which was one of the main legacies of the first part of the Han dynasty (the Former, or Western, Han, 206 B.C.–A.D. 8).

From the Zhou and the Qin, certain elements of bureaucratic government had been inherited: these included rotation of office, short-term appointments and promotion by merit. Under the Han, bureaucracy became highly developed. In 196 B.C., examinations for entry to official posts were introduced. In 124 B.C., 12 years after Confucianism had been proclaimed as the recognized state cult, an imperial university was established in Chang'an, the capital, with a curriculum founded upon the Confucian canon. This institution acted as a training ground for the highest officials of the administration. The expansion of higher education was facilitated by the standardization of the Chinese script, a reform introduced under the Qin.

The Han government had a state monopoly on the lucrative iron and salt trade, and the production of alcohol was taxed. The Emperor Wu Di (140–87 B.C.) established public granaries which officials had to stock when prices were low; the grain was then sold in times of shortage. The government's economic measures were in part the result of costly campaigns against the Xiongnu, fierce nomads of the north.

In A.D. 9, a reaction to the Han, as a result of recurring economic difficulties and renewed pressure from the Xiongnu, helped the courtier Wang Mang to usurp the throne. But his interregnum (A.D. 9–23) ended when he proposed radical land reforms. After rebellions, Guangwu Di, a member of the Han, continued the dynasty by becoming emperor in A.D. 25.

During the time of the Han Empire, watchtowers, similar in design to this ceramic model (RIGHT), were built inside the defensive compounds of large homesteads. Made of wood with projecting tiled roofs, the towers were also constructed on city walls and other defensive structures, such as the Great Wall.

The Han horse and carriage (BELOW), shown in this bronze model dating from the second century A.D., was used for the conveyance of officials as they traveled the country on tours of inspection. Two bronze chariots were found in the area surrounding the tomb of the first emperor, but they were drawn by four horses. However, the design, with its two wheels and parasol-like canopy, is similar to the carriages depicted on tomb bricks of the Han period.

THE HAN EMPIRE (2)

*The Han city of Chang'an,
part of which is shown in this
reconstruction based on
contemporary evidence as well as
that from the later Tang period,
was the imperial capital from
202 B.C. to A.D. 8. The city
was based on a grid system of
boulevards — whose traffic would
have included canopied carriages
(1) and freight wagons (4) —
intersected by narrow lanes; it
was divided into a number of
quarters subdivided into 160
smaller li, or wards, each
surrounded by a wall.*

*The houses (2) of
Chang'an's residential areas
were packed together "as closely
as the teeth of a comb" and were
divided from the marketplaces
(3), of which there were several
in the city. Here, musicians,
jugglers and storytellers could be
seen mixing with people selling
their wares. A drum in a tower
(5) may have been sounded to
signal the market's opening and
closing hours.*

*In these lively, crowded
bazaars, a wide variety of
materials and products could be
obtained, ranging from silk,
wood, leather and bronze to
sweetmeats and cakes. Other
produce which might have been
on offer included ginger, melons,
onions, turnips, millet, barley,
dried beef, persimmons and
plums. In addition to buying and
selling, marketplaces were used
for other purposes, such as the
popular practice of divination
and even for public executions.*

Guangwu Di's restoration of the Han dynasty in A.D. 25 was
made possible by the support of the big landowners whose
holdings the usurper Wang Mang had sought to reduce. As a
result, the later Han emperors (A.D. 25–220) were much less
independent than their dynastic predecessors, and this inherent
weakness meant that feudalism was gradually restored.

There was still a wealthy nobility under the early Han emperors, but later rulers effectively disposed of this old aristocracy.
The wealth of these nobles is evident from their rich tombs and
grave goods, as can be seen in those of the Marquis of Dai, who
died in 186 B.C., and his wife and son. The jade shrouds of the
marquis and marchioness each had more than 2,000 jade
plaques held together with knotted gold wire and would have
been immensely costly.

The capital of the Western Han had been Chang'an on the
Wei River, but under the later Han, it was moved to Luoyang in
the lower Huang He (Yellow River) valley, (for which reason
the later Han are also known as the Eastern Han). At Chang'an,
details of the construction and layout of the Weiyang Palace
have been uncovered, together with the imperial government
archives. Weiyang Palace was built for Liu Bang by the prime
minister Xiao He. It covered some 40 miles and was enclosed by
walls and towers. Large quantities of armor and arms found at
the southwestern watchtower would suggest that the palace was
heavily guarded. Behind three ascending halls, in the first of
which the emperor dealt with affairs of state, were the luxurious
quarters of the empress and concubines.

The city was surrounded by a rammed-mud wall with a
moat, and towers and gates large enough for four carriages to go
through side by side. The archives discovered here included lists
of supplies to the government, specifying type, quality and the
date of contribution. The changing pattern of tribute can be
followed over two centuries and shows the evolution of the
bureaucracy, its management system and revenue collection.

Much of Chang'an was destroyed in disturbances that
occurred from A.D. 9 to 27; but the main reason for the move to
Luoyang was the rise in importance of the east and south as
economic centers. The Chang Jiang (Yangtze) and Huai river
valleys had outstripped Shaanxi as the most developed part of the
empire. Irrigation schemes had raised agricultural productivity
and population; whereas in the north, marginal land was abandoned to herders and the population declined.

Luoyang, the new capital, was much smaller and thus more
crowded than Chang'an. Although the emperors tried to make
it elegant, by comparison with Chang'an it appears to have been
modest. By contrast, great wealth was concentrated in private
lands. There were vast landholdings, and the owners of these
estates often had thousands of retainers and traded extensively.
As with the early Han nobility, the wealth of this class can be
observed from their extravagant burials. The tombs were built of
brick and were ornately decorated and lavishly furnished.

The owners of the great landholdings accumulated even more
wealth and property as they gained exemptions from taxation.
The economic conditions deteriorated, and the government
became increasingly unable to control and organize the country.
In the third century A.D., the dynasty collapsed from famine,
flood, peasant risings, insurgent groups, such as the Yellow
Turbans, and the military strength of great generals.

THE END OF THE EARLY EMPIRE

Between A.D. 221 and 265, China was divided into three kingdoms (BELOW), each under separate ruling houses. In the north was the Wei, which had displaced the Han; in the west lay the kingdom of Shu, centered on Chengdu; while in the south, the Wu ruled from Danyang (Nanjing). The struggle between these kingdoms ended in 280, when the house of Wei was defeated by the Western Jin. The latter, in turn, lasted until the barbarians took Luoyang and Chang'an in 311 and 316, respectively. Thereafter, the Eastern Jin was formed in Danyang, and China was divided until the sixth century.

THE ART OF WRITING

The Chinese system of writing was originally pictographic; later it was extended so that ideas that could not be drawn were shown by phonetic loans – words which had the same or a similar sound. To avoid confusion, idea signs, or ideograms – known as "category markers" or "radicals" – were used, and most Chinese characters are still made up of a phonetic element and a radical.

The earliest known surviving Chinese characters date from the 11th century B.C. – by this time they were already quite complex, and radicals appear among the pictographs. At the end of the third century B.C., under the Qin emperor, the script was standardized and reformed. From then until this century, the formal versions of the characters remained relatively stable. However, the complexity of the system of loans and the use of cursive shapes have destroyed most traces of pictorial representation. Also, different writing implements, such as the brush and the stylus, and materials, such as bone, bamboo, wood, paper and silk, used by scribes have affected the design of the characters. For instance, the narrow bamboo strips (RIGHT) of this Han period text resulted in a neat script of uniform width. The main different styles of script have been: seal scripts, ranging from oracle writing to the small seal style adopted by the Qin; regular brush scripts used from the Han; running script, a looser, cursive version of regular script; and grass script, a very stylized cursive form.

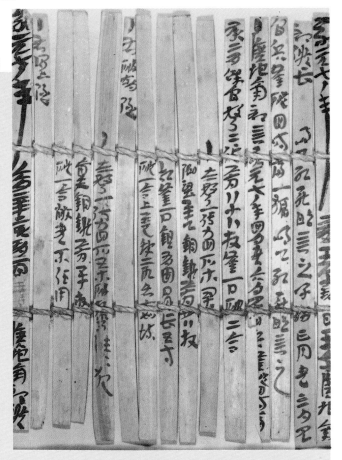

The Three Kingdoms

During the final years of the later Han dynasty in the third century A.D., there was anarchy and lawlessness as the empire disintegrated. A symptom of this was that owners of large estates fortified their homes and recruited personal armies for their own protection. In 208, the general Cao Cao had been forced to accept the division of China after being defeated by the Sun dynasty of Danyang (Nanjing) on the Chang Jiang (Yangtze River). Twelve years later, Cao Cao's son, Cao Pi, deposed the last Han emperor and became the first Wei ruler in A.D. 220. Shortly afterward, the Sun family declared itself the ruling dynasty Wu. And in Sichuan Province, at Chengdu, Liu Bei now proclaimed himself the ruler of Shu.

The struggle between these three kingdoms into which China was now divided continued for about half a century, a period that was romanticized by later Chinese tradition. In 265, the house of Wei was brought down by the Western Jin dynasty. Sima Yan, the latter's first ruler, briefly reunited China after defeating the Shu in 264 and the Wu in 280. And under his rule, Chinese authority was once again asserted over the south and southwest. Improved agricultural techniques, which increased production, as well as the use of water for transportation, benefited the economy and thus made possible a strengthening of imperial military power. The local magnates were stripped of their private armies, and barbarians were permitted to settle within the Great Wall. Although the barbarians now provided extra and necessary manpower (as was the case with the Roman Empire), the policy of allowing barbarian settlement was to have adverse military and political consequences, which in time outweighed such short-term advantages.

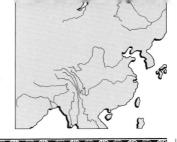

Sericulture (silk production) has been practiced in China since Neolithic times, and old methods (LEFT) are still in use today. This piece of silk (ABOVE) is made from threads of five different colors and is some 1,500 years old.

In traditional sericulture, the fiber of the silkworm cocoon is first unwound before being twisted and doubled to achieve various thicknesses. The silk is then dyed and woven.

The treatment of silkworms is a delicate operation: after being raised in conditions of controlled warmth, light and humidity, the silk moths are selected and mated. Weaker eggs are killed off and others carefully stored. Once hatched, the silkworms are fed with mulberry leaves until they spin their cocoons. They are then placed in boiling water which loosens the thread so that it can be reeled out.

Silk was a valuable export in ancient times, and bolts of silk were given as royal gifts; but the export of silkworm eggs was punishable by death. Silk was traded along the silk routes running through central Asia. From northwestern China, a route ran along the Gansu corridor and eventually branched into two main routes: one ran north to Ferghana, near the northern border of modern Afghanistan, the other went south to Bactria and then west.

Another factor which would have longer-term implications was Sima Yan's policy of giving his many sons separate provinces to govern. This fatally weakened the central government because the realm became fragmented by the development of quasi-feudal holdings and conflicts within the imperial family.

The conciliatory policy toward the steppe people had begun under the later Han, and what followed was the logical extension of such an approach. In time, one faction or another in China became accustomed to enlisting the help of the steppe tribes. In 304, the Xiongnu (Huns) backed one prince and the Xianbei (Tartars) backed another. In 311, Luoyang was sacked, and by 316 most of the northern provinces had fallen into the hands of the barbarians. In that year, with the fall of Chang'an, the last Western Jin ruler was taken prisoner.

Members of the imperial family fled to Danyang (Nanjing) and established the Eastern Jin dynasty. This much-diminished state, ruled by Sima Yan's descendants, had a disciplined and well-equipped army, and defeated the barbarians at Feshui in 383; thereafter it retained control of China south of the Huai River until 420. In the north, the Tartars ruled the former domains of the Han Empire and the ancient Chinese heartland in the Huang He area.

With the sacking of Luoyang and Chang'an, there had been an exodus of scholars and officials to Danyang in the south. Here the ancient traditions were continued, and it was at this time that Buddhism began to spread among the educated upper classes. Although in time the barbarian rulers of the north became increasingly sinicized, the Eastern Jin dynasty nevertheless saw itself as the preserver of ancient Chinese culture.

THE COMING OF BUDDHISM

Buddhism, in its Mahayana form (pp.154–55), began to reach China during the first century A.D., coming from northern India and Kashmir via the central Asian Buddhist kingdoms and along the silk route through Gansu to Chang'an. The spread of Buddhism to China can be traced by the temples, such as the Bingling temple (BELOW), which came to prominence especially in the Tang period (618–907), and shrines decorated with paintings and sculpture that followed the trade routes to Dunhuang and other centers in Gansu. By A.D. 65, there was a community of Buddhist monks in an area now located in the eastern provinces of Jiangsu and Shandong.

By the second century A.D., there was a Buddhist community in Luoyang, and the translation of sacred texts from Indian into Chinese had begun. After the division of China into north and south in the early fourth century, Buddhism, which had at first been a religion of foreigners, began to be adopted by members of the aristocracy in the south, perhaps because of a feeling of disillusion with Confucianism. The influence of Daoism led to the foundation of monastic communities, and in the south there were several such institutions, which, like the great noble estates, functioned semi-independently. In the north, the barbarian rulers adopted Buddhism as their state cult. Following the reunification of China in A.D. 581, Buddhism continued to flourish until the ninth century.

THE AMERICAS

"What thoughts must crowd the traveler . . . as he treads over the ashes of generations who reared these colossal fabrics, which take us . . . into the very depths of time."

AMERICAN HISTORIAN WILLIAM PRESCOTT (1796–1859) ON THE SITE OF TEOTIHUACÁN

Gold face masks, such as this one, were often attached to the mummies of high-ranking Chimú, a South American people who flourished from about A.D. 1000 to 1476. Made from hammered gold and cut to shape, the mask was adorned by dangling ear and nose ornaments that were designed to catch the light. The eyes were sometimes represented by semiprecious stones, such as turquoise, and blood-red cinnabar (mercury oxide) was often painted on the mask, possibly as a symbol of the renewal of life.

For over 40,000 years, the peoples of the Americas lived unaware of the existence of other continents. Apart from links between Inuit groups in Alaska, Siberia, northern Canada and Greenland, and the fleeting exploration and settlement of part of the eastern seaboard by Viking voyagers around the year A.D. 1000, the first external contacts took place after Christopher Columbus's fateful landfall in 1492.

Within 50 years of that contact, two major world civilizations, the Aztec and the Inca, and many other smaller societies had been destroyed by the newcomers. Within a century, the population of the New World had been reduced from 100 million to 10 million by the sword, slave raids and disease. Native religions were outlawed, and traditions, history and knowledge acquired over millennia were obliterated. Few Europeans were interested in these matters, and little was recorded of them. As a result, historical documents are scarce and archaeology, supplemented by ethnohistory, is the prime means of access to ancient American cultures.

Many aspects of ancient American civilizations are different from those of the Old World. Perhaps the most frustrating dissimilarity is that only one group, the Maya of Mesoamerica, was truly literate. Other cultures, for example the Mixtec and the Aztec, had forms of writing, but these were only suited to the lists of taxes and almanacs. It has taken over 150 years for Maya writing to be deciphered, with the big breakthrough coming in the 1970s; even so, many glyphs have still to be decoded.

The Maya, whose city temples tower above the jungle canopy; the Aztecs, whose island capital city housed 100,000 people; and the Incas, famous for their megalithic architecture, all operated without the use of the world's most basic machine: the wheel. All goods were carried either on human backs or, in the Andes, (with a maximum load of 100 pounds) on the backs of llamas.

Huge stone building blocks were hauled by muscle power. There were no simple rotary machines — for example, no pulleys or winches, no water wheels, no millstones, nor even the potter's wheel. Before European contact, Amerindian smiths worked gold, silver, copper and bronze with consummate skill, but there were virtually no iron tools or weapons. No coins circulated; in the Aztec Empire, cacao beans or bird quills filled with gold dust were accepted as standard units of value.

Many of the foodstuffs taken for granted in the Old World originated in the Americas. Aztec emperors drank a beverage made from cacao beans which, in their Nahuatl language, they called *xocolatl* – chocolate in English. Central America was also the original home of tomatoes, avocados, maize and many varieties of bean and squash. From South America came potatoes (some 700 different types are cultivated in the Andes), peanuts and manioc (yucca). Medicinal plants of great importance also came from the Americas, such as tobacco, quinine and coca, from which cocaine is refined.

In contrast to the wealth of plants domesticated in the Americas is the small number of domesticated animals. The fauna of the Americas contained few species suitable for draft-power, milking or meat. Most animal protein in the diet came from hunting or fishing; however, turkeys and guinea pigs were bred for eating, and llamas and alpacas, primarily sources of wool, were occasionally eaten.

Animals and plants bred by Amerindians now play an important part in world nutrition, medicine and economics. Recent studies of these extinct American cultures show that there were other aspects of their societies that might also have had an influence in the modern world.

The **Cliff Palace** at the site of Mesa Verde in Colorado was occupied from about A.D. 1100 to 1300 by the Anasazi people of the Southwest. The complex has 200 rooms and provided shelter from both the elements and intruders with its rock canopy high in the canyon wall. At the front of this village are circular-plan, semi-subterranean kivas (ceremonial meeting houses for male kin groups). Originally, kivas had flat plastered roofs that formed a plaza for the inhabitants' use.

Structures in the gloomy depths of the rock shelter were storehouses, while people lived in small, square, mud brick apartment buildings. The village was abandoned soon after 1300, after some 20 years of drought, crop failure and attacks by the forebears of the Navajo and Apache peoples.

Tenochtitlán, the great Aztec capital, is depicted in murals in the National Palace, Mexico City, by the 20th-century Mexican artist Diego Rivera. This city of 100,000 people was destroyed by the Spanish, and its ruins lie under the modern capital.

The Spanish conquistadores' lust for gold in the New World is perhaps epitomized by tales of El Dorado that lured many adventurers to their deaths. Lake Guatavita (ABOVE) in Colombia was the reality behind the legend — countless offerings of gold were made here during ceremonies performed by the local Muisca people.

FROM FARMERS TO TOWN DWELLERS

The first humans to reach the Americas were big game hunters who had followed herds of mammoth, mastodon and bison across the wide bridge of land which linked northeast U.S.S.R. with Alaska from about 40,000 to 10,000 B.C. Then, at the end of the last glacial period in about 10,000 B.C., the ice cap melted and the rise in sea level effectively isolated the American continent. Human settlement was, however, already widespread: there is evidence of hunters living in caves in the extreme south of South America in 9000 B.C. Gradually, throughout the

In the vast American continent, virtually isolated from outside influences after 10,000 B.C., animals and plants not found elsewhere in the world were domesticated, and unique civilizations developed. The Pacific coast and high Andes of South America and the heartland of Mesoamerica were the cradles of cultures whose influences spread deep into Amazonia and northward into the present-day United States. The map shows the major sites of the Americas, from the earliest times to the arrival of the Spanish in the early 16th century. The sites of Mesoamerica are shown on the inset map.

Americas, the wild animals on which the hunters depended became extinct, mainly due to climatic changes, and greater reliance was placed on plant foods. *Manos* and *metates* (grinding stones) used for milling gathered grain have been dated to about 8000 B.C., and it was at about this time that the initial domestication of food plants began in Mexico and Peru.

It is difficult to identify the first stages of plant cultivation because the seeds of wild and sown plants are identical. The pioneering areas of domestication of both plants and animals must, however, have been where their wild forebears existed. In the Tehuacán Valley in Mexico, for example, the wild grass *teosinte* was gradually modified by selection of bigger ears of corn until, by 5000 B.C., it was recognizably a domesticated type of maize. At first, yields were low, but by 2000 B.C. they had improved considerably through continued selection and hybridization. Similar slow advances were also made in Mexico before 5000 B.C. in the domestication of beans, chili peppers, avocados, gourds and squash.

In South America, high altitude Andean grasses were ancestral to important cultivated grain crops such as quinoa, tarwi and cañihua. They were initially cultivated, together with squash, peppers and beans, in about 8500 B.C. in the area of Ayacucho. Maize arrived in the region approximately 3,000 years later. Root crops were also an important food source in South America, and there is evidence that potatoes, manioc, oca and ulluco were all domesticated by 6300 B.C.

Vegetable foods were always of major significance in the Americas since there were few domesticated animals. In the Andes, wild camelids were tamed and bred by 5400 B.C., eventually producing llamas and alpacas, principally beasts of

Maize *was the staple food for many ancient American cultures and is still important in modern American nutrition. Served as tortillas or porridge, maize combined with beans provides a balanced diet of starch, protein and amino acids.*

Llamas and alpacas *were domesticated in the Andes by about 5000 B.C., providing the only beasts of burden in the whole of the Americas. Llamas (BELOW) could carry loads of 100 pounds for 10 to 12 miles a day and were important sources of wool, hides, meat, fat for lamps and candles, and dung for fertilizer and fuel. Their wild relative, the vicuña, whose wool is very fine and warm, is still hunted with a bola (a weighted rope device thrown to entangle the legs), shown on this post-conquest Inca cup (BELOW RIGHT).*

Many Mesoamerican peoples *worshipped a maize god, such as this Zapotec deity shown here on a funerary urn. His headdress is made of corn tassels and cobs hang from his chest ornament.*

burden and sources of wool. Little of their meat was eaten, and in about 7500 B.C., almost half of the animal protein in the Andean diet came from domesticated guinea pigs. In Mesoamerica, even fewer animals were domesticated; small dogs, turkeys and Muscovy ducks were bred for meat.

As ancient Americans gradually became better farmers, ever larger numbers of people could be fed. Estimates suggest that by 2500 B.C., populations in Mesoamerica and Peru had increased 25-fold. Reliable food supplies and surpluses led to great changes in everyday life. Permanent settlements were built, and farmsteads, villages and even towns with up to 4,000 inhabitants grew up. Specialist craftworkers developed their skills in weaving, pottery and making ground stone tools. They also produced luxury goods, such as jewelry, featherwork and polished stone mirrors, for elite ruling families. Numerous clay female figurines made at this time may indicate the existence of a fertility cult; and the first evidence of organized religion, temple platforms and shrines, appeared in about 2600 B.C. at various places on the central coast of Peru.

A shift toward irrigable river valleys took place on the Peruvian coast in about 2500 B.C., when more complex ceremonial centers and small towns were built of mud brick and stone. At Sechín Alto, Aspero and Huaca de los Reyes, sunken courts, ritual pits and massive platforms established an architectural and cultural pattern which was to influence all later Andean and coastal civilizations.

In Mesoamerica, the development of urban societies was slower. Permanent villages of five to ten houses existed in the Tehuacán Valley by 3000 B.C., but much of the villagers' food was still gathered rather than cultivated. The transition from a partially agricultural economy to full dependence on agriculture took place only after 1500 B.C. Excavations at San Lorenzo in Veracruz, the oldest site of the Olmec civilization, have shown that it developed as a significant population center and the scene of massive civil engineering works only after 1350 B.C. In Oaxaca, a large village of up to 100 whitewashed, thatched houses existed at San José Mogote in about 1150 B.C. Here, Olmec influence can be detected in pottery decoration, suggesting that the spread of the "mother culture" of Mesoamerica had by this time already begun.

Evidence for the emergence of complex, large-scale societies in the Andes begins in about 1200 B.C. with the spread of works of art or images in the distinctive Chavín style. Chavín culture, which is named after the site of Chavín de Huantar in the central Andes, flourished until 200 B.C.; it was distinguished by its large freestanding stone sculptures as well as grand temples with U-shaped plans and sunken courts. It is, however, the widespread dissemination of a single art style, which has been discovered throughout the length of present-day Peru, that indicates the influential role that Chavín culture played in Andean prehistory.

Chavín influence was imposed, however, not by conquest or colonization, but peacefully — through the spread of a religious cult. Sculptures decorating the temples at Chavín de Huantar depict caymans, jaguars, snakes, eagles and combined human and animal creatures. Many have snarling mouths with projecting curved fangs, serpentine hair and off-center pupils in their eyes. Chavín designs and religious motifs have been found on various artifacts, including textiles, sheet gold, marine shells and small stone and bone objects elsewhere in Peru.

As Chavín influence waned, more varied local cultures developed. Large cemeteries of the Paracas culture, located on the south coast of Peru, contain thousands of mummified bodies, each wrapped in multiple layers of cotton clothing embroidered with brightly colored wool yarn.

The wealth of evidence from these Paracas textiles reveals not only the artistry of Paracas needleworkers but also the long-lasting influence of Chavín: the famous image of a large-eyed deity, known as the Oculate Being, can be identified with the Smiling God of Chavín. Polychrome ceramics found in Paracas graves also reflect northern influences, for example in vessels which have a double spout and bridge; but, over the centuries, Chavínoid traits faded as the Nazca people became the dominant group of the south coast.

The Nazca continued the tradition of fine textile working, but excelled at tapestry and brocade rather than embroidery. They adopted many ceramic decoration motifs from Paracas, and over their 700-year existence, which lasted from about 350 B.C. to A.D. 450, they elevated the art of the potter to sublime heights. Rich polychrome designs were painted on the pottery before it was fired. Up to 14 different colored slips could be used to depict a variety of animals, birds, plants and fish.

Supernatural beings were also shown, as were decapitated human bodies and trophy heads. This evidence for the practice of headhunting is further substantiated by the discovery of caches of skulls in Nazca cemeteries. Few traces of major public buildings or engineering schemes have been found from Nazca times apart from the famous Nazca Lines. These mysterious designs were laid out on a gigantic scale in the desert between Palpa and Cahuachi. Also near Cahuachi lies an impressive stepped pyramid, made of adobe and reaching a height of more than 60 feet. Stone buildings were virtually unknown; the vast majority of structures were made of flimsy cane tied together.

In contrast to the Nazca, their contemporaries on the north coast of Peru, the Moche people, constructed some of the largest buildings in ancient South America. At Moche, their capital, the massive Temple of the Sun was constructed of solid adobe brick. Today it measures 130 feet in height and 1,150 feet in length, perhaps representing only one third of its original size.

Flourishing during the first six centuries A.D., the Moche people expanded the territory under their control by force, ultimately controlling the area from the Lambayeque Valley in the north to Huarmey in the south. Roads were built throughout their lands to link strongly fortified outposts. Civil engineers created irrigation channel networks which allowed the cultivation of peppers, maize, sweet potatoes and peanuts in the otherwise unproductive semidesert valleys.

Moche leaders were buried in great splendor, their tombs filled with elaborate goldwork, textiles and pottery. Specialist craft production reached a high level in the Moche realm: goldsmiths developed techniques such as the making of alloys and gilding; and they could cast objects in molds or by using the "lost wax" technique. Potters also used molds in their workshops to mass-produce vessels. High and low relief-decorated pots were sometimes hand-modeled and decorated with scenes from everyday life, warfare, religious ceremonies and myths.

A crouching warrior, armed with mace and shield, forms the body of a fine stirrup-spouted Moche vessel (RIGHT). Moche potters were renowned for the superb naturalistic modeling and painting of such pots, which were made to be buried in graves. During the Moche period, there was a revival of Chavín-style ornamental designs and Chavín religion. Traces of the earlier civilization's influence can be seen on this piece.

TEXTILES OF PARACAS

The stable, dry conditions of the Peruvian coastal desert, like the desert sands of Egypt, have preserved thousands of mummy bundles in large cemeteries. The embroidered garments found with the mummies reveal that ancient Peruvian clothing was colorful and untailored, and conveyed messages about the wearer's status and religious beliefs. Paracas textiles display an elaborate iconography: the feline deity (ABOVE) with a long tongue terminating in a face has two tails; one represents an animal, the other ends in a human head with streaming hair. Another famous Paracas image is that of a deity known as the Oculate Being, a figure that resembles the Smiling God of Chavín culture.

The production of cloth still plays an important part in the everyday life of Andean village women. The simple spinning and weaving equipment of their ancestors is still familiar to them as they continue to use similar spindles, distaffs and back-strap looms. Locally made garments immediately identify the wearer's ethnic or regional group according to the distinctive patterns and colours.

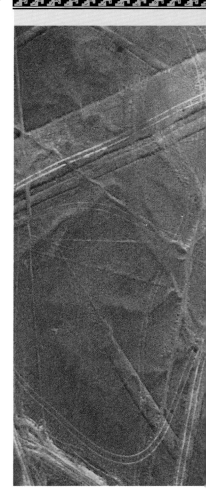

Three Moche figure vessels *depict a helmeted warrior with a disk-shaped shield, a potter modeling a vase with a spatula, and a musician playing the flute.*

THE NAZCA LINES

One of the most fascinating puzzles in South American archaeology is the purpose and age of the large-scale geometric and representational figures carved on some 200 square miles of coastal desert landscape in southern Peru near the town of Nazca. The Nazca Lines were constructed more than 1,000 years ago when the dark-colored surface layer of the desert was cleared away to expose the paler layer of gravel beneath. The soil that was removed was carefully placed in the levee-like banks on each side of the line, defining it and preventing a blurring of the edges.

Some figures are simply straight lines which run absolutely true for six miles or more across otherwise featureless desert. Other straight lines converge on central points or form geometric shapes such as trapezoids. Much rarer are the gigantic depictions of animals. These include a hummingbird, a duckling, a sea bird, a killer whale, a monkey more than 100 yards long, and a spider (LEFT). Stylistic similarities with creatures painted on Nazca-period pots and woven in Nazca textiles suggest that these images may have been made by the Nazca people, but accurate dating is difficult.

The precision of planning and layout of these figures is remarkable, and the achievement can only be truly appreciated from the air, a viewpoint not available to ancient Americans. This fact has led to the growth of many unusual theories about the origins of the Nazca Lines – even, for example, their creation by visiting extraterrestrials. The more probable explanation is that the straight lines were associated with astronomical observations, while the animal figures may have been made as offerings to the mountain and sky gods.

THE RISE OF THE INCAS

This tumi, *a ceremonial knife with a semicircular blade, was made by a craftsman of the Chimú people of cast and hammered gold set with turquoise. The Chimú dominated the north of Peru from the demise of the Huari Empire to the late 15th century, when they suffered defeat at the hands of the Incas. Chimú metalsmiths were so highly esteemed by the Incas that they were taken to Cuzco to work for the emperor.*

Ruins of mud brick walls *eroded by wind and rain still stand at the Chimú capital of Chan Chan on the desert coast of northern Peru. These are the remains of the ten palaces of the ten Chimú kings, each of whom was buried in a mausoleum at his residence.*

After about A.D. 500, the focus of South American civilization shifted from the Pacific coast to the high Andean basins. From about 500 to 1000, two empires, Tiahuanaco and Huari, grew to dominate much of the central and southern Andes and parts of the coast. Although they were contemporary and probably practiced the same religion, it is uncertain how they related to each other. The city of Huari could have been the capital of an independent northern state or the political headquarters of a much larger empire whose religious center was at the city of Tiahuanaco.

Tiahuanaco itself was certainly a major place of pilgrimages, attracting travelers from all regions of the Andes and Pacific coast. It was a large city, located at 11,800 feet above sea level on a windswept, treeless plain 12 miles south of Lake Titicaca, occupied by up to 40,000 people. The cult center consisted of stone-built temples, megalithic gateways, monolithic sculptures of figures up to 25 feet high and sunken courtyards surrounded by a moat. The sculptures are covered with low-relief carvings of felines, running winged figures shown in profile, and an anthropomorphic figure holding a staff and always depicted frontally. Some motifs have their roots in Chavín art, while the Staff God may be an early representation of Viracocha, the Creator God of later Andean civilizations.

Designs found on Tiahuanaco sculptures adorn the pottery — albeit in a cruder form — made in the Huari-dominated lands. By 600, the leaders of the Huari state had conquered territory extending 300 miles along the mountain chain on both sides of the capital and controlled the coast in the district of present-day Lima, the capital of Peru. Huari itself, a city of 100,000 inhabitants, was very different from Tiahuanaco. Its massive fortifications, barrack blocks, special areas for craftsmen and large stone houses give an overwhelming impression of a strong centralized power. Huari's expansion was achieved by military force, and its power maintained in provincial regions through control centers and strategically positioned storehouses. The Huari Empire was, however, short-lived. By 800, the capital had been abandoned, apparently suddenly; but Tiahuanaco continued to thrive and even extended its contacts southward into what is now Chile and western Argentina.

As the Huari Empire fell apart, a people known as the Chimú began to emerge as a power in the north of Peru, a region which they dominated until their defeat by the Incas in 1476. Led by semi-divine kings, their realm was enlarged through force of arms and secured by an efficient administrative system. The capital, Chan Chan, lies on the Pacific coast in the Moche Valley and was constructed entirely of mud brick. At its center, surrounded by walls six times the height of a man, lay ten vast labyrinthine compounds which served as both palaces and tombs of kings. When a king died, his compound became his mausoleum, and the new king ordered his workmen to build him a new one. The compounds consisted of a large courtyard, storerooms, wells, lesser courtyards and an area designated as the royal living quarters.

The empire they ruled eventually stretched for about 1,000 miles along the coast north and south of Chan Chan. Each newly colonized territory was duly given its own specially built governmental center for the better military and economic control of the various subject peoples. Some scholars have suggested that the Chimú learned their imperial skills through early contacts with Huari, as well as from their predecessors the Moche. What is certain, however, is that the Incas, the most rampant imperialists of all time in ancient South America, could not have managed their vast territories without the traditions of government established by Huari and the Chimú.

The Incas are first heard of in about 1200, when they entered the high Andean valley near the city of Cuzco as a small, warlike tribe engaging in local feuds. Gradually their chiefdom became more significant as they won more land around Cuzco, their timber-and-thatch capital. In the 1440s, Pachacutec Inca, the architect of the Inca Empire, began a series of long-distance campaigns which, within 30 years, brought South America, from Quito to Lake Titicaca, under Cuzco's rule.

The Gateway of the Sun (BELOW) is the largest and most highly decorated of the megalithic portals at Tiahuanaco, a major religious center situated just south of Lake Titicaca. The frieze depicts a central figure, dressed in an elaborate tunic, who holds a staff or scepter in each hand. Flanking him are three rows of winged attendants.

Guaman Poma de Ayala, a 17th-century Peruvian of mixed Inca and Spanish blood, wrote an illustrated account of everyday life in the Inca Empire which is a rare and valuable source of information for archaeologists and historians. In one of Poma's original woodcuts (ABOVE), agricultural work for the month of May is depicted: a

man cuts grain crops, which are being stacked by a woman. The drawing of September (ABOVE RIGHT) shows sowing taking place. A man uses a foot plow to break up the shallow Andean soil. One woman plants maize seeds, while the other's job is to cover them with soil.

About 25,000 miles of roads were built by the Incas to link all parts of their empire (ABOVE LEFT), which stretched down the west coast of South America from what is now Ecuador in the north to Chile in the south. Virtually every type of terrain was crossed: desert, tropical forest, mountain crags and high-altitude grasslands. Engineers spanned deep ravines with suspension bridges and dug tunnels.

THE INCA EMPIRE

The white granite ruins of the Inca town of Machu Picchu were discovered as recently as 1912. Although only 43 miles from Cuzco, its remote location on a narrow ridge 2,000 feet above the Urubamba River concealed it from the conquistadores and prevented it from being sacked. This small town of 150 houses is a triumph of Inca engineering and architectural achievement.

Machu Picchu

In only 90 years, the Inca Empire rose and fell. At its height, just before its destruction at the hands of the Spaniard Francisco Pizarro in 1532, it covered over 380,000 square miles and incorporated numerous diverse conquered populations, ranging from the hunter-gatherer tribes of the Upper Amazon to the sophisticates of Chimú city life. The rapid development of a state in which virtually all aspects of life were controlled from the center was only achieved by refining governmental techniques tried and tested by earlier Andean empires.

Inca society and government were hierarchical and pyramidal in form. The Sapa Inca, or emperor, was believed to be a descendant of the sun god and stood at the apex of the pyramid as the absolute ruler of Inca lands. His senior councilors and provincial governors, each of whom was responsible for 10,000 people, were chosen from the aristocracy which consisted principally of his relatives. Beneath them came lesser bureaucrats and military officers, some drawn from the trusted leaders of assimilated conquered peoples, who in turn controlled smaller numbers of imperial citizens. This system continued downward to the smallest unit, the nuclear family, with each official responsible to the Sapa Inca through the administrator who was ranked directly above him.

The success of the empire depended on not only a vast number of efficient bureaucrats, but also the existence of an excellent communications network, tight control of all agricultural and industrial production, a ruthless tax system and strict monitoring of the movements of citizens. There were also well-organized armed forces loyal to the emperor.

The Incas took over a pattern of existing roads from preceding states such as the Chimú kingdom, and extended and improved them with considerable engineering skill. Major north-south highways, running along the coast and through the interandean basins, were linked by lesser paths to produce a total of more than 25,000 miles of paved roads.

The roads, built by labor levied as tax on local peasants, facilitated the movement of Inca troops, the transport of supplies and the rapid transmission of information vital to the control of the empire. Series of relay runners could carry a message over 150 miles in a single day. Soldiers from the well-trained standing army could be dispatched to deal with rebellious subjects as soon as news of insurrection reached the authorities.

Sometimes forced mass movements of defeated hostile tribes seemed the efficient solution to potential revolt. Such peoples were evacuated to secure areas of the empire, where they were more easily supervised, and their former lands were distributed to trustworthy subjects.

The empire's infrastructure was created by highly skilled engineers and architects, who designed bridges, causeways, irrigation schemes, agricultural terraces, food warehouses, industrial buildings, fortresses and complete towns.

Taxes were uniform throughout the empire: a massive 66 percent of local production (for example, food, maize beer, stone tools, mats and cloth) was claimed for the state. Huge, strategically sited warehouses were built to store foodstuffs and other goods obtained as tax for future redistribution. The scale of stockpiling of supplies is illustrated by the fact that one storehouse at Huánuco Pampa could contain a staggering total of nine and half million gallons of grain.

The most sacred temple in Cuzco was the Coriancha, the Temple of the Sun, whose curved lower walls of Inca masonry survived the devastation of the city by Pizarro's troops in 1533. Today they form the foundation of the colonial-period church of Santa Domingo.

High taxes went with a degree of social security: during famines, the state provided rations and regularly distributed food and clothing to the old and infirm. It is astonishing that such a tightly organized state, dealing with the receipt and redistribution of vast quantities of taxes and the welfare of a huge population, was run without written records. The Incas did, however, have one device which assisted their bureaucratic control: the *quipu*. This was a set of strings with knots tied at particular intervals which was used by Inca administrators to record and transmit statistical information.

The center of this ultracentralized state was the Sapa Inca himself, and the efficient running of the empire depended on his ability. Without an authoritative head of state, there was little to bind together the various layers of Inca society. A second problem was that there was no clear line of succession to the throne. Pizarro and his small band of conquistadores arrived at a moment of crisis resulting from these two faults and took advantage of them. A war of succession between the half brothers Huascar and Atahualpa had strained and divided the system. When Atahualpa, the victor who became Sapa Inca, was seized by Pizarro and murdered, the whole structure collapsed and the greatest state in the ancient Americas disintegrated.

In their quest for riches, Spanish adventurers explored South America in search of El Dorado — a legendary land of gold. One of the most intrepid was Orellana, whose expedition across the Andes into Amazonia was dramatized by the film director Werner Herzog in Aguirre, Wrath of God.

The still (RIGHT) shows the conquistadores' steel armour and weapons. Their horses, never seen before by native Americans, also proved to be terrifying weapons. But the horses and armor did have their disadvantages: roads were poor and fodder was hard to find; and in addition, high temperatures often led to heat exhaustion among the soldiers.

Captured by a daring ruse at Cajamarca, the last effective Inca emperor, Atahualpa, was held to ransom by the Spanish conquistadores under their leader Francisco Pizarro. This evocative painting by the British artist Sir John Everett Millais (1829–96) entitled Pizarro seizing the Inca of Peru *was inspired by this crucial moment of South American history.*

To pay the ransom, the Incas' temples and treasuries throughout the realm were emptied to fill a large hall at Cajamarca with gold and silver to just below ceiling height. Pizarro did not release his captive, but required him to convert to Christianity, which Atahualpa refused to do. Then, after a show trial, the emperor was garotted and burned at the stake as a heretic. Thus, the only effective leader who could organize resistance to the Spanish invaders was removed.

THE FIRST MEXICAN CIVILIZATIONS

Colossal stone heads, such as this one, weighing up to 20 tons each have been discovered at La Venta, San Lorenzo and Tres Zapotes, three major Olmec sites. The source of the basalt boulders from which they were hewn lies in the Tuxtla Mountains, approximately 60 miles from their find spots. Although superficially very similar, these baby-faced sculptures are portraits of individual Olmec rulers, who are identified by the decorative motifs that can be seen on their helmetlike headgear.

From about 1000 B.C. for two and a half thousand years, successive civilizations of Mexico consisted of cultural variations on a theme. The principal components common to each were monumental architecture, planned ceremonial and religious centers with pyramid and plaza complexes, accurate astronomical observations, meticulous calendrical computations and hieroglyphic writing.

The first great Mexican civilization, the Olmec, was born in the humid, swampy lands of the present-day states of Tabasco and Veracruz on the Gulf of Mexico. Silt from annual floods continually renewed the high fertility of the farmland where at least two harvests of maize and root crops could be guaranteed each year. Intensive agriculture produced large, reliable food surpluses, which fed the large labor forces of craftsmen and artists needed for massive Olmec building projects.

The Olmecs seem to have spread their influence more through trade networks than by conquest. Their heartland, a small region measuring about 30 miles by 125 miles, contains major sites dating from about 1200 to 300 B.C. From such places as La Venta and the earlier San Lorenzo, numerous examples of Olmec art have been recovered. These include stone sculptures, often in the form of colossal human heads 10 feet tall, and exquisitely worked jade figurines and axes. Many of the supernatural beings depicted appear in later Mexican cosmologies.

Few Olmec habitations have been discovered, and it is mainly through their ceremonial centers that the Olmecs are known. At La Venta, a ritual area contains a fluted clay

The Pyramid of the Niches at El Tajín, so called because 365 niches decorate its seven steps, is one of the few buildings so far excavated at this "type site" for Classic Veracruz culture. Each niche is reputed to have once held the image of the god appropriate to each day of the year.

After the decline of Olmec power in Veracruz, little is known about developments on the Gulf coast until about A.D. 600, when the large city of El Tajín was constructed. Classic Veracruz culture is famous for its stone replicas of equipment used in the ritual ballgame, as well as for the large number of ballcourts which have been found at El Tajín itself.

pyramid more than 110 feet high and three pavements made of serpentine blocks arranged to form stylized jaguar masks. The pavements were covered up soon after they were made as an offering to the gods, and many Olmec sites contain caches of small carvings in jade or serpentine which had been deposited for similar purposes.

Olmec trading networks reached as far as Oaxaca and the Valley of Mexico, where white pottery Olmec-style figurines have been found in graves. The desire for raw materials such as cinnabar, jade, iron ore, serpentine, basalt and obsidian brought the Olmecs into contact with suppliers in many regions of Mexico, and essential elements of their culture continued to be important in the region well after their own decline by 300 B.C.

The next great peak of Mexican civilization was achieved at the great city of Teotihuacán. As early as 1500 B.C., this site in the Valley of Mexico was a pilgrimage place of tremendous religious importance: a cave there was believed to be the birthplace of the Sun and Moon. In the first century A.D., major developments occurred. The huge Pyramid of the Sun, the largest artificial structure in pre-Columbian America, was created and a planned city laid out around it. The rural population moved to the city, and for the next five centuries, as temple after temple was constructed, Teotihuacán flourished as one of the dozen largest cities in the world.

At least 200,000 people – 90 percent of the area's population – lived in the city. The ruling elite dwelt in palaces in the city center, skilled artisans and farmers occupied single-story apartment compounds, while laborers had flimsier adobe huts. Laid out on a north-south axis, the grid plan of the city was maintained for more than 500 years, during which time the workers in shell, kitchen pottery, tableware, semiprecious stones and obsidian blades continued to inhabit their allocated quarters.

The city's influence was evidently spread by diplomacy and trade; at Kaminaljujú in the Maya highlands of Guatemala, the graves of eminent Teotihuacán merchants have been found. Depictions of soldiers are rare until the final century of Teotihuacán's existence; they appear with ominous frequency in the period from 650 to 750, and the rise of military power may be connected with the city's decline at this time. It is still unclear what caused the city's final collapse and the destruction of its center by fire during the eighth century. Even so, it remained a place of pilgrimage until the Spanish came 800 years later.

Teotihuacán was subdivided into four districts. In the center was the ceremonial complex (BELOW) where the Avenue of the Dead linked the Pyramid of the Moon and the 230-foot-high Pyramid of the Sun. Almost 100 smaller shrines and temples faced the avenue, while to the east lay the six-tiered Temple of Quetzalcoatl. Elite residential districts surrounded the ceremonial complex; beyond these lay the apartments and workshops of craftsmen, while the farming population lived on the outer edges of the city.

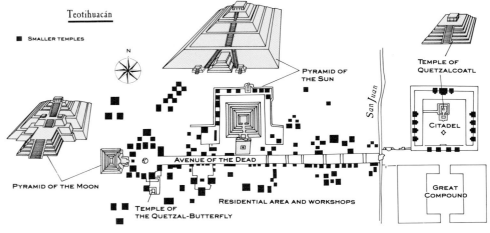

Other, less well-known civilizations flourished in Mexico at the time of the Olmecs and Teotihuacán. In the region of Oaxaca, the Zapotec civilization was centered on Monte Albán (LEFT). Established as a Zapotec settlement in about the middle of the first millennium B.C., this hilltop site consisted of a number of plazas, platforms for temples and a huge pyramid. Also, more than 150 stone slabs decorated with low-relief carvings known as the Danzantes ("Dancers") (ABOVE LEFT) survive from about 500 B.C. The reliefs may in fact have formed a war memorial with the figures shown writhing in agony after mutilation in battle.

THE MAYA (1)

Present-day rural Maya *often live in one-room houses (*BELOW*), similar to those of their ancestors, as this copy of a Maya mural (*RIGHT*) shows. The huts are built around slim poles lashed together; a thatched roof keeps out rain and heat. These houses were copied in stone by the ancient Maya for the temple shrines that stood atop their pyramids.*

The Maya city of Copán, *in Honduras, shown in this reconstruction, was a complex of stone-built temples, palaces, ballcourts and plaster-floored plazas. The huge Temple 11 (6), with its painted "roof comb," looked north across the 650-foot-long Great Plaza (1) and North Plaza. Adjacent was the Court of the Hieroglyphic Stairway (4), named after the 2,500-glyph long inscription carved on the stone steps of a temple (3), the longest known Maya inscription.*

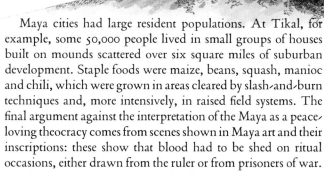

Maya civilization, the only one to achieve true literacy in pre-Columbian America, flourished between A.D. 300 and 900 in Guatemala, western Honduras, Belize, Yucatán and eastern Campeche in Mexico. This area encompasses a great variety of terrain and many ecological zones among which raw materials and products were being traded as early as 2000 B.C. Maya civilization reaches back to this period; excavations at Cuello, Belize, have revealed a proto-Maya culture with characteristic groupings of Maya-type buildings, including a temple on low mounds around a plaster-floored central plaza.

From 300 B.C. to A.D. 300, sizable cities were being constructed in both lowland and highland zones. By the start of the Classic Maya phase, in about A.D. 300, extraordinary stone-built cities, such as Tikal in Guatemala and Palenque in Campeche, had come into existence. Maya cities contained multistoried buildings, often called palaces, temple-topped pyramids up to 150 feet high, ballcourts in which a ritual game was played, and astronomical observatories, all grouped around central plazas.

Such gigantic enterprises depended on a large population and sociopolitical mechanisms to control its labor. The nature of this control has been disputed. Formerly, the predominance of religious buildings in the undefended cities led them to be interpreted as purely ceremonial centers, used only for periodic festivals. Recent breakthroughs in deciphering Maya hieroglyphs and further excavations have shown this to be untrue. The inscriptions refer to particular events involving members of ruling dynasties, for example accession to the throne, and emphasize their legitimate descent. Public sculptures and wall paintings stressed the unity of the gods with the hereditary rulers and commemorated political and matrimonial alliances and victorious campaigns.

Maya cities had large resident populations. At Tikal, for example, some 50,000 people lived in small groups of houses built on mounds scattered over six square miles of suburban development. Staple foods were maize, beans, squash, manioc and chili, which were grown in areas cleared by slash-and-burn techniques and, more intensively, in raised field systems. The final argument against the interpretation of the Maya as a peace-loving theocracy comes from scenes shown in Maya art and their inscriptions: these show that blood had to be shed on ritual occasions, either drawn from the ruler or from prisoners of war.

Classic Maya culture was neither homogenous nor closed to outside influence. Each major city-state developed its own art and architectural style. Regional products, such as cacao, copal

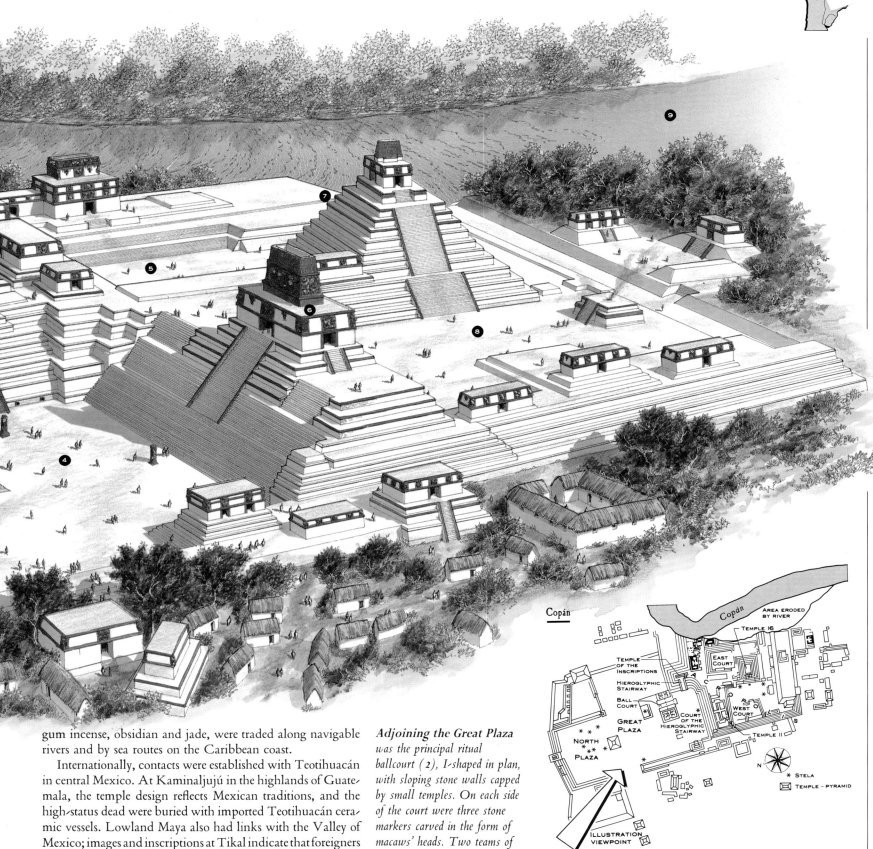

gum incense, obsidian and jade, were traded along navigable rivers and by sea routes on the Caribbean coast.

Internationally, contacts were established with Teotihuacán in central Mexico. At Kaminaljujú in the highlands of Guatemala, the temple design reflects Mexican traditions, and the high-status dead were buried with imported Teotihuacán ceramic vessels. Lowland Maya also had links with the Valley of Mexico; images and inscriptions at Tikal indicate that foreigners from Teotihuacán married into the ruling dynasty. Mexican influence declined after A.D. 500, leading to a resurgence of Maya civilization. Many splendid new buildings were constructed at Copán, Palenque and Naranjo, while Tikal was virtually reconstructed, the new edifices covering earlier ones.

Adjoining the Great Plaza was the principal ritual ballcourt (2), I-shaped in plan, with sloping stone walls capped by small temples. On each side of the court were three stone markers carved in the form of macaws' heads. Two teams of players competed to score points by hitting a solid rubber ball, without using hands or feet, against one of the macaw markers.

Facing the West Plaza (8) towered Temple 16 (7), behind which lie the remains of the East Plaza (5) and other temples, largely destroyed by river erosion. In fact the Río Copán (9) was diverted in 1930 to avoid further damage.

Copán

TEMPLE OF THE INSCRIPTIONS
HIEROGLYPHIC STAIRWAY
BALL COURT
GREAT PLAZA
NORTH PLAZA
COURT OF THE HIEROGLYPHIC STAIRWAY
EAST COURT
TEMPLE 16
WEST COURT
TEMPLE II
Copán
AREA ERODED BY RIVER
ILLUSTRATION VIEWPOINT
✳ STELA
▦ TEMPLE - PYRAMID
N

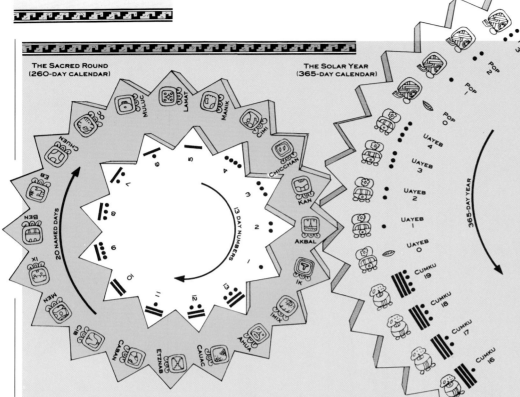

THE SACRED ROUND
(260-DAY CALENDAR)

THE SOLAR YEAR
(365-DAY CALENDAR)

CALCULATING TIME

The Maya numerical system was based on units of 20 and included the concept of zero. Numbers were written down using a system of horizontal bars for units of five, dots for one, and a stylized shell for zero. The Maya possessed three major calendars: the Solar Year; the Sacred Round; and the Long Count. The Solar Year consisted of 365 days which made 18 named months, each of 20 numbered days, with an extra five-day period at the year's end.

The Maya did not allow for Leap Years, even though they knew perfectly well that the Solar Year was really $365\frac{1}{4}$ days long. The Solar Year calendar (LEFT) intermeshed with the Sacred Round (FAR LEFT): this was made up of a cycle of 20 named days which permutated with the numbers 1 to 13 and returned to its starting point every 52 years. This 52-year-cycle was called the Calendar Round.

The third calendar was the Long Count, used principally for giving historical dates outside the compass of the Calendar Round. Starting on August 13, 3114 B.C., in the Christian calendar, the number of days elapsed since that date were counted in units of 144,000, 72,000, 360, 20 and 1 day. Each unit had its own glyph, and the numbers of units were indicated by bars and dots preceding the unit glyph.

In the ninth century, Maya civilization collapsed. The causes are still unclear. It has been proposed that the agricultural system was simply too fragile to support the demands placed upon it, or that invasion or internal strife destroyed a society which had concentrated so much labor and wealth in glorifying its rulers.

Maya cities survived longer in Yucatán, where Chichén Itzá was remodeled by the Toltecs in about A.D. 1000. Abandoning Chichén Itzá in about A.D. 1220, the Maya built a new capital at Mayapán in 1283. Significantly, this city had defensive walls to protect its 10,000 inhabitants, but these could not prevent its destruction during civil wars of the 15th century. In the 1520s, the invading Spanish met only a few scattered and degenerate groups of Maya, their old traditions and intellectual achievements obscured by the passage of time.

It was the Maya's ruined cities and huge carved monuments, overgrown by tropical forest, which first seized the imagination of European and North American explorers and scholars in the 1800s. Only later did the great intellectual achievements lying behind them come to be appreciated.

Above all, ideas about time played a central role in Maya life. The construction of several elaborate intermeshing calendars, and mathematical calculations and astronomical observations of the movements of heavenly bodies in conjunction with the calendars, were areas in which the Maya surpassed all other Mesoamerican peoples.

Time, writing and the activities of Maya rulers were all intimately connected. Virtually all monuments bear glyphs detailing the exact date when the rituals and events they depict were performed. The days for performing ceremonies were carefully chosen according to their auspices. Maya sculptural monuments were the physical markers of time: for example,

stelae (upright stone slabs) were erected to mark the lapse of units of 144,000 days; portraits of rulers were inscribed with their genealogy and achievements; the lintels of buildings were dated and the person on whose authority they were constructed named. Maya texts, so far, consist of terse factual statements.

Not all Maya writing was carved in stone; four books written on treebark paper have survived, and many pots have painted texts as long as most monumental inscriptions. The outer surface of thin-walled cylindrical pots was painted with polychrome scenes of ritual activities, such as the ballgame and events in the underworld. Hieroglyphs identify the participants and date the events like a cartoon caption. On a larger scale, wall paintings on the interior plaster of tombs and temples equally demonstrate the excellence of Maya artists.

The high level of Maya artistic production indicates the existence of talented, trained specialist craftsmen working for the elite of their society. Some of the raw materials in which they worked were both valuable and very difficult to handle. Jade carving was one of their greatest arts; jade in all its shades of green was prized far more than gold and was traded from its principal source in the Motagua River far into Maya lands. The extremely hard stone was sawn, ground and polished with string saws, drills and various grades of abrasive. In this way, jade was made into flowerlike flares for the enlarged perforations in the ear lobes of high-ranking Maya, pectoral plaques, pendants, beads and small masklike human faces, which were worn as jewelry and sometimes deposited in votive caches or as grave goods.

Pink spondylus shell was also valued for ornament making, and feather work was highly developed. Perhaps the most fragile medium in which Maya artist-craftsmen worked was obsidian. This dark volcanic glass was chipped into translucent waferlike blades or eccentric shapes and incised with designs.

At Chichén Itzá in the center of the Yucatán peninsula, the Classic Maya city was largely rebuilt and extended during the tenth and eleventh centuries A.D. The result is a unique blend of Classic Maya and Toltec architecture and ornament, best displayed in the 73-foot-high stepped pyramid (ABOVE RIGHT), known as the Castillo, which stands in the center of the main plaza. To the west is the Temple of the Warriors, whose entrance is guarded by open-jawed carved stone representations of the god Quetzalcoatl, the Feathered Serpent.

Principal Maya sites

Classic Maya cities flourished in parts of Guatemala, El Salvador, Belize, Honduras and Mexico for almost 600 years.

DISCOVERING THE MAYA

In the 19th century, the exploration and revelation of the Maya civilization was dramatic and puzzling. So impressive were the Maya monuments that many scholars considered them to be beyond the capability of Native Americans and attributed them to white migrants, such as the legendary Ten Lost Tribes of Israel.

It was the work of John L. Stephens, an American lawyer, and Frederick Catherwood, a British artist, that brought the Maya to public notice and supported the theory of an indigenous origin of Maya civilization. In 1839, they set out for Copán to study its ruins and any others they could find. Stephens's account gives the first accurate description of 44 Maya sites, and Catherwood, who was compelled to wear gloves to ward off the mosquitoes, produced equally accurate drawings of Maya monuments and writing.

Another later Maya pioneer was the Englishman Alfred Percival Maudslay, who visited the Maya area between 1881 and 1894, during which time he saw various sites including Chichén Itzá, Copán, Tikal and Palenque. Maudslay's site plans, scale drawings, photographs and papier-mâché molds of many sculptures and inscriptions set standards for later research in Maya studies.

Maya stelae come in many sizes and shapes. At Quiriguá, Guatemala, Alfred Maudslay photographed the plain rectangular monolith (LEFT) in 1885, while his predecessor Frederick Catherwood drew an accurate picture of the rococo "stone idol" at Copán in 1884.

Screen-folded deerskin books were used by Aztec priests to keep count of the complex rituals appropriate to each day of their calendar. This book (BELOW RIGHT), the Codex Borgia, is partly concerned with the process of divination. In the center of the page, back to back, are two gods: Quetzalcoatl, also shown (BELOW) in a detail from the colonial period Codex Florentine, is on the left, manifested as the winged god Ehecatl; while Mictlantecuhtli is represented as a human skeleton on the right. The margins of the page contain the signs which represent each day of the Aztec month.

The disintegration of Classic Maya civilization in the Yucatán peninsula and the abandonment of the central Mexican city-state Teotihuacán left power vacuums in two large areas of Mexico. During the tenth century A.D., tribes of land-hungry nomads from the northwestern deserts of the Sierra Madre Mountains swept into the Mexico basin, the zone formerly dominated by Teotihuacán. Tribal warlords conducted a series of full-scale campaigns which reduced their enemies to tribute-paying vassals, whose forced contributions, often in the form of foodstuffs, supplied the conquerors' armies for further advance. These barbarians brought with them the Nahuatl language and bloodthirsty religious practices.

By 950, a single dominant group of these invaders had emerged. They were the Toltecs, who rapidly absorbed surviving remnants of Teotihuacán civilization. They adopted architectural styles, pottery technology, myths, legends and traditions and adapted them to produce a hybrid culture which became the model for all subsequent Mexican states until the European conquest some 500 years later. Indeed, the days of the Toltecs were idealized as a golden age by later ancient Mexicans.

In fact, Tula, the Toltec capital, was a much smaller city than Teotihuacán, but like its progenitor, the central area contained a planned complex of stepped pyramids and platforms, none more than 40 feet high. In the first decades of Tula's existence, from 950 to 987, the most important city god was Quetzalcoatl (Feathered Serpent), a benign deity inherited from Teotihuacán. But

according to legend, Quetzalcoatl was exiled from Tula in A.D. 987 by a traditional Toltec tribal god, Tezcatlipoca (Smoking Mirror), patron of sorcerers and warriors.

Tezcatlipoca and his fellow tribal gods could only be prevented from destroying the world by frequent offerings of human hearts and blood. At this time, large-scale human sacrifice became a central feature of ancient Mexican religious ritual. Basalt sculptures of reclining human figures discovered at Tula were carved to have human hearts placed on their hollow stomachs, and storage racks for the skulls of victims kept a literal head count of the number of offerings.

Virtually identical sculptures of skull racks have been found more than 620 miles away from Tula at Chichén Itzá in the center of the Yucatán peninsula. Soon after 987, this abandoned Maya city underwent a major remodeling in Toltec style, becoming a far more impressive city than Tula itself. This creation of a Toltec city in distant lands may perhaps be reflected in the legend of Quetzalcoatl's exile from Tula.

Eventually, Toltec influence stretched from the Gulf coast to the Pacific coast of Chiapas and deep into what are now the countries of Guatemala and Belize. Long-range trade routes were established, with fine quality multicolored painted pottery being imported from Costa Rica and large quantities of turquoise from the American Southwest. In the 1170s, however, Tula was sacked by Chichimec tribesmen raiding from their increasingly desiccated, famine-struck homelands situated in

northwestern Mexico. Just as the Toltecs' barbarian ancestors had established many petty kingdoms in the Mexican basin, so the Chichimec created small city-states which were almost continuously at war with each other.

Finally gaining supremacy among these different groups were a people known as the Aztecs, who settled in the Valley of Mexico in 1325. Over the following three generations, the Aztecs served as mercenaries to the powerful city-states already established on the lake shores, gaining enough military and political expertise to attack and defeat their former masters, the Tepanec of Azcapotzalco, in 1428. For most of the next 100 years, the growth of the Aztec Empire seemed to fulfill the myth that Tenochtitlán was to be the center of the world and the Aztecs the rulers of it.

The Aztec emperor Moctezuma's headdress, four feet high, was made of irridescent green quetzal feathers woven into a cloth backing and embellished with tiny blue plumes and gold disks.

At Tula, the capital of the Toltecs, lying about 45 miles northwest of present-day Mexico City, four Toltec warriors (BELOW) carved in basalt stand on the summit of the best-preserved pyramid. This, probably the Temple of Quetzalcoatl, is decorated with reliefs of coyotes, jaguars and eagles devouring hearts. Each column stands 15 feet high and is made of four sections fitted together with mortice and tenon joints to form massive columns which once supported the temple roof. These powerful Atlantean figures wear full battledress, clearly displaying the military essence of Toltec culture.

THE AZTEC EMPIRE

In theory, the Aztec state consisted of a triple alliance among the rulers of Texcoco, Tlacopán and Tenochtitlán, but it was dominated by the last, the Aztec capital city. After 1428, Aztec history is a story of expansion until the Aztecs ruled an area that stretched from the Pacific to the Atlantic with an estimated ten million people.

Aztec society was profoundly militaristic in both organiza-tion and spirit. The large professional army drew many of its officers from the aristocracy, whose young men might enter one of the military orders of knighthood, the Eagles or the Jaguars. Officers could rise from the ranks, and prowess in battle often led to high status and power. Soldiers were protected by padded cotton armor and disk-shaped shields and fought with darts and serrated-edged sword-clubs made of hardwood set with razor-sharp obsidian blades.

One of the aims of Aztec warfare was to acquire new lands, not for colonization, but as a source of income. Conquered peoples, governed by puppet rulers, were expected to pay heavy taxes, collected by efficient Aztec officials based at administrative centers defended by military garrisons. Careful accounts were kept of what taxes were due from each province twice a year. Massive tonnages of beans, maize and other grain crops were levied, together with manufactured goods, such as mats, stools, clothing, weapons and luxuries that included incense, cacao, gold, turquoise and feathers. These goods poured into Tenoch-titlán, as did prisoners of war — spoils which were, in fact, of even greater importance to the Aztecs.

Like the Toltecs, from whom they claimed descent, the Aztecs believed the continuity and safety of the world could be guaranteed only by the regular and abundant sacrifice of human victims. Captured enemies formed the majority of offerings, and to provide a continuous, plentiful supply, "Flowery Wars" with nearby states of Tlaxcala and Huexotzinco were arranged. These ritualized combats resulted in thousands of captives being taken to Tenochtitlán, where their blood — "flowers" in Aztec poetic language — would be spilled.

In less than 200 years, the once uninhabited island at the swampy edge of Lake Texcoco was transformed by the Aztecs into a major stone-built city with over 100,000 inhabitants. The island capital was crisscrossed by narrow canals which reminded the first European visitors of Venice. At the heart of the city lay a ceremonial precinct where the emperor, elected from a royal lineage by the hereditary aristocracy, lived in splendor in a vast stone-built palace. Lesser palaces and schools also lay near the ritual center of the empire. Here, temples were dedicated to Tezcatlipoca, the warrior god, and other Toltec-derived deities.

CORTÉS: THE RETURNING GOD

The Aztecs believed that the world had passed through four creations which had been destroyed by jaguars, fire, wind and water. The fifth and current creation, they thought, was in danger of being ended by earthquakes at the whim of earth monsters. Every 104 years, when the cycles of the 260-day Aztec calendar, the 365-day solar calendar and 584-day Venus cycle all coincided, the world was threatened with destruction.

Calculation of such danger periods was important, and the great Aztec calendar stone (LEFT), nearly 13 feet in diameter, exemplifies Aztec fears. In its center is the face of the Earth Monster, surrounded by symbols of previous creations. Twenty glyphs representing the names of each day in the Aztec month occupy the innermost circular band. But the stone was unusable as a calendar, and computations were made by priests using texts and tables written in skin books.

Other destructive events were dreaded by the Aztecs. Each day the sun god needed to be fed with human hearts and blood to give him strength to survive the night and to rise the next day. The return of the god Quetzalcoatl was also expected, fulfilling the Toltec myth which said that before leaving on his journey into exile across the Gulf of Mexico on a raft of snakes, the god vowed to return to the Valley of Mexico to reclaim his rightful kingdom and, presumably, to end Aztec power.

Greatly to the advantage of the Spaniard Hernán Cortés, the year 1519 was considered one of the probable dates for Quetzalcoatl's return, and wild storms and other phenomena seen in Tenochtitlán that year prepared the emperor and his people for unusual events. As soon as Cortés made landfall on the Gulf coast of Mexico, news of the arrival of pale-skinned, bearded exotic strangers was relayed to Moctezuma. Believing Cortés to be Quetzalcoatl, the emperor allowed the Spanish adventurers into the city where they seized and murdered him.

Aztec gods were worshipped at the Great Temple, at the summit of which stood shrines to Huitzilopotchli, the sun god, and Tlaloc, the god of rain. Human sacrifices were usually carried out on a platform outside the shrine by stretching a victim over a stone altar and cutting out the heart, which was offered to the god. The body was rolled down the pyramid steps. It is said that in one four-day period of great celebration, 20,000 victims were killed.

The stench of blood and the clotted locks of priests horrified the Spaniard Hernán Cortés and his followers when they reached the Aztec capital in 1519. Having landed at Cempoala on the Gulf coast, the Spanish force soon discovered that the discontented Tlaxcalans, weary of the Aztecs' "Flowery Wars," were willing informants, spies and allies. Defeat of the last Aztec emperor, Moctezuma II, was made easier by traditional beliefs in the return of the god Quetzalcoatl, which led the ruler to identify Cortés with the god and welcome him to his city. Cortés took his host prisoner, killed him, and by 1521, had stifled all Aztec resistance. In a campaign lasting only two years, a small force of Europeans destroyed a Mesoamerican civilization which had roots that stretched back 3,000 years.

Tenochtitlan.

This post-conquest Aztec drawing (RIGHT) *from Tlaxcala shows Cortés, seated on the right, talking to Moctezuma II. Behind Cortés stands his interpreter and mistress, Malinzin, who, along with the people of Tlaxcala, helped Cortés achieve success.*

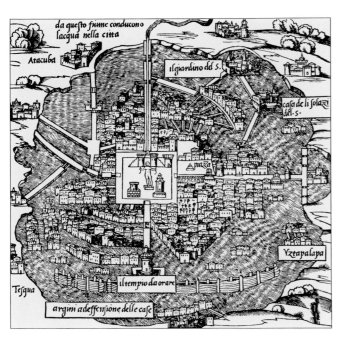

Only seven years after the Conquest, the artist Benedetto Bordone drew Tenochtitlán (ABOVE) *as a city of European-style pitched roofed houses defended by castlelike fortifications. The causeways linking the island to the mainland are reasonably accurate, as is the aqueduct running to the square center precinct. Although Tenochtitlán lies beneath modern Mexico City, it is known that it conformed to a rigid grid plan, and that the flat-roofed Aztec houses were often served by both streets and canals.*

In 1325, the nomadic Aztecs are said to have sighted an eagle grasping a snake while perching on a prickly pear cactus. This bizarre occurrence, depicted on this post-conquest Aztec codex (RIGHT), *was the prophetic sign that there they should found their capital city, Tenochtitlán, "Place of the Prickly Pear Cactus." This ancient symbol of the Aztec capital now adorns the national flag of Mexico.*

THE MOUND BUILDERS

From about 1000 B.C. to A.D. 1450, eastern North America witnessed the rise and fall of three distinctive prehistoric cultures known as the Adena, Hopewell – both named after find-sites – and the Mississippian. Each culture was characterized by the building of mounds. The eastern woodlands, a zone that was centered in Ohio and which extends into Pennsylvania, West Virginia, Kentucky and Indiana, was the birthplace of the Adena culture.

Between 1000 B.C. and 300 B.C., the Adena people constructed large scale earthen monuments, some of which, known as effigy mounds, are in the shape of living creatures. More frequently, the earthworks form enclosures, many perfectly circular, consisting of a low embankment with a parallel internal ditch. These "sacred circles" are thought to have been used for ceremonies, and some enclose burial mounds. Inside the burial mounds are the remains of people who merited elaborate funerary rites. The rich burials and political organization required to build the sacred circles indicate that Adena was a chiefly society.

Hopewell culture (c.300 B.C.–A.D. 500) can be seen as a continuation and elaboration of basic patterns established in Adena times. Hopewell earthworks were large and sometimes built in complexes, where circular, rectangular and polygonal enclosures were linked by long, embankment-edged causeways. Burial mounds were built inside or near the enclosures and covered multiroomed log tombs. Several rooms were needed: one for the important first burial; another to contain subsequent interments of cremated human bones; and a third for the very large quantities of grave goods which included flint and obsidian dart tips, spearthrowers, stone knives and polished axes.

Tobacco smoking was a widespread ceremonial custom in much of prehistoric North America. Tobacco pipes are among the most beautiful artifacts made by the Adena and Hopewell peoples, who lavished great skill on their manufacture from pipestone. The Adena pipe (LEFT), made up to 3,000 years ago, represents a standing human figure wearing a loin cloth and large ear ornaments.

Hopewell effigy pipes, made between 300 B.C. and A.D. 500, are different in form. The one shown here (BELOW LEFT) is in the shape of a frog, whose body contains the tobacco bowl and sits on a curved, pierced platform through which the smoke was drawn. The frog's front faced the smoker.

Adena and Hopewell sites are shown on the maps below (LEFT and CENTER) and those of the Mississippian culture (A.D. 700–1450) on the map on the right.

Most archaeologists of the 18th and early 19th centuries dug into ancient American mounds with little regard for the scientific data they were destroying. One apparent exception was Dr. Montreville Dickenson, who claimed to have "investigated" more than 1,000 mounds. In the painting (RIGHT) he is shown directing an unusually careful excavation, which clearly depicts the stratification, skeletons and other objects that he discovered.

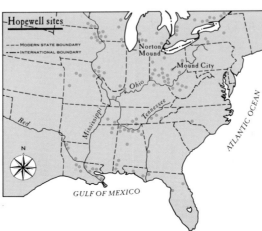

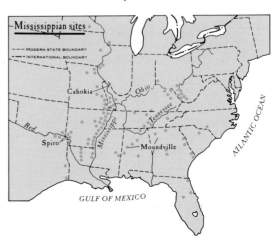

Hopewell-derived cultures covered North America from western New York to Kansas and from the Gulf of Mexico to Lake Huron. Their trading contacts extended even farther, proved by finds in burial mounds. Conch shells from the Gulf coast have been found in Wisconsin and Michigan; shark's teeth in Illinois, obsidian and grizzly bear teeth from the far west in Illinois and Ohio.

The Mississippian culture, which extended from the Atlantic coast to Oklahoma and from Minnesota to Mississippi, first became predominant in the Middle Mississippi Valley from about A.D. 700. It was characterized by rectangular flat-topped mounds which formed platforms for timber temples, mortuary houses and chiefly residences. About 20 mounds, grouped around a plaza and encircled by a stout pallisade fence, formed the center of the oldest towns known in North America. Urban centers, such as Cahokia, housed populations of up to 10,000; and rural zones contained permanent villages with dense populations supported by intensive maize cultivation.

Many Mississippian burials contain valuables, including copper and mica sheet ornaments, pearls, monolithic stone axes, pottery vessels in the form of trophy heads, and shell vessels. They are decorated with incised motifs, such as weeping eyes, flying winged human figures, and sunburst designs that relate to a religion known as the Southern Cult. Mississippian culture peaked in about A.D. 1250, then declined until, by A.D. 1450, the Middle Mississippi had become a depopulated area. The densely packed town dwellers had fallen victim to epidemic disease, a fate which was to befall many of their fellow Americans, who had no defense against the illnesses brought by Europeans.

The famous Serpent Mound in Ohio is the most striking of the enigmatic effigy mounds. Raised only some three feet above the surrounding land surface, it coils over 1,300 feet from head to tail, and appears to be open-jawed, swallowing an egg.

CULTURES OF THE SOUTHWEST

During the first millennium B.C., the hunter-gatherer societies of the American Southwest – New Mexico, Utah, Arizona and parts of Colorado – were transformed into settled communities by the introduction of horticultural crops, as well as cultural influences from Mexico: maize had come to the region about 1000 B.C., and squash and beans arrived somewhat later. After 300 B.C., three major prehistoric cultures can be identified in the region: the Hohokam, Mogollon and Anasazi.

The area occupied by the Hohokam, in present-day southern Arizona and northern Sonora in Mexico, receives little rain, and the Hohokam survived only because of their expertise in irrigation. Their settlements of half-buried houses were near large rivers from which they could divert the water into their fields. Their culture is remarkable for the labor dedicated to canal building and water conservation.

Richard Wetherill, on the far right of the picture, was the discoverer of the remarkable cliff village of Mesa Verde in Colorado, built into the side of a canyon by craftsmen of the Anasazi culture (A.D. 1100–1300). This photograph was taken in 1894 when Wetherill was guiding some visitors around the site.

Highly valued Mimbres ware, *such as the bowl (*ABOVE*), is a prime target for treasure hunters and collectors. This bichrome piece is decorated with two human figures wearing waist bands, loincloths and body paint. Made in the 11th century A.D. and deposited in a grave, it has been broken deliberately in order to allow the owner's spirit to escape.*

*The destruction of an ancient burial ground at Slack Farm, Kentucky, in 1987 brought protests about the ransacking of graves for commercial purposes. Here, a native American (*RIGHT*) inspects the desecration of his ancestors' bones.*

PROTECTING THE PAST

Stylish bowls made in the Mimbres Valley from about A.D. 1050 to 1200 are objects coveted by collectors; and the insatiable market for these pieces has resulted in bulldozing of Mimbres sites by treasure hunters. Such destruction of archaeological sites and the desecration of the graves of the ancestors of native Americans also occur elsewhere in the country.

In 1987, a group of treasure hunters virtually destroyed an important Mississippian village at Slack Farm, western Kentucky. The site, inhabited from about A.D. 1450 to 1650, covered some 40 acres near the Ohio River. In all, 450 small craters were dug into it seeking the graves of native Americans who had been buried with offerings of pots, jewelry, tobacco pipes and weapons, for all of which there is a ready market. The bones of at least 650 individuals were scattered like refuse.

Unusually, the state of Kentucky has a law under which the diggers could be charged: desecration of a venerated object. The looters were prosecuted, and archaeologists were called in to try to piece together the jumbled pieces of the past. After scientific study, the human bones were returned to native Americans for traditional burial.

The Slack Farm case may lead to new legislation in other states or even at federal level, but it poses many difficult questions about the ownership and protection of archaeological sites and who has the right to permit or deny their disturbance.

Excellent farming techniques enabled the Hohokam to produce two crops of cotton, maize, beans and squash a year, supplemented by wild fruits and seeds, fish and game. Excavations at the sites of Pueblo Grande and Snaketown have produced evidence of strong links with the major civilizations of Mexico to the south. Ballcourts have been discovered, as have platform mounds of broadly Mesoamerican form. Luxury goods such as cast-copper bells, macaw and parrot feathers, pyrite mirrors and turquoise mosaics suggest trade links or even the actual northward migration of people from Mexico.

Changes in funerary practices and the fortification of Hohokam settlements in the period from A.D. 1200 to 1400 suggest major upheavals in the region. After 1200, much Hohokam territory came under Anasazi dominance, and after 1400 many sites were abandoned.

The Mogollon culture, which lasted until c.A.D. 1200, was located in the rugged mountains of southwestern New Mexico and eastern Arizona. Farming was established early in this area; domesticated maize was grown in the first millennium B.C., but agriculture had to be supplemented by hunting and gathering. Small settlements of pit houses were located along river tributaries, near horticultural plots which benefited from occasional flooding. Shell and turquoise ornaments recovered from graves indicate links with Mexican cultures. These links became stronger after A.D. 1000, when the town at Casas Grandes, Chihuahua, may have been founded by Mexicans seeking to establish a trading and administrative center in the Southwest.

Farther north in the Mogollon area, changes occurred in village art and architecture. Pit dwellings were replaced by houses of stone above ground, containing several linked rooms. Underground circular ritual rooms for men also appeared for the first time. Their form and function continue in the present-day kivas of New Mexico. The earlier brown pottery decorated in red was replaced by white slipped vessels with black decoration. The finest of these come from the Mimbres Valley – many have been pierced with a central hole to "kill" them ritually. Mimbres ware coincided with the final phase of Mogollon culture.

Like the Mogollon, the Anasazi were not builders of irrigation schemes, but relied on rainfall and flash floods to water their fields. After A.D. 700, they abandoned their semi-subterranean houses, replacing them with houses built above ground with the exception of kivas. Over the following 400 years, the Anasazi settled previously unexploited territories, occupying much of Utah, Colorado, New Mexico and Arizona.

At this time the villages were easily accessible and undefended, but external threats led to the construction of villages in defensible positions. These, built from about 1100 to 1300, are among the most impressive sites in North America. At Mesa Verde, for example, watchtowers protected settlements sited in high and almost inaccessible rock shelters in the canyon wall. And at Chaco Canyon, there are over 100 villages, each consisting of multistory apartment dwellings and kivas.

Settlements within Chaco Canyon were connected by roads which also extended far into the surrounding regions, suggesting that the canyon may have been a focus for trading activities or a ceremonial center. Twenty years of drought, consequent crop failures and invasions led to the abandonment of both the cliff and open-site type settlements soon after A.D. 1300.

Pueblo Bonito in Chaco Canyon was a planned Anasazi village occupied from about A.D. 950 to 1300. Within the D-shaped exterior defensive wall are the remains of 800 rooms where the inhabitants lived. In the central areas stood some three dozen kivas, circular meeting houses for male kin groups.

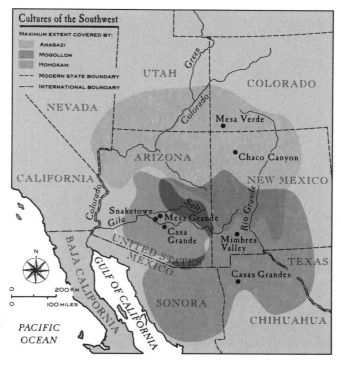

The "Four Corners" area of the American Southwest, where the state boundaries of Colorado, Utah, Arizona and New Mexico meet, was the heartland of the Anasazi culture. Earlier Hohokam sites lie to the southwest, in Arizona, while the principal Mogollon towns and villages are located in northern Mexico, New Mexico and extend into central Arizona. The map (LEFT) shows the chief sites of the three cultures as well as the territorial limits of their influence.

CHRONOLOGY
OF THE
ANCIENT WORLD

❝ *'My name is Ozymandias, King of Kings:*
Look on my works, ye Mighty, and despair!'
Nothing beside remains. Round the decay
Of that colossal wreck, boundless and bare
*The lone and level sands stretch far away.***❞**

BRITISH POET SHELLEY (1792–1822)

MESOPOTAMIA AND THE NEAR EAST

B.C.

c.15,000	Hunter-gatherers start to harvest wild grains.
c.9000	Jericho is settled and grain cultivation begins.
c.8000	Jericho expands to cover more than ten acres and is surrounded by a huge stone wall.
c.7000	Agriculture and livestock rearing become widespread.
c.6800	Çatal Hüyük, in Asia Minor, has over 5,000 inhabitants.
c.4500	A temple at Eridu, on the Euphrates, shows certain features, such as its small altar and offering table, which become standard in the first cities.
c.3300	Along with the rise of the early cities comes evidence of the first writing, a pictographic script, found at Uruk.
c.2370	Sargon of Akkad conquers Sumer and founds the city of Agade.
c.2350	Lugalzaggesi of Umma conquers Uruk and other Sumerian cities.
2334	Sargon overthrows Lugalzaggesi and takes his territory.
c.2200	Sargon's dynasty is overrun by Gutians, mountain people from the east.
2112	The Sumerian king Ur-Nammu founds the Third Dynasty of Ur, and a period of prosperity ensues. He builds the famous ziggurat of Ur, the best-preserved Mesopotamian tower.
2006	The Elamites sack the city of Ur.
c.1900	The Amorites infiltrate Mesopotamia and take control of several cities, including Mari, Ashur and Babylon.
1814	The Amorite Shamsi-Adad becomes king of Assyria.
1792	Hammurabi becomes the king of Babylon.
1757	The city of Mari is destroyed by Hammurabi of Babylon.
c.1755	Hammurabi's Law Code is carved on a stele.
c.1750	Samsu-iluna succeeds Hammurabi; in Anatolia, the Hittites become dominant.
c.1700	The use of horses revolutionizes warfare.
c.1650	Under Hattusilis I, the Hittites seize control of important trade routes and the Mediterranean ports of Byblos and Ugarit.
c.1600	In the Levant, the Phoenicians begin to use the Canaanite script – the first alphabetic script.
c.1550	The Hittites plunder Babylon.
c.1525	In Egypt, powerful Eighteenth Dynasty pharaohs expand their empire to the Euphrates, incorporating Palestine, the Levant and some of Syria.
c.1430	The Mitanni Empire, which stretches from the Zagros Mountains to the Mediterranean Sea, is at its height for the next 80 years.
c.1380	Under Suppiluliumas, the Hittites regain their power. They defeat Mitanni and its vassal states and seize Syria from Egypt.
c.1300	The Hittites and the Egyptians clash at Qadesh. The battle ends in stalemate.

c.1200	The Hittite Empire ends suddenly for unknown reasons.
c.1100	Syria and Palestine are settled by nomadic tribes.
c.1165	The Kassite dynasty of Babylon ends.
1125	Nebuchadrezzar I seizes power in Babylon.
c.1000	The Aramaeans, a nomadic group, settle beside the Euphrates in Syria. Their kingdoms spread into Assyrian territory. Meanwhile, David is king of Israel and Judah.
c.930	With the death of David's son Solomon, the united monarchy is split into the two kingdoms of Israel and Judah.
883–859	Ashurnasirpal II rules Assyria.
824	At the end of Shalmaneser III's reign, Assyrian territory reaches to the Euphrates.
745–727	Tiglath-Pileser III reigns over Assyria.
729	Tiglath-Pileser captures Babylon and becomes its king. He then takes Damascus and the Syrian states and imposes direct imperial rule.
721–705	Under Sargon II, Assyria defeats the Urartians.
704–681	Sennacherib, king of Assyria, campaigns in the west to the Mediterranean coast, repels Egypt and besieges Jerusalem. Sennacherib moves his capital to Nineveh.
680–669	Esarhaddon, king of Assyria, campaigns in Egypt and captures Memphis.
668–627	Ashurbanipal, king of Assyria, destroys the Elamites, recaptures Memphis and sacks Thebes. This brings the Assyrian Empire to its greatest extent.
609	The Assyrian Empire is conquered by the Medes and Babylonians. Babylon becomes the greatest Mesopotamian city in an empire that reaches to the borders of Egypt.
604	Nebuchadrezzar II rebuilds Babylon. He captures Jerusalem and takes the Hebrews into exile.
539	Cyrus of Persia captures Babylon.

EGYPT

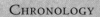

B.C.

c.3500	A uniform predynastic culture emerges across the Nile Valley and delta.
c.3100	Unification of Egypt and the beginning of the Dynastic period. The first four dynasties are known as the Old Kingdom.
c.2650	The Step Pyramid at Saqqara is built for King Djoser, a Third Dynasty ruler.
c.2590	The Great Pyramid of Khufu (Cheops) at Giza is the largest built by the Fourth Dynasty kings and the largest in the world.
c.2181	End of the Old Kingdom: the First Intermediate Period begins.
2060	The Middle Kingdom period begins with Mentuhotep II of Thebes who establishes the Eleventh Dynasty at Herakleopolis.
c.2010	Mentuhotep III makes sure that Egyptian ships can trade again in the Mediterranean.
1991	Amenemhet I founds the Twelfth Dynasty and moves the capital to It-Towy in the Fayum.
1878	Sesostris III comes to power. He suppresses the *nomarchs*, or provincial governors, and consolidates Egypt's control over the supply of gold from Nubia.
1786	End of the Middle Kingdom: the Second Intermediate Period begins.
1783	The independent Fourteenth Dynasty rules much of the delta and some of Lower Egypt from their capital Xois.
c.1650	A new dynastic line emerges at Thebes and forms the Seventeenth Dynasty. The fourth ruler, Kamose, takes Avaris and starts to drive the Hyksos from Egypt.
1633	The Hyksos, an Asiatic people, take control of much of Egypt from their capital Avaris and form the Fifteenth and Sixteenth Dynasties.
c.1570	Ahmosis finally rids Egypt of the Hyksos and becomes first ruler of the Eighteenth Dynasty. This marks the start of the New Kingdom that continues until the end of the Twentieth Dynasty.
c.1500	Queen Hatshepsut, the fifth ruler of the Eighteenth Dynasty, begins her 21-year reign.
1482	Tuthmosis III comes to power.
1450	Amenophis II suppresses Nubia, giving Egypt control of the Nile down to the Fourth Cataract.
1417	Egyptian power, prestige and prosperity reach their high point under Amenophis III.
1379	Amenophis IV abandons the worship of Amun in favor of the Aten, the sun-disk. He changes his name to Akhenaten and moves his capital from Thebes to Akhetaten, now the site known as Tell el-Amarna.
1362	Tutankhaten, who is advised to give up Aten worship, returns to Thebes and changes his name to Tutankhamun. The discovery of his burial treasures in 1922 have made him the most famous of pharaohs.

c.1320	Ramesses I is appointed king by the vizier Horemheb. He is the first ruler of the Nineteenth Dynasty.
c.1310	During the reign of Ramesses' son, Seti I, Egypt first becomes aware of a possible future power struggle with the Hittites.
1304	Accession of Ramesses II, grandson of Ramesses I. He rules for 67 years.
c.1300	Ramesses II fights the Hittites under King Muwatallis at the battle of Qadesh. Ramesses claims victory, but the result was probably a stalemate. Some years after the battle, a peace treaty, sealed by the marriage of Ramesses II and a Hittite princess, is signed. The treaty lasts until the end of the Hittite Empire in about 1200 B.C.
c.1245	Ramesses II moves his capital to the new city Pi-Ramesse, where he lives out his reign. During this period, the rock-cut temples at Abu-Simbel and monuments at Tanis are made.
1182	Ramesses III defeats marauders known as the Sea People. All subsequent rulers of the Nineteenth Dynasty are named Ramesses.
1045	The Twentieth Dynasty and the New Kingdom end. The Late Period starts as Egypt is divided between the Amun priests at Thebes and Smendes, vizier of Lower Egypt, who is based at Tanis.
945	Friction between Tanis and Thebes leads to civil war. By the mid-eighth century, Egypt has divided into several small states.
747	Beginning of domination by the Nubian Twenty-fifth Dynasty.
667	The Assyrians plunder Memphis and Thebes, ending the Nubian Dynasty.
663–525	Egypt again becomes independent, and the Twenty-sixth Dynasty rules from Sais. The last great period of splendor.
605	The Babylonians conquer Egypt.
539	The Babylonians are defeated by the Persians, who now represent the new threat to Egypt.
525	Egypt falls to the Persians under Cambyses and is incorporated into the Persian Empire. Despite revolts, the Persians maintain their control for nearly 200 years.
332	Alexander the Great conquers Egypt and lays the foundations of his new city Alexandria.
305	Death of Alexander IV; Ptolemy I declares himself the King of Egypt.
c.196	The Rosetta Stone is written in Greek, Egyptian hieroglyphs and Demotic, a late form of the Egyptian language. It was discovered by French soldiers in 1799 and provided the key that allowed Jean François Champollion to decipher the Egyptian script.
30	The last of the Ptolemies, Cleopatra VII, commits suicide, and Egypt becomes part of the Roman Empire.

B.C.

c.6000	Evidence of several cultures in Iran.
c.3000	Decorated wheel-made pottery is being produced at this time.
c.2700	The earliest kings of the Old Elamite Period.
c.2300	The pictographic writing system known as Proto-Elamite is in use – examples have been found at Susa and Shahr-i Sokhteh.
c.2000	Start of the Elamite rock carvings. Objects of bronze, silver and gold, as well as terra-cotta figures are being made.
c.1400	Gray ware pottery first appears around Marlik.
c.1300	Iranian people found in the Marlik area.
c.1260	The Elamite king, Untash-Napirisha, builds a new capital and temple complex at Choga Zanbil.
1168	The Elamites under Shutruk-Nahtunte attack Babylon and take the Law Code of Hammurabi to their capital of Susa.
c.1100	Defeat by the Babylonians ends this period of Elamite history.
c.640	Brief Elamite revival before total defeat by Assyria.
615	Cyaxares, the Median ruler, makes an alliance with the Babylonian king Nabopolassar against Assyria.
612	Nineveh falls to a combined force of Medes and Babylonians.
559	Cyrus II, known as Cyrus the Great, comes to the Achaemenid throne.
549	Cyrus defeats Astyages, the last Median king, and becomes king of both the Medes and Persians. He builds the city of Pasargadae.
546	Cyrus defeats the Lydian king Croesus; Lydia becomes a Persian province.
539	Cyrus takes Babylon, apparently without bloodshed. This victory makes him master of the Babylonian Empire.
530	Death of Cyrus the Great on the northeastern frontier. His body is taken to Pasargadae, where he is succeeded by his son Cambyses.
526	The Persians under Cambyses conquer Egypt.
522	When Cambyses is killed, Darius, his spearbearer, puts down widescale revolts and becomes ruler.
518–486	The Persian Empire reaches its greatest extent. Darius moves the capital to Susa, in winter, and to Ecbatana, in summer.

500	Revolt by the Greek cities of Ionia.
490	A Persian expedition sent to Greece is defeated at Marathon and forced to retreat.
486	Darius dies and is succeeded by his son Xerxes, who crushes rebellions in Egypt and Babylon.
480	Xerxes invades Greece. After an initial victory at Thermopylae, the Persians are later defeated at Salamis, Plataea and Mycale.
465	Xerxes is murdered; Artaxerxes comes to the throne.
336	Accession of Darius III.
331	The battle of Gaugamela ends with Alexander the Great's final defeat of Darius III. Darius is later killed, and the Achaemenid Empire ends.
323	Death of Alexander.
c.300	Seleucus, founder of the Seleucid dynasty, gains control of Iran, Mesopotamia, northern Syria and much of Asia Minor.
247	Arsaces founds the Arsacid, or Parthian, dynasty.
c.175	Phraates I begins to expand Parthian rule.
171	Mithridates I succeeds Phraates I. He founds the Parthian Empire.
141	Capture of Seleucia-on-the-Tigris, the old Seleucid capital by the Parthians. They now control Mesopotamia.
124	Accession of Mithridates III. Under him, the Parthian Empire reaches its greatest extent.
53	The Parthians defeat the Romans at Carrhae (Harran) in northern Syria.

A.D.

116	The Romans capture Ctesiphon, the Parthian capital; they later withdraw, but Parthian power is waning.
164	The Romans attack and sack Ctesiphon.
225	The last Parthian king, Artabanus V, is defeated by Ardashir I, founder of the Sasanian Empire.
240	Shapur I extends the Sasanian Empire; he defeats three Roman emperors, including Valerian.
272–293	Persecution of non-Zoroastrians by Sasanian kings.
309	Accession of Shapur II; nomadic groups threaten the empire's frontiers.
615	The last Sasanian king, Yazdigird III, is defeated by an Arabic Islamic army. Ctesiphon falls; the last Iranian empire ends.

PREHISTORIC EUROPE

B.C.

c.6500 Agriculture spreads from Anatolia into Neolithic southeastern Europe.

c.5000 The first metal objects made by hammering pure gold and copper are produced during this Chalcolithic ("copper-stone") period in the Balkans.

c.4500 The transition from hunter-gathering to settled faming in western Europe. Meanwhile, in the Balkans, metalworking is becoming more sophisticated as smelting and casting techniques are used.

c.4200 The Neolithic groups of Brittany in northwestern France build chamber tombs.

c.4000 In east-central Europe, the Chalcolithic period marks the beginnings of hierarchical societies. The burials of wealthy people at Varna in Bulgaria include metal ornaments, jewelry and beads. By contrast, the poorer graves contain only stone and pottery objects.

c.3700 In some parts of northern Europe the Bronze Age begins and coexists with other Stone Age societies. Trade and migration assist the spread of ideas across the continent. Copper and tin, the metals used to make bronze, are found together only in parts of western Britain, France, northwestern Spain and northern Italy.

c.3600 Megalithic chambers of the longbarrow at West Kennet in the west of England are being used for burials.

c.3300 Stone tombs are constructed across Britain, Denmark and western Europe. They range from crude designs, for example a simple chamber covered with large stones, to huge gallery or circular tombs.

c.3200 The people of Britain and northwestern France start erecting standing stone monuments and henges – circular ditch and bank enclosures – a practice which continues until around 1500 B.C.

c.2500 Finds of Bronze Age central European beaker and corded-ware pottery found in Neolithic western and northern Europe show that long-distance trade was occurring about this time.

c.2300 The Bronze Age begins in western Europe and Italy soon after reaching central and eastern parts.

c.2000 Settlements are fortified in eastern and central Europe, a phenomenon that spreads westward by 1200 B.C.

c.1800 Stonehenge, erected in southern England by Bronze Age people, is now complete. By this time, Bronze Age society is becoming increasingly stratified. Some wealthy people are buried with expensive grave goods under large mounds, or barrows, away from the settlement.

c.1200 In the Danube area, a new culture emerges known as Urnfield after the tradition of cremating the dead and placing ash-filled urns in communal burial fields, or urnfields.

c.1000 Bronze becomes widespread, suggesting a period of prosperity. Iron working reaches Europe from the Near East.

c.800 The first Celtic Iron Age societies develop in Austria and southern Germany. Some of the earliest iron objects are found at Hallstatt in Austria. This site gives its name to the earliest Iron Age culture in Europe, which roughly lasts from the eighth to the fifth centuries B.C.

c.750 Scythians, nomadic horsemen, are driven westward from the Steppes, toward the Black Sea area. In Scythian burials, wagons, furs, silks and horses are deposited along with the tattooed bodies of the dead.

c.600 Iron working spreads westward across Europe. In southern Germany and eastern France, defensive hilltop fortresses are built. At first iron goods are rare, but as supplies increase and tools and weapons are made of the metal, it revolutionizes warfare, agriculture and craftsmanship.

c.500 The Iron Age Germanic peoples of northern Europe start expanding their territories.

c.450 A Celtic culture named La Tène after a Swiss site emerges. It is known for its superb metalwork, remains of which are found across Europe.

390 The Celts help to bring about the end of the Etruscans. In this year, the Gauls sack early Rome.

272 The Gauls sack Delphi on their way to Asia Minor.

c.200 A Germanic group, the Bastarnae, threaten the Greek cities on the Black Sea coast. The next century sees massive migrations into Belgium and the area of the Rhine.

61 The Germanic Suevi under the leadership of Ariovistus ally themselves with the Celtic Sequani and attack the Celts of central Gaul. This causes the Roman general Julius Caesar to intervene to restore order.

A.D.

180 The Romans make peace with the Marcommanni barbarians and give them subsidies.

c.300 The barbarians attack the Roman Empire with greater success, and there are massive invasions of Germans into Gaul and the Balkans.

410 Visigoths under Alaric capture and sack Rome.

B.C.

c.3000 — Early Bronze Age Cycladic culture in the Aegean.

c.2200 — Minoan civilization is established on the island of Crete. The first palaces at Knossos and Phaistos are built.

c.2000 — A pictographic script is in use and continues to be in existence until about 1600 B.C.

c.1900 — Linear A script comes into use. It has yet to be deciphered.

c.1700 — An earthquake damages the Minoan palaces, and grander ones are built.

c.1600 — The Mycenaeans become the dominant power on the Greek mainland.

c.1500 — The Minoan settlement of Thera is destroyed by an earthquake, followed by a massive volcanic explosion which causes the whole island to be abandoned.

c.1450 — The ideogram-based script Linear B is used at Knossos. Most of the Cretan palaces and settlements are destroyed, and Knossos is occupied by the Mycenaeans.

c.1400 — The palace of Knossos is burned down and abandoned, never to be rebuilt.

c.1300 — Athens's central fortress, later known as the Acropolis, is enclosed by massive walls during this late Mycenaean period.

c.1100 — The Mycenaean world comes to a sudden end. Greece enters its Dark Age that lasts until about 800 B.C.

c.1000 — Colonists migrate from mainland Greece to the coast of Asia Minor and the eastern Aegean islands.

776 — The first athletics festival is held at the sanctuary of Zeus in Olympia.

c.750 — During the Archaic period, Athens and Sparta become powerful.

733 — Corinth establishes the city of Syracuse on Sicily.

715 — Sparta conquers Messenia and continues its annexation of the Peloponnese.

706 — Tarentum in southern Italy is founded by Sparta.

c.650 — The oracle of Apollo at Delphi reaches the height of its influence.

594 — Athens's laws are reformed by Solon.

540 — Peisistratus seizes control of Athens and rules as a tyrant.

510 — After one of Peisistratus's sons is killed and the other flees Athens, far-reaching reforms are introduced by Cleisthenes.

490 — Greek cities in Asia Minor revolt against Persian rule. To punish the Athenians for supporting them, Darius sends an invasion force. It is defeated at Marathon by the Athenians.

480 — Xerxes leads a huge army to invade Greece. After an initial victory at Thermopylae, the Persians are defeated at Salamis, and later at Plataea and Mycale.

478 — Establishment of the Delian League, an alliance of cities with a common treasury and military strategy under the leadership of Athens.

471 — Naxos's attempts to leave the Delian League are put down by Athenian forces.

469 — Socrates, the famous philosopher, is born.

448 — Construction of the Parthenon begins; it takes 16 years to complete.

443 — Pericles heads the board of ten generals elected annually by popular vote. He leads Athens until his death in 429.

431–404 — The Peloponnesian War between Sparta and Athens.

429 — Plato, a pupil of Socrates and author of numerous philosophical works, including the *Republic*, is born.

404 — Athens is defeated by Sparta, now the most powerful city-state.

401 — Sparta and Persia go to war against each other, despite being allies against Athens a few years before.

399 — Socrates receives the death sentence for allegedly corrupting the youth of Athens.

395 — A coalition of Athens, Argos, Corinth and Thebes defeats Sparta. For the next 40 years, these states war among themselves.

384 — The philosopher and scientist Aristotle is born.

362 — Thebes destroys Sparta at the battle of Mantinea; by now, all the Greek states are weak from years of warfare.

359 — Philip II becomes king of Macedon. Within 20 years, his territory extends from the lower Danube to the Aegean, and from the Adriatic coast to the Black Sea.

338 — Philip II defeats the Greek states at Chaeronea.

336 — Philip is succeeded by his son Alexander.

331 — Alexander the Great defeats the Persians under Darius III.

332 — Alexander is welcomed to Egypt where he founds the city of Alexandria.

323 — Alexander dies in Babylon; the empire he founded disintegrates in the War of Successors.

278 — Three main Hellenistic kingdoms are formed: the Ptolemies in Egypt; the Seleucids in Babylonia and Syria, and Antigonids in Macedonia.

146 — Macedonia and Greece are annexed by Rome.

86 — The Romans sack Athens.

30 — The last remaining Hellenistic kingdom, Egypt, is annexed by Rome after the suicide of Cleopatra VII.

B.C.

c.1000	The earliest villages on the Palatine and neighboring hills.
814	Carthage is founded by the Phoenicians.
c.800	Etruscan civilization begins to flourish in what is now Tuscany.
753	Traditional date of the founding of Rome by Romulus.
c.650	Rome expands under the Etruscan kings.
509	Expulsion of Tarquinius Superbus. Foundation of the Roman Republic.
499	Roman victory over Latin tribes at Lake Regillus.
c.450	The Law of the Twelve Tables, the codified law of the city, is published.
390	Rome is sacked by the Gauls.
343–290	Samnite Wars.
340–338	Latin Wars.
312	Construction of the *Via Appia* and *Aqua Appia*.
c.280	The first Roman coinage comes into use.
275	Roman territorial expansion continues. Defeat of Pyrrhus of Epirus.
264	The earliest recorded Roman gladiator fight.
264–241	The First Punic War.
218–201	The Second Punic War. Hannibal crosses the Alps and invades northern Italy.
217	Carthaginian victory at Lake Trasimene.
218	Carthaginian victory at Cannae.
202	Carthaginian defeat at Zama in north Africa.
168	Roman victory at Pydna ends the Macedonian wars. Beginning of Rome's eastward expansion.
149–146	The Third Punic War. Final defeat and destruction of Carthage.
73	Spartacus leads a slave rebellion which ultimately fails.
67	Pompey clears the Mediterranean of pirates. Defeat of Mithridates of Pontus.
60	Pompey, Crassus and Julius Caesar form the First Triumvirate.
58–51	Caesar's Gallic conquests.
46	After the defeat of Pompey two years before, Julius Caesar is appointed dictator for ten years; he starts a huge reform program.
44	Julius Caesar murdered on the Ides (the 15th) of March.
43	Octavian, Caesar's heir, returns from Greece and forms the Second Triumvirate with Marc Antony and Lepidus.
31	Octavian defeats Antony and Cleopatra at the naval battle of Actium.
27	Octavian granted special powers and becomes Augustus. He is now emperor in all but name.
19	Death of Virgil; his great epic, the *Aeneid*, is published posthumously.

A.D.

14	Augustus dies and is succeeded by his stepson Tiberius.
37	Tiberius is succeeded by Caligula who is assassinated four years later.
41	Claudius becomes emperor.
54	Accession of Nero.
68	Nero commits suicide, thus ending the Julio-Claudian dynasty.
69	The year of the four emperors: Vespasian finally becomes emperor and restores order.
70	The Jewish Revolt: Jerusalem falls to the Romans under Vespasian's son Titus.
79	Eruption of Vesuvius buries Pompeii and Herculaneum with ash and lava. In Rome, the Colosseum is dedicated.
96	The Emperor Domitian is murdered: the Senate elects Nerva, who adopts Trajan as his heir.
114	The Roman Empire reaches its greatest extent under Trajan.
117	Hadrian succeeds Trajan.
138–161	The reign of Antoninus Pius. He is followed by Marcus Aurelius, who rules until 180.
192	With the death of Commodus, Marcus Aurelius's successor, a period of civil war erupts with several emperors following each other.
193–235	The reign of the Severan emperors.
235	Alexander, the last Severan emperor, is killed by the army. For the next 50 years there is internal instability.
284	Diocletian becomes emperor and restores some political stability.
293	The tetrarchy, rule of four, is established by Diocletian, who divides the empire into two.
312	The tetrarchy system collapses, and civil war ensues.
324	Constantine becomes sole ruler of the Roman Empire.
337	Constantine is baptized as a Christian on his deathbed; from this time, almost every emperor is at least nominally Christian.
391	Theodosius I suppresses pagan worship and makes Christianity the religion of the empire.
395	After the death of Theodosius, the empire is partitioned between his sons Arcadius, in the east, and Honorius, in the west.
404	The western capital is moved to Ravenna.
410	Visigoths under Alaric capture and sack Rome.
451	Attila the Hun attacks Gaul and, four years later, enters Italy. After negotiations he withdraws.
476	In the west, soldiers proclaim the German Odoacer as their king. He deposes the last western emperor Romulus Augustulus, so ending the western empire.

INDIA

B.C.

c.4000 A diverse and extensive urban civilization develops in areas bordering the Indus Valley.

c.3500 Several villages are established on the fertile flood plain of the Indus.

c.2500 By now the Indus, or Harappan, civilization has developed. This unified culture covers an area of about 500,000 square miles. The Indus people use a hieroglyphic script, and the grid layouts of their cities suggest a strong, centralized society.

c.1750 End of the Indus civilization, for reasons that remain unknown.

c.1500 The Aryans move into northern India. These pastoral nomads speak an Indo-Aryan language and are named for linguistic, rather than ethnic, reasons.

c.1300 The Aryans expand eastward, establishing small kingdoms and fighting among themselves. Their history is reflected in the later epic poems, *Mahabharata* and *Ramayana*.

c.1000 The *Rig-Veda*, a collection of hymns, is being composed and passed down orally from generation to generation.

c.600 Some 16 Aryan kingdoms have now emerged across northern India. At the center of these states are the great cities of Kaushambi, Rajgir and Hastinapura, the starting place of the *Mahabharata*.

c.566 Gautama the Buddha – "the Enlightened One" – is born in the foothills of the Himalayas. Gautama rejects his life as a rich nobleman and lives as an ascetic. He reaches enlightenment, or Buddhahood, after meditation.

543 Bimbisara, the ruler of the state of Magadha, expands his territories and introduces an efficient administration for tax collection.

c.540 Vardhamana, the ascetic who founds Jainism, is born. He is known to his followers as *Mahavira*, "Great Hero," and *Jina*, "Victor," after which the religion Jainism is named.

533 Gandhara becomes one of the satrapies of the Achaemenid Empire of Persia.

491 Ajatasatru, Bimbisara's son, continuing his father's expansionist policy, takes control of much of the Ganges basin.

459 At the death of Ajatasatru, a series of ineffective leaders rule Magadha until a new dynasty is founded by Sisunaga. This lasts only 50 years until it is ousted by Mahapadma Nanda, the first of the Nanda dynasty.

327 Alexander the Great of Macedon enters India. He temporarily occupies Punjab and Sind.

c.320 Chandragupta Maurya defeats the last of the Nandas and takes control of Magadha. He advances across to the Indus and down into central India.

305 With the defeat of the Seleucid king, Seleucus I Nicator, eastern Afghanistan is added to the Mauryan Empire, which now reaches from Kandahar in the west across to the Ganges.

c.297 Chandragupta, said to have converted to Jainism, abdicates in favor of his son Bindisura, who extends the empire south as far as Mysore.

c.272 Following Bindisura's death, there are dynastic disputes until his son Ashoka seizes the throne.

c.260 Ashoka has a spiritual crisis as the result of a particularly bloody campaign in Kalinga (Orissa). He converts to Buddhism, becomes a pacifist and sets up many Buddhist stupas, and carves edicts on rocks and pillars to spread his word around the empire.

232 With the death of Ashoka, the Mauryan Empire begins to disintegrate. Within 50 years, it has been reduced to only a part of the Ganges Valley.

c.200 With the decline of the Mauryans, Bactrian Greeks establish themselves in small kingdoms in the Punjab and the Kabul Valley. These kingdoms slowly give way to the Sakas.

185 The last of the Mauryans, Brhadratha is assassinated by Pusyamitra, his Brahmin commander, first of the Sunga dynasty. The Sungas rule Magadha for around 110 years. Buddhism declines, and Brahmanism enjoys a revival.

c.155 The reign of Menander begins; the best known of the Indo-Greek kings, he controls Punjab and Gandhara.

c.90 Gandhara and its capital Taxila fall to the Sakas.

c.30 Having overrun the Indo-Greek kingdoms, the Sakas occupy the Indus Valley, Gujarat and the south as far as Ujjain. Their prosperous kingdom lasts until the fourth century A.D.

A.D.

c.80 The Kushans, one of the Yueh-chih tribes, unite the other tribes to form a single people. They advance to Gandhara and on to Punjab. Around A.D. 80, their greatest king, Kanishka, comes to the throne. From his capital Purusapura near Peshawar, he extends the kingdom until it reaches from Benares to Kabul and south to Sanchi.

c.120 After Kanishka's death, the Kushans lose the Ganges Valley, the Sakas become independent, and by the middle of the third century the Kushans have become Persian vassals.

320 The Gupta period starts with the expansion of an obscure Magadhan family under Chandra Gupta I.

c.330 Chandra Gupta I is succeeded by his son Samudra Gupta, who makes further conquests in northern and eastern India.

376 Samudra Gupta's son, Chandra Gupta II, defeats the Saka rulers of Ujjain, taking the Gupta rule to its greatest extent, stretching from the Arabian Sea to the Bay of Bengal. The Guptas emulate the Mauryans and also have their capital at Pataliputra.

c.414 Prosperity and peace continue under Kumara Gupta until toward the end of his 50-year-reign when there are signs of a White Hun invasion.

c.460 Skanda Gupta rallies the Gupta forces in the face of a full-scale Hun invasion. He is successful for a while, but after his death, the situation worsens, and the Gupta Empire starts to disintegrate.

c.500 When the Huns attack again, the Gupta area has been split between many local kings. Although the Huns are defeated, the last of the great Indian empires is destroyed.

B.C.

*c.*6000   Agriculture first emerges in the central Asian desert. Neolithic people, such as the Banpo of Shaanxi Province, establish settlements.

*c.*5000   By this time, rice is being farmed on the eastern coast of China.

*c.*4000   In the northwest, the Yangshao people produce painted pottery and live in settlements that are partly underground. Toward the east and northeast, the Longshan, another Neolithic group, produce jade carvings and black pottery. They also practice divination by scapulimancy, a tradition continued by the Shang dynasty.

*c.*3500   Contact between the Yangshao and Longshan Neolithic groups appears to happen at this time.

*c.*3000   In the east, an advanced Longshan culture, whose burials already show signs of a hierarchy, moves westward and becomes widespread during the third millennium.

*c.*2740   According to tradition, Shen Nong invents agriculture in China.

*c.*1750   In the provinces of Henan and Shaanxi, a Bronze Age culture develops from one which includes elements of both the Yangshao and advanced Longshan cultures. This culture is characteristic of the Shang dynasty, founded by Tang at about this time, which dominates northern China until the end of the second millennium.

*c.*1300   The Shang dynasty has several capitals – the last one is thought to be at Anyang. In addition to producing bronze helmets, armor and ritual vessels for their almost constant sacrifices, the Shang introduce new techniques such as irrigation, a writing and measurement system, and a calendar; they continue to practice divination, jade working and the use of rammed-earth walls for building.

*c.*1050   The Shang dynasty ends when their king, Di Xin, is defeated by the Zhou. The first 200 years of the new dynasty, the Western Zhou, is a time of prosperity and good kings. Although much of the Shang culture is continued, some of the excesses, such as human sacrifice, are limited. The Zhou consider their king to be the "son of heaven" who possesses the "mandate of heaven," the right to rule the whole world as long as it is with justice and concern for the people.

*c.*770   The Western Zhou period ends in the eighth century when central authority collapses – former fiefdoms become rival states, and the capital is moved to Luoyang. The Eastern Zhou period is also known as the Spring and Autumn period, named after Confucius's *Annals*.

*c.*600   With iron becoming increasingly common, farming implements, as well as weapons, are made, which leads to greater agricultural productivity. In addition, this is a period when crafts such as silk painting, lacquerware and ceramics become highly skilled.

*c.*480   Confucius, the great philosopher, dies.

*c.*350   The Qin, regarded as unethical barbarians by the other states, employ Shang Yang, from the ruling house of Wei, as an adviser. Under him a new political and economic system is introduced.

*c.*300   To protect themselves and keep out barbarians, some states build huge walls and ditches; however, endless conflicts lead to all the states becoming weaker.

221   The Qin emerge triumphantly from this period of warfare, and their leader Shi Huangdi declares himself emperor of all China. The walls and ditches built by the warring states are joined together to create the Great Wall, which stretches from Liaoyang Province in the east to Gansu Province in the west.

210   Shi Huangdi's death leads to revolts around the empire.

206   The Qin dynasty is overthrown as various groups struggle for control. Finally, Liu Bang becomes the first Han emperor, under the name Gao Zu, and establishes his capital at Chang'an.

136   Confucianism is proclaimed the state religion.

124   An imperial university for training the highest officials of the empire is established in Chang'an. Based on a grid, the city grows to cover 40 miles enclosed by massive walls and towers.

A.D.

9   Expensive campaigns against the Xiongnu northern nomads cause economic difficulties which allow the courtier Wang Mang to seize the throne, ending the Western Han and founding the Xin dynasty.

23   When Wang Mang attempts to introduce land reforms, he is overthrown.

25   Guangwu Di, a member the Han, finally puts down the Red Eyebrow Rebellion and continues the dynasty as the Eastern, or Later, Han.

*c.*65   The first entry of Buddhism into China from India is recorded.

*c.*220   The Han dynasty succumbs to a combination of famine, flood and rebellions. China is divided into three kingdoms – the Wei, Wu and Shu.

264   The imperial Shu dynasty is overthrown by the Western Jin dynasty, a new, important group who overthrow the house of Wei the next year.

280   When the isolated Wu are finally overcome, Sima Yan, first ruler of the Jin dynasty, unifies China.

291   The weak Jin dynasty allows rich landowners to struggle for power. For about 15 years, the Troubles of the Eight Princes, as the period is known, continue. At the same time, the barbarians, who are allowed to live inside the boundary of the Great Wall, join in ethnic uprisings.

311   Luoyang is sacked by the barbarians, who within five years take control of most of the northern provinces.

316   When Chang'an falls, so does the Western Jin. However, members of the imperial Jin flee east to Nanjing, where they found the Eastern Jin. China is divided, north and south, for more than 250 years.

The Americas

B.C.

c.8500 The first cultivation of grains in the Americas occurs in the Ayacucho area of the Andes.

c.8000 Plant cultivation begins in Mexico.

c.6300 Root crops such as potatoes, manioc and ulloco are all being cultivated.

c.5400 The ancestors of the llama and alpaca are being domesticated.

c.5000 The first recognizably domesticated maize is grown around this period, as are beans, avocados and squash.

c.3500 First cultivation of cotton.

c.3000 In Mexico, permanent settlements of five to ten houses are established in the Tehuacán Valley; however, much of the food is still gathered rather than cultivated.

c.2500 The populations of Mesoamerica and Peru have increased an estimated 25-fold by this time, bringing far-reaching changes to society. Permanent settlements of up to 4,000 people are established. In central Peru, coastal settlements show evidence of both organized religion and an artisan class making pottery, stone artifacts, jewelry and woven goods.

c.1500 The site of Tiahuanaco in Peru is first occupied, although it does not reach its zenith for 2,000 years.

c.1200 A complex, large-scale society known as Chavín, named after the site Chavín de Huantar, emerges in the Andes. In the Olmec heartland area of Veracruz in Mexico, San Lorenzo, the first city of the Olmec civilization, is flourishing.

c.1000 In eastern North America, the Adena culture develops.

c.850 In Peru, the Chavín cult, based on were-jaguar worship, reaches its height around this time, and large stone sculptures and temples with sunken courts are being built.

c.500 Across Peru, Chavín influence begins to wane as other cultures develop. On the southern coast, the Paracas culture, famed for its bright textiles, becomes important.

c.350 The Nazca become the dominant group of the southern Peruvian coastal area. They are most famous for the huge figures and shapes carved out of the desert, known as the Nazca Lines.

c.300 The first Maya cities emerge. In North America, the Adena culture declines as the Hopewell culture emerges. This continues and elaborates upon the Adena mound culture.

A.D.

c.10 On the northern coast of Peru, the Moche culture develops. The Moche build the largest structures in South America. In addition, they produce superb ceramics and elaborate gold work.

c.50 The city of Teotihuacán in central Mexico increases in size.

c.250 Monte Albán, in the Mexican state of Oaxaca, develops as a major Zapotec temple complex.

c.300 Teotihuacán has become a city of around 200,000 people. Meanwhile across Guatemala, Honduras, Belize and the Yucatán peninsula of Mexico, the Maya civilization and the classic cities of Tikal, Palenque and Copan begin to flourish.

c.500 In Peru, two centers, Tiahuanaco and Huari emerge. Over the next century, the Huari state conquers a territory that extends 300 miles along the Andes mountain chain. In North America the Hopewell Mound Builders decline.

c.600 Power in Peru shifts from Moche to Tiahuanaco and Huari. Tiahuanaco, close to Lake Titicaca, grows to become a city of around 40,000 people; while farther north the population of Huari grows to around 100,000. El Tajín develops as the major site of the Classic Veracruz civilization.

c.700 The Middle Mississippian Valley in North America becomes the center of the mound-building Mississippian culture. In the southwestern United States, three cultures emerge: the Hohokam, Mogollon and Anasazi.

c.750 Teotihuacán is destroyed by fire, but remains a place of pilgrimage.

c.800 The fortified city of Huari is suddenly abandoned. Meanwhile Tiahuanaco continues to thrive and extend its contacts across the continent. As the Huari Empire falls apart, the Chimú emerge from their capital Chan Chan to become the new power in northern Peru.

c.900 The Maya civilization begins to decline in the south; farther north in the Yucatán peninsula, centers such as Chichén Itzá and Uxmal are built.

c.950 The Toltecs begin to dominate central Mexico. They quickly build a huge empire across Mesoamerica. In the Yucatán, they remodel the now abandoned Maya city of Chichén Itzá.

c.1000 People of the Mogollon culture of the southwestern United States are building stone houses and round underground ceremonial rooms, known as *kivas*.

c.1100 The Anasazi, contemporaries of the Mogollon and Hohokam, begin to occupy areas of Arizona, New Mexico, Utah and Colorado.

1175 Tula, the Toltec capital, is sacked by the Chichimec, a tribe from northwestern Mexico; as a result, small warring city-states are created.

c.1200 The Incas, led by Manco Capac, enter and settle an Andean valley near Cuzco. The irrigated lands of the Hohokam in the southwestern United States are captured by the Anasazi and later abandoned around A.D. 1400.

1325 The Aztec people settle in the Valley of Mexico.

1428 The Aztecs defeat their former enemies and begin to build the city of Tenochtitlán, on an island in Lake Texcoco. Their empire grows to cover much of Mesoamerica.

c.1440 Pachacutec Inca begins a series of long-distance campaigns across Peru.

1476 The Inca, under Sapa Inca, defeat the Chimú, and their lands are incorporated into the vast Inca Empire.

1521 The last native Mesoamerican civilization ends when Moctezuma II, the Aztec ruler, is taken prisoner by the Spaniard Hernán Cortés.

1532 The Inca Empire is destroyed by the Spanish under Francisco Pizarro.

BIBLIOGRAPHY

GENERAL

Bickerman, E.J. *Chronology of the Ancient World* Thames & Hudson, London, 1968; revised ed., 1980

Branigan, K. (ed.) *The Atlas of Archaeology* Macdonald, London, 1982

The Cambridge Ancient History Cambridge University Press, Cambridge, 2nd ed., 1970–84

Cameron, A. & Kuhrt, A. (ed.) *Images of Women in Antiquity* Croom Helm, London, 1983

Casson, L. *Travel in the Ancient World* G. Allen & Unwin, London, 1974

Chamberlain, R. *Loot! The Heritage of Plunder* Thames & Hudson, London, 1983

Cotterell, Arthur (ed.) *The Encyclopedia of Ancient Civilizations* Mayflower Books, New York, 1980

Daniel, G. *150 Years of Archaeology* Duckworth, London, 1950; 2nd ed., 1975

Finley, Moses I. (ed.) *Aspects of Antiquity* Viking Press, New York, 1968

————*The Ancient Economy* Chatto & Windus, London, 1973

————*Atlas of Classical Archaeology* Chatto & Windus, London, 1977

Hall's Dictionary of Subjects & Symbols in Art John Murray, London, 1974

Hawkes, Jacquetta *The Atlas of Early Man* Book Club Associates, London, 1976

Kinder, Hermann & Hilgemann, Werner *The Penguin Atlas of World History: Vol 1* Penguin, London and New York, 1974

Norwich, John Julius (ed.) *Great Architecture of the World* Mitchell Beazley, London, 1975

The Oxford Classical Dictionary Oxford University Press, Oxford, 2nd ed., 1970

Raymond, R. *Out of the Fiery Furnace: the impact of metals on the history of mankind* Pennsylvania State University Press, Pennsylvania, 1984

Renfrew, C. *Before Civilization* Penguin, London, 1976

Rogerson, John *The New Atlas of the Bible* Macdonald, London, 1985

Schreiber, H. *The History of Roads* Barrie & Rockliffe, London, 1961

Tait, Hugh (ed.) *Seven Thousand Years of Jewellery* British Museum Publications, London, 1986

Warry, John *Warfare in the Classical World* Salamander Books, London, 1980

Whitehouse, Ruth *The First Cities* Phaidon, Oxford, 1977

MESOPOTAMIA AND THE NEAR EAST

Barnett, R.D. *Assyrian Palace Reliefs* Batchworth Press, London, 1959

Budge, E.A.T. Wallis *Babylonian Life and History* The Religious Tract Society, London, 1885

Contenau, Georges *Everyday Life in Babylon and Assyria* Edward Arnold, London, 1954

Curtis, John (ed.) *Fifty Years of Mesopotamian Discovery* The British School of Archaeology in Iraq, London, 1982

Dougherty, Raymond Philip *Nabonidus and Belshazzar: a study of the closing events of the Neo-Babylonian empire* Yale University Press, New Haven, 1929

Frankfort, Henri *The Art and Architecture of the Ancient Orient* Penguin, London, 4th revised ed., 1969

————*Kingship and the Gods; a study of ancient Near Eastern religion* University of Chicago Press, Chicago, 1978

Frankfort, H. & Others *Before Philosophy; the intellectual Adventure of Ancient Man* Pelican, London, 1949

Grayson, Albert Kirk *Assyrian Royal Inscriptions: Part 2* Otto Harrassowitz, Wiesbaden, 1976

Gurney, O.R. *The Hittites* Pelican, London, 1952

Hooke, S.H. *Middle Eastern Mythology* Penguin, London, 1963

Kramer, Samuel Noah *The Sumerians* University of Chicago Press, Chicago, 1963

Kramer, Samuel Noah and Time-Life Books (eds.) *Cradle of Civilization* Time-Life Books, Amsterdam, rev. ed., 1969

Lane, W.H. *Babylonian Problems* John Murray, London, 1923

Layard, Austen Henry *Nineveh and its Remains: Vols I & II* John Murray, London, 1849

————*Early Adventures in Persia, Susiana and Babylonia: Vol I* John Murray, London, 1887

Lloyd, Seton *The Archaeology of Mesopotamia* Thames & Hudson, London, 1978

Macqueen, J. *The Hittites and Their Contemporaries in Asia Minor* Thames & Hudson, London, 1975

Macqueen, James G. *Babylon* Robert Hale, London, 1964

Madhloom, T.A. *The Chronology of Neo-Assyrian Art* The Athlone Press, University of London, London, 1969

Mellaart, J. *Earliest Civilizations of the Near East* Thames & Hudson, London, 1965

Mitchell, T. *The Bible in the British Museum* British Museum Publications, London, 1988

Mallowan, Max E.L. *Nimrud and its Remains: Vol I* Collins, London, 1966

————*The Nimrud Ivories* British Museum Publications, London, 1978

Moscati, Sabatino *The World of the Phoenicians* Weidenfeld & Nicolson, London, 1968

Oates, D. & J. *The Rise of Civilization* Phaidon, Oxford, 1976

Oates, Joan *Babylon* Thames & Hudson, London, 1979

Olmstead, A.T. *History of Assyria* University of Chicago Press, Chicago, 1951

Oppenheim, A. Leo *Ancient Mesopotamia: Portrait of a Dead Civilization* The University of Chicago Press, Chicago and London, 1964

Reade, J. *Assyrian Sculpture* British Museum Publications, London, 1983

Roaf, Michael *Cultural Atlas of Mesopotamia and the Ancient Near East* Facts on File, New York and Oxford, 1990

Saggs, H.W.F. *Everyday Life in Babylonia and Assyria* Dorset Press, New York, 1987

Sandars, N.K. *The Sea Peoples* Thames & Hudson, London, 1978

Tubb, J.N. & Chapman R.L. *Archaeology and the Bible* British Museum Publications, London, 1990

Wiseman, D.J. (ed.) *Peoples of the Old Testament Times* Oxford University Press, Oxford, 1973

EGYPT

Aldred, C. *Egypt to the end of the Old Kingdom* Thames & Hudson, London, 1965

————*Jewels of the Pharaohs, Egyptian jewellery of the dynastic period* Thames & Hudson, London, 1971

Andrewes, Carol *Egyptian Mummies* British Museum Publications, London, 1984

Baines, John & Malek, Jaromir *Atlas of Ancient Egypt* Phaidon, Oxford, 1984

Bowman, Alan K. *Egypt after the Pharaohs, from Alexander to the Arab conquest* Oxford University Press, Oxford, 1990

Carter, Howard *The Tomb of Tutankhamen* Book Club Associates, London, 1972

Clayton, Peta *The Rediscovery of Ancient Egypt, Artists and Travellers in the 19th century* Thames & Hudson, London, 1982

David, A. Rosalie *Ancient Egypt* Phaidon, Oxford, 2nd ed., 1988

Drower, Margaret *Flinders Petrie, a life in archaeology* Victor Gollancz, London, 1985

Emery, Walter *Egypt in Nubia* Hutchinson, London, 1965

Frankfort, H. *Ancient Egyptian Religion* Harper & Row, New York, 1961

Gardiner, Sir Alan *Egypt of the Pharaohs* Oxford University Press, Oxford, 1961

Hobson, Christine *Exploring the World of the Pharaohs: A Complete Guide to Ancient Egypt* Thames & Hudson, London, 1987

Hoffman, Michael A. *Egypt before the Pharaohs* Routledge & Kegan Paul, London, 1980

James T.G.H. *An Introduction to Ancient Egypt* British Museum Publications, London, 1979

James T.G.H. & Davies W.V. *Egyptian Sculpture* British Museum Publications, London, 1983

Lauer, J.P. *Saqqara, the Royal Cemetery of Memphis* Thames & Hudson, London, 1976

Kees, Hermann *Ancient Egypt, a cultural topography* University of Chicago Press, Chicago, 1961

Lichtheim, Miriam *Ancient Egyptian Literature: A Book of Readings: Vol II: The New Kingdom* University of California Press, Berkeley, 1976

Stead, Miriam *Egyptian Life* British Museum Publications, London, 1986

Trigger, Kemp, O'Connor & Lloyd *Ancient Egypt: A Social History* Cambridge University Press, Cambridge, 1983

Watson, Philip J. *Costume of Ancient Egypt* B.T. Batsford, London, 1987

PERSIA

Bengston, Herman *et. al.* *The Greeks and the Persians from the sixth to the fourth centuries* Weidenfeld & Nicolson, London, 1968

Boyce, Mary *Zoroastrians, their religion, beliefs and practices* Routledge & Kegan Paul, London, 1979

Cambridge History of Iran: Vol 2: The Median and Achaemenian periods Cambridge University Press, 1985

Colledge, Malcolm *The Parthians* Thames & Hudson, London, 1967

Collins, Robert *The Medes and Persians: Conquerors and Diplomats* Cassell, London, 1974

Cook, J.M. *The Persian Empire* J.M. Dent & Sons, London, 1983

Curtis, J. *Ancient Persia* British Museum Publications, London, 1989

Dalton, O.M. *The Treasure of the Oxus* British Museum Publications, London, 1964

Ghirshman, R. *Iran: from the earliest times to the Islamic conquest* Pelican, London, 1954

Lamb, W.H. *Cyrus the Great* Robert Hale, London, 1961

Matheson, S. *Persia: An archaeological guide* Faber & Faber, London, 1972

Moorey, P.R.S. *Ancient Iran* Ashmolean Museum, Oxford, 1975

————*Ancient bronzes from Luristan* British Museum Publications, London, 1974

Olmstead, A. *History of the Persian Empire* University of Chicago Press, Chicago, 1948

Rice, David Talbot *Islamic Art* Thames & Hudson, London, 1965

PREHISTORIC EUROPE

Briard, Jacques *The Bronze Age in Barbarian Europe: from the Megaliths to the Celts* Book Club Associates, London, 1979

Burl, A. *Megalithic Brittany* Thames & Hudson, London, 1985

Chadwick, Norah *The Celts* Pelican, London, 1971

Champion T., Gamble, C., Shennan, S., Whittle, A. *Prehistoric Europe* Academic Press, London, 1984

Collis, John *The European Iron Age* Batsford, London, 1984

Cunliffe, Barry *Rome and the Barbarians* The Bodley Head, London, 1975

Ellis Davidson, H.R. *Gods and Myths of Northern Europe* Pelican, London, 1964

Harding, D.W. *Prehistoric Europe* Elsevier, Oxford, 1978

Jettmar, Karl *Art of the Steppes: The Eurasian Animal Style* Methuen, London, 1967

Longworth, I.H. *Prehistoric Britain* British Museum Publications, London 1985

Phillips, Eustace D. *The Royal Hordes: Nomad Peoples of the Steppes* Thames & Hudson, London, 1965

Rice, Tamara Talbot *The Scythians* Thames & Hudson, London, 1957

Rudenko, Sergei I. *Frozen Tombs of Siberia: the Pazyryk Burials of Iron Age Horsemen* J.M. Dent & Sons, London, 1970

Todd, Malcolm *The Northern Barbarians, 100 B.C.–A.D. 300* Hutchinson, London, 1975

Wallace-Hadrill, J.M. *The Barbarian West; 400–1000* Basil Blackwell, Oxford, 1967

Wilson, David M. (ed.) *The Northern World* Thames & Hudson, London, 1980

GREECE AND THE AEGEAN

Boardman, John *The Greeks Overseas, their early colonies and trade* Thames & Hudson, London, 1964

———*Greek Art* Thames & Hudson, London, 1964

Chadwick, J. *The Decipherment of Linear B* Cambridge University Press, Cambridge, 1958

Finley, M. I. *The World of Odysseus* Pelican, London, 1956

———*Early Greece: the Bronze and Archaic Ages* Chatto & Windus, London, 1970

Green, Peter *Alexander to Actium, the Hellenistic Age* Thames & Hudson, London, 1990

Herodotus *The Histories* tr. A. De Sélincourt, Penguin, London, 1954

Higgins, R. *The Greek Bronze Age* British Museum Publications, London, 1970

———*Minoan and Mycenean Art* Thames & Hudson, London, revised ed., 1981

Hopper, R.J. *The Acropolis* Weidenfeld & Nicolson, London, 1971

Kuhrt, Amélie & Sherwin White, Susan (eds.) *Hellenism in the East* Duckworth, London, 1987

Lane-Fox R. *Alexander the Great* Allen Lane, London, 1973

Levi, Peter *Atlas of the Greek World* Phaidon, Oxford, 1984

Ling, Roger *Classical Greece* Phaidon, Oxford, 2nd ed., 1988

Murray, Oswyn *Early Greece* Fontana, London, 1980

Parke, H.W. *Greek Oracles* Hutchinson, London, 1967

Sekunda, Nick *The Army of Alexander the Great* Osprey Publishing, London, 1984

Swaddling, Judith *The Ancient Olympic Games* British Museum Publications, London, 1980

Vermeule, Emily *Greece in the Bronze Age* University of Chicago Press, Chicago, 1972

Wallbank, F.W. *The Hellenistic World* Fontana, London, 1981

Warren, P. *The Aegean Civilizations* Phaidon, Oxford, 1975

THE ROMAN WORLD

Balsdon, John P.V.D. *Rome: The Story of an Empire* Weidenfeld & Nicolson, London, 1971

Boethius, Carl Axel & Ward-Perkins, J.B. *Etruscan and Roman Architecture* Penguin, London, 1970

Brunt, P.A. *Social Conflicts in the Roman Republic* Chatto & Windus, London, 1978

Cornell, Tim & Matthews, John *Atlas of the Roman World* Phaidon, Oxford, 1982

Crawford, Michael *The Roman Republic* Fontana, London, 1976

Foss, Clive & Magdalino, Paul *Rome and Byzantium* Phaidon, Oxford, 1977

Grant, Michael *The Roman Emperors: a biographical guide to the rulers of Imperial Rome 31 B.C.–A.D. 476* Weidenfeld & Nicolson, London, 1983

Grimal, P. *Hellenism and the Rise of Rome* Weidenfeld & Nicolson, London, 1965

Hopkins, K. *Conquerors and Slaves* Cambridge University Press, Cambridge, 1978

Horizon Magazine (eds.) *Ancient Rome* American Heritage Publishing Co, New York, 1966

Macdonald, William L. *The Pantheon: Design, Meaning, and Progeny* Allen Lane, London, 1976

Millar, Fergus *The Roman Empire and its Neighbours* Duckworth, London, 1981

Norwich, John Julius *Byzantium, the Early Centuries* Viking, London, 1988

Ogilvie, R.M. *Early Rome and the Etruscans* Fontana, London, 1976

Pallatino, M. *The Etruscans* Pelican, London, 1955

Quennell, Peter and Newsweek Book Division (eds.) *The Colosseum* The Reader's Digest, London, 1973

Robinson, Cyril E. *A History of Rome: from 753 B.C. to A.D. 410* Methuen, London, 4th ed., 1949

Sellis, Salvatore *The Land of the Etruscans* Scala, Florence, 1985

Simkins, Michael *The Roman Army from Caesar to Trajan* Osprey Publishing, London, 1974

Syme, Ronald *The Roman Revolution* Oxford University Press, Oxford, 1939

Symons, David J. *Costume of Ancient Rome* B.T. Batsford, London, 1987

Talbot-Rice, David *Art of the Byzantine Era* Thames & Hudson, London, 1988

Trevelyan, Raleigh *The Shadow of Vesuvius: Pompeii A.D. 79* Folio Society, London, 1976

Vickers, Michael *Ancient Rome* Phaidon, Oxford, 2nd ed., 1989

Wise, Terence *Armies of the Carthaginian Wars: 265–146 B.C.* Osprey Publishing, London, 1982

INDIA

Craven, Roy *Indian Art, a concise history* Thames & Hudson, London, 1976

Davies, C. Collin *An Historical Atlas of the Indian Peninsula* Oxford University Press, Oxford, 2nd ed., 1959

Le Bon, G. *The World of Ancient India* Minerva, Geneva, 1974

Keay, John *India Rediscovered* Collins, London, 1988

Marshall, John (ed.) *Mohenjo-Daro and the Indus Civilization: Vols I and III* Indological Book House, Delhi, 1973

Piggott, Stuart *Prehistoric India* Pelican, London, 1950

Rawson, Philip *Indian Asia* Phaidon, Oxford, 1977

Schulbert, Lucille and Time-Life Books (eds.) *Historic India* Time-Life Books, Amsterdam, 1968

Thapar, Romila *A History of India (Vol 1)* Penguin, London, 1966

Thapar, B.K. "New Traits of the Indian Civilization at Kalibangan: an appraisal" in *South Asian Archaeology* ed. Norman Hammond, Duckworth, London, 1973

Watson, Frances *A Concise History of India* Thames & Hudson, London, 1974

Wheeler, Mortimer *Civilizations of the Indian Valley and Beyond* McGraw-Hill, New York, 1966

———"The Indian Civilization" in *Cambridge History of India Supplement* Cambridge University Press, Cambridge 3rd ed., 1968

Zwalf, W. *The Shivas of Gandhara* British Museum Publications, London, 1979

CHINA

Blunden, C. & Elvin, M. *Cultural Atlas of China* Phaidon, Oxford, 1983

Cotterell, Arthur *The First Emperor of China* Macmillan, London, 1981

———*China: A Concise Cultural History* John Murray, London, 1988

———(ed.) *The Encyclopedia of Ancient Civilizations* Mayflower Books, New York, 1980

Dawson, Raymond *Confucius* Oxford University Press, Oxford, 1981

FitzGerald, Patrick *Ancient China* Elsevier Phaidon, Oxford, 1978

Hartman-Goldsmith, Joan *Chinese Jade* Oxford University Press, Oxford, 1986

Hookham, Hilda *A Short History of China* Longmans, Green and Co, London, 1969

Loewe, Michael *Everyday Life in Early Imperial China: During the Han Period 202 B.C.–A.D. 220* B.T. Batsford, London, 1968

Medley, Margaret *The Chinese Potter: A Practical History of Chinese Ceramics* Phaidon, Oxford, 1976

Rawson, Jessica *Ancient China: Art and Archaeology* British Museum Publications, London, 1980

Schafer, Edward H. and Time-Life Books (eds.) *Ancient China* Time-Life Books, Amsterdam, 1969

Temple, Robert K.G. *China: Land of Discovery* Patrick Stephens, Wellingborough, 1986

Tregear, Mary *Chinese Art* Thames & Hudson, London, 1980

Whitfield, R. & Farrer A. *Caves of the Thousand Buddhas, Chinese art from the Silk Route* British Museum Publications, London, 1990

Yap, Yong & Cotterell, Arthur *The Early Civilization of China* Weidenfeld & Nicolson, London, 1975

THE AMERICAS

Bankes, George *Peru Before Pizarro* Phaidon, Oxford, 1977

Bray, Warwick M., Swanson, Earl H. & Farrington, Ian S. *The Ancient Americas* Phaidon, Oxford, 2nd ed., 1989

Coe, Michael, Snow, Dean & Benson, Elizabeth *Atlas of Ancient America* Facts on File, New York, 1986

Davies, Nigel *The Ancient Kingdoms of Mexico: a magnifi{ re-creation of their art and life* Penguin, London, 1982

Heyden, Doris & Gendrop, Paul *Pre-Columbian Architecture of Mesoamerica* Faber & Faber, London, 1988

Keatinge, Richard W. (ed.) *Peruvian Prehistory: An Overview of Pre-Inca and Inca Society* Cambridge University Press, Cambridge, 1988

Leonard, Jonathan Norton and Time-Life Books (eds.) *Ancient America* Time-Life Books, Amsterdam, 1968

Miller, Mary Ellen *The Art of Mesoamerica* Thames & Hudson, London, 1986

The Reader's Digest Mysteries of the Ancient Americas: The New World Before Columbus Reader's Digest, New York, 1986

Rivet, Paul *Maya Cities* Elek Books, London and G.P. Putnam's Sons, New York, 1966

Time-Life Books (eds.) *Empires Ascendant: Time Frame 400 B.C.–A.D. 200* Time-Life Books, Alexandria, Virginia, 1987

INDEX

INDEX

118, *120*, *141*; Visigoths *88*, *145*; *see also* Gauls
Franks *88*, 89, 142

G

Gades 30
Gaius 130
Gaius Caesar 136
Gaius Octavius *see* Augustus
Galatia *116*, 117, *117*, 136; "Galatians" 85
Galba 136
Galerius 143
games: ballgame *118*, 190, *191*, 192, 201; Greece 90, *110*, 112; Rome 120, 129, *134–5*
Gandhara 68, 117, *117*, 153, 156, 159, *159*
Ganges 151, 153, *153*, 154, 156, 158–9
Gansu *162*, *165*, 166, 171, 177
Gao Zu (Liu Bang) 172–3, 174
Gaskas 23, *69*
Gaugamela 114
Gauls 84–5, 89, *89*, 126, 132, 136, 142, *145*; Galatia 85, *116*, 117, *117*, 136
Gaumata 72, 74
Gautama, Siddhartha (Buddha) *147*, 153, *154–5*, *159*, 160; *see also* Buddhism
Germanic people 78, 88–9, 132, 136, 142, 145
Germany 80, 83, 84–5, 88
Gilgamesh 16, 42
Girnar: Rock of Girnar 157
Giza 45, *45*, 46, *46*, 47
Gla 96
gladiators 131, *134–5*
Godin 66
gold: Near East *19*, 21, 30; Nubia (and Egypt) 41, 42, 49, 51, 52, 56; Persia 62, *62*, 64, 66, *67*, 68, *75*; early Europe 78, 81, 82, *82*, *83*, 85, 87, *87*; Greece 96, 98, 100–01, 112, 115, *133*; China *170*, 174; Americas 178, *178*, *179*, 182, 192
Gordion 69
Gordium: and Gordian knot 114
Goths 89, 142, 145
Gournia 94
Gracchus (Tiberius Gracchus) 130
grain 12, 27, 34, 41, 151, 180; Greece 101, 107, 109; Rome 130, *130*, 131, 138; China 163, 164, 173
Granicus River 112
Great Wall of China *163*, 171, *172*, 173

H

Hadrian 138, 140; Hadrian's Wall 138, *141*, 145
Haft Tepe 64
Halicarnassus *105*, 114, 120
Hallstatt 78, 84, *84*
Hamadan *see* Ecbatana
Hammurabi *20*, 23, 24, *36*; law and Law Code *20*, 36, 64
Han dynasty *162*, *170*, *172–5*, 176, *176*, 177
Hanging Gardens of Babylon 36
Hannibal *128*, 129
Harappa 146, *148–9*, 151
Harappan culture *148–9*
Harkhuf 47
Harpagus 68
Harran (Carrhae) 34, 71, 76, 132
Harrison, Thomas: Elgin Marbles *106*
Hasan Dağ 15
Hasanlu 66
Hasdrubal *128*
Hastinapura 153
Hatra 77
Hatshepsut *50*, 52

Hatti 22
Hattic people 22
Hattusas 22, *23*
Hattusilis I 22
Hebei *170*
Hebrews 28, *31*
Heliopolis 46
Helladic culture 96
Hellenism 63, *69*, 101, *116–7*; in Rome 90, 117, 118–9, 129, *131*, *139*
helots 103
Henan Province 165
Hephaestion 114–5
Hepthalites 77, 160
Heracleopolis 48
Herculaneum *139*
Herodotus 90, *105*; as source 30, 36, 37, 38, 87, 92, 100, 120, on Persian conflict 62, 72, 74, 104
Hesiod 101
Heuneburg fortress 84
Hierakonpolis 42, *42*
Hindu religion 146, *146*, *149*, 151, 152–3, *158*, 160, *160*; caste *152*, 154, 160, *160*
Hindu Kush 152, 158
Hindush 156
Hittites 10, *18*, *22–3*, 24, 26, 28, *69*; conflict with Egypt 22–3, 26, 52, 54–5; Neo-Hittites 28, 29
Hochdorf: tomb 84
Hohokam culture *200–01*
Holland: prehistory 80, 88–9
Holy Roman Empire: Charlemagne 118
Homer 92, 96, *96*, 99, 100–01, *100*, 131
Honan: cauldron 166
Honduras: Maya 190, *190–1*, 191, *193*
Honorius 145
Hopewell culture *198–9*
hoplites *102*, 103
Horace 134
Horemheb 54
horses *13*, 24, 32, 78, 112, *187*; chariots 23, 24, 51, 85, 90, *152*, 153, *173*, Trundholm Sun Chariot 78, 83; Scythian horsemen 78, *86–7*
Horus 26, *43*, 44, 48
houses and other dwellings 42, 80, 94, 151; Near East 12, *14*, 15, 28, 30; Rome (city) 122, *131*, *133*, *139*; China 164, 165, *173*, *174*; Americas 180, 189, 190, 197, 199, 201, *201*
Hrozny, Bedrich 23
Huai River valley 174
Huang He (Yellow River) *162*, 164, *165*, 166, 174, 177

Huari *184–5*
Huascar 187
Huexotzinco 196
Hunan 168
Hunas (White Huns) 77, 160
Huns 77, 89, 145, *145*, 173, 177
Hunt, Arthur: papyri 61
hunting, esp. hunter-gatherers 10, 12, *13*, 78, 80, 164–5, 167, 168; Americas 180, *181*, 186, 200, 201
Hurrians 10, *20*, 23, 24, 26
Hydaspes 112
Hyksos *50–1*

I

Iberia 78
Iceni *89*
Imhotep 44
Inanna *see* Ishtar
Incas 178, *184–7*
incense 47, 48, 72
India *19*, 62, 66, *146–61*; food 152–3, *153*; languages 146, *152–3*, 157; Persians 72, 76–7, 153; Greeks 112, 117, *117*, 156, 158–9; Sakas (Scythians) 87, *158–9*; Indus Valley *19*, *146–51*, 159; Northwest 146, *148*, 152, 158
Iolkos 96
Ionia 100, 101, *105*, 114; and Persia 62, 68, 104, 109, 110
Iran 12, 62, 68, 71, 76, *76*, 77, 87, *117*; *see also* Elam
Iraq 11, *14*, 28, 77, 114
Ireland, prehistoric 80, 81, *81*, *82*, 85
iron 23, 28, 59, 66, 112, 120, 153, 178; early Europe 78, *83*, *84–5*, 89; China 168, *170*, 173
irrigation: Near East 15, 16, 17, *21*; Nile 40–1, 42, 44, 61; China 162, *165*, 167, 174; Americas 181, 182, 200
Ishtar (Astarte; Inanna) *14*, 21, 32, 36
Ishtar Gate, Babylon *10*, 36, *70–1*
Isis 44, 48, *58*, *133*, *139*
Islam 28, 76, 77, 146, 151
Isocrates 110
Israelites 10, 28, 30, 33, 47, 57; *see also* Palestine
Issus *112*, 114, *139*
Istakhr *76–7*
It-towy 48, 49
Italy: early 83, 84, 85, *88*; Greek colonies 84, *101*, *101*, 126, 127; and Roman Republic 126, 127, *128–9*, 130, 132; Attila 145; *see also* Ravenna; Rome

ivory 30, 67, 72, *101*, 159; Egypt 42, *42*, 47, 52; Greece 90, 98, *98*, 115

J

jade: China *162*, *165*, *167*, *170*, 173, 174; Maya 192
Jainism 153, *153*, 154, 157
Japan: Buddhism 161
Jebel Barkal 59
Jehoiachin 36
Jericho 12, *13*, *13*, 14
Jerusalem and Jews 30, *31*, 33, 36, *137*, 138; *see also* Israelites
Jesus of Nazareth: early church *143*
jewelry *19*, 30, 94, 121, 159, *181*; Egypt 42, 44, 45, 52, 58–9, *58*; early Europe 82, 85, 87; Persia 67, 74, 75
Jews *see* Israelites; Jerusalem
Jin: Eastern Jin *176*, 177; Western Jin *176–7*
Josephus: on Jewish revolt 137
Jovian 144
Judaea 136, 138, *143*
Judah 28, 33; *see also* Jerusalem
Judaism 28
Jugurtha 130
Julian 144
Julius Caesar *60*, 89, *89*, 131, 132, 134; Julio-Claudian dynasty *136*
Jupiter 120, 122, *123*, 133
Justinian *144*
Jutes 88
Jutland 83, 84, 88, *88*

K

Kabnak 64
Kabul Valley 158, 159
Kalhu (Nimrud) *11*, 30, *32*, *34–5*
Kalidasa 160
Kalinga: Ashoka 157
Kamenskoye 87
Kaminaljujú 189, 191
Kamose 51
Kanesh 21
Kanishka 159, 161
Kapilavastu 154
karma 154–5
Karnak 59
Kashta 59
Kassites 24, *24*
Kaushambi 153
Kentucky: Slack Farm *200*
Kerman 64
Kermanshah: Bisitun *74*
Khafre (Khephren) *44*, 45, *45*, 46, *46*

Index

ACKNOWLEDGMENTS

The publishers and author would like to thank the following people and institutions for their invaluable help in the making of this book:

Maggi McCormick (Editorial)
Lindsay McTeague (Editorial)
Tim Probart (Editorial)
Glenda Tyrrell (Design)
Valerie Chandler (Index)
Brian Harkins
British Museum Education Department
Sally Hopkins

Catherine Keats
Amélie Khurt
Susan Rollin
School of Oriental and African Studies Library
Patsy Vanags
Dr. Frances Wood
Elizabeth Wyse

PICTURE CREDITS

Front Cover: L. Villota/Zefa Picture Library
Back Cover: t   Mardoon/Zefa Picture Library
            b   Israel Museum/Ancient Art & Architecture

1 Michael Freeman/Bruce Coleman; 2 Lee Boltin; 6/7 Bridgeman Art Library; 10 Robert Harding Picture Library; 10/11 Dr. Georg Gerster/The John Hillelson Agency; 11l British Museum/Michael Holford; 11r Robert Harding Picture Library; 12 F. Jackson/Robert Harding Picture Library; 13 Institute of Archaeology, University College London; 14t Tor Eigeland/Susan Griggs Agency; 14b British Museum; 15 Margaret Oliphant; 16 Robert Harding Picture Library; 17l Scala; 17r Michael Jenner/Robert Harding Picture Library; 18l British Museum/Michael Holford; 18r The Hulton Picture Company; 18/19 British Museum/The Bridgeman Art Library; 19 British Museum/Michael Holford; 20l Louvre, Paris/The Bridgeman Art Library; 20r Archiv für Kunst und Geschichte, Berlin; 21t Michael Jenner/Robert Harding Picture Library; 21bl Ankara Museum/Michael Holford; 21bc The Mansell Collection; 21br Photographie Giraudon/The Mansell Collection; 22l G. Tortoli/Ancient Art & Architecture; 22r Konrad Helbif/Zefa Picture Library; 23 John Bulmer/Susan Griggs Agency; 24 Hirmer Fotoarchiv; 26/27 Louvre, Paris/The Bridgeman Art Library; 27l Ronald Sheridan/Ancient Art & Architecture; 27c/r Hirmer Fotoarchiv; 28 Desmond Harney/Robert Harding Picture Library; 32t/l Mary Evans Picture Library; 33 The Mansell Collection; 36 Dr. Georg Gerster/The John Hillelson Agency; 37t The Hulton Picture Company; 37l Erich Lessing/Magnum Photos; 37r British Film Institute; 38t image processed by NRSC Farnborough; 38l Christies, London/The Bridgeman Art Library; 38r Weltbild Verlag; 39 Bildarchiv Preussischer Kulturbesitz; 40 Tor Eigeland/Susan Griggs Agency; 41t British Museum/Michael Holford; 41b Rene Burri/Magnum Photos; 42 Ronald Sheridan/Ancient Art & Architecture; 42/43t Petrie Museum; 42/43b Hirmer Fotoarchiv; 43 Explorer; 44 The Hulton Picture Company; 45 J. Jack Jackson/Robert Harding Picture Library; 46t The Hulton Picture Company; 46l John Stevens/Ancient Art & Architecture; 46r John G. Ross/Susan Griggs Agency; 47c The Mansell Collection; 47t The Hulton Picture Company; 47b Guildhall Art Gallery, Corporation of London/The Bridgeman Art Library; 49 British Museum/Michael Holford; 48/49 The Hulton Picture Company; 50 Zefa Picture Library; 51/52 Peter Clayton; 53l British Museum; 53c Bildarchiv Preussischer Kulturbesitz; 53r Ronald Sheridan/Ancient Art & Architecture; 56l Bildarchiv Preussischer Kulturbesitz; 56r British Museum/Michael Holford; 57 Staatliche Museen zu Berlin; 58 Albert Shoucair/Thames & Hudson; 59l Werner Forman Archive; 59r British Museum; 60l/tr Bildarchiv Preussischer Kulturbesitz; 60br The Kobal Collection; 61t Scala; 61l Peter Clayton; 61r Sandra Lousada/Susan Griggs Agency; 62 Scala; 63 Bridgeman Art Library; 64 British Museum; 65l Anthony Howarth/Susan Griggs Agency; 65r Josephine Powell; 66 Dr. J.E. Curtis; 67 British Museum; 68 Lauros-Photographie Giraudon; 69t Museum of Anatolian Civilisations, Ankara; 69b Robert Harding Picture Library; 72 Maroon/Zefa Picture Library; 74t British Museum; 74b Robert Harding Picture Library; 75t British Museum/Bridgeman Art Library; 75b British Museum; 76t British Museum/Bridgeman Art Library; 76b Ronald Sheridan/Ancient Art & Architecture; 77l Jehangir Gazdar/Susan Griggs Agency; 77r Scala; 78/79 Robert Harding Picture Library; 79 Archiv für Kunst und Geschichte, Berlin; 81t Zefa Picture Library; 81bl James Harpur; 81br Zefa Picture Library; 82 National Museums of Scotland; 83l Novosti; 83r Erich Lessing/Magnum Photos; 84 Archiv für Kunst und Geschichte, Berlin; 85t Musée Archaeologique Châtillon-sur-Seine/Bridgeman Art Library; 85b Archiv für Kunst und Geschichte, Berlin; 87 Lee Boltin; 88 National Museum, Copenhagen/Werner Forman Archive; 89 The Mansell Collection; 90 James Harpur; 91tl Ronald Sheridan/Ancient Art & Architecture; 91tr Harald Sund/Image Bank; 91b Zefa Picture Library; 93tl British Museum; 93tr Reflejo/Susan Griggs Agency; 93b/94 Scala; 95 Ashmolean Museum; 96/97tl The Hulton Picture Company; 97tr Alison Frantz/Robert Harding Picture Library; 97b National Anthropological Museum, Athens/Robert Harding Picture Library; 98 Zoë Dominic; 99t Bridgeman Art Library; 99b Ekdotike Athenon; 100 John Bulmer/Susan Griggs Agency; 101l Scala; 101r Hirmer Fotoarchiv; 102 James Harpur; 103 K. Kerth/Zefa Picture Library; 104tl Peter Clayton; 104tr The Hulton Picture Company; 104b Cornell Capa/Magnum Photos; 105 James Harpur; 106 Richard Philpott/Zooid Pictures; 108t The Mansell Collection; 108b Ronald Sheridan/Ancient Art & Architecture; 109t Staatliche Antikensaamlung, Munich/Bridgeman Art Library; 109b Giraudon/Bridgeman Art Library; 110 Scala; 111t Robert Harding Picture Library; 111b British Film Institute; 112 Richard Neave/The Manchester Museum; 114 Bridgeman Art Library; 115t Ekdotike Athenon; 115b Bildarchiv Preussischer Kulturbesitz; 116 Scala; 117l L. Villota/Zefa Picture Library; 117r Ian Yeomans/Susan Griggs Agency; 118t Obrenski/Image Bank; 118b Fred Mayer/Magnum Photos; 119/121tl Ronald Sheridan/Ancient Art & Architecture; 121bl Museo di Villa Giulia, Rome/Robert Harding Picture Library; 121r The Mansell Collection; 122 Robert Harding Picture Library; 123/124 Scala; 127t Ronald Sheridan/Ancient Art & Architecture; 127b Scala; 128l British Museum; 128r The Mansell Collection; 129 Scala; 130 Biblioteca Apostolica Vaticana; 131t Metropolitan Museum of Art, Rogers Fund, 1903/Bridgeman Art Library; 131b Scala; 132t British Museum; 132b/133t The Mansell Collection; 133b Archiv für Kunst und Geschichte, Berlin; 135/136 Scala; 137 The Mansell Collection; 138 John Flowerdew/Zefa Picture Library; 139l Bridgeman Art Library; 139r Adrianne Leman/Susan Griggs Agency; 139b Krafft/Explorer; 142l British Museum; 142t Werner Forman Archive; 142b Sonia Halliday Photographs; 143 British Museum; 144/145 The Mansell Collection; 146r Nick Sidle/The Dance Library; 146l Scala; 147l Alain Thomas/Explorer; 147r Scala; 148 Christine Osborne; 149t Robert Harding Picture Library; 149b Hanif Reza/Zefa Picture Library; 151 J.L. Nou/Explorer; 152 Ronald Sheridan/Ancient Art & Architecture; 153 Ann & Bury Peerless; 154 Robert Harding Picture Library; 155t Ann & Bury Peerless; 155b P & G Bowater/Image Bank; 156l Indian High Commission; 156r Michael Holford; 157 British Library; 158l Bruno Barbey/Magnum Photos; 158r/159 Scala; 160 Josephine Powell; 161t Steve Satushek/Image Bank; 161b Michael Holford; 162 Östasiatiska Museet, Stockholm; 163 Dr. Georg Gerster/The John Hillelson Agency; 165l Victoria & Albert Museum/Michael Holford; 165r Hiroji Kubota/Magnum Photos; 166l Courtesy of the Freer Gallery of Art, Smithsonian Institution, Washington D.C.; 166r Robert Harding Picture Library; 167 Courtesy of The Institute of History and Philology; 168l Marie Antoinette Evans Fund, Courtesy Museum of Fine Arts, Boston; 168r/169l Ronald Sheridan/Ancient Art & Architecture; 169r Sally & Richard Greenhill; 170/171 Laurie Lewis/Frank Spooner Pictures; 170 Robert Harding Picture Library; 172 Popperfoto; 173l Robert Harding Picture Library; 173r Bridgeman Art Library; 176 Courtesy of The Institute of History and Philology; 177tl Robert Harding Picture Library; 177bl/r G & P Corrigan/Robert Harding Picture Library; 178 Israel Museum/Ancient Art & Architecture; 179t David Muench; 179r/181tl Tony Morrison/South American Pictures; 181tr Lee Boltin; 181c ET Archive; 181b Tony Morrison/South American Pictures; 182 Israel Museum/Ancient Art & Architecture; 182/183 Cornell Capa/Magnum Photos; 183l ET Archive; 183r/184t Michael Holford; 184b Robert Harding Picture Library; 185 Tony Morrison/South American Pictures; 186t Michael Holford; 186b Tony Morrison/South American Pictures; 187t The Kobal Collection; 187b Bridgeman Art Library; 188t Inge Morath/Magnum Photos; 188b Michael Holford; 189t Heather Magrill; 189b Michael Holford; 190t Heather Magrill; 190b B, Norman/Ancient Art & Architecture; 193t Werner Forman Archive; 193bl British Museum; 193br Tony Morrison/South American Pictures; 194l ET Archive; 194r Biblioteca Apostolica Vaticana; 195t Ronald Sheridan/Ancient Art & Architecture; 195b Tony Morrison/South American Pictures; 196 National Museum of Anthropology/Werner Forman; 197t Fotomas Index; 197b ET Archive; 198l Ohio State Museum/Werner Forman Archive; 198r Ohio Historical Society; 199t Tony Linck/Shostal Associates/Superstock; 199b The Saint Louis Art Museum, Eliza McMillan Fund; 200t McNitt Collection, State Records Center, Santa Fe, New Mexico; 200bl Maxwell Museum of Anthropology/Werner Forman Archive; 200br David Lucas/Evansville Courier, Indiana; 201 David Muench.

ILLUSTRATION CREDITS

Harry Clow: 30–31, 54–55, 70–71, 86–87.
Stephen Conlin: 106–107, 134–135, 150–151t, 190–191,
Maxine Hamil: Decorative borders throughout
Richard Hook/Linden Artists: 29, 34–35, 82, 102b, 113, 126, 127, 174–175,
Janos Marffy/Jillian Burgess: 8–9, 12, 24–25, 30, 33, 40, 51, 65, 72–73b, 80, 84, 92, 120, 148t, 164b, 180l.
Technical Art Services: 13, 15, 17, 18, 20, 23, 27, 32, 34, 36, 45, 55, 69, 95, 98, 100, 102t, 107, 112, 117, 124, 125, 128, 138, 140–141, 145, 148b, 150b, 152, 157, 164t, 167, 176, 180r, 185, 189t, 189b, 191b, 193, 198, 201t, 201b.
Roger Wade-Walker/Jillian Burgess: 44, 48, 73t, 141 INSETS, 192.

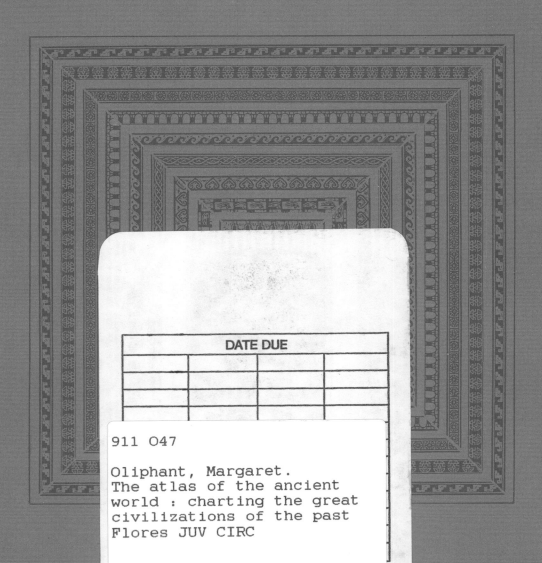